Lempicka

1898-1980

Grange
BOOKS

Page 4:
Self-Portrait in the Green Bugatti, 1929
Oil on panel, 35 x 27 cm
Private Collection

Designed by:
Baseline Co Ltd
19-25 Nguyen Hue
Bitexco Building, Floor 11th
District 1, Ho Chi Minh City
Vietnam

Published in 2005 by Grange Books
an imprint of Grange Books Plc
The Grange Kingsnorth Industrial Estate
Hoo, nr Rochester, Kent ME3 9ND
www.grangebooks.co.uk

ISBN 1-84013-775-4

Printed in China

It can be argued that the Art Deco spirit expressed itself more naturally through portraiture than through any other kind of painting. The quintessential Art Deco portraitist is undoubtedly Tamara de Lempicka. The Fashionable society of the 1920s and 30s is now perceived very largely through her eyes.

— Edward Lucie-Smith

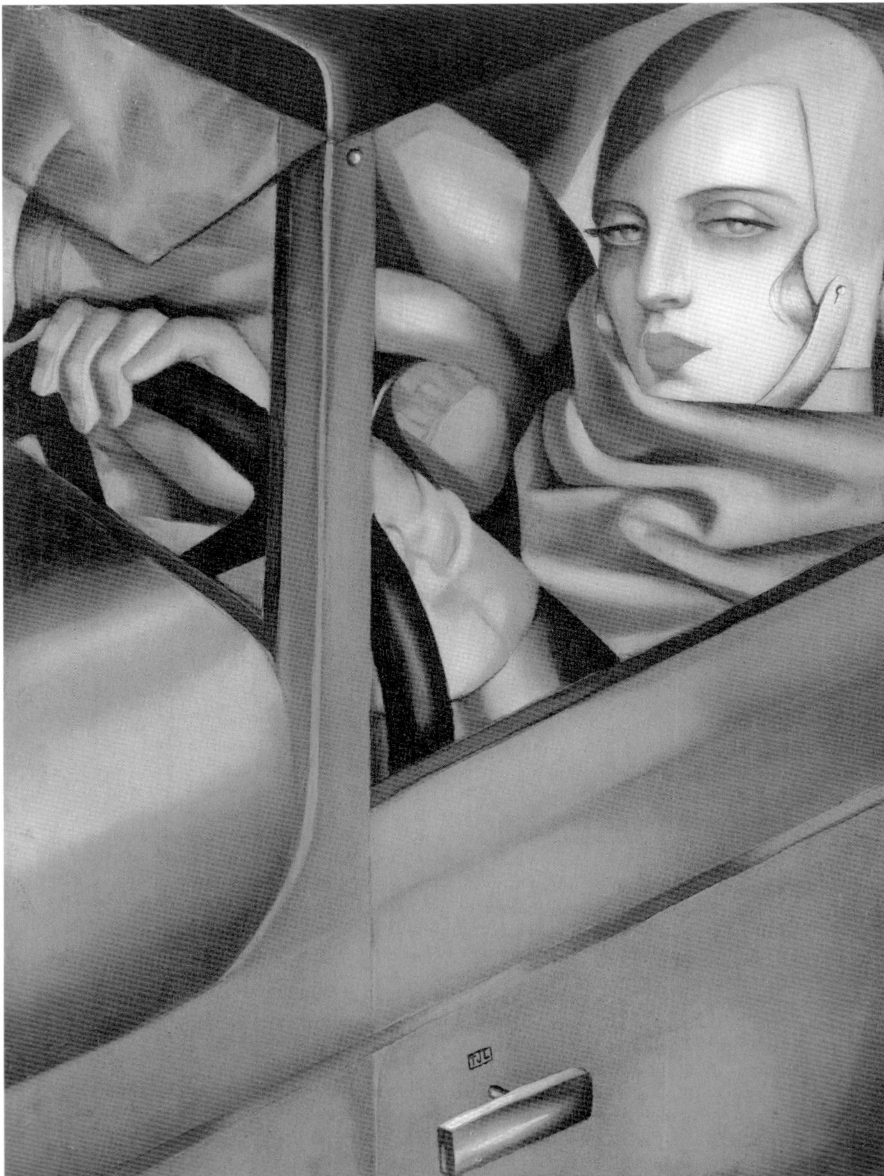
TJL

Biography

1898 Born Tamara Gurwik-Gorska in Warsaw to wealthy, upper-class Polish parents. Her father, Bolris Gorski, was a lawyer with a French firm. Her mother was Malvina Decler.

1911 A trip to Italy with her grandmother helps Tamara discover her passion for art.

1914 Tamara moves in with her aunt Stephanie in St Petersburg, resenting her mother's decision to remarry. She meets her future husband, Tadeusz Lempicki, a handsome lawyer from a wealthy Russian family.

1916 Tamara and Tadeusz marry in Petrograd in the chapel of the Knights of Malta.

1917 Russia is engulfed in revolution after the rise of the Bolsheviks and the new regime.

1918 Tadeusz is arrested as a counter-revolutionary. Tamara enlists the help of the Swedish consul to help him escape. They both manage to flee the country and are reunited in Paris, their home for the next 20 years.

1920 Birth of Kizette de Lempicka. Tamara takes classes with Maurice Denis and Andre Lhote. She takes the name Tamara de Lempicka and begins to develop her worldly, modish and erotic style.

1922 She sells her first paintings from the Gallerie Colette Weill, later exhibiting her work for the first time at the Salon d'Automne in Paris.

1925 De Lempicka makes a name for herself with a one woman show at the Bottega di Poesia in Milan and at the world's first Art Deco exhibition, held in Paris. The German fashion magazine *Die Dame* commissions one of her most famous paintings, the *Self-Portrait in the Green Bugatti*.

1926 The great Italian poet and playwright, Gabriele d'Annunzio, makes a failed attempt to seduce de Lempicka at his villa on the Italian coastline.

1927 De Lempicka completes several controversial paintings of her daughter Kizette. She meets the beautiful Rafaela in the Bois de Boulogne who inspires some of her most sensuous and erotic works.

LEMPICKA

1928 She begins work on her Boucet family commissions and paints a portrait of her husband Tadeusz before their divorce later in the year. She meets Baron Raoul Kuffner and moves into a spacious apartment in rue Méchain designed by the fashionable modernist architect Robert Mallet-Stevens.

1929 De Lempicka becomes Kuffner's mistress and makes her first trip to America.

1933 She marries Baron Kuffner. Her work and creativity suffer after the sobering realities of Hitler's ascension to power in Germany and the Wall Street Crash. She enters a long period of depression.

1939 De Lempicka and Baron Kuffner move to America and settle in Los Angeles after Kuffner sells off most of his Austrian and Hungarian estates. De Lempicka continues to paint and slips easily into the glamorous world of Hollywood high society.

1942 Tired of their life in Hollywood, Kuffner insists they move back to New York. Kizette joins them in America where she meets her husband, Harold Foxhall, a geologist from Texas.

1943 Her new life as a New York socialite detracts from her art. Her figurative paintings and experiments with abstract expressionism fail to attract any interest. Her career begins to stall and she fades slowly into obscurity.

1962 Baron Kuffner dies. A distraught de Lempicka moves in with her daughter and husband in Houston.

1973 A renewed interest in her work leads to a hugely successful retrospective show of her work at the Galerie du Luxembourg.

1974 Her fame restored, she moves in with her daughter in Cuernavaca, Mexico, living the rest of her life marred by her irascibility in her dealings with her family and the rest of the world.

1980 Tamara de Lempicka dies on March 18th leaving instructions for her ashes to be scattered over the crater of the volcano Popocatepetl.

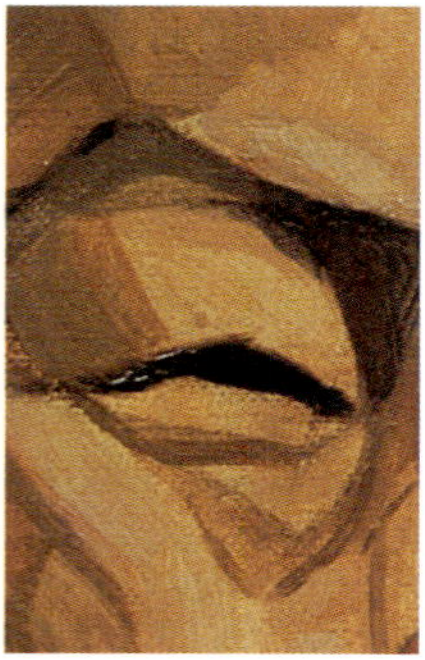

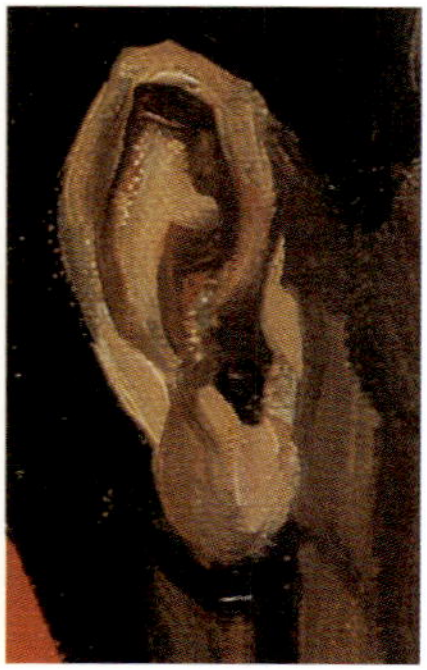

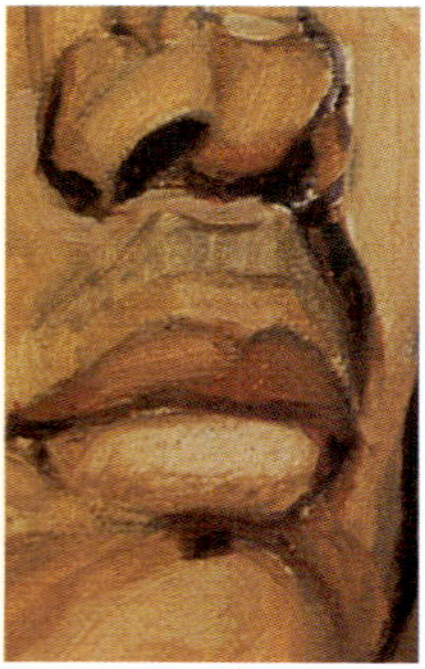

Tamara de Lempicka created some of the most iconic images of the twentieth century. Her portraits and nudes of the years 1925-1933 grace the dust jackets of more books than the work of any other artist of her time. Publishers understand that in reproduction, these pictures have an extraordinary power to catch the eye and kindle the interest of the public. In recent years, the originals of the images have fetched record sums at Christie's and Sotheby's. Beyond the purchasing power of most museums, these paintings have been eagerly collected by film and pop stars. In May 2004, the Royal Academy of Arts in London staged a major show of de Lempicka's work just one year after she had figured prominently in another big exhibition of Art Deco at the Victoria and Albert museum.

The Chinese Man

c. 1921
Oil on canvas, 35 x 27 cm
Musée des Beaux-Arts du Havre

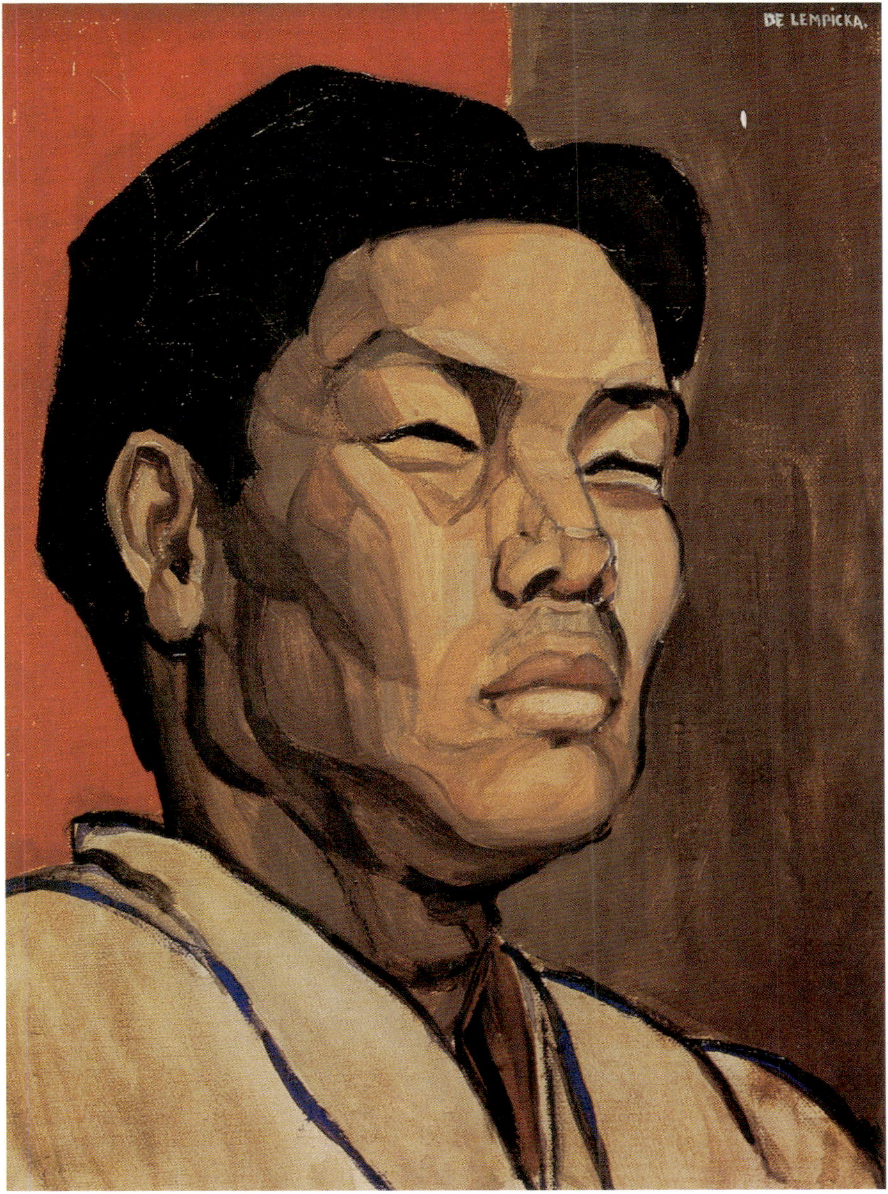
DE LEMPICKA.

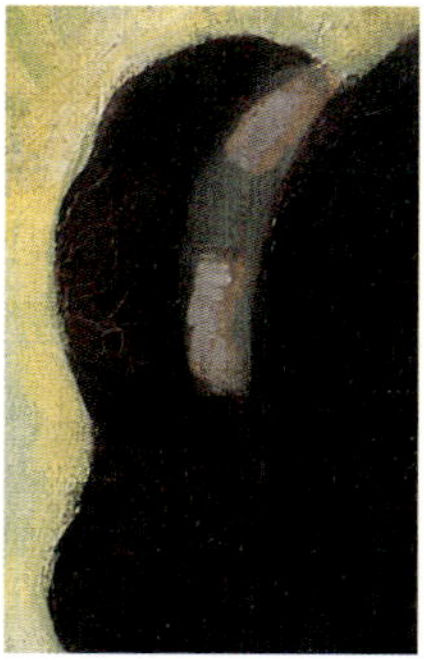

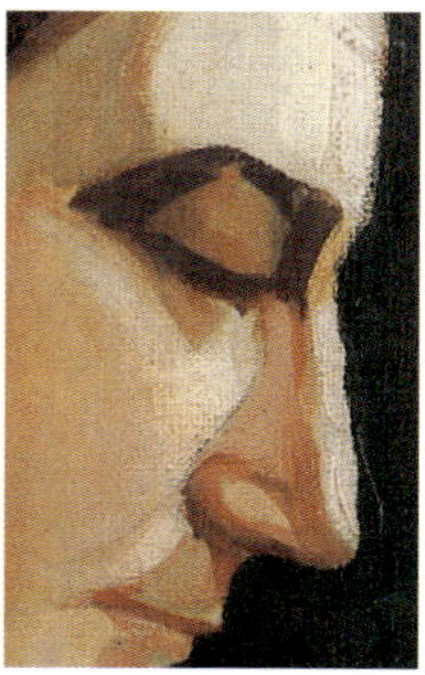

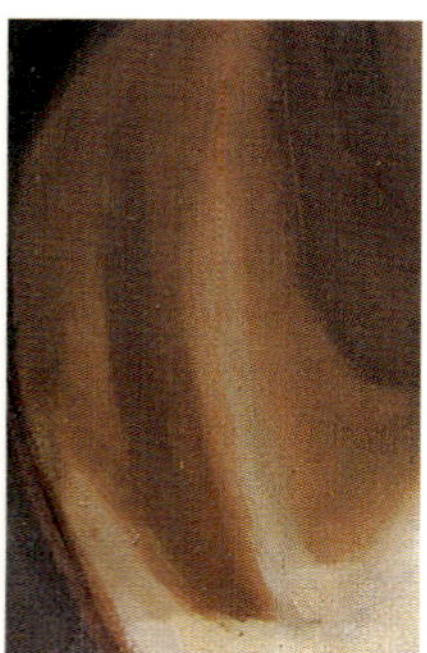

The public flocked to the show despite a critical reaction of unprecedented hostility towards an artist of such established reputation and market value. In language of moral condemnation hardly used since Hitler's denunciations of modern art at the Nuremberg rallies and the Nazi-sponsored exhibition of *Degenerate Art*, the art critic of the Sunday Times, Waldemar Januszczak, fulminated "I had assumed her to be a mannered and shallow peddler of Art Deco banalities. But I was wrong about that. Lempicka was something much worse. She was a successful force for aesthetic decay, a melodramatic corrupter of a great style, a pusher of empty values, a degenerate clown and an essentially worthless artist whose pictures, to our great shame, we have somehow contrived to make absurdly expensive."

Woman Wearing a Shawl, in Profile

c. 1922
Oil on canvas, 61 x 46 cm
Barry Friedman Ltd, New York

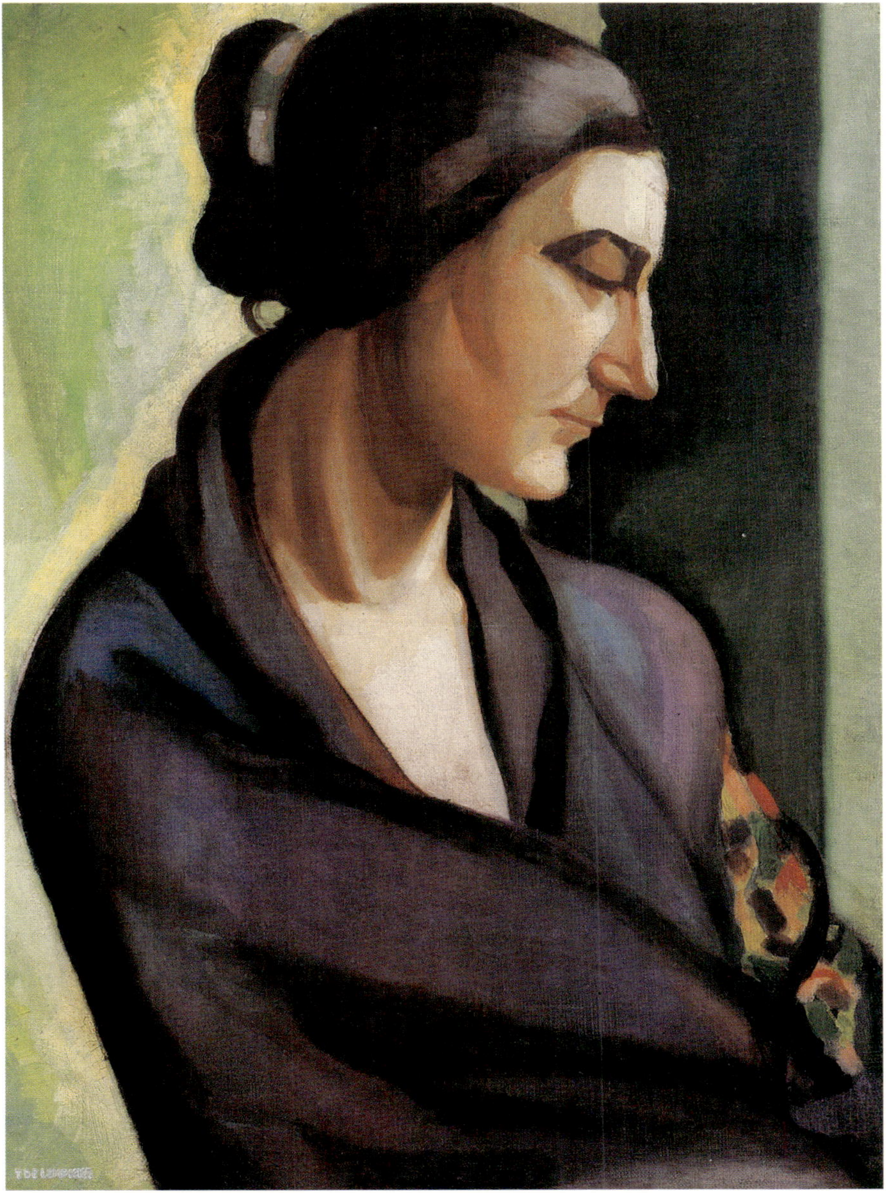

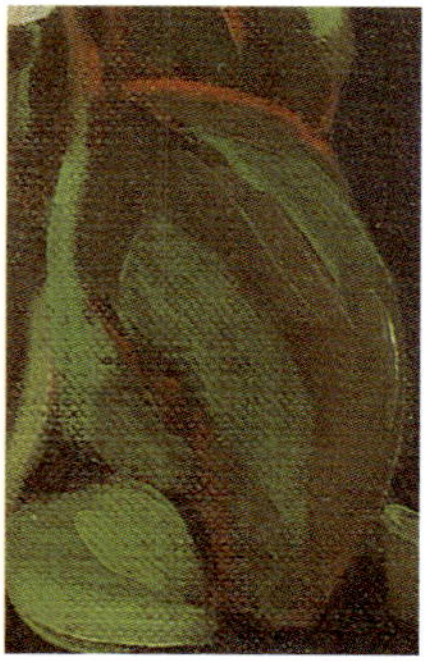

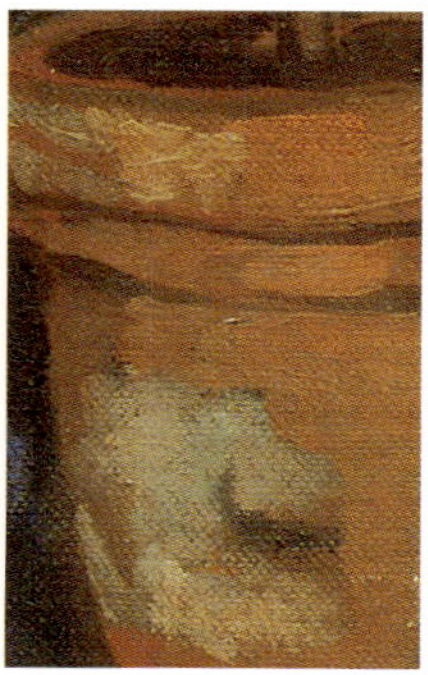

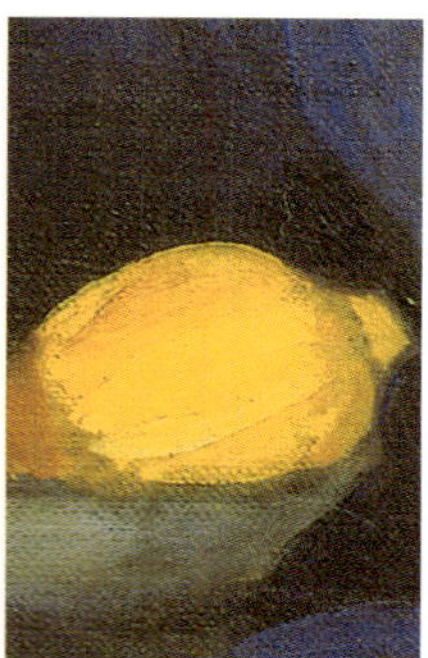

According to Januszczak, de Lempicka did not arrive in Paris in 1919 as an innocent refugee from the Russian Revolution but on a sinister mission, intending "an assault on human decency and the artistic standards of her time". One cannot help wondering what it was about de Lempicka's art that should bring down upon it such hysterical vituperation. There is a clue perhaps in his waspish observation "Luther Vandross collects her, apparently. Madonna. Streisand. That type." The hostility is perhaps more politically than aesthetically motivated and what really got under the skin of certain critics was the glamorous life style of Tamara's collectors as well as of her sitters.

Bouquet of Hortensias and Lemon

c. 1922
Oil on canvas, 55.2 x 45.7 cm
Barry Friedman Ltd, New York

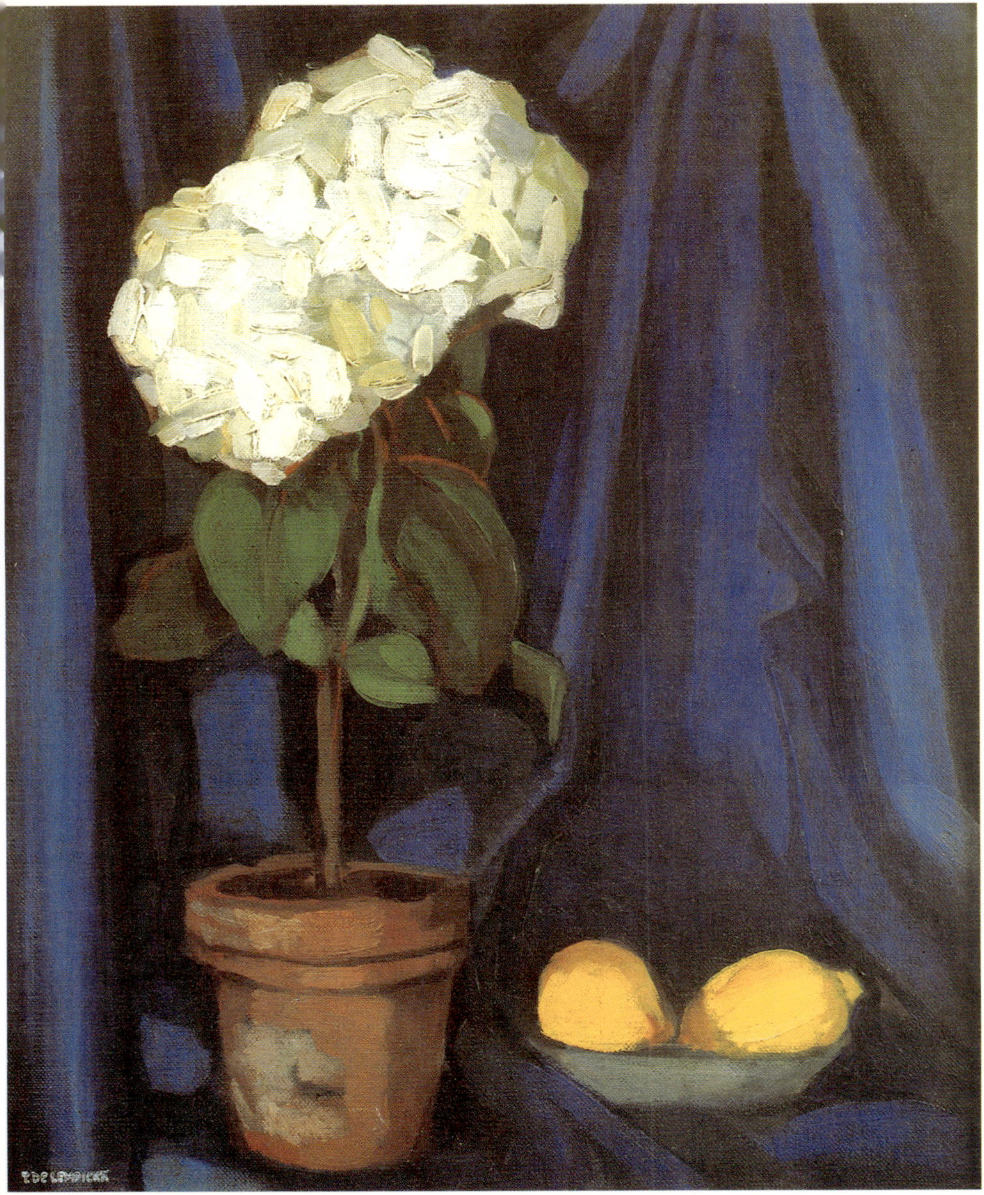

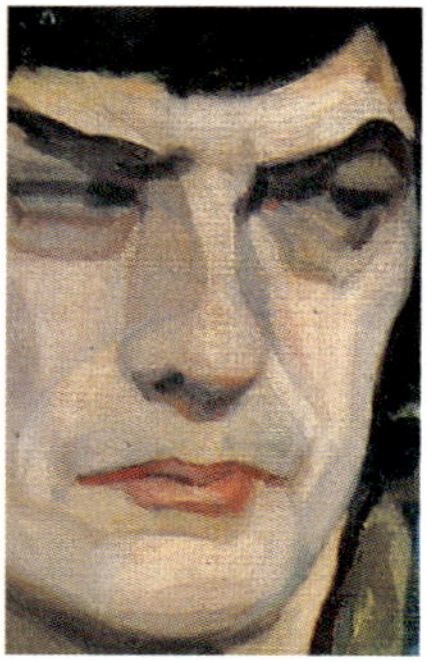

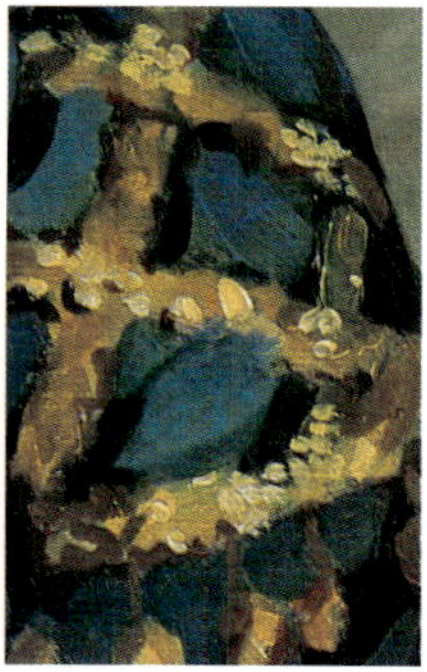

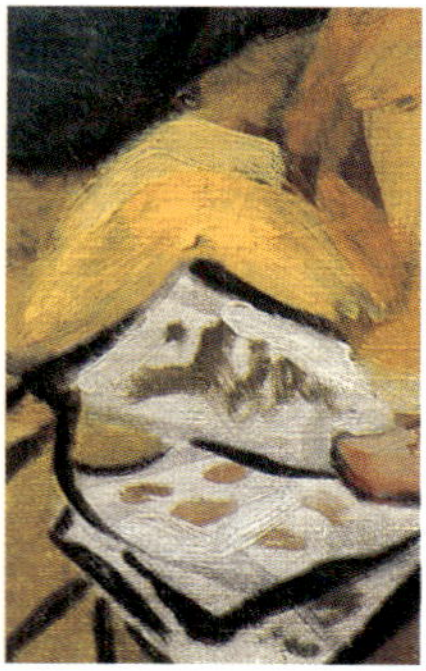

Both the place and the date of de Lempicka's birth vary in different accounts. According to some, de Lempicka changed her birth place from Moscow to Warsaw which could be more significant. There has been speculation that de Lempicka was of Jewish origin on her father's side and that the deception over her place of birth resulted from an attempt to cover this up. Certainly the ability to reinvent oneself time and again in new locations, manifested by de Lempicka throughout her life was a survival mechanism developed by many Jews of her generation. The prescience of the danger of Nazi Germany in a woman not usually politically minded and her desire to leave Europe in 1939 might also suggest that she was part Jewish. The official version was that Tamara Gurwik-Gorska was born in 1898 in Warsaw into a wealthy and upper-class Polish family.

The Fortune Teller

c. 1922
Oil on canvas, 73 x 59.7 cm
Barry Friedman Ltd, New York

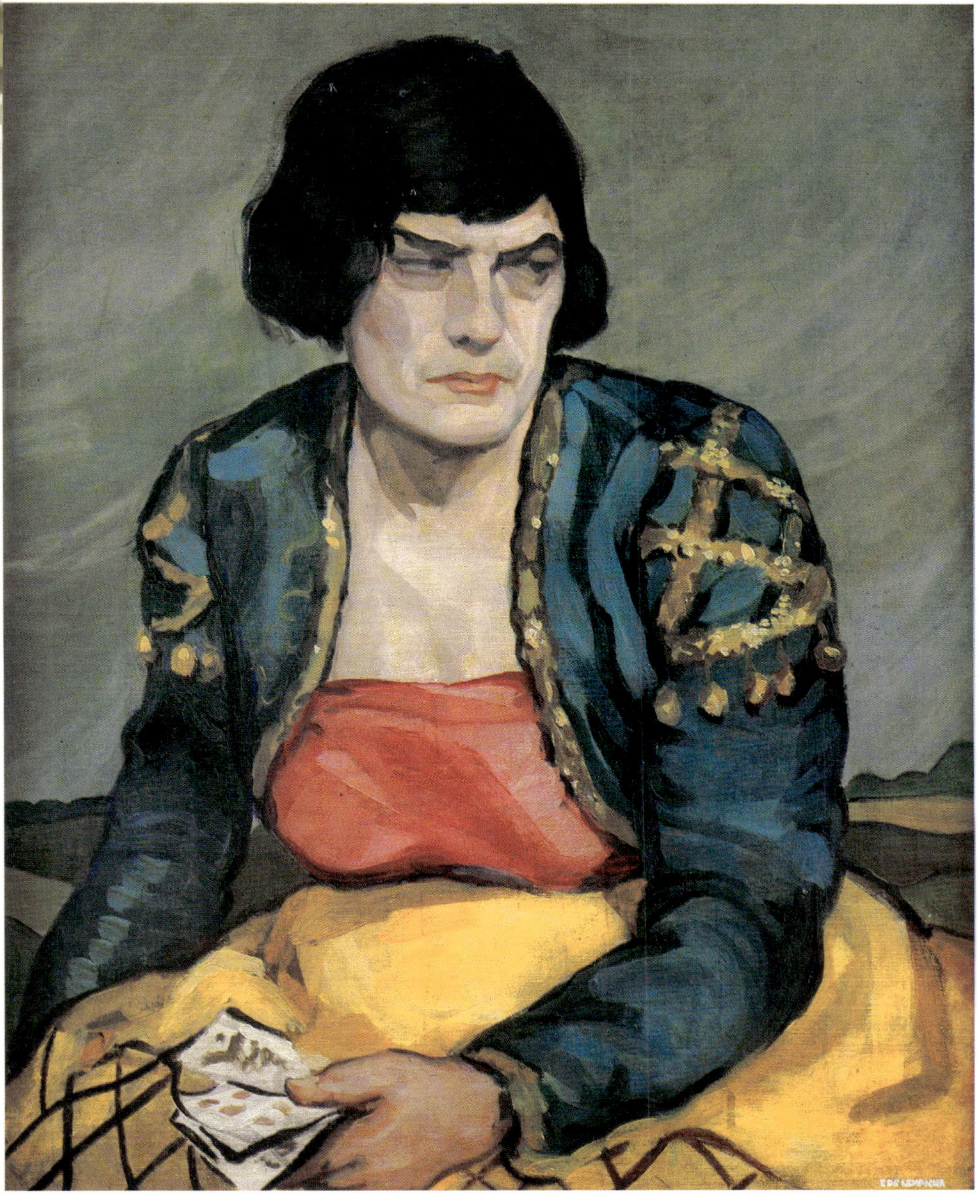

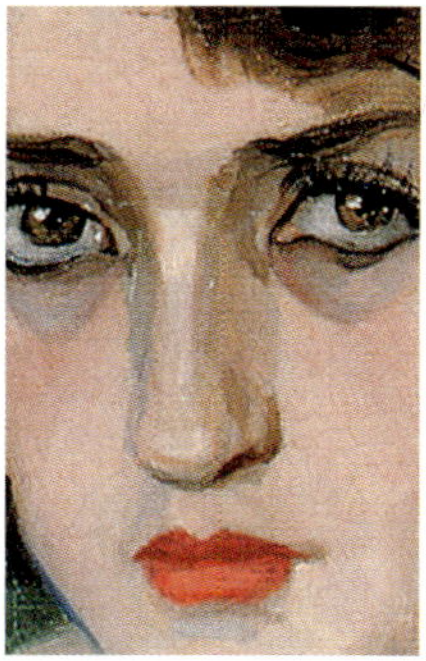

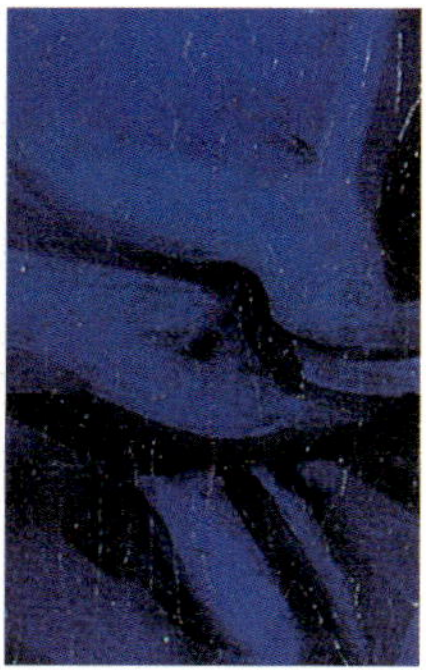

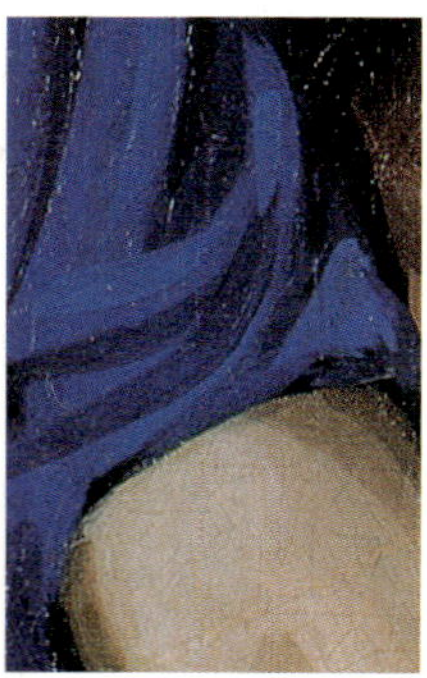

Following three partitions in the late eighteenth century, the larger part of Poland including Warsaw was absorbed into the Russian Empire. The rising tide of nationalism in the nineteenth century brought successive revolts against Russian rule and increasingly harsh attempts to Russify the Poles and to repress Polish identity. There is little to suggest that Tamara ever identified with the cultural and political aspirations of the Polish people. On the contrary, she seems to have identified with the ruling classes of the Tzarist regime that oppressed Poland. It is telling that in 1918 when she escaped from Bolshevist Russia she chose exile in Paris along with thousands of Russian aristocrats rather than to live in the newly liberated and independent Poland. From what Tamara herself later said, she seems to have enjoyed a happy childhood with her older brother Stanczyk and her younger sister Adrienne.

Portrait of a Young Lady in a Blue Dress

1922
Oil on canvas, 63 x 53 cm
Barry Friedman Ltd, New York

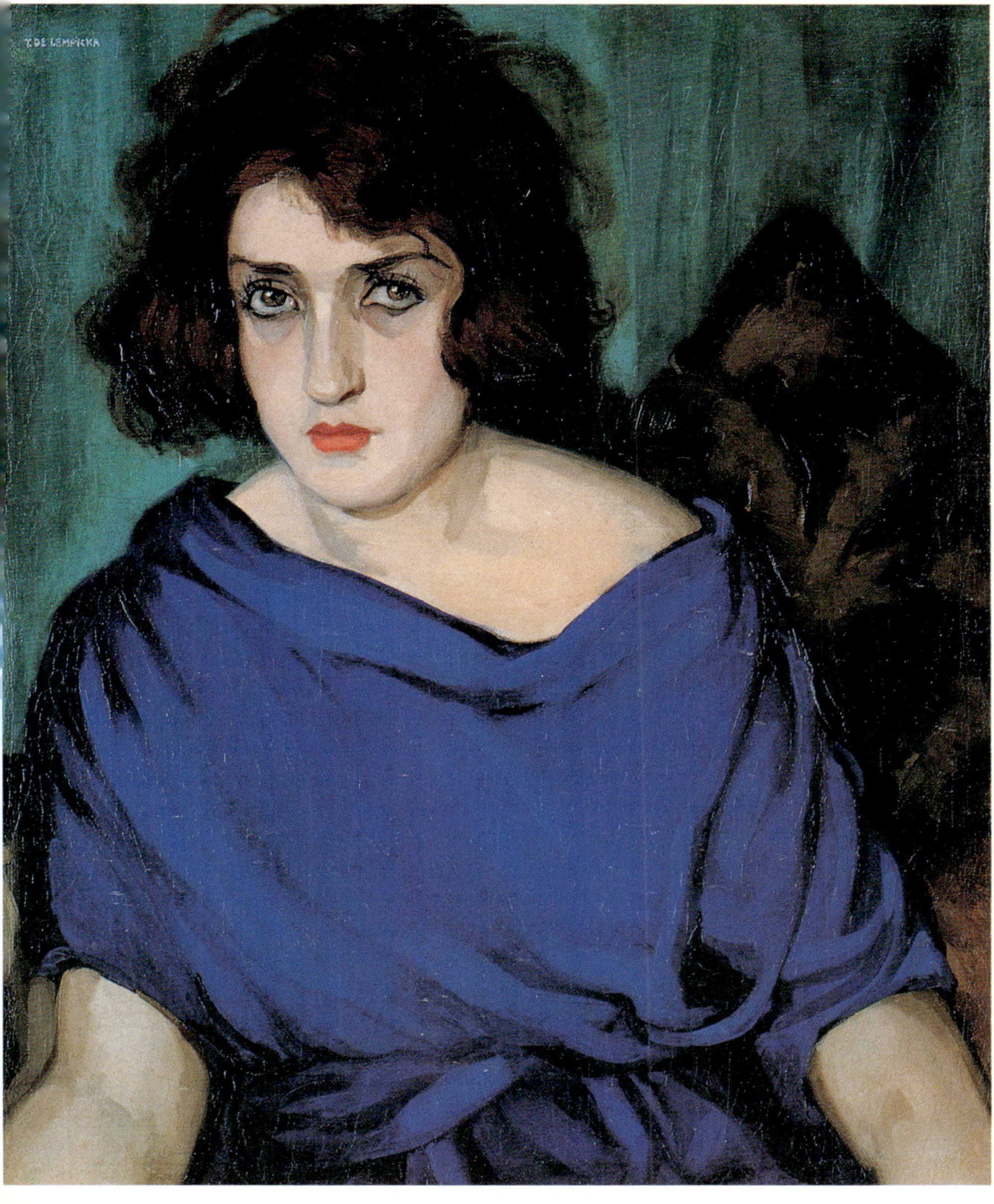
T. DE LEMPICKA

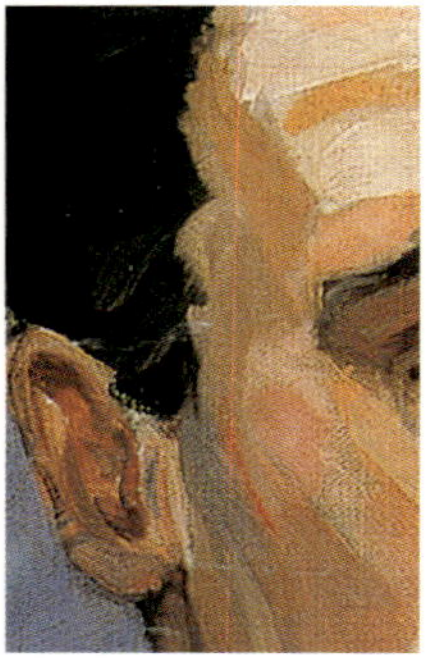
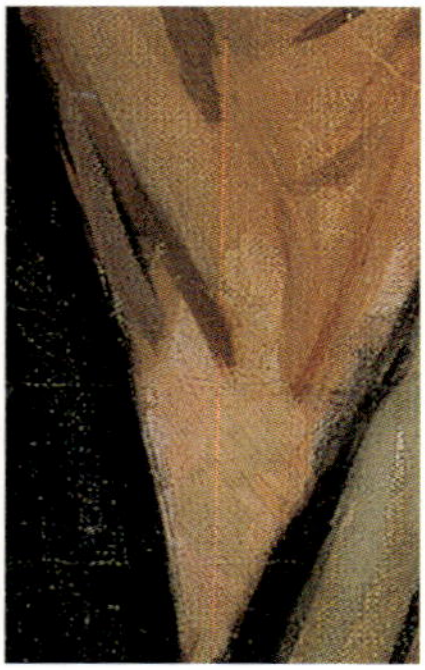
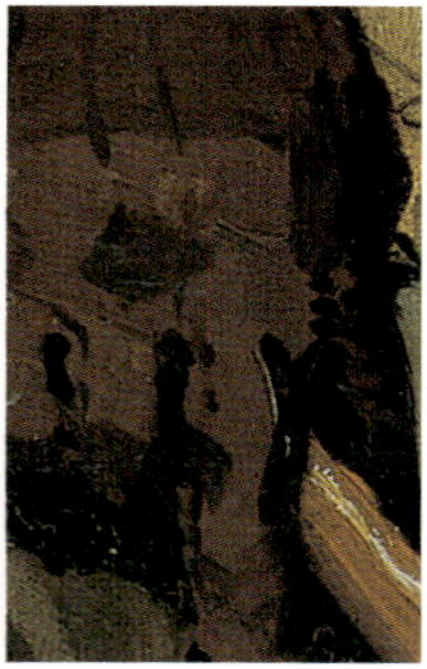

The wilfulness of her temperament, apparent from an early age, was indulged rather than tamed. The commissioning of a portrait of Tamara at the age of twelve turned into an important and revelatory event. "My mother decided to have my portrait done by a famous woman who worked in pastels. I had to sit still for hours at a time...more...it was a torture. Later I would torture others who sat for me. When she finished, I did not like the result, it was not... precise. The lines, they were not *fournies*, not clean. It was not like me. I decided I could do better. I did not know the technique. I had never painted, but this was unimportant. My sister was two years younger. I obtained the paint. I forced her to sit. I painted and painted until at last, I had a result. It was *imparfait* but more like my sister than the famous artist's was like me."

Portrait of a Polo Player

c. 1922
Oil on canvas, 73 x 60 cm
Barry Friedman Ltd, New York

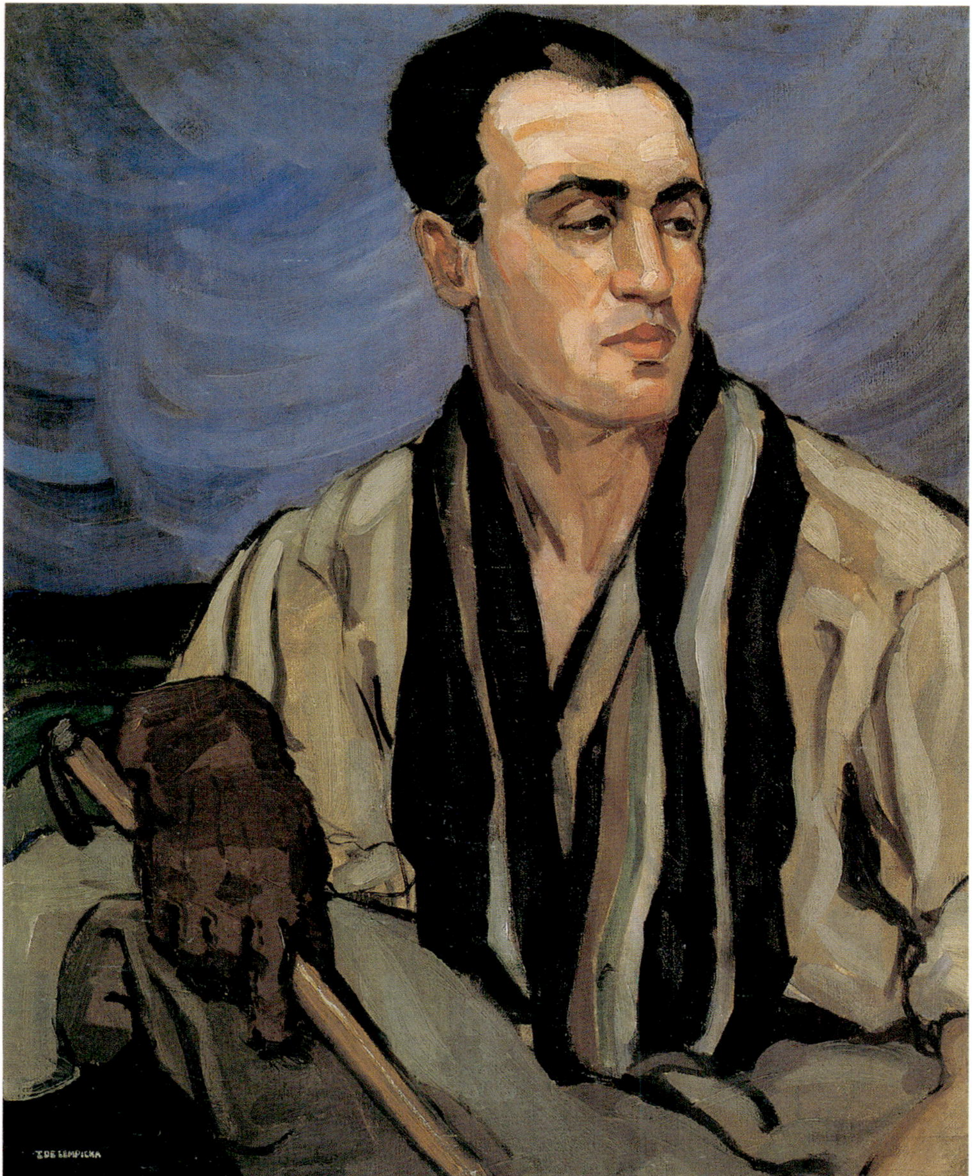
T. DE LEMPICKA

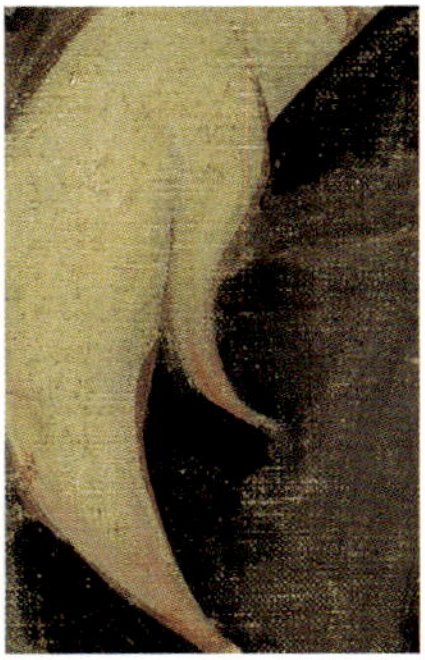

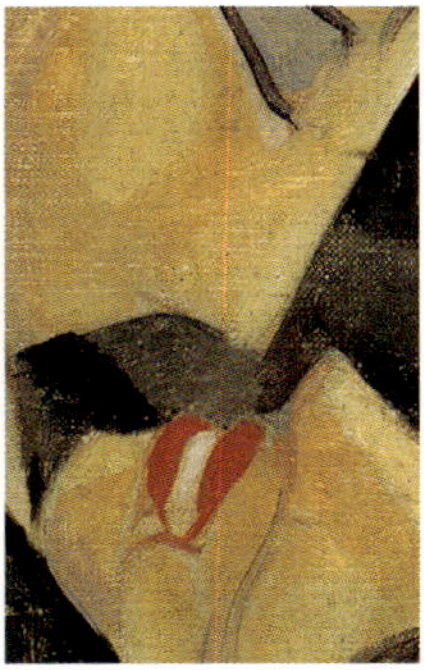

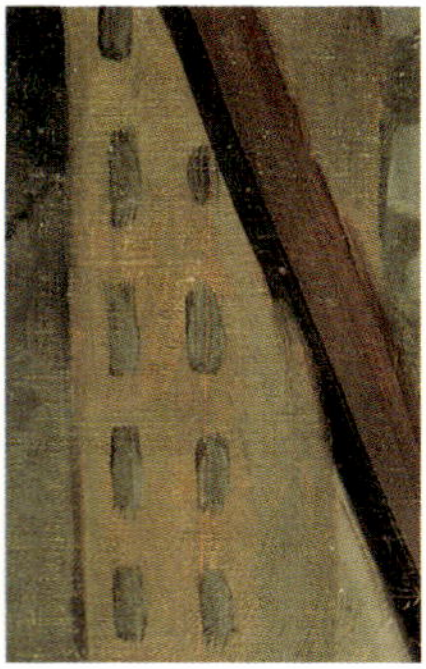

If Tamara's vocation was born from this incident as she suggests, it was encouraged further the following year when her grandmother took her on a trip to Italy. Visits to museums in Venice, Florence and Rome lead to a life long passion for Italian Renaissance art that informed de Lempicka's finest work in the 1920s and 30s. A torn and crumpled photograph of Tamara taken in Monte Carlo shows her as a typical young girl *de bonne famille* of the period before the First World War. Her lovingly combed hair cascades with Pre-Raphaelite abundance over her shoulders and almost down to her waist. She poses playing the children's game of diabolo but her voluptuous lips and coolly confident gaze belie her thirteen years. It would not be long before she would be ready for the next great adventure of her life — courtship and marriage.

The Kiss

c. 1922
Oil on canvas, 50 x 61 cm
Private Collection

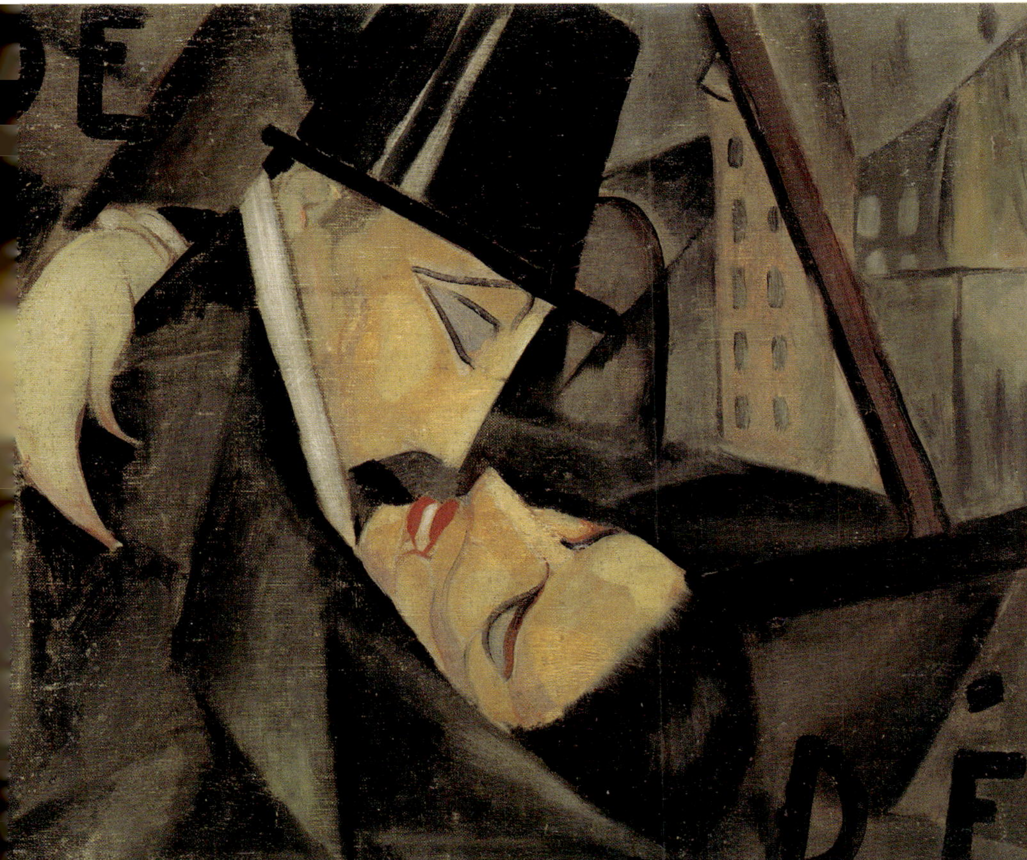
DE
DÉ

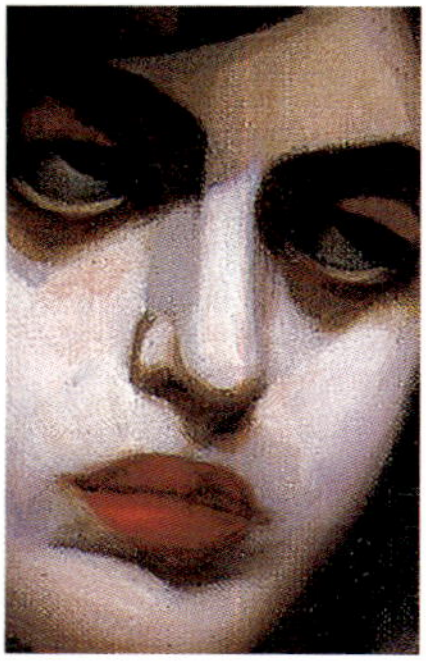

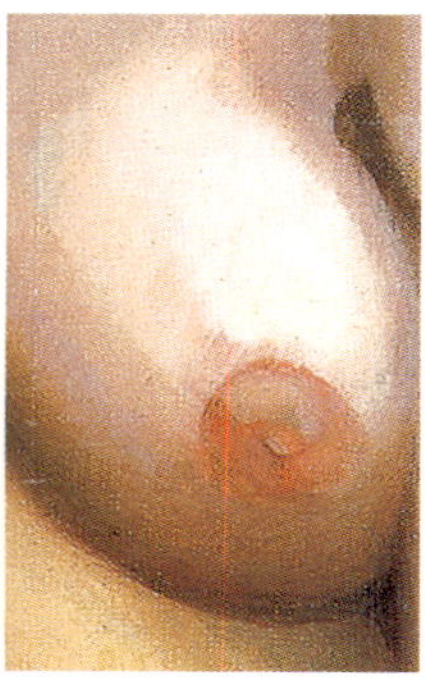

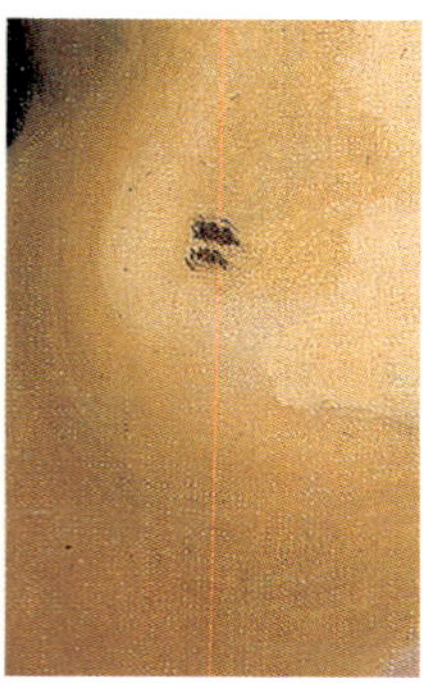

Played against the backdrop of the First World War and the death throes of the Russian monarchy, the story as passed down by Tamara and her daughter is, as so often in de Lempicka's life, worthy of a popular romantic novel or movie. When Tamara's mother remarried, the resentful daughter went to stay with her Aunt Stephanie and her wealthy banker husband in St. Petersburg, where she remained trapped by the outbreak of war and the subsequent German occupation of Warsaw. Just before the war when Tamara was still only fifteen, she spotted a handsome young man at the opera surrounded by beautiful and sophisticated women and instantly decided that she had to have him. His name was Tadeusz Lempicki.

Nude, Blue Background

1923
Oil on canvas, 70 x 58.5 cm
Private Collection

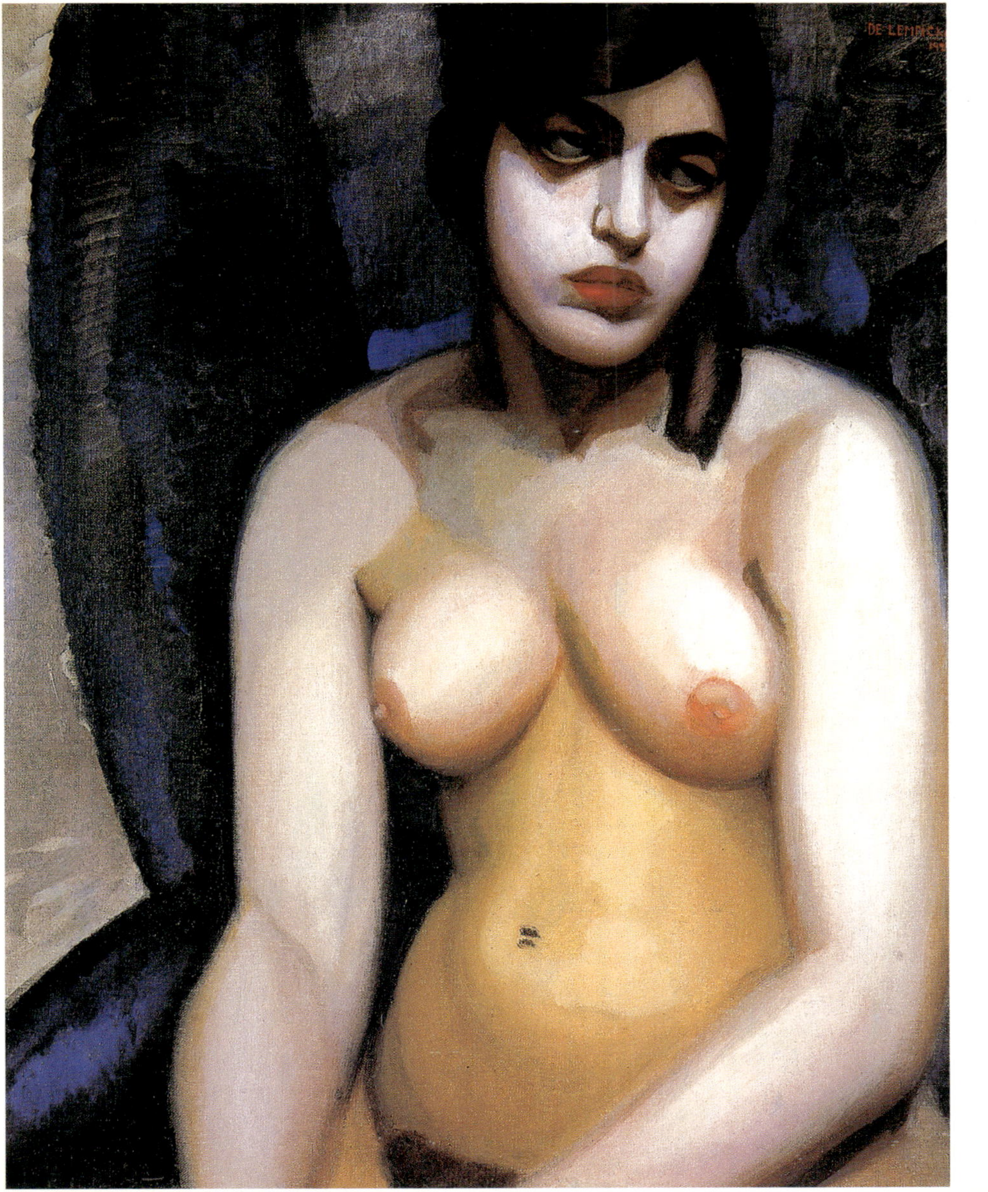

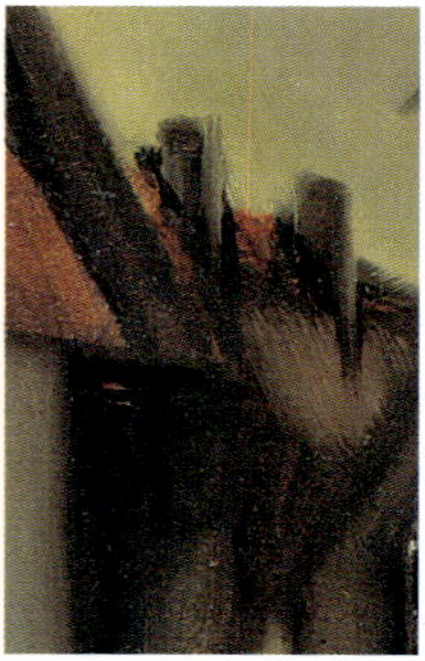

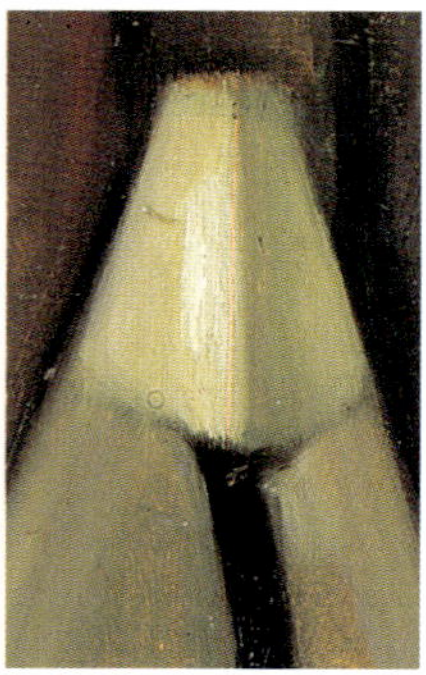

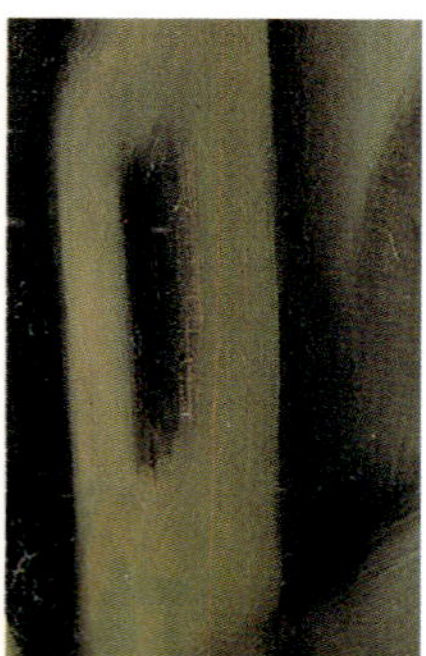

Though qualified as a lawyer, he was something of a playboy, from a wealthy land-owning family. With her customary boldness and lack of inhibitions, the young girl flouted convention by approaching Tadeusz and making an elaborate curtsey. Tamara had the opportunity to reinforce the impression she had made on Tadeusz at their first meeting when later in the year, her uncle gave a costume ball to which Lempicki was invited. In amongst the elegant and sophisticated ladies in the Poiret-inspired fashions of the the day, Tamara appeared as a peasant, goose-girl leading a live goose on a string.

A Street at Night

c. 1923
Oil on canvas, 50 x 33.5 cm
Private Collection

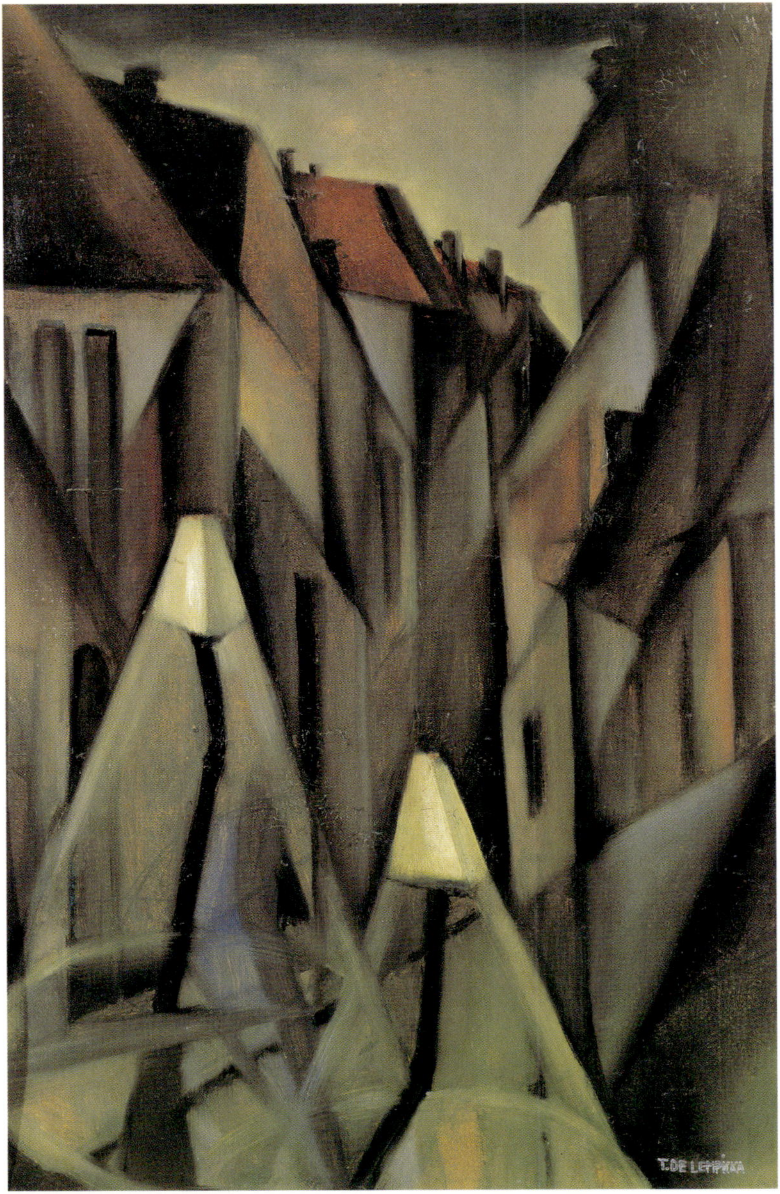
T. DE LEMPICKA

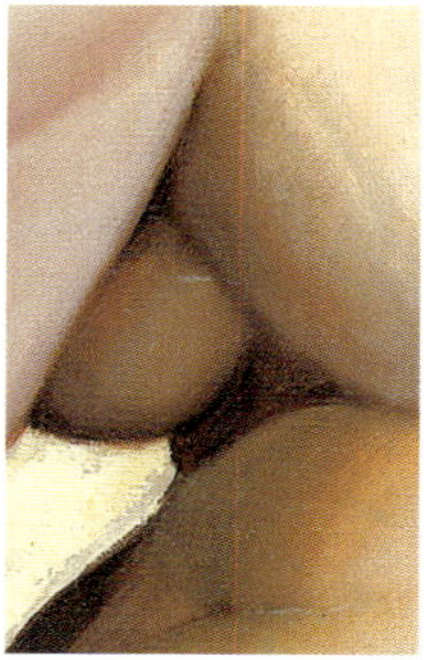

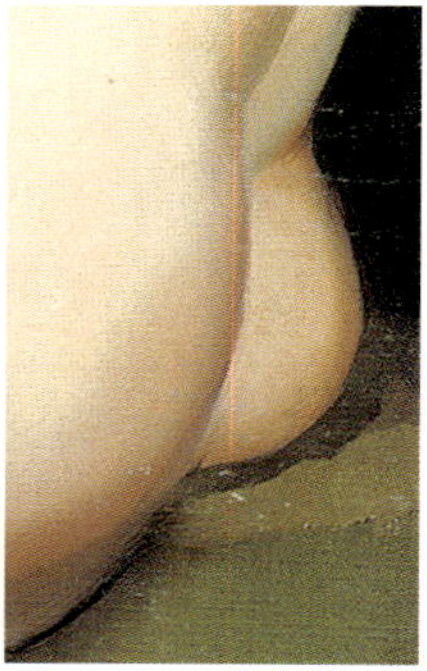

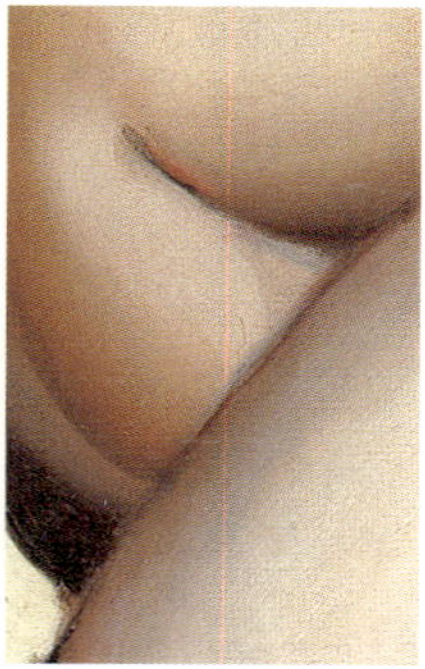

Barbara Cartland and Georgette Heyer could not have invented a ploy more effective for catching the eye of the handsome hero. In an account that has the ring of truth to it, Tamara admitted that the brokering of her marriage to Tadeusz by her Uncle was less than entirely romantic. The wealthy banker went to the handsome young man about town and said "Listen. I will put my cards on the table. You are a sophisticated man, but you don't have much fortune. I have a niece, Polish, whom I would like to marry. If you will accept to marry her, I will give her a dowry. Anyway, you know her already."

Seated Nude in Profile

c. 1923
Oil on canvas, 81 x 54 cm
Barry Friedman Ltd, New York

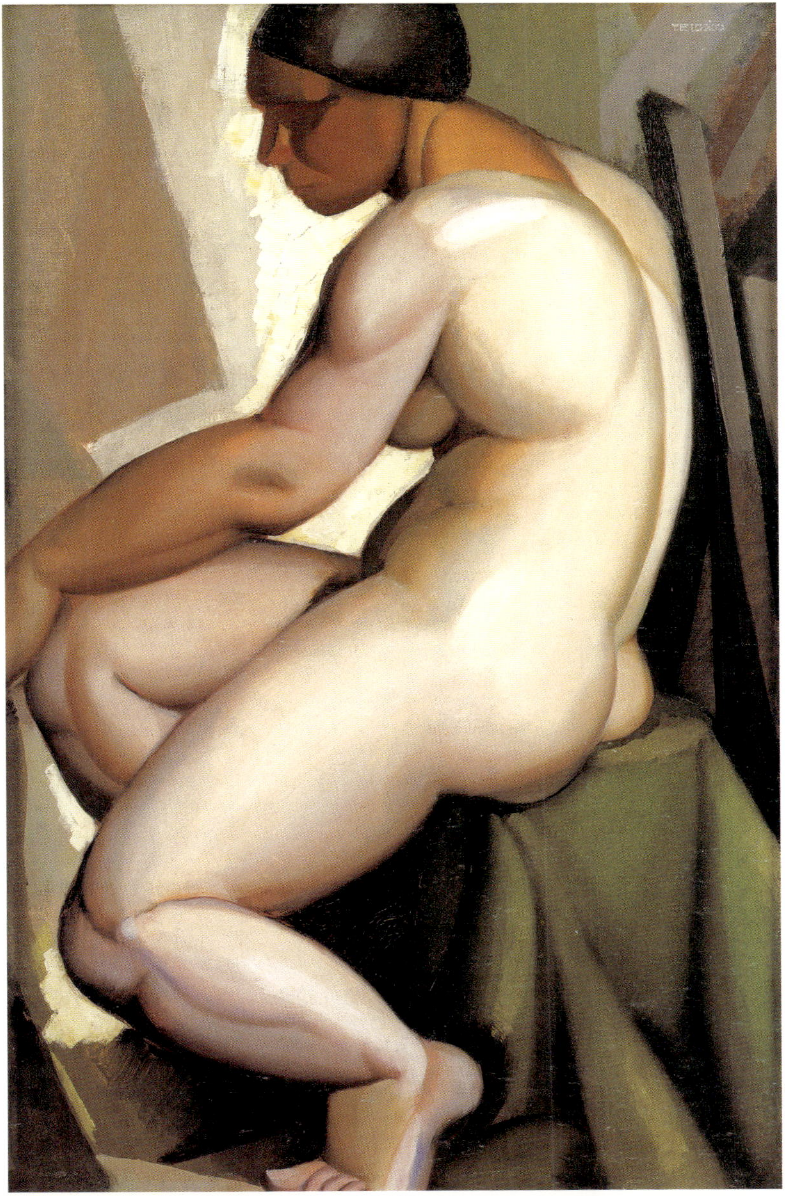

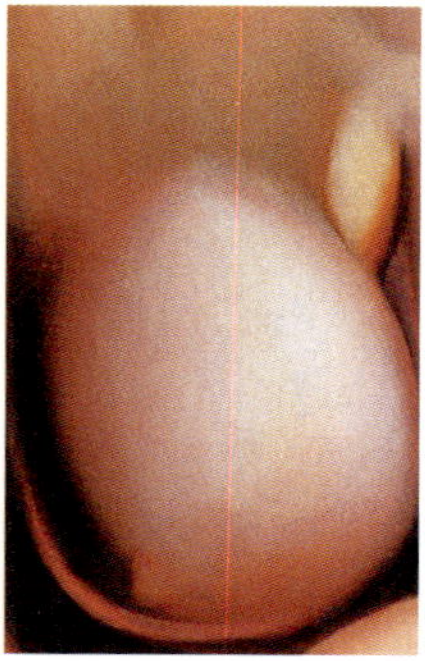

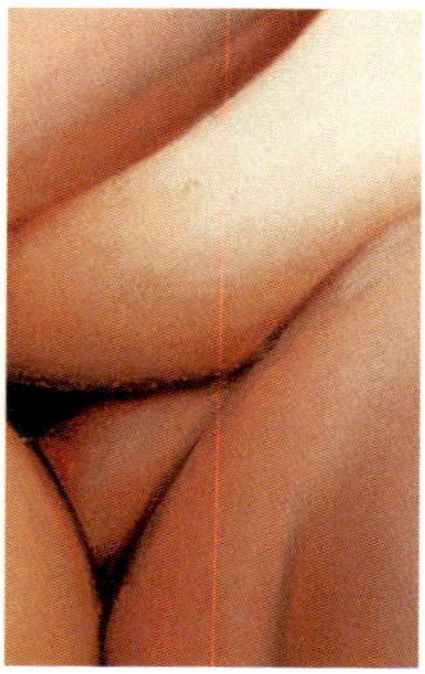

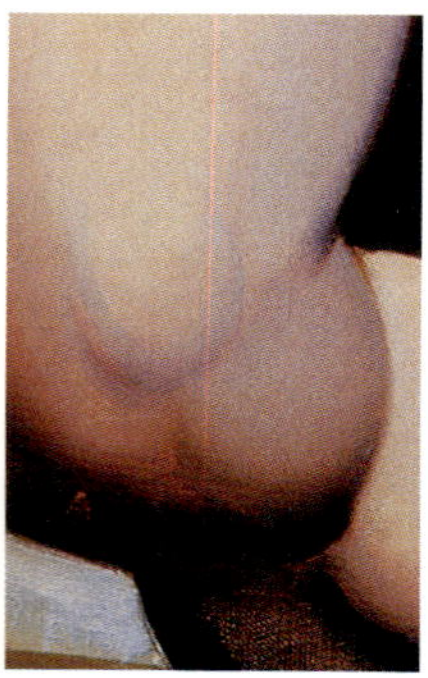

By the time the marriage took place in the chapel of the Knights of Malta in the recently re-named Petrograd in 1916, Romanov Russia was on the verge of collapse under the onslaught of the German army and on the point of being engulfed in revolution. The tribulations of the newly married couple after the rise of the Bolsheviks belong not so much to the plot of a novel as of an opera, with Tamara cast in the role of Tosca and Tadeusz as Cavaradossi. Given the background and life-style of the couple and the reactionary political sympathies and activities of Tadeusz, it was not surprising that he should have been arrested under the new regime. Tamara remembered that she and Tadeusz were making love when the secret police pounded at the door in the middle of the night and hauled Tadeusz off to prison.

Seated Nude

c. 1923
Oil on canvas, 94 x 56 cm
Private Collection

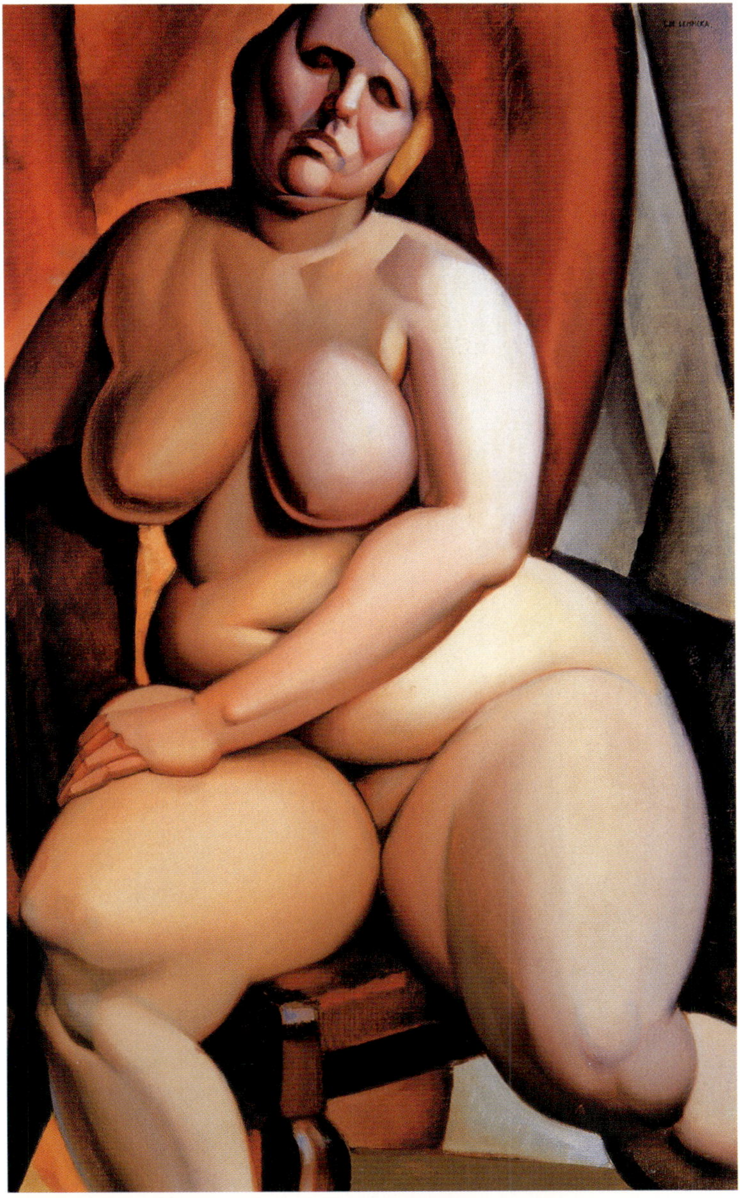

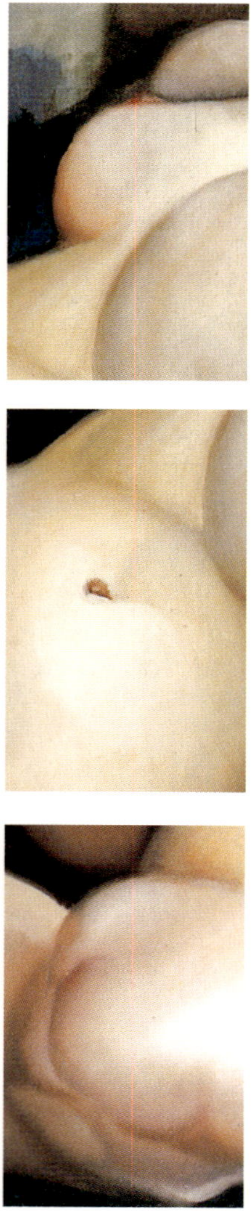

In her efforts to locate her husband and to arrange for his escape from Russia, Tamara enlisted the help of the Swedish consul who like Scarpia in Puccini's operatic melodrama, demanded sexual favours. Happily the outcome was different from that of Puccini's opera and neither party cheated the other. Tamara gave the Swedish consul what he wanted and he honoured his promise, not only to aid Tamara's escape from Russia but also the subsequent release and escape of her husband. Tamara travelled on a false passport via Finland to be re-united with relatives in Copenhagen.

The Sleeping Girl

1923
Oil on canvas, 89 x 146 cm
Private Collection

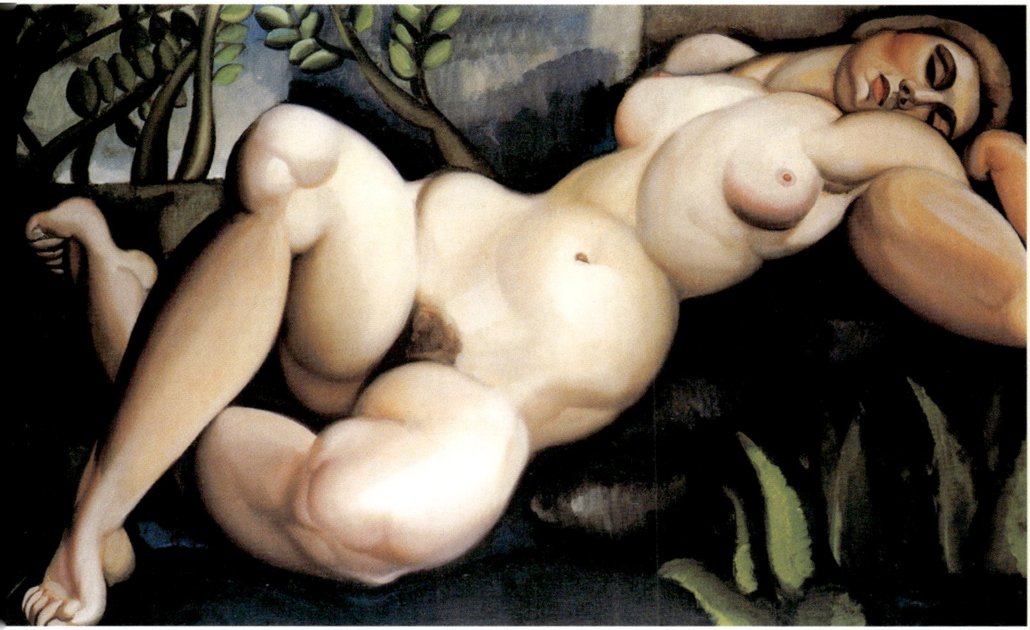

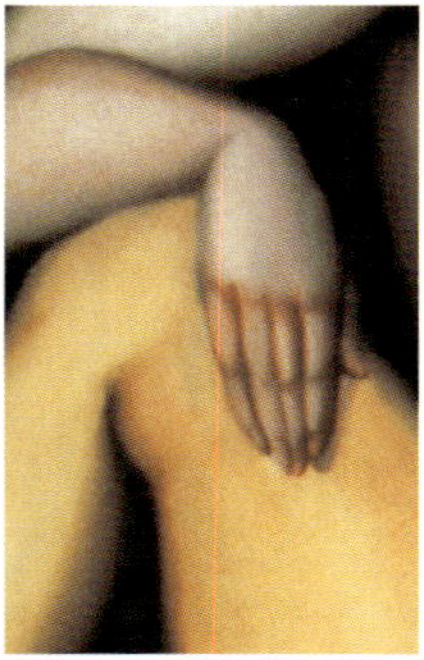

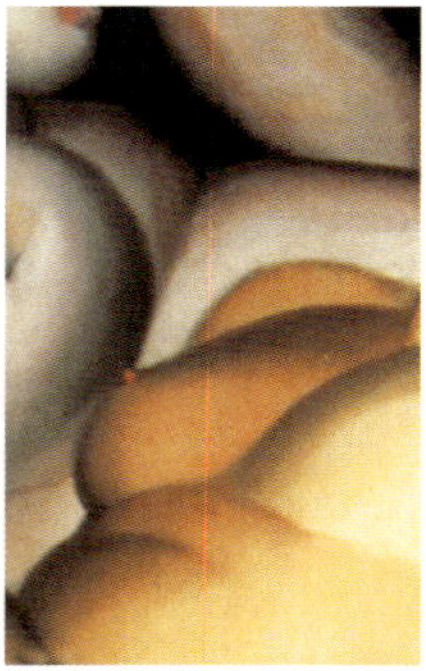

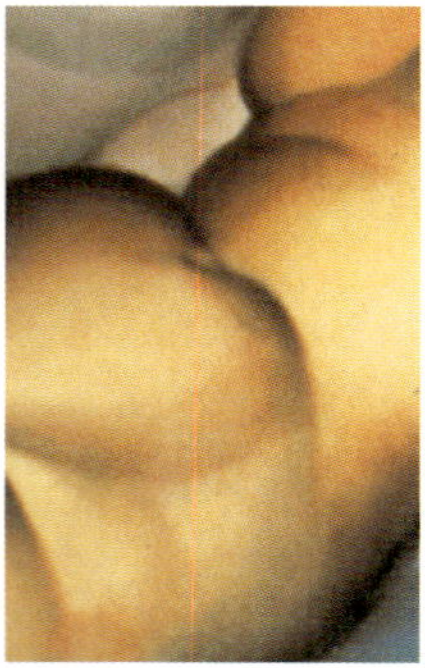

Refugees from the Russian Revolution fanned out across the globe, but Paris which had long been a second home to well-healed Russians, became a Mecca for White Russians in the inter war period. Inevitably Tamara and Tadeusz were drawn there along with Tamara's mother and younger sister (her brother was one of the millions of casualties of the war). Unlike so many refugees who arrived there penniless and friendless they could at least rely upon help from Aunt Stefa and her husband who had managed to retain some of his wealth and to re-establish himself in his former career as a banker.

Perspective

1923
Oil on canvas, 130 x 162 cm
Musée du Petit Palais, Genève

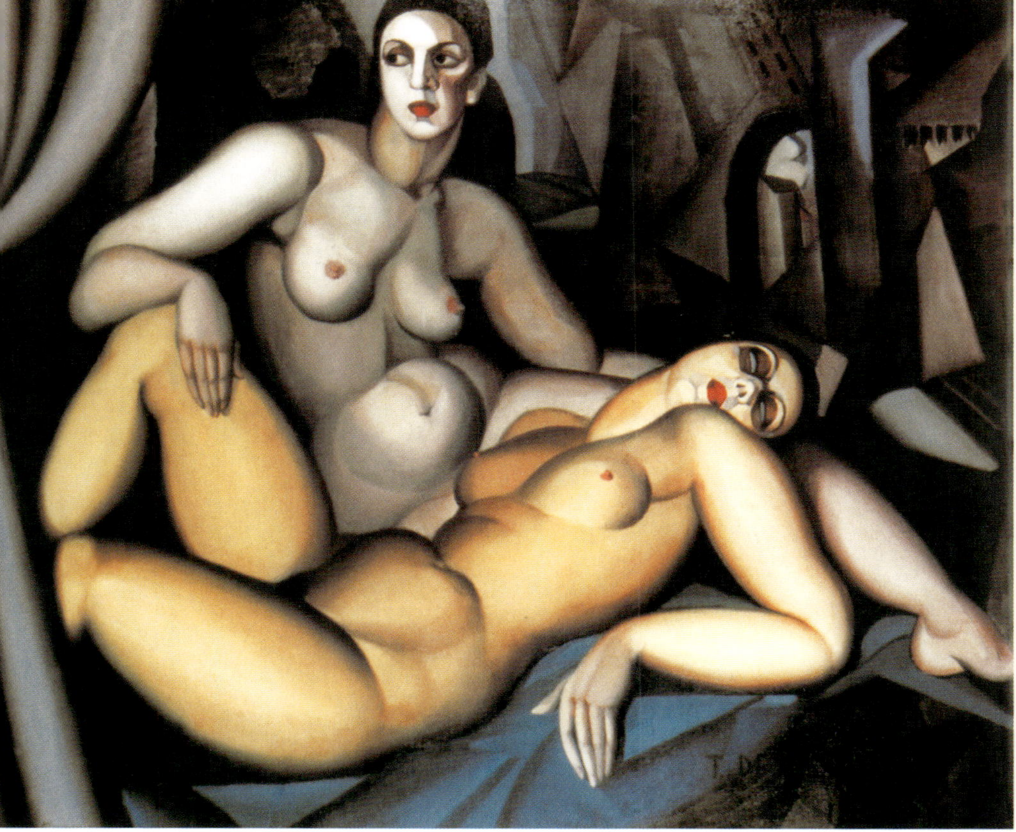

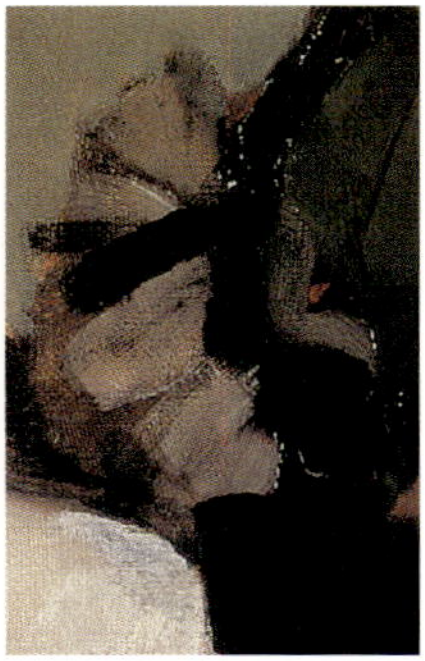

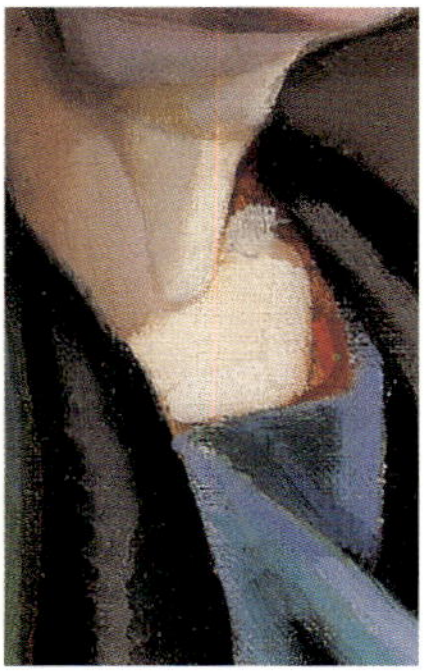

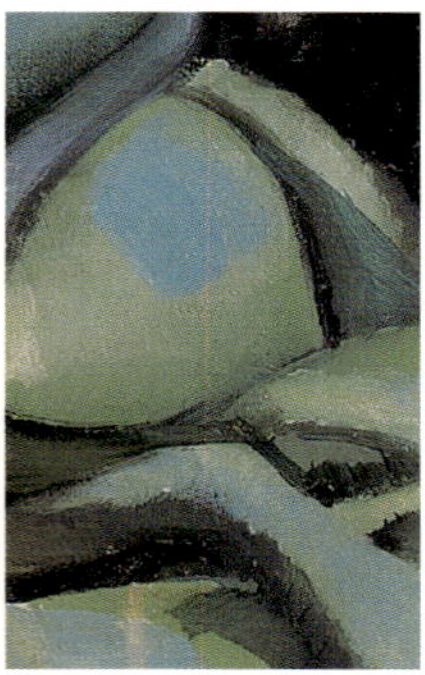

From the turn of the century the political alliance between Russia and France — aimed at containing the menace of Wilhelmine Germany — encouraged the growth of cultural links between the two countries. The great impresario Sergei Diaghilev took advantage of this political climate to establish himself in Paris. In 1906, Diaghilev organised an exhibition of Russian portraits at the Grand Palais that pioneered a more imaginative presentation of paintings and sculptures. Following this success, he arranged concerts that for the first time presented to the French public the music of such composers as Glazunov, Rachmaninov, Rimsky-Korsakov, Tchaikovsky and Scriabin.

The Gypsy

c. 1923
Oil on canvas, 73 x 60 cm
Private Collection

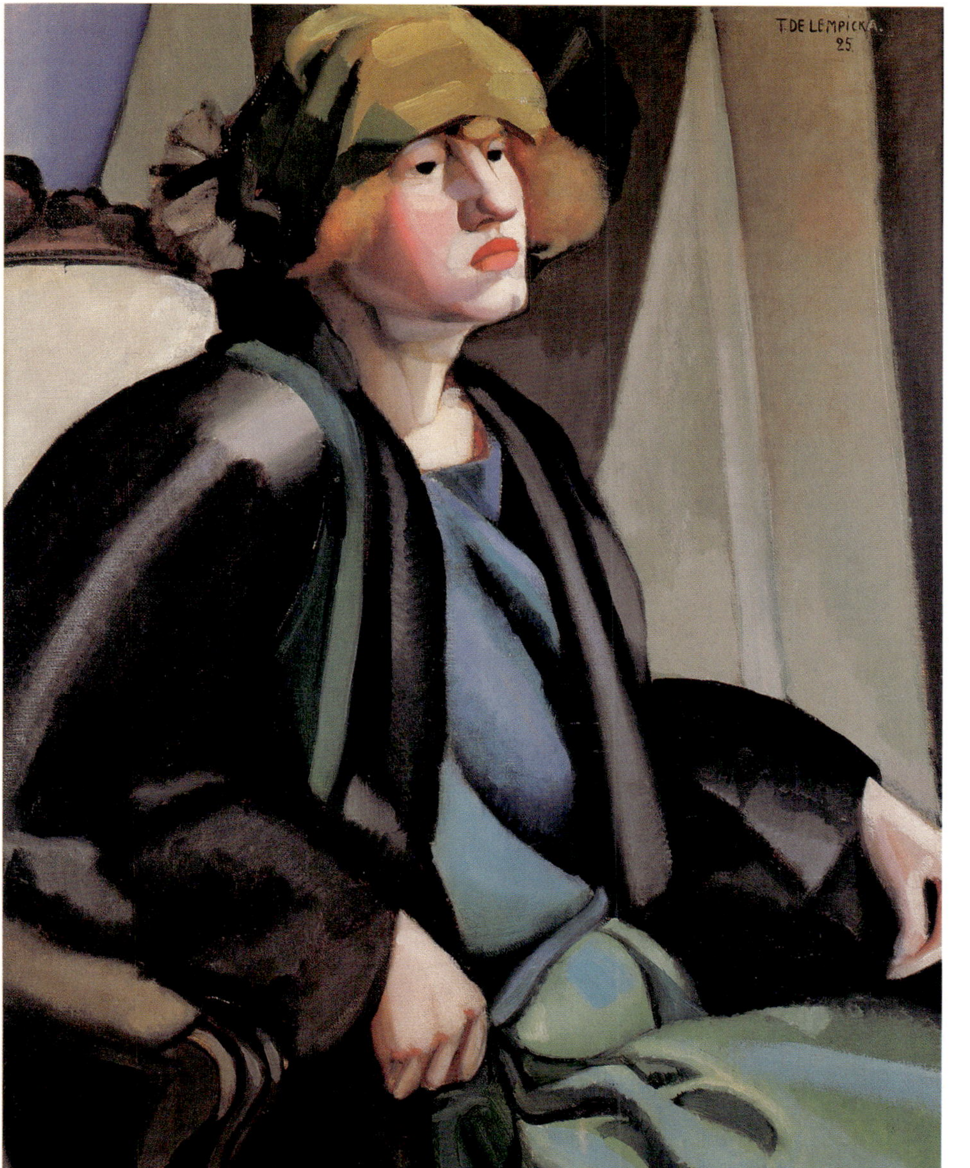
T. DE LEMPICKA
25

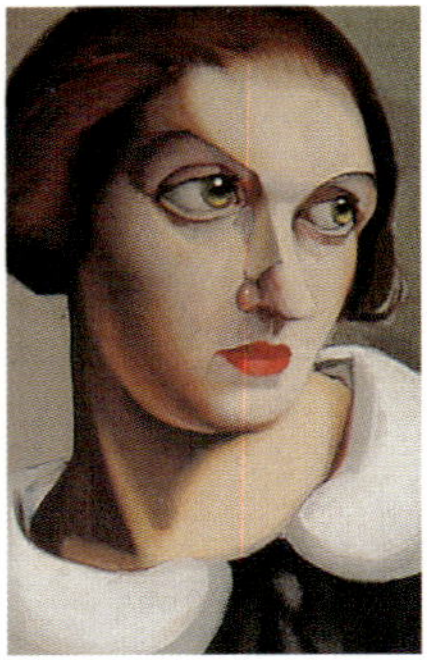

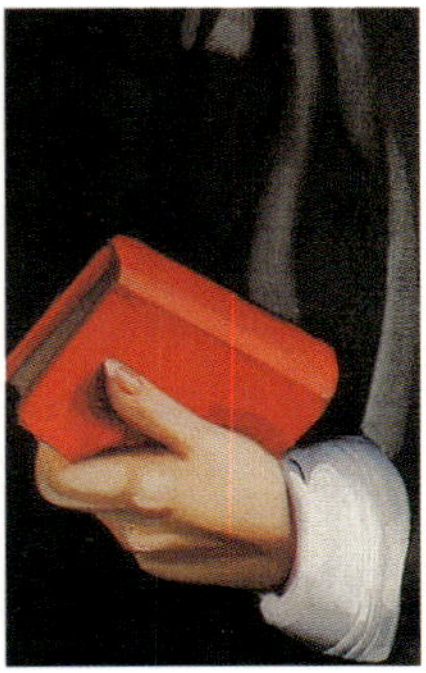

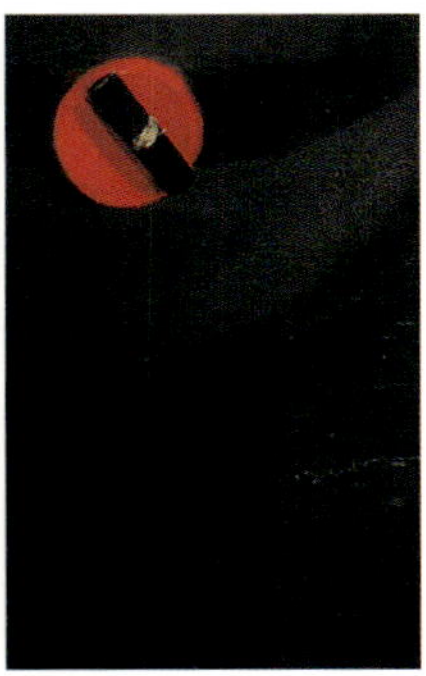

Diaghilev's designers, notably Leon Bakst, played a vital role in developing the Art Deco style with which de Lempicka became associated. In particular Bakst's designs for the 1910 production of *Sheherazade* had an extraordinary impact on fashion and interior design. For the next generation, fashionable Parisian hostesses dressed themselves and decorated their salons as though for an oriental orgy. Even in the late 1920s, photographs of Tamara de Lempicka's bedrooms show decors which, though much pared down from the lushness of Bakst's designs, make them look as if Nijinsky's sex slave would not be out of place as an overnight guest.

Woman in a Black Dress

1923
Oil on canvas, 195 x 60.5 cm
Private Collection

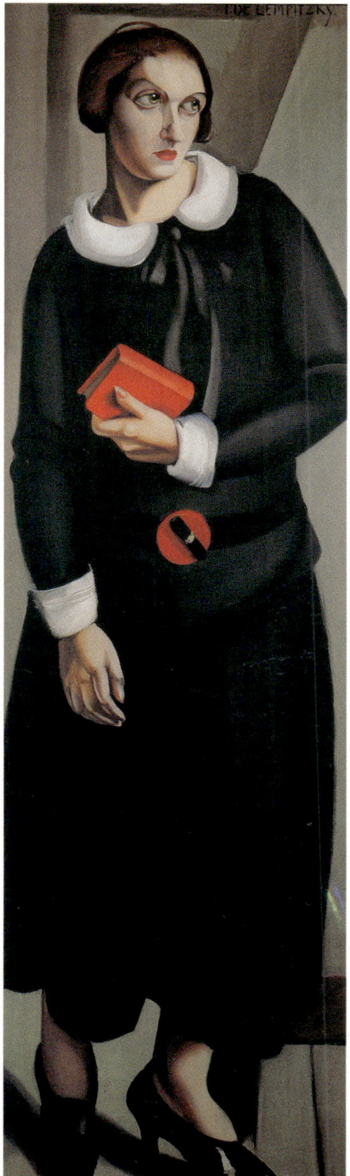

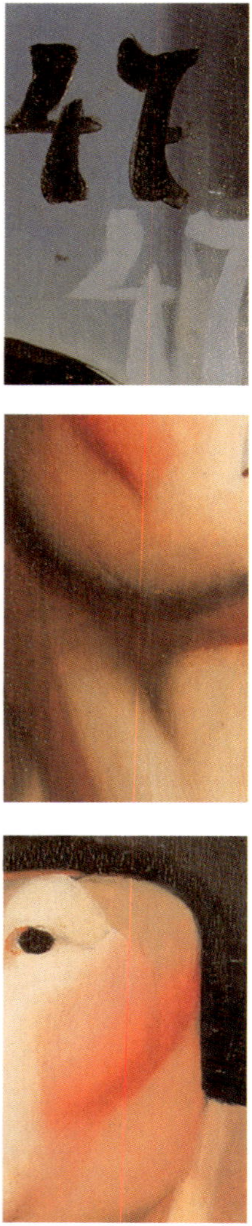

Paris in the inter-war period was teeming with Russian refugees. It was jokingly said that every second taxi driver in Paris was either a real or pretend Grand Duke.

De Lempicka's early years in Paris were not happy. Though never reduced to the penury of so many of her refugee compatriots, she was nevertheless dependent upon the largesse of her wealthier relations. Despite the birth of her daughter Kizette, Tamara's love match with Tadeusz was turning sour as a result of her own infidelities and his frustrations. He refused as demeaning the offer of a job in her uncle's bank. According to her own account it was out of this grim situation and a desire for financial and personal independence that de Lempicka's artistic vocation was born.

Double "47"

c. 1924
Oil on panel, 46 x 38 cm
Private Collection

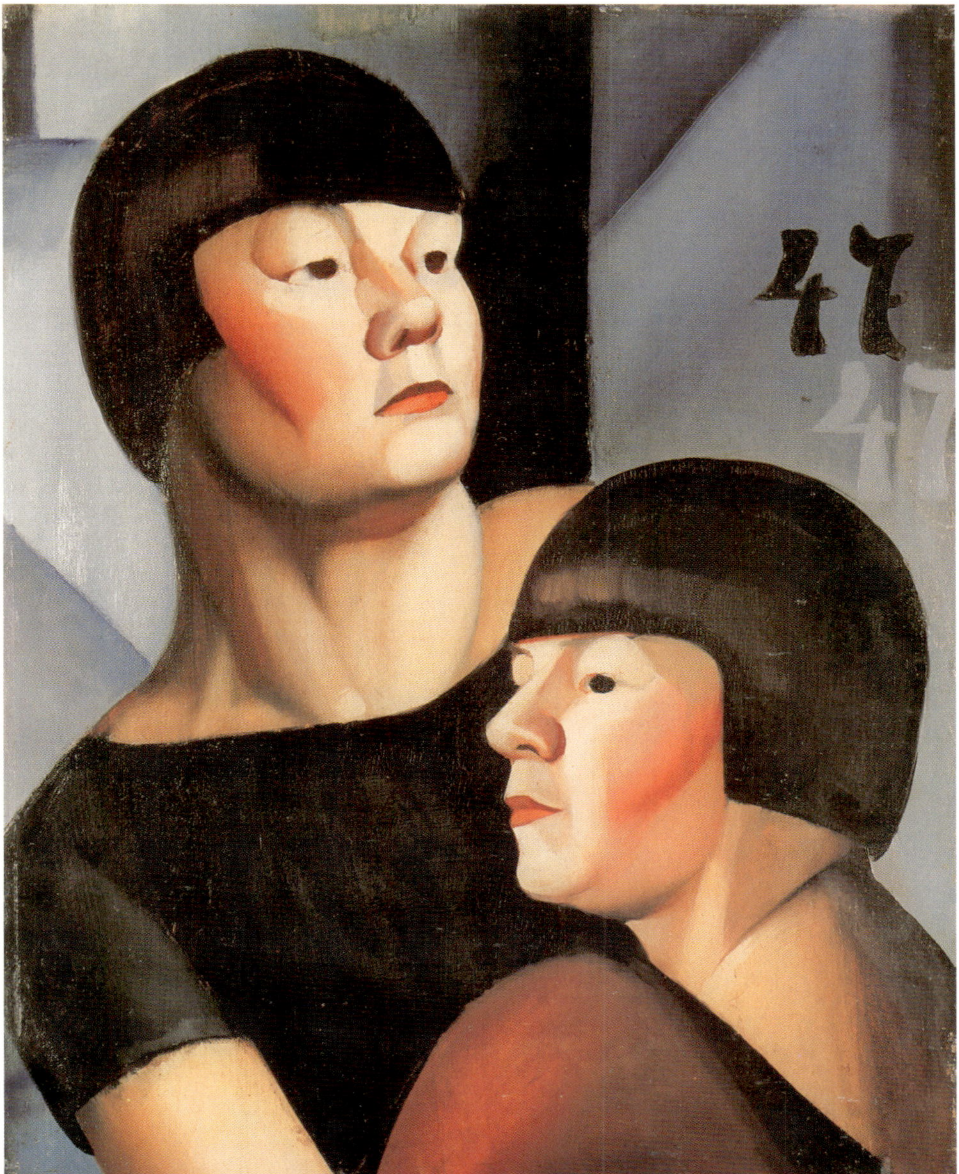
47

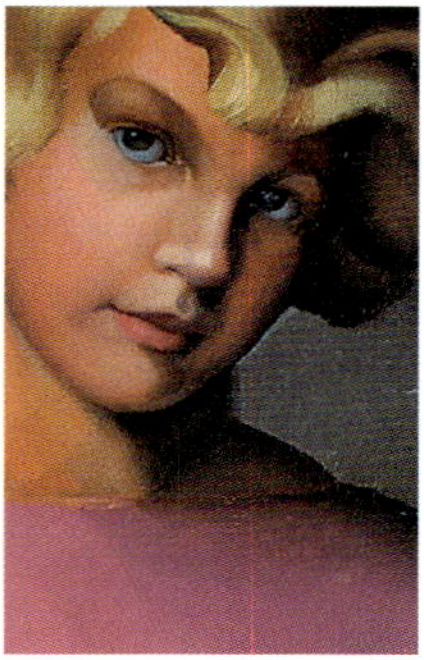

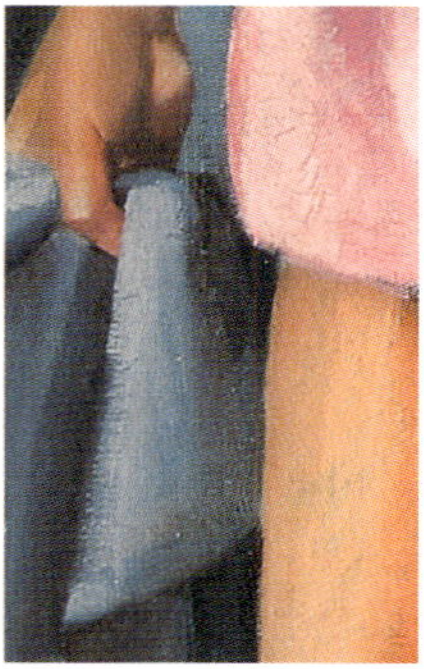

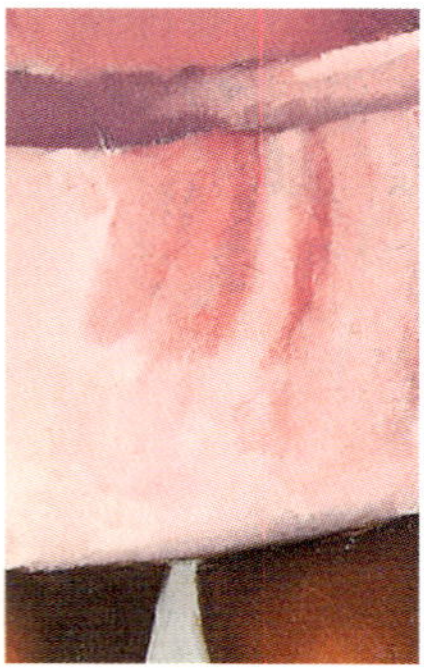

Tamara confessed her plight to her younger sister Adrienne, resulting in the following conversation between the sisters; — "Tamara, why don't you do something — something of your own? Listen to me, Tamara. I am studying architecture. In two years I'll be an architect, and I'll be able to make my own living and even help out Mama. If I can do this, you can do something too" "What? What? What?" "I don't know, painting perhaps. You can be an artist. You always loved to paint. You have talent. That portrait you did of me when we were children...." The rest, as they say, was history. Tamara bought the brushes and paints, enrolled in an art school, sold her first pictures within months and made her first million (francs) by the time she was twenty-eight.

Portrait of Kizette

c. 1924
Oil on canvas, 135 x 57 cm
Private Collection

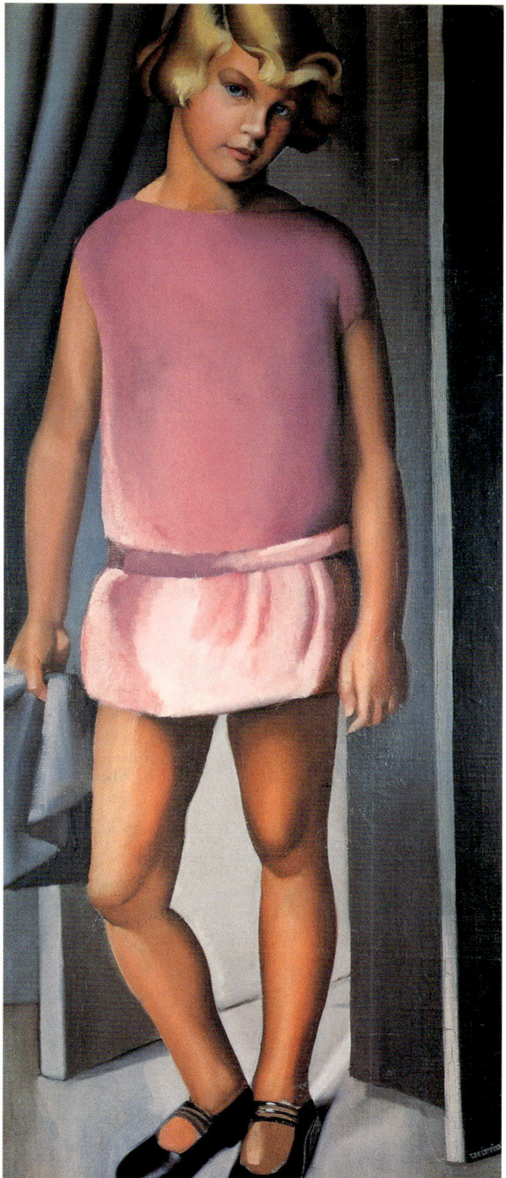

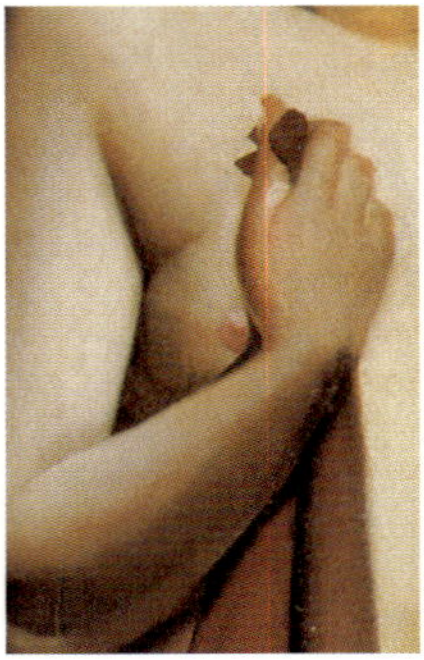

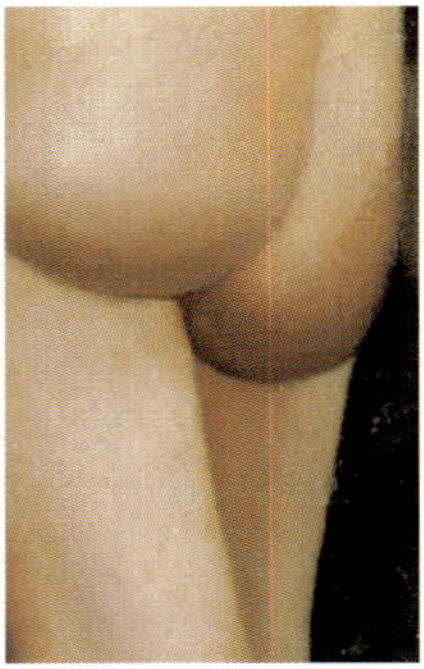

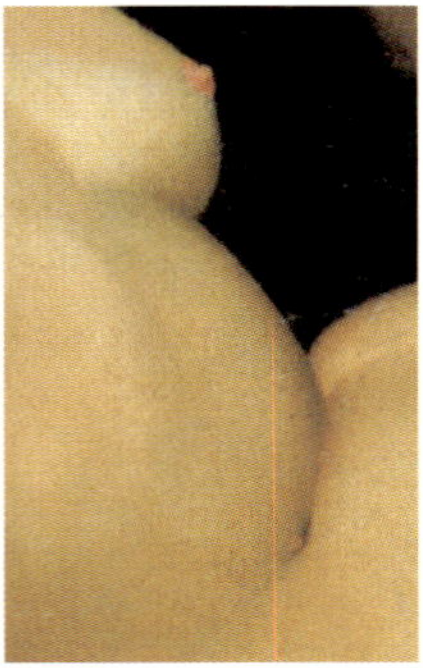

Tamara took herself for tuition to two distinguished painters in succession: Maurice Denis (1870-1943) and André Lhote (1885-1962). De Lempicka later claimed that she did not gain much from Denis. It is indeed difficult to imagine that the intensely Catholic Denis would have been much in sympathy with the worldly, modish and erotic tendencies that soon began to display themselves in Tamara's work. Nevertheless Denis was an intelligent initial choice as a teacher for the aspiring artist. For a brief period in the early 1890s Denis had been at the cutting edge of early modernism as a leading member of the Nabis group that included Vuillard, Bonnard, Serusier, Ranson and Vallotton.

Rhythm

1924
Oil on canvas, 160 x 144 cm
Private Collection

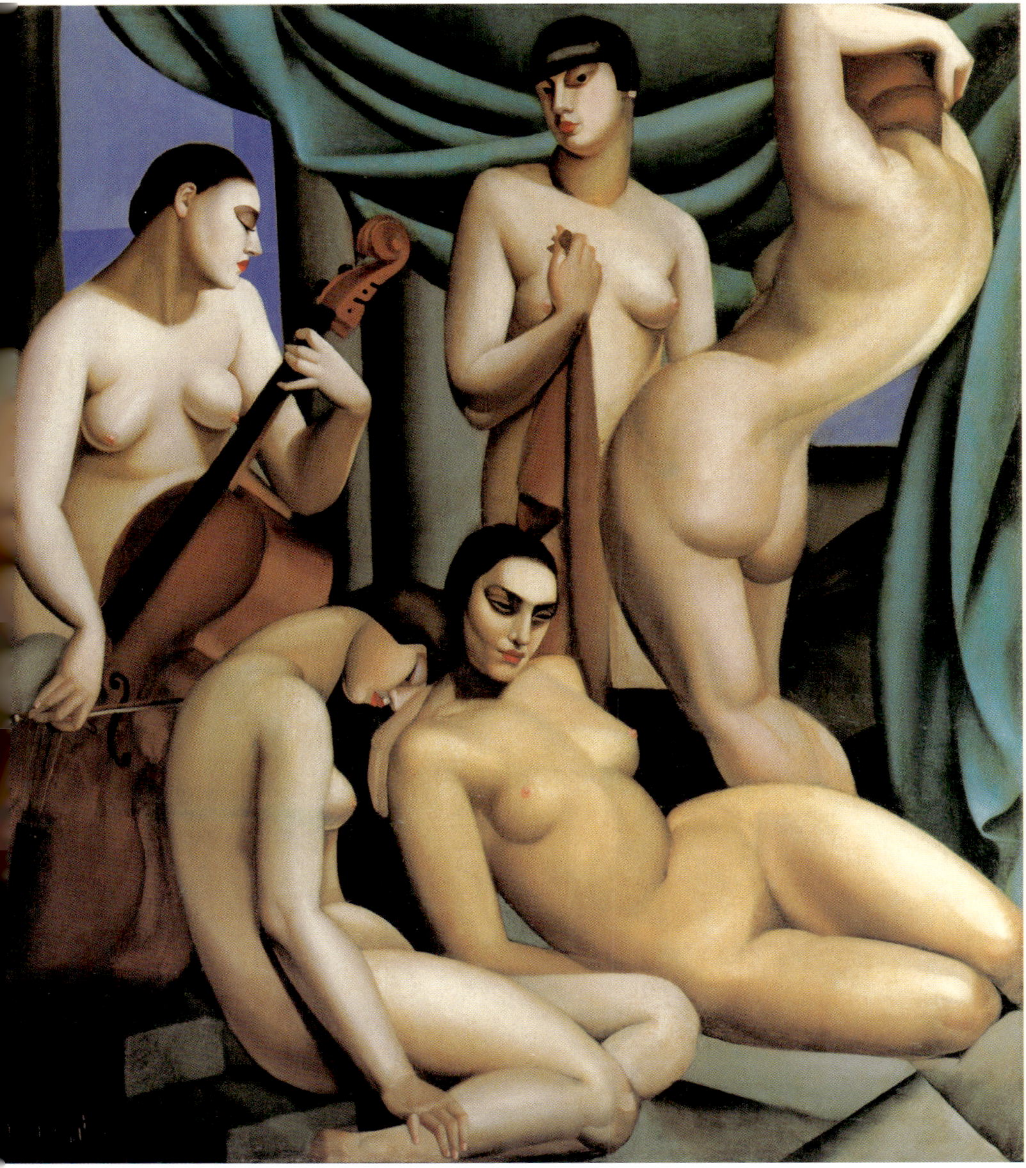

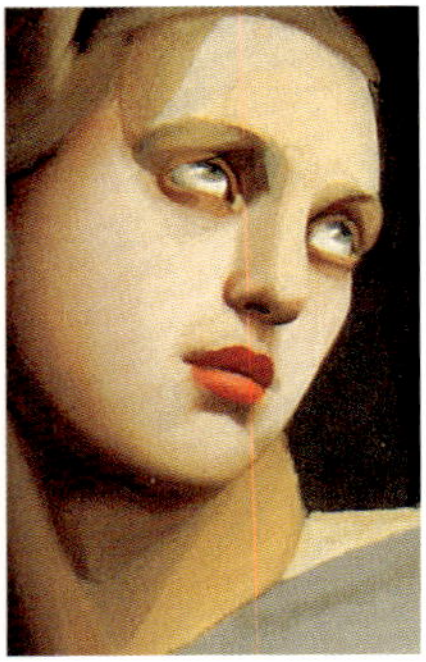

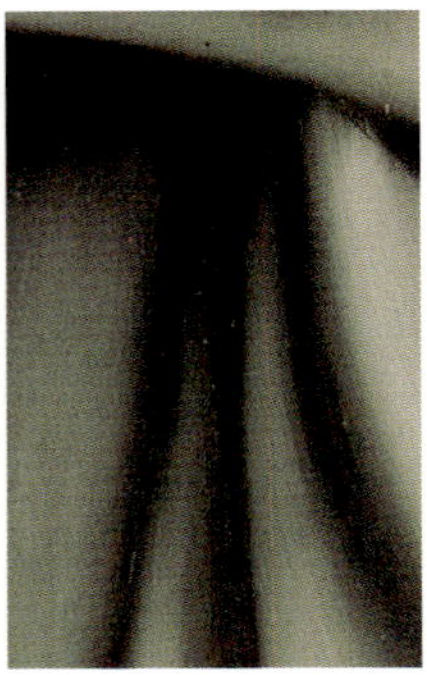

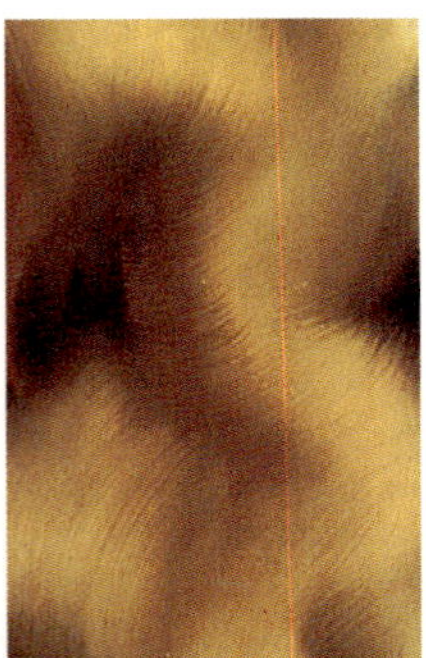

Inspired by the Synthetism of Gauguin's Breton paintings, Denis and his friends broke with the naturalism of Salon painting and the very different naturalism of the Impressionists who were tied to sensory perception and painted small pictures in flat patches of bright, exaggerated colours. However the firm linearity and smooth modelling of the forms in Denis' later works as well as his attempts to marry modernity with the classical tradition can hardly have failed to influence the young de Lempicka. The aesthetic expressed by Denis in his 1909 publication *From Gauguin and Van Gogh to Classicism* was surely one with which she would have agreed. "Art is not simply a visual sensation that we receive, ... a photograph however sophisticated of nature. No, it is a creation of the mind, for which nature is merely the springboard." This is surely true of de Lempicka's strangely cerebral and abstracted portraits of the 1920s.

Irene and Her Sister

1925
Oil on canvas, 146 x 89 cm
Irena Hochman Fine Art Ltd, New York

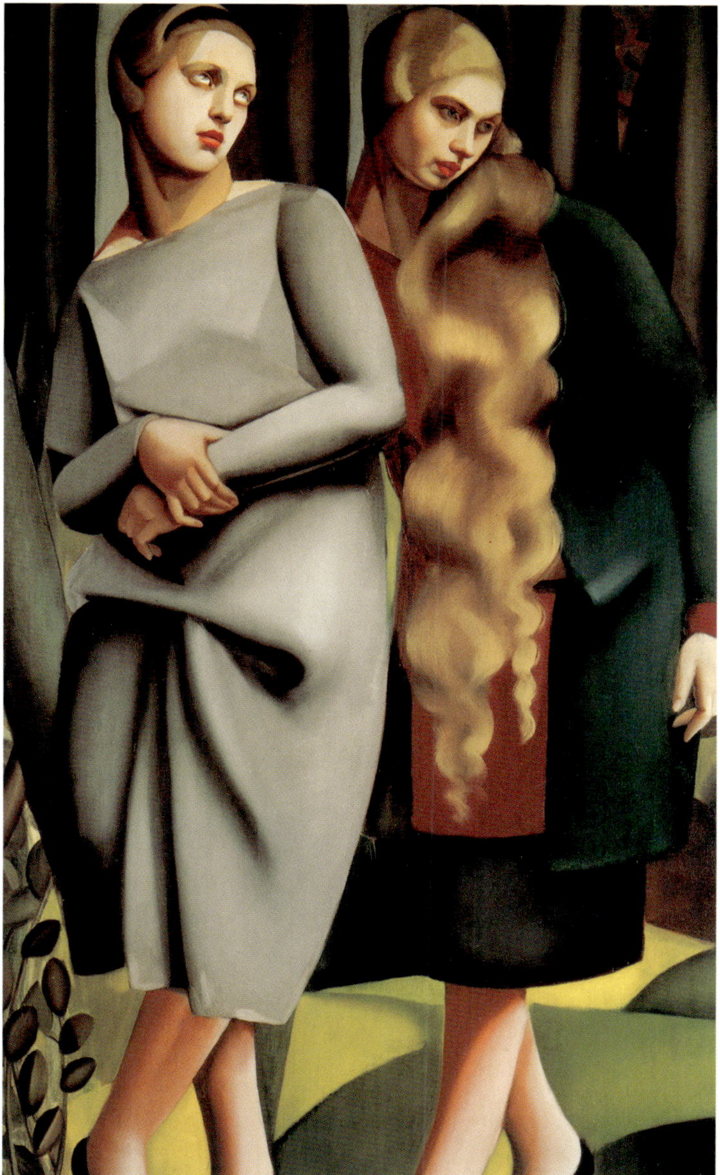

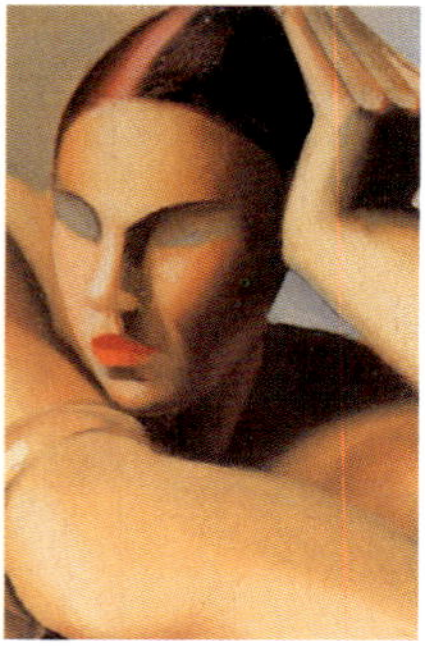

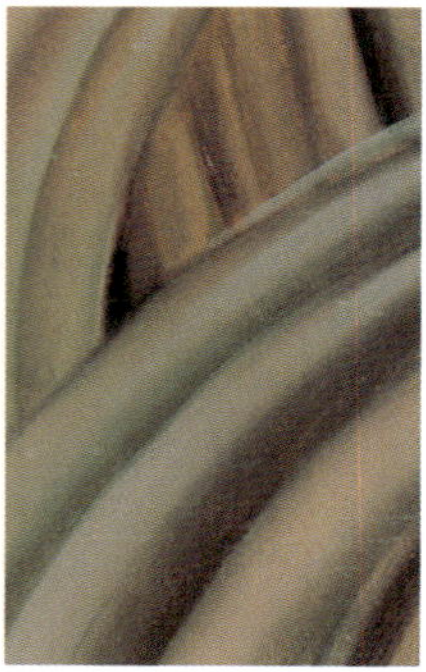

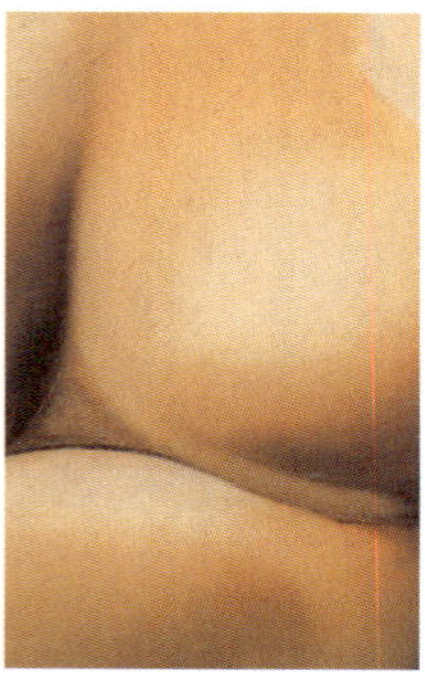

De Lempicka was far more ready to acknowledge the influence of her second teacher André Lhote. Whilst Denis must have seemed like a relic of the nineteenth century, Lhote, born in 1885, was not much more than a decade older than de Lempicka herself and was much closer to her modern and worldly outlook. Lhote had been associated with cubism since 1911 when he exhibited at the Salon des Independents and the Salon d'Automne alongside artists such as Jean Metzinger, Roger de La Fresnaye, Albert Gleizes and Fernand Leger. Rather than following the radical experiments in the dissolution of form in Picasso and Braque's Analytical Cubism, he was attracted to the brightly coloured and more representational Synthetic Cubism of Juan Gris, Albert Gleizes and Jean Metzinger.

Nude on a Terrace

1925
Oil on canvas, 37.8 x 54.5 cm
Private Collection

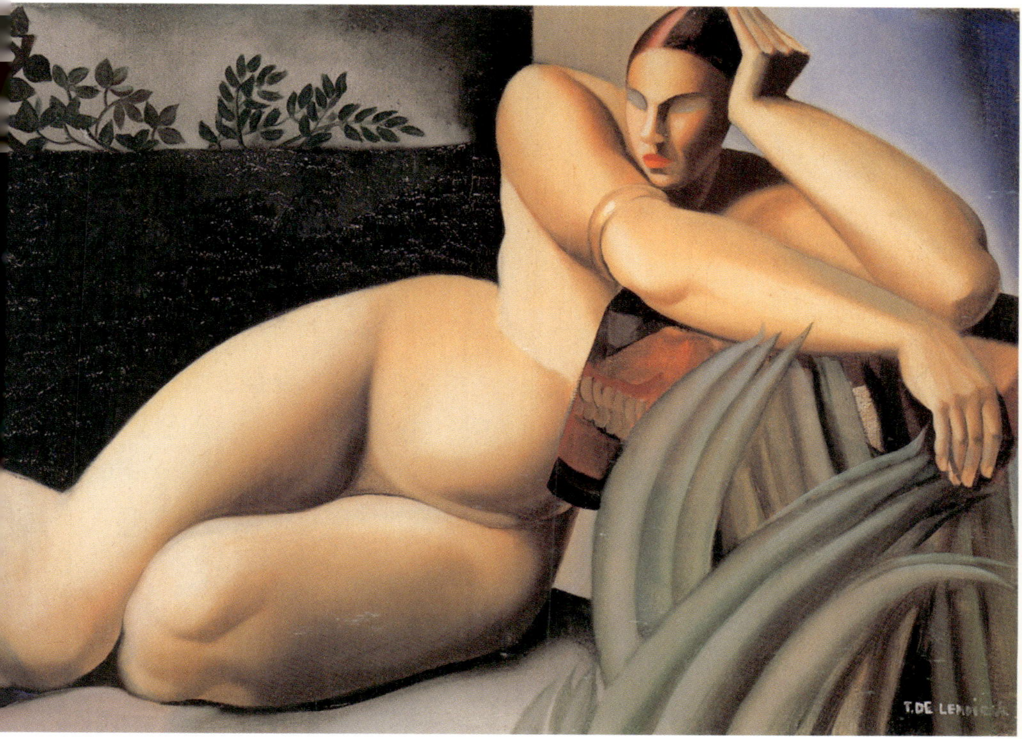
T. DE LEMPICKA

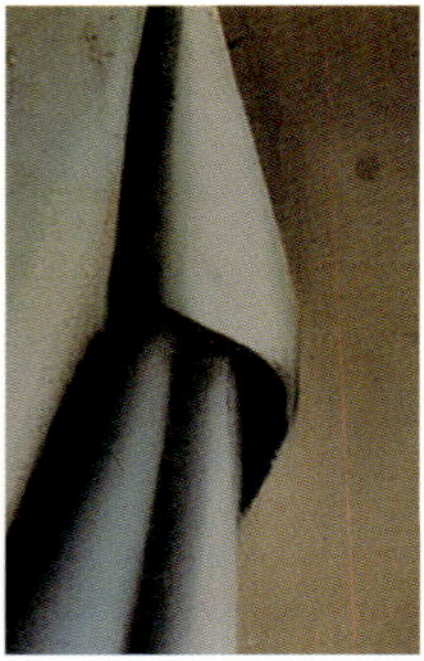

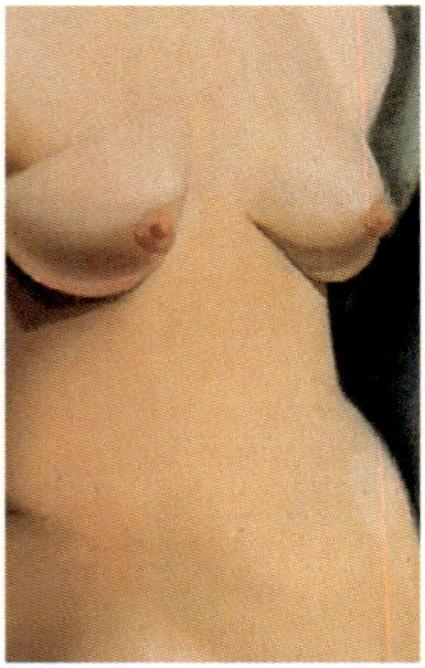

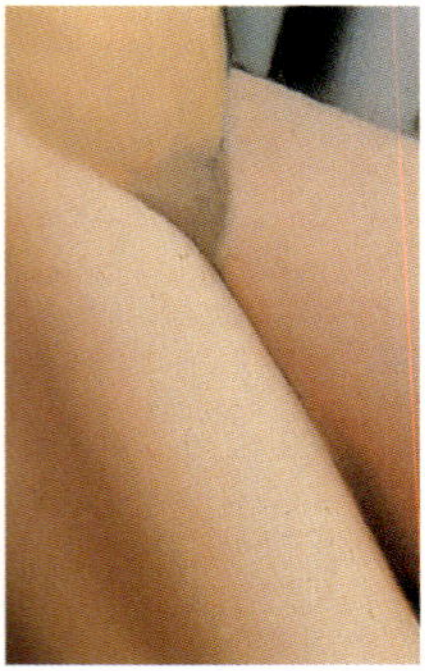

For Lhote, painting was a "plastic metaphor…pushed to the limit of resemblance. " In words not so different from those of Denis, he maintained that artists should aim to express an equivalence between emotion and visual sensation, rather than to copy nature. What made Lhote particularly useful to de Lempicka as an example and as a teacher was the acceptance of the decorative role of painting and also his attempt to fuse elements of cubist abstraction and disruption of conventional perspective with the figurative and classical tradition. If the artist de Lempicka did not spring to life fully formed and fully armed like Athena from the head of Zeus as she would have us believe, the gestation period of her mature art was remarkably short — lasting two or three years at most.

Seated Nude

c. 1925
Oil on canvas, 61 x 38 cm
Private Collection

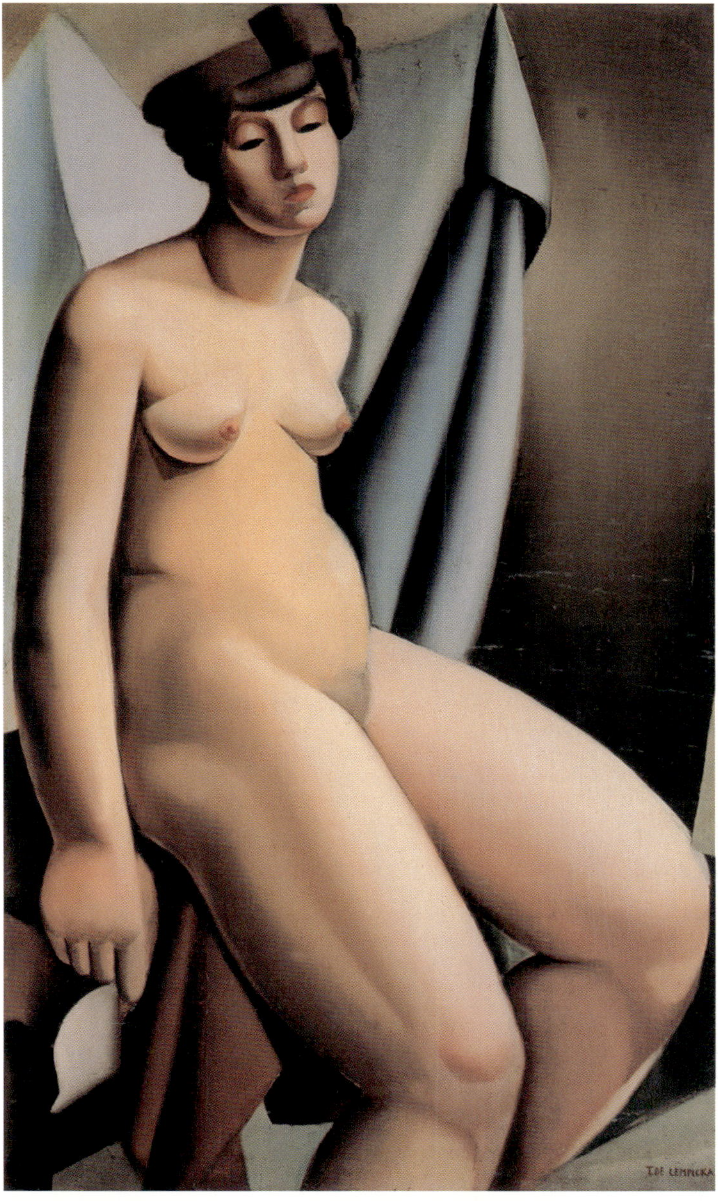
T. DE LEMPICKA

Her *Portrait of a Polo Player* painted around 1922 already shows her predilection for the smart set but could otherwise have been painted by any competent artist trained in Paris in these years. It has a looseness of touch and a painterly quality that would soon disappear from her work. The modelling of the face in bold structural brush strokes shows an awareness of Cezanne that would undoubtedly have been encouraged by both Denis and Lhote. Similarly lush and painterly is the portrait of Ira Perrot later re-titled *Portrait of a Young Lady in a Blue Dress*. In its original form, as exhibited at the Salon d'Automne and photographed at the time with the model in front of it, it showed Ira Perrot seated cross-legged in front of cushions piled up exotically in the manner of Bakst's Sheherazade designs.

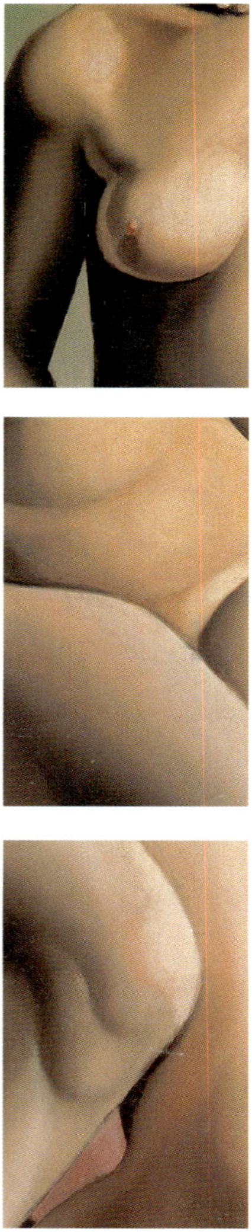

Seated Nude

1925
Oil on canvas, 61 x 38 cm
Private Collection

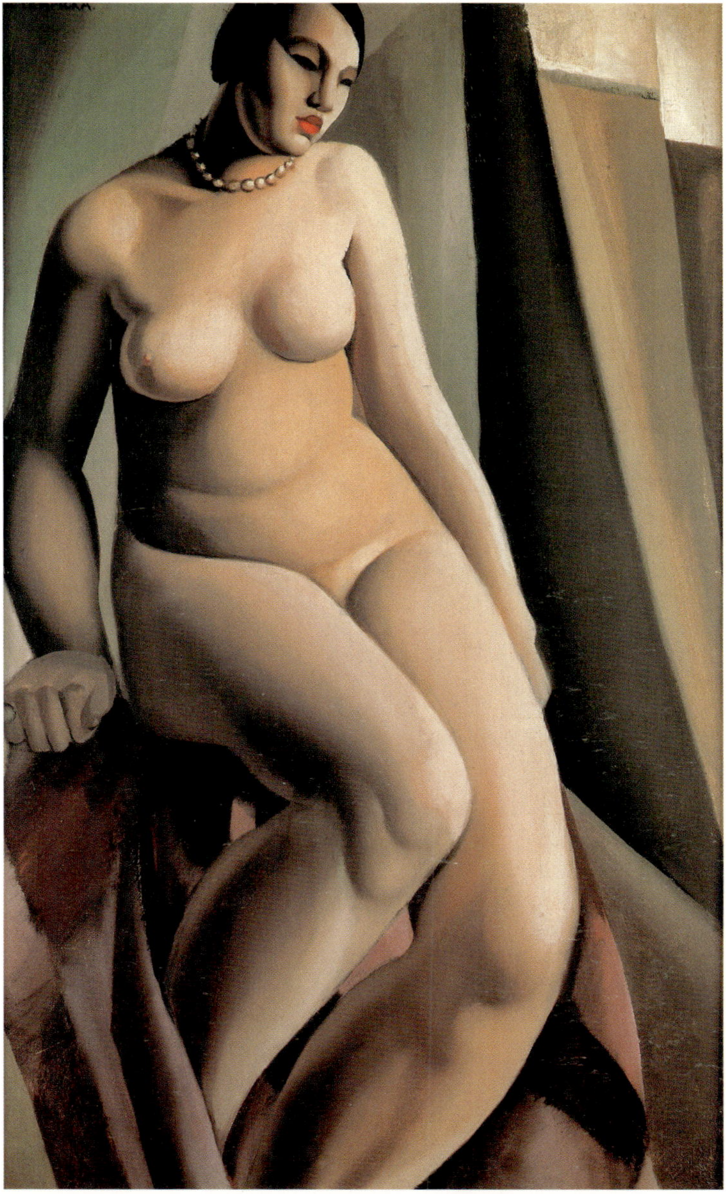

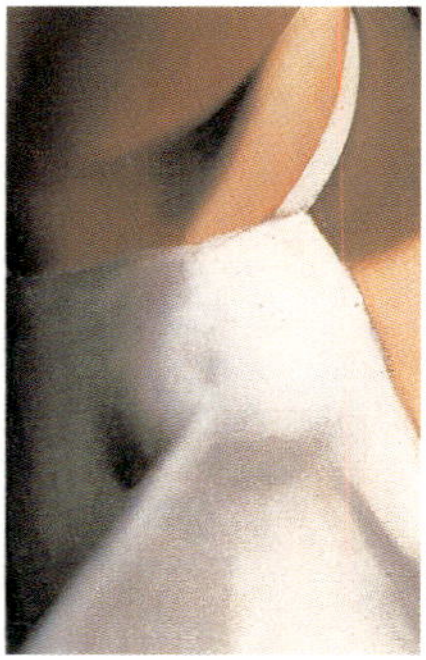

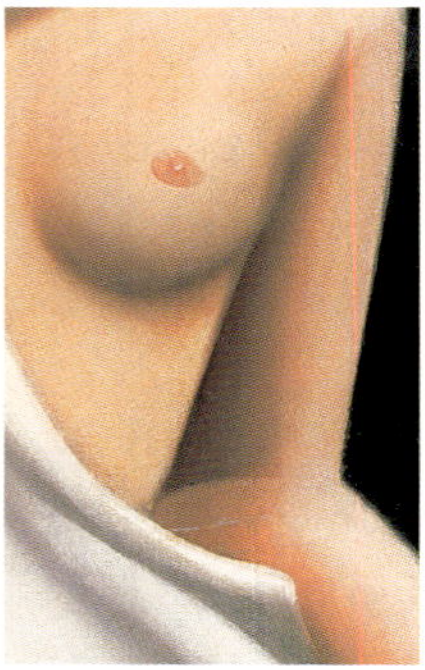

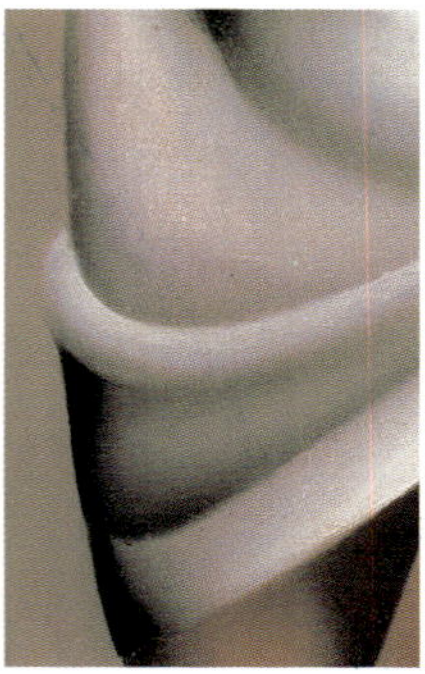

More prophetic both stylistically and in subject matter than these two portraits is another canvas of the same period entitled *The Kiss*. The erotic theme, played out against an urban back-drop, the element of cubist stylisation that gives the picture an air of modernity and dynamism and the metallic sheen on the gentleman's top hat all anticipate de Lempicka's artistic maturity. The crudeness of the technique is as yet far from the enamelled perfection of her best work. Naivety is not in general a quality we associate with de Lempicka but this picture has the look of a cover for a lurid popular novel.

The Model

1925
Oil on canvas, 116 x 73 cm
Barry Friedman Ltd, New York

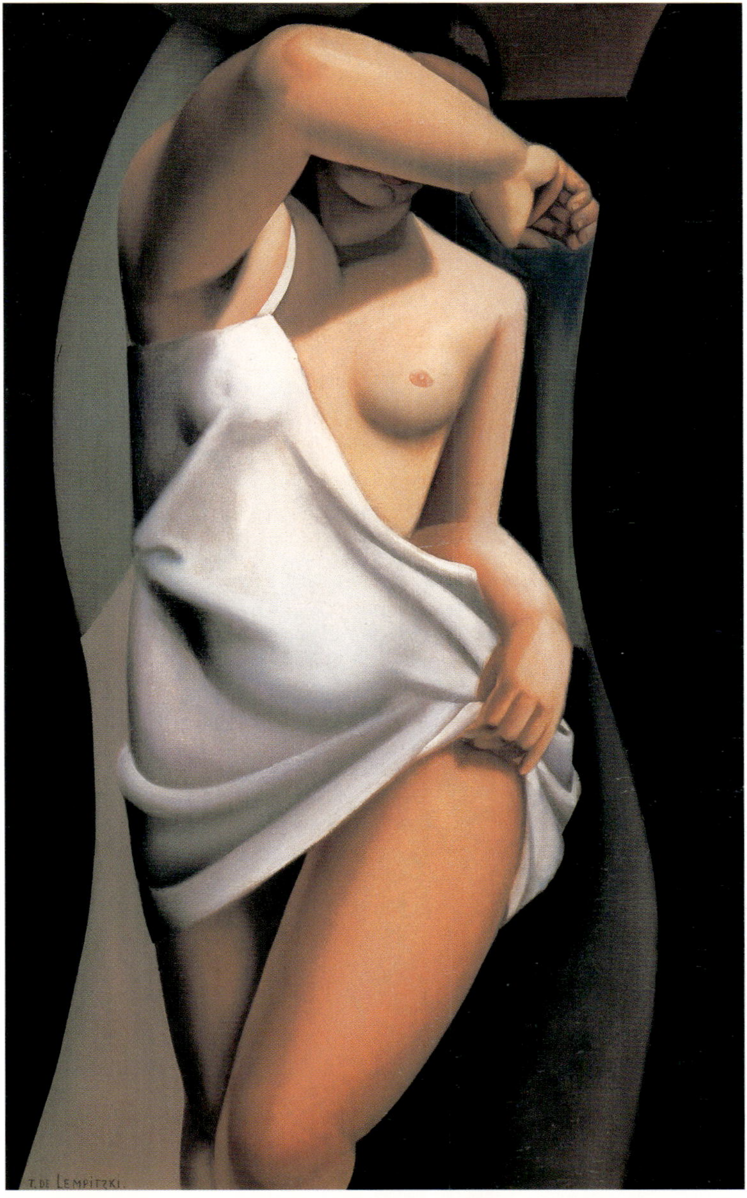
T. DE LEMPITZKI.

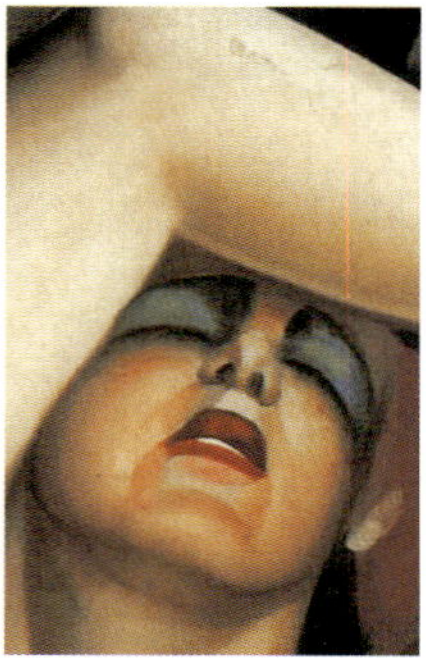
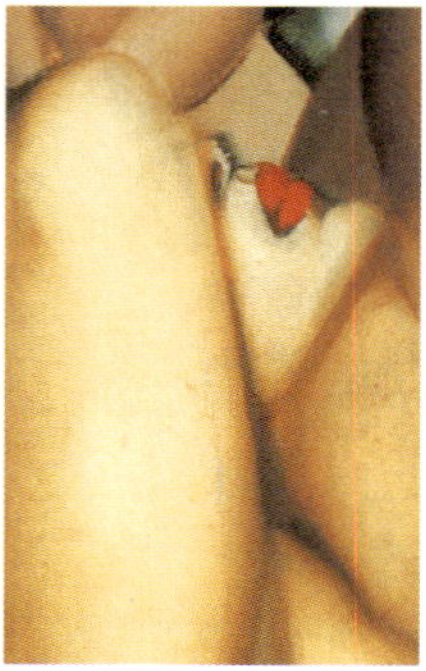
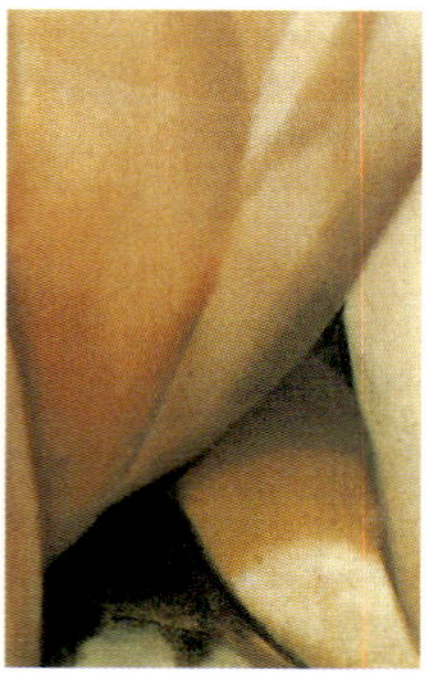

The following year we find de Lempicka working on a series of large scale and monumental female nudes that might be described as *cubified* rather than Cubist. These works reflect an interest in the classical and the monumental that was widespread in Western art following the First World War and throughout the inter-war period.

The entire history of Western art from the Ancient world onwards can be seen in terms of a series of major and minor classical revivals. In an essay of 1926 entitled *The Call to Order*, Jean Cocteau presented the post-war return to classicism as a necessary reaction to the chaos of radical experimentation during the anarchic decade that had preceded the First World War. There was undoubtedly some element of truth in this, though the roots of inter-war classicism can be traced back much further.

Group of Four Nudes

c. 1925
Oil on canvas, 130 x 81 cm
Private Collection

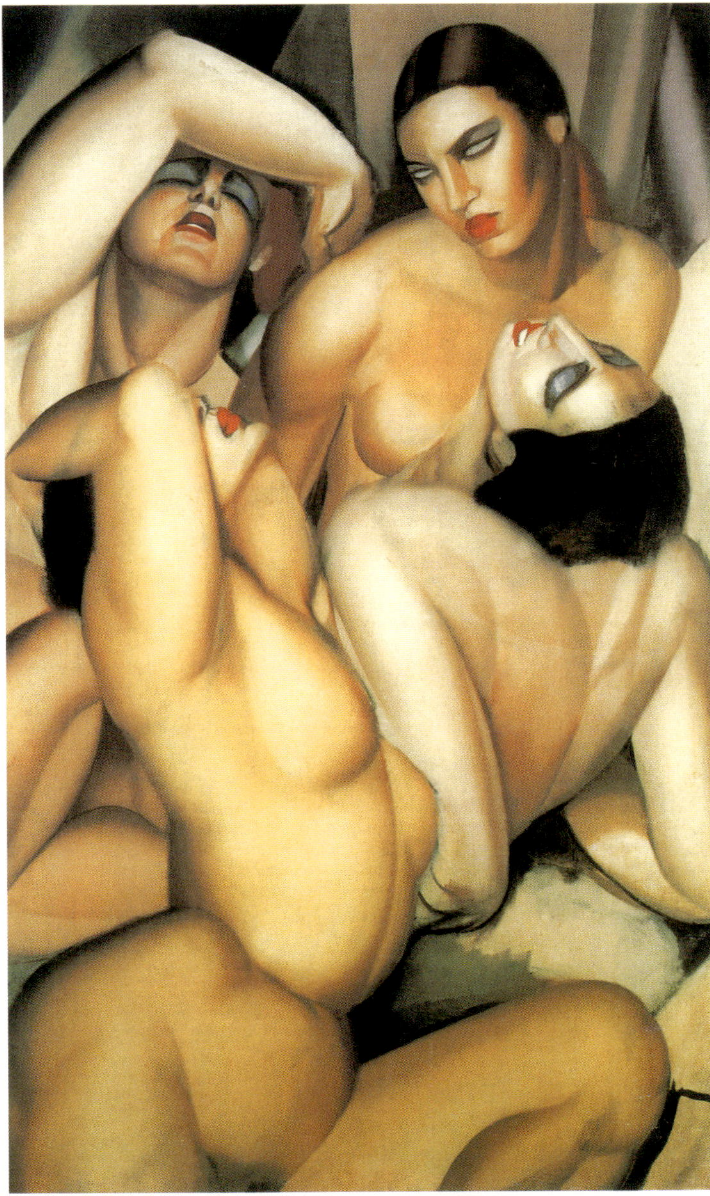

A specifically French version of classicism can be seen as a continuing thread in French art running back as far as Poussin in the seventeenth century. The classicist most often cited in connection with de Lempicka is the nineteenth century painter Jean-Auguste-Dominique Ingres (1780-1867). The taste for hard, bright colours and enamelled surfaces, the combination of abstraction and quasi-photographic realism, the eroticising of the female body through the radical distortion of anatomy and the love of luxurious and fashionable accessories link the female portraits of Ingres and de Lempicka.

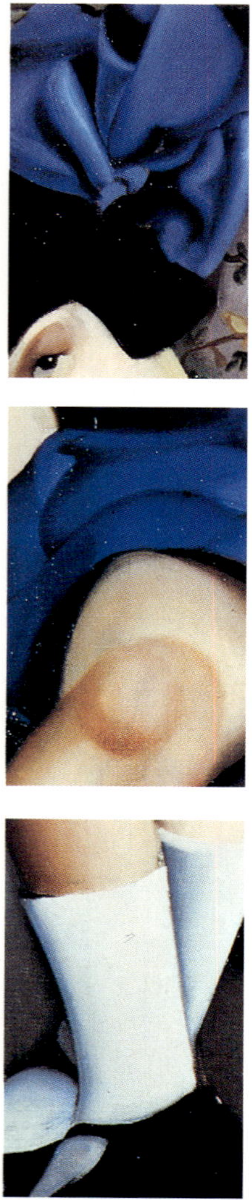

Two Little Girls with Ribbons

1925
Oil on canvas, 100 x 73 cm
Dr George and Mrs. Vivian Dean's Collection

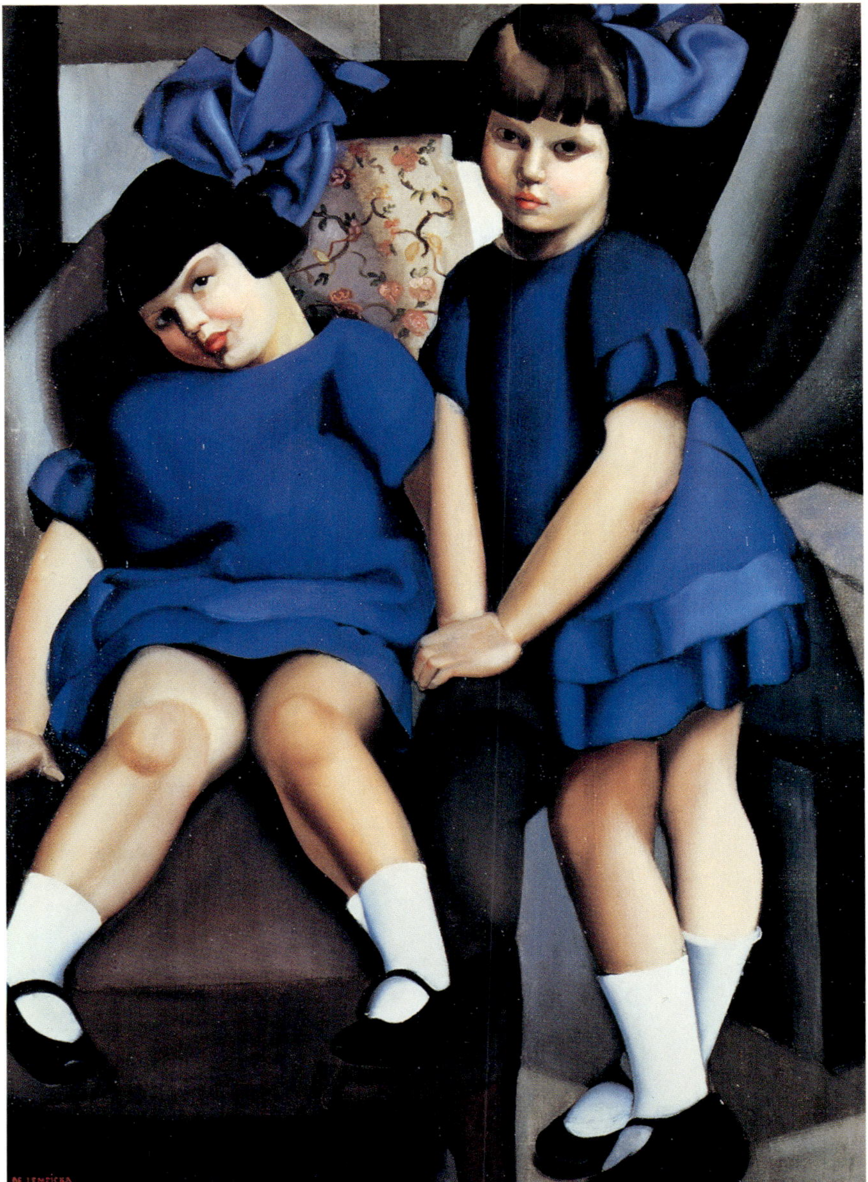
DE LEMPICKA

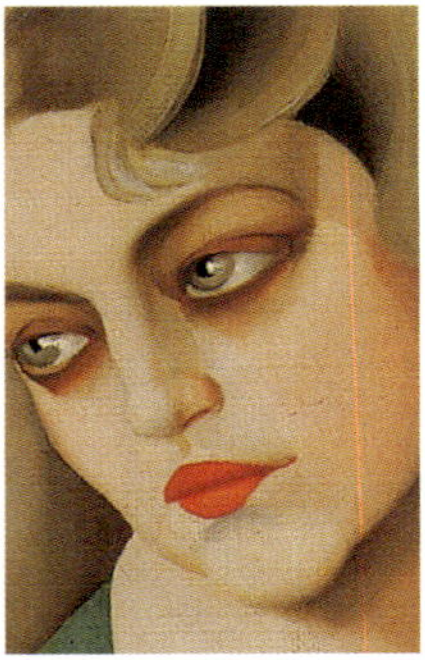

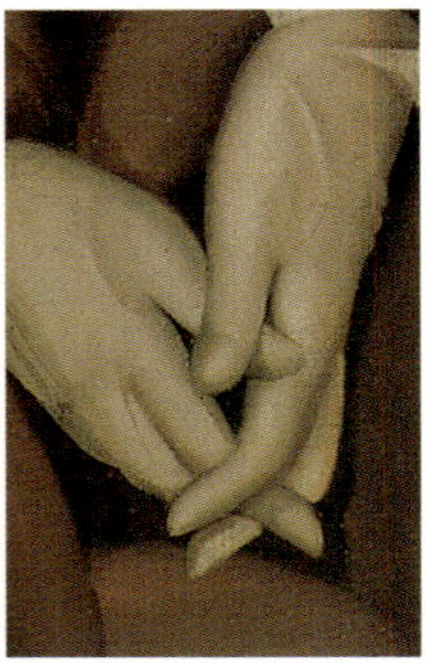

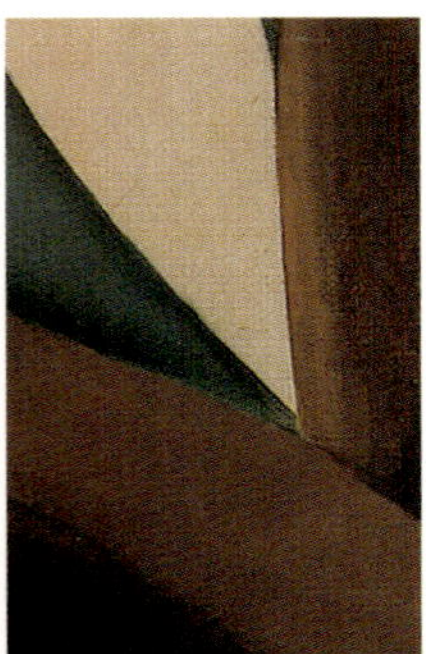

Baudelaire's bitchy comment that Ingres' ideal was "A provocative, adulterous liaison between the calm solidity of Raphael and the affectations of the fashion plate" could apply equally well to de Lempicka. What is perhaps more surprising is the way de Lempicka follows Ingres' example in treating women as passive sex objects. Like Ingres she shows virtually no interest in the individual psychology or personality of her female sitters. De Lempicka's female nudes are still more closely linked to Ingres. Her chained and swooning Andromeda with her upturned eyes and head thrown further back than anatomy should allow, against a cubified urban backdrop, is clearly an updated version of Ingres' Angelica. Her groups of female nudes piled up like inflatable dolls, descend from Ingres' notorious *Turkish Bath.*

Portrait of Baroness Renata Treves

1925
Oil on canvas, 100 x 70 cm
Barry Friedman Ltd, New York

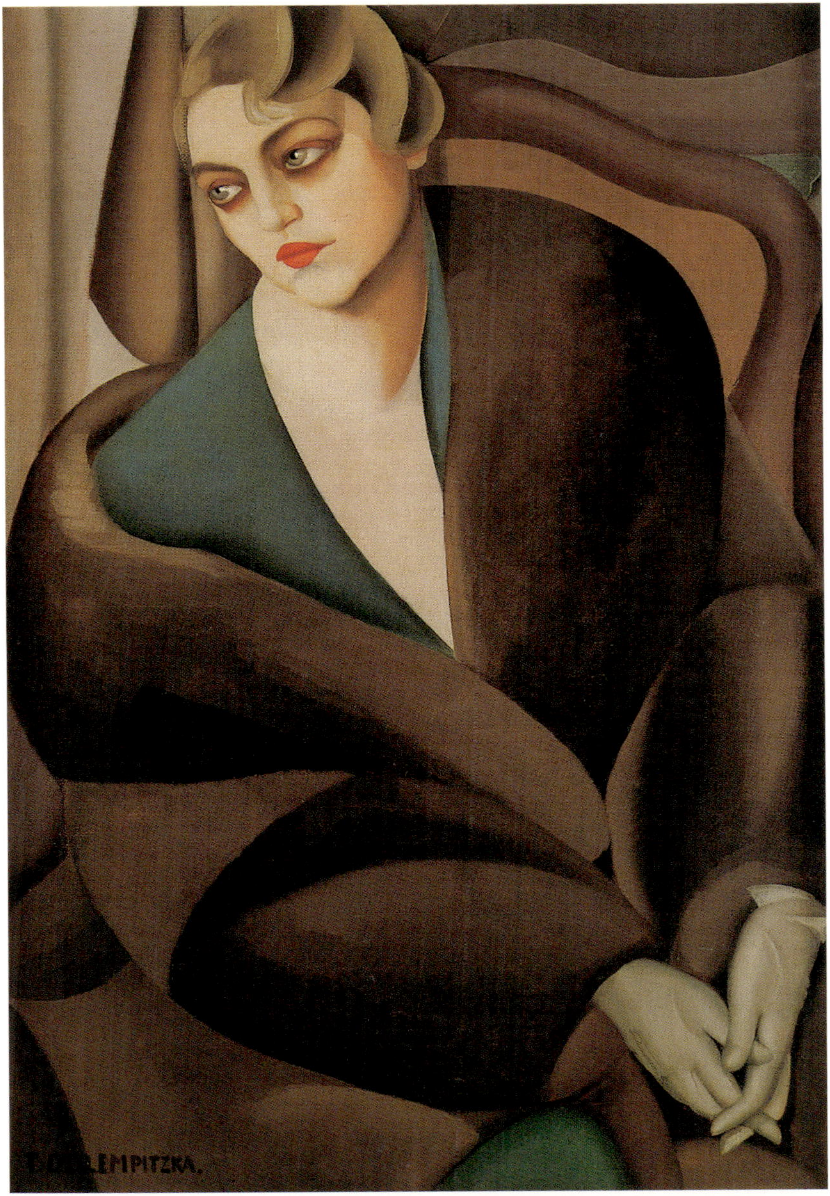

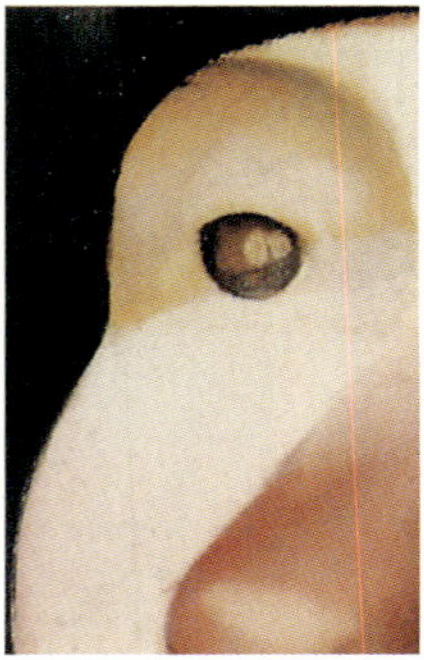

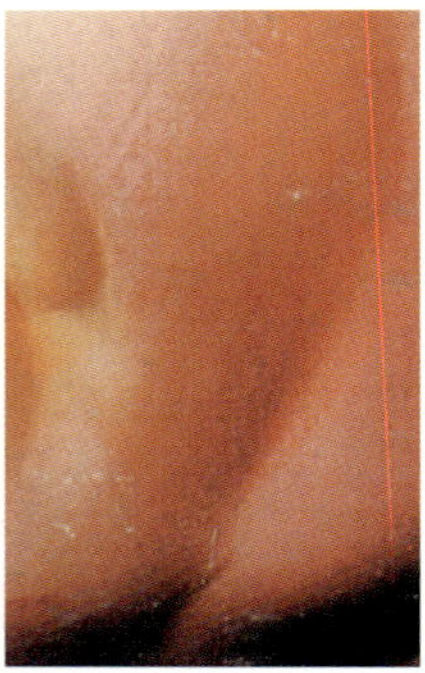

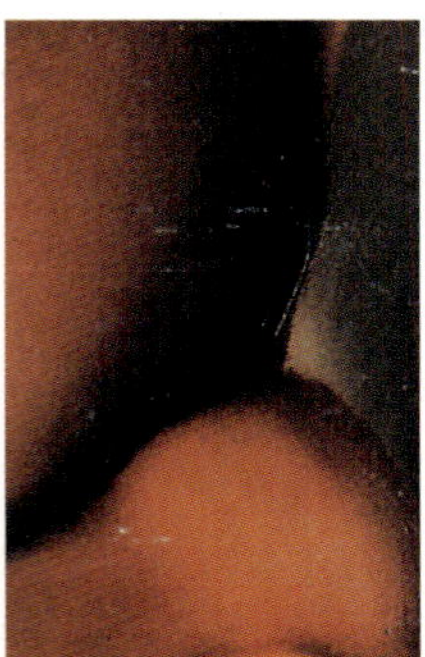

The crisis of confidence suffered by all the Impressionists to a greater or lesser degree in the 1880s caused Renoir to turn back to the classical tradition. It was the simple lines and large sculptural volumes of Renoir's late nudes that encouraged Aristide Maillol to break with the pathos and "unsculptural" qualities of Rodin's expressively modelled sculptures. The key work for the re-launching of a monumental classical style in twentieth century sculpture was Maillol's *La Méditerranée* modelled in 1902 and exhibited in bronze in 1905 in the very same Salon d'Automne that saw the controversial debut of the Fauve group.

Head of Slavic Woman

c. 1925
Oil on canvas, 46 x 38 cm
Private Collection

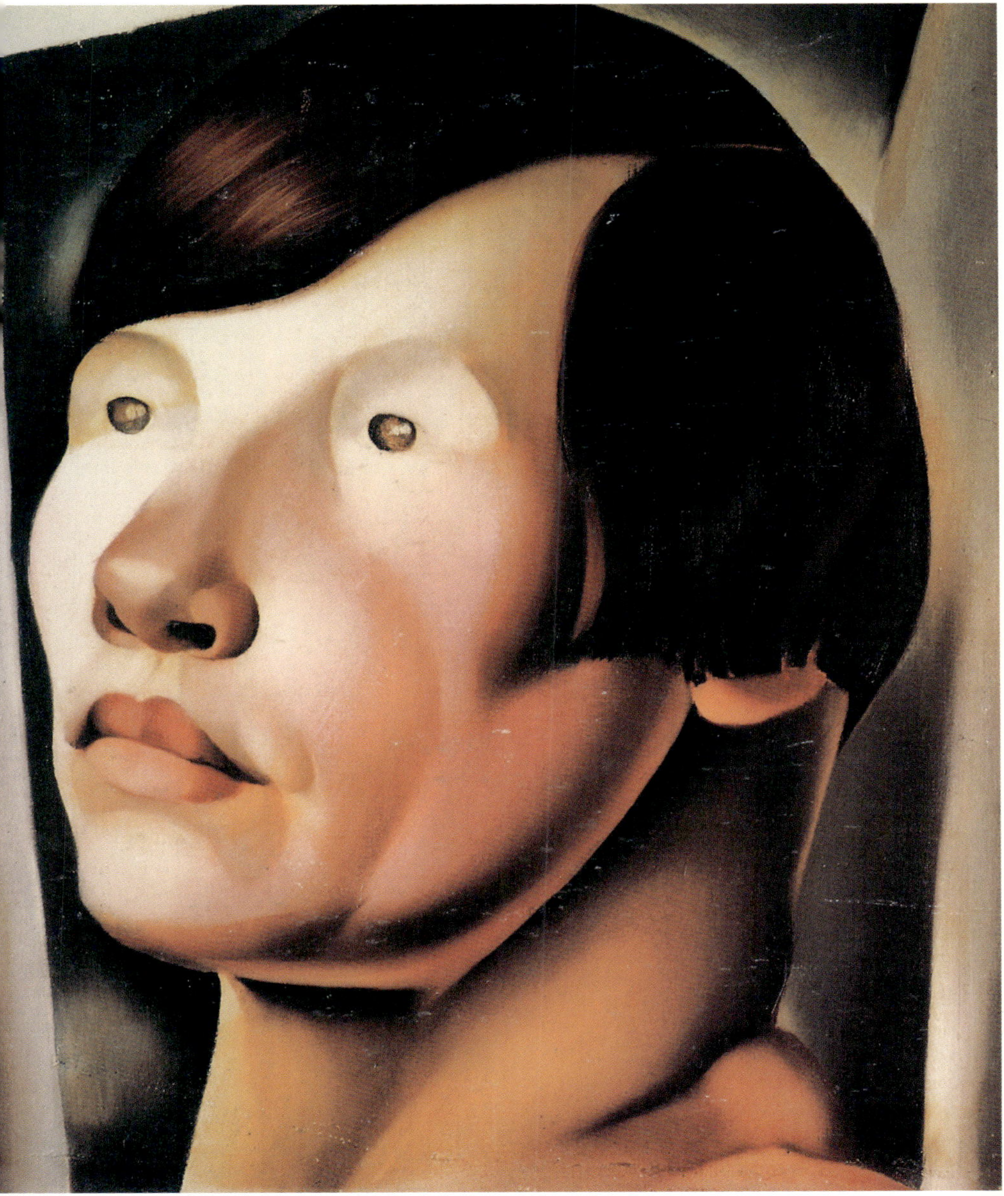

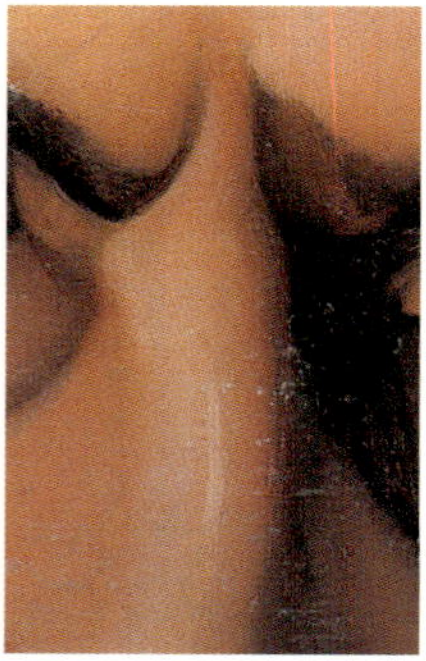

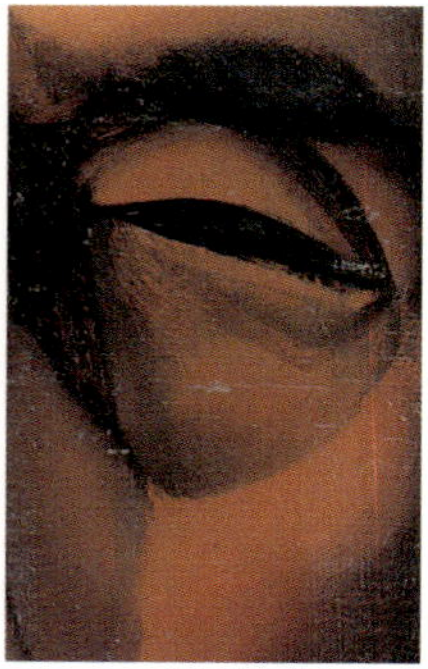

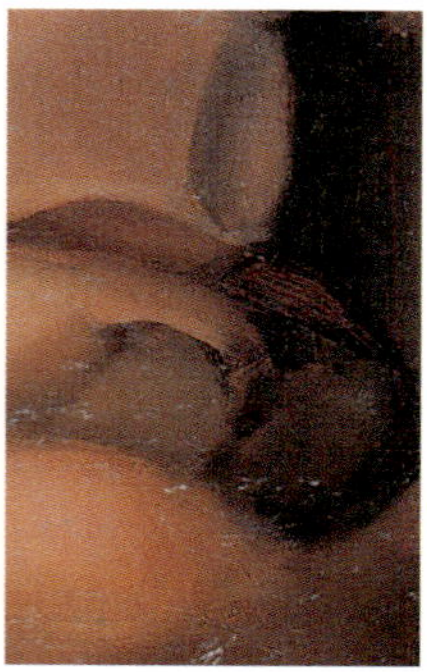

The return to classicism regarded by some followers as a betrayal and even a blasphemous provocation was given the stamp of approval by the king of the Parisian avant-garde Pablo Picasso. In the close and somewhat incestuous artistic and intellectual circles of Paris between the wars, it was inevitable that de Lempicka would have come into contact with most of the leading artists and intellectuals. Amongst the artists and writers she mixed with were Gide, Marinetti, Cocteau, Marie Laurencin, Foujita, Chagall, Kiesling and Van Dongen. Cocteau, who warned her that she risked ruining her art by too much socialising, would have provided her closest contact with Picasso.

Portrait of André Gide

c. 1925
Oil on cardboard, 50 x 35 cm
Private Collection

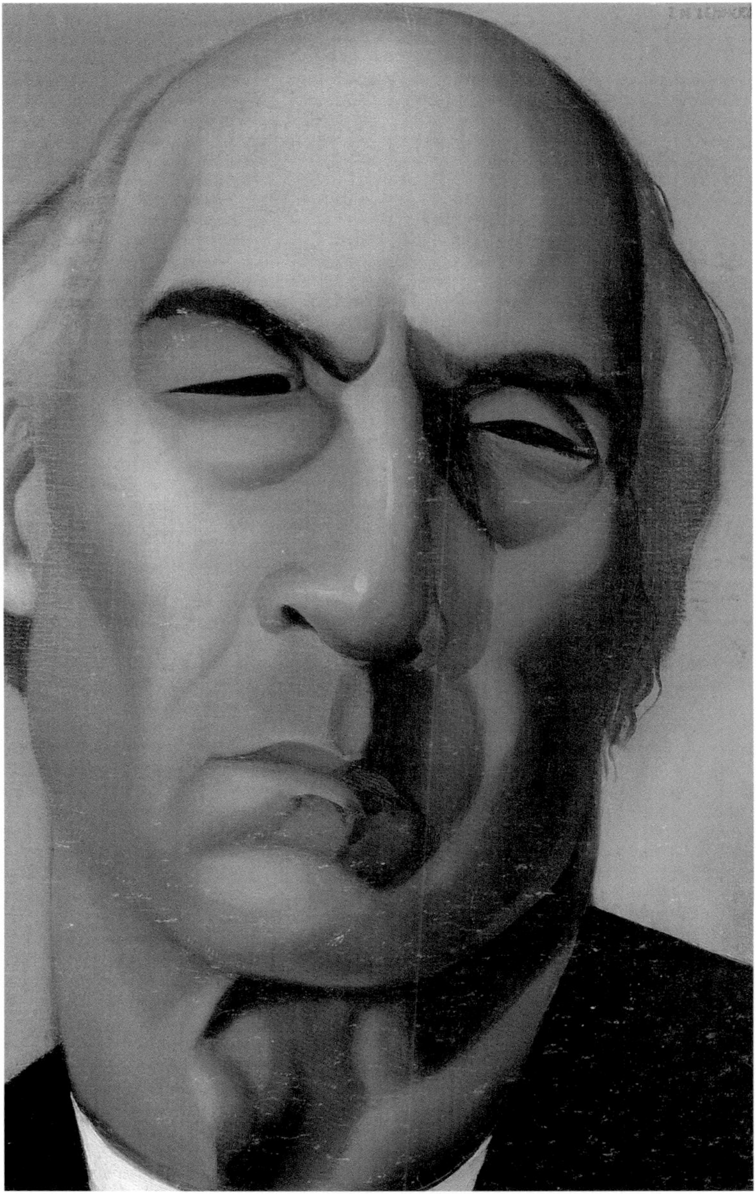

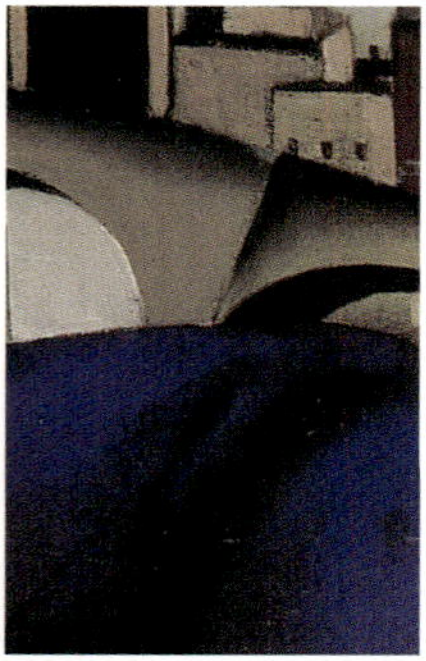

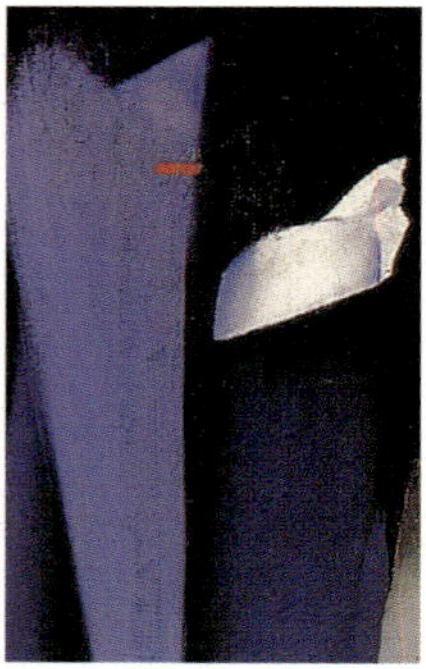

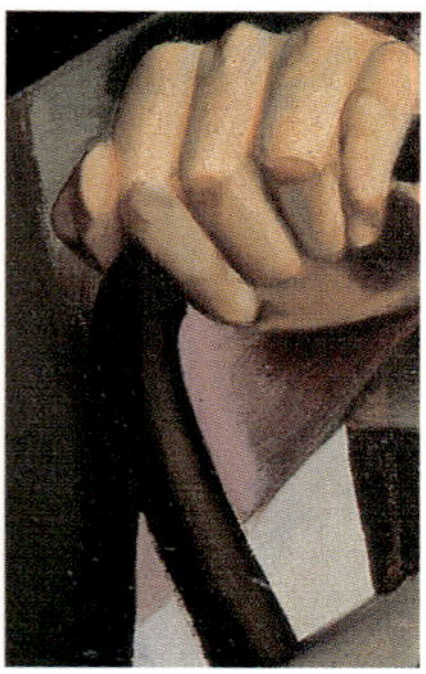

Cocteau's own dazzlingly clever and sophisticated erotic drawings would have provided de Lempicka with an example of how to combine the avant-garde, the classical and the slickly commercial. Lifting nude male figures straight from Michelangelo's Sistine ceiling and other Renaissance and classical sources, Cocteau added the enlarged genitals, curling pubic hair and other attributes of homosexual pornography, all drawn in a spare linear style closely based on Picasso's neo-classical drawings. The result is Michelangelo and Picasso crossed with Tom of Finland. If the eroticism in de Lempicka's work is never quite as blatant as Cocteau's she certainly managed to achieve a similar synthesis of the modern, the illustrational and the commercial in her mature work of the late 1920s.

Portrait of Prince Eristoff

1925
Oil on canvas, 65 x 92 cm
Private Collection

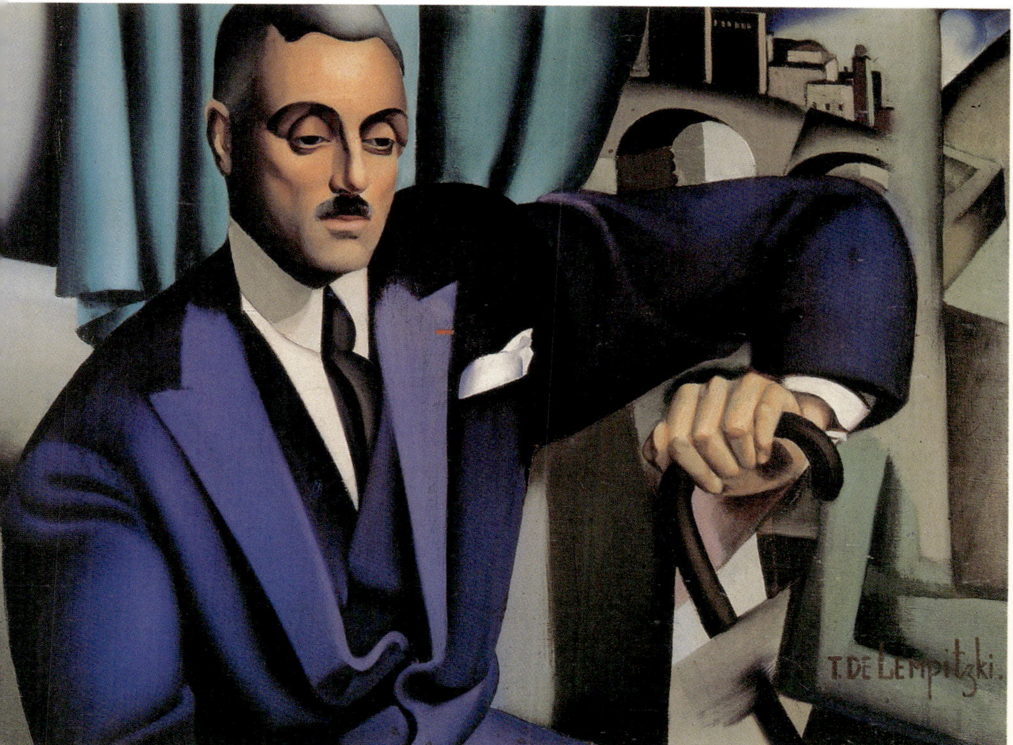
T. DE LEMPITZKI.

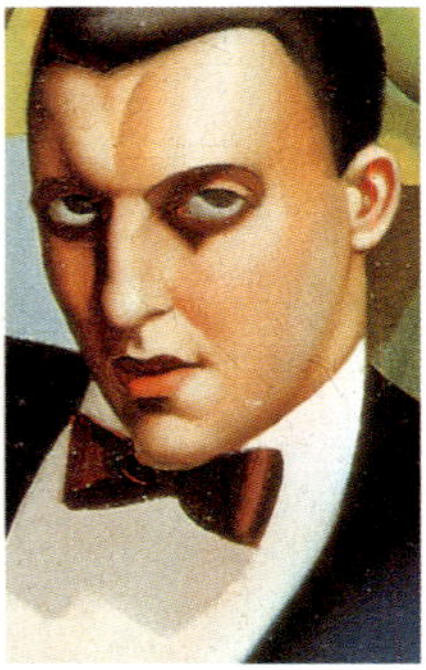

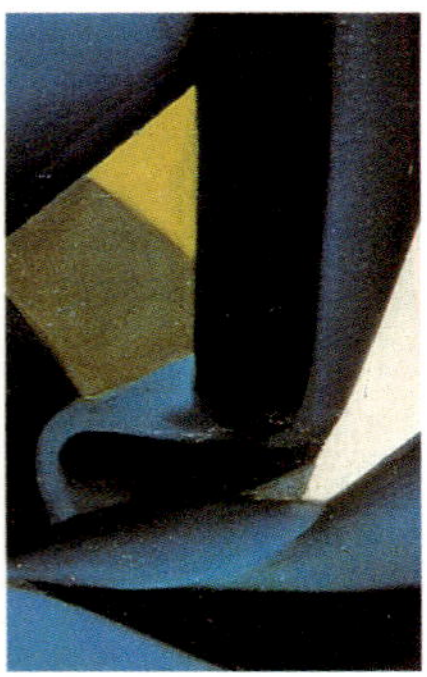

The "intense modernity" and "chilliness" of de Lempicka were both expressed through a devotion to the mechanical and the metallic that are characteristic of the period. One of the most distinctive aspects of de Lempicka's art is the way she paints everything from human flesh to permed hair and crumpled drapery with metallic sheen. One is reminded of Manet's cutting remark on the military paintings of Ernest Meissonier, that everything looked as though it was made out of metal except the weapons. In de Lempicka's work though, the metallic quality comes from an aesthetic that is in thrall to the machine. As industrialisation spread through the Western world in the nineteenth century the machine began to influence every area of human endeavour. It was not till after the turn of the century that architects and designers such as Richard Riemerschmid and Peter Behrens began to perceive the machine as opportunity rather than a threat.

Portrait of the Marquis d'Afflito

1925
Oil on canvas, 81 x 130 cm
Private Collection

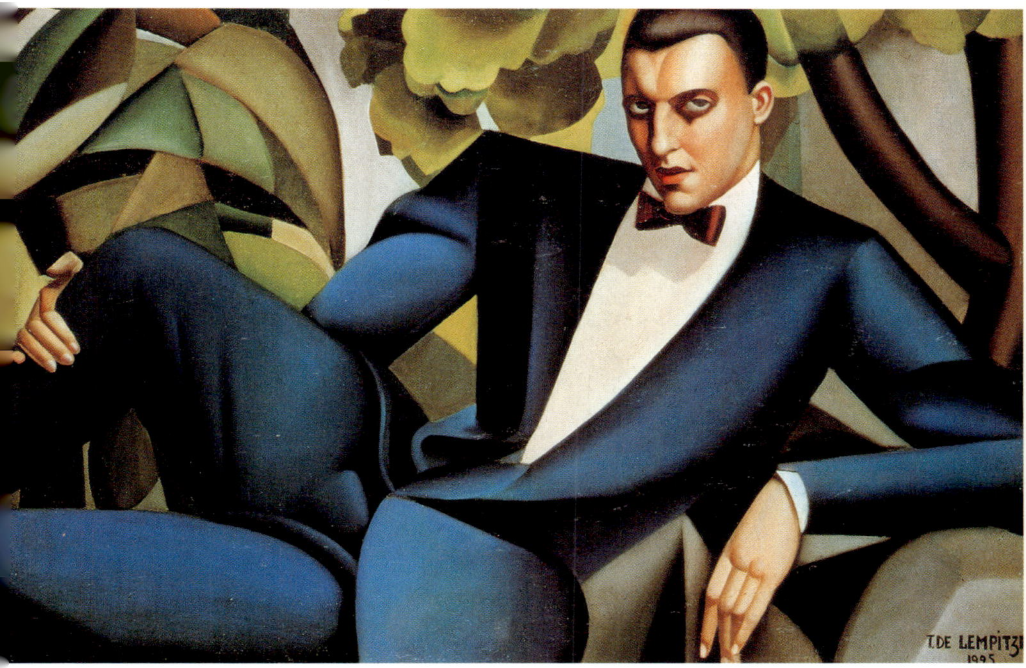
T.DE LEMPITZ

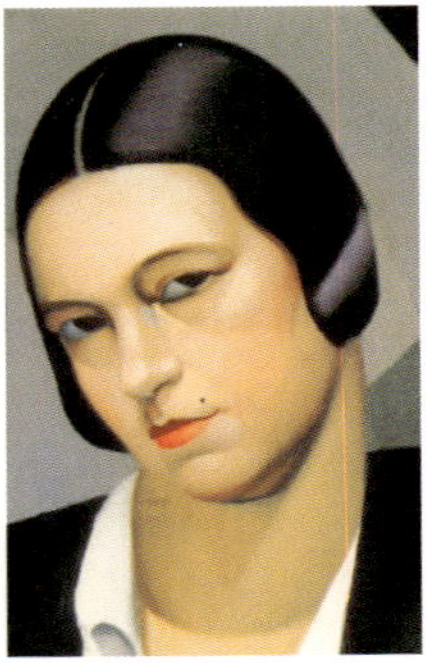

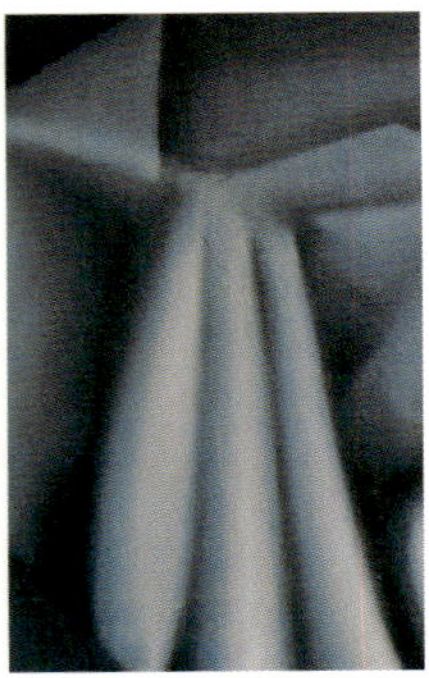

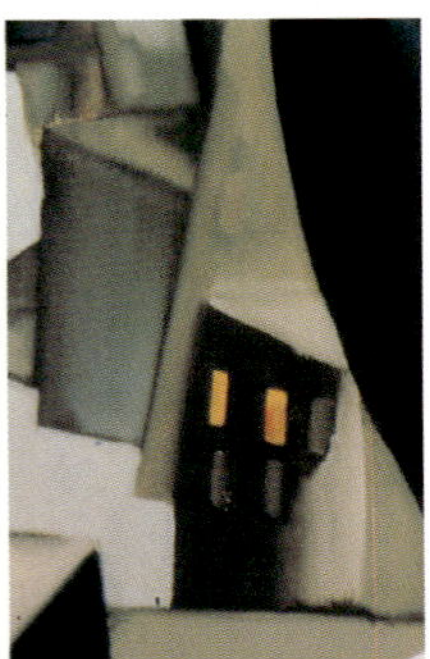

In the inter war period, the cult of the machine permeated every aspect of culture and society. Motor cars, express trains, aeroplanes, zeppelins and ocean liners replaced nymphs and caryatids as decorative motifs on the façades and ceilings of department stores such as Barker's in London and Bullocks Wilshire in Los Angeles. Le Corbusier described a house as "a machine for living in". Buildings such as Broadcasting House in London and the Coca-Cola Bottling Plant in Los Angeles took on the appearance of immobilised ocean liners, while ocean liners such as the Ile de France, the Normandie, the Queen Mary and the Queen Elizabeth represented the aspirations and ethos of the Art Deco period in a way that cathedrals had done for the Middle Ages and museums and railway stations for the nineteenth century.

Portrait of the Duchess of La Salle

1925
Oil on canvas, 162 x 97 cm
Private Collection

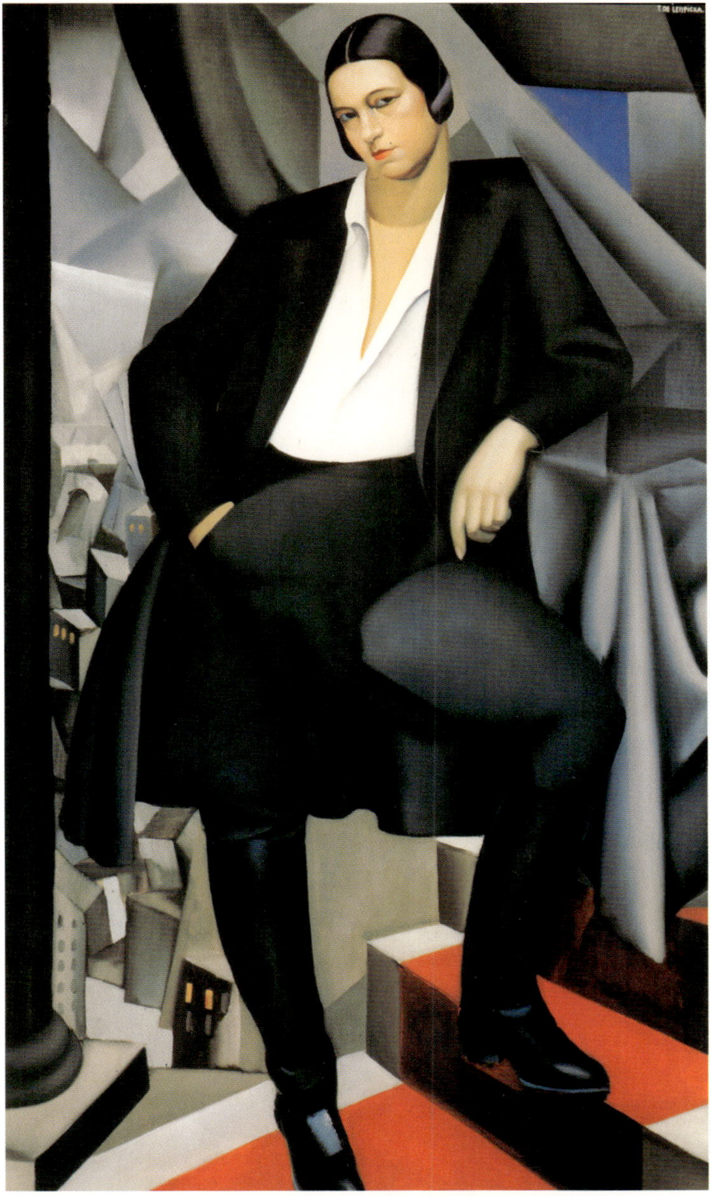
T. DE LEMPICKA

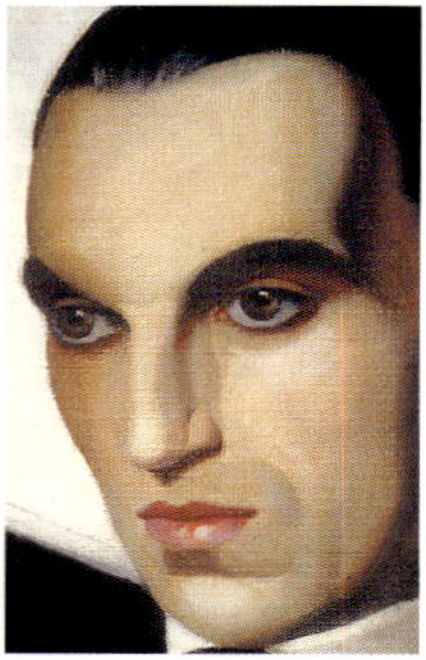

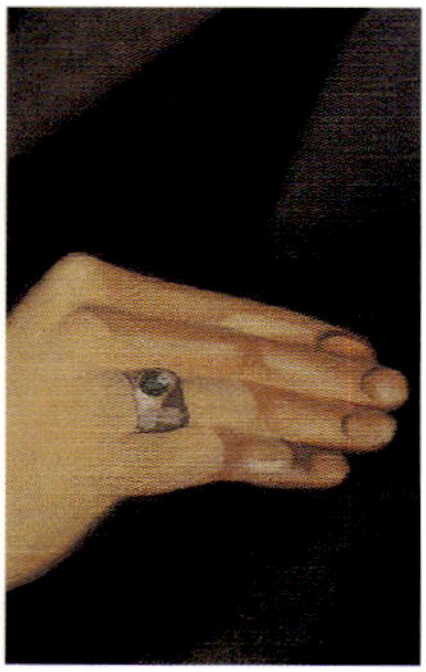

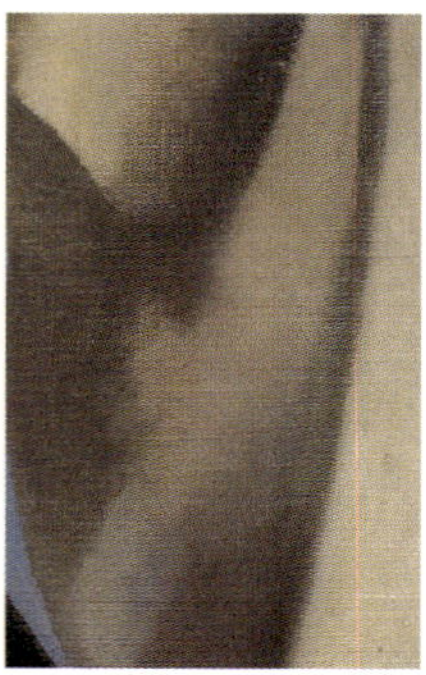

The smooth reflective surfaces of the Art Deco style that we see throughout de Lempicka's best work and in particular in works such as *Arlette Boucard with Arums* of 1931 with its glass topped table and transparent vase, also express a new found desire in Western culture for hygiene. The idea that "cleanliness is next to godliness" had not been central to Christian culture prior to the nineteenth century (unlike Jewish and Muslim traditions that had always put great emphasis on personal hygiene). After the notion of germs and the connection between health and hygiene had been established by Louis Pasteur and others in the mid nineteenth century, cleanliness and bathing received greater emphasis in Europe too.

Portrait of Marquis Sommi

1925
Oil on canvas, 100 x 73 cm
Private Collection

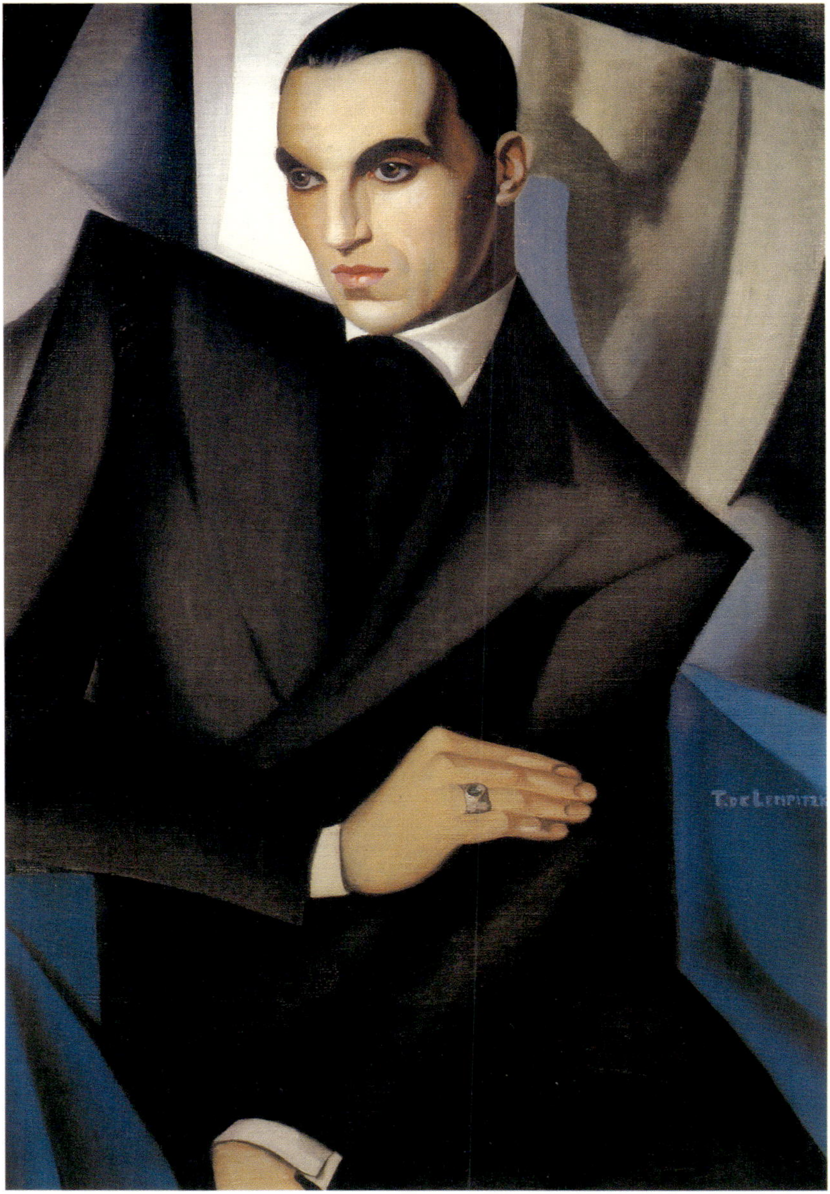

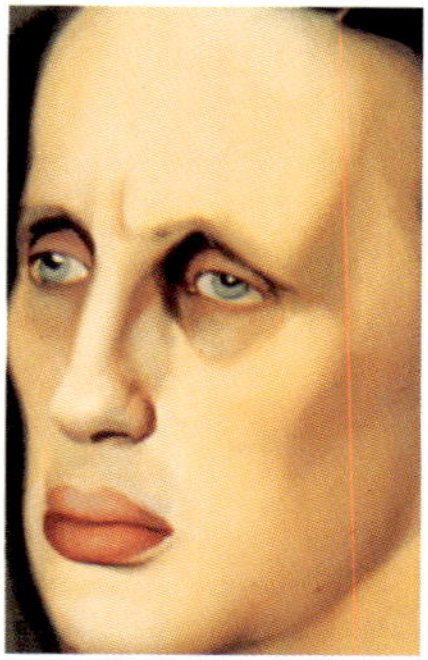

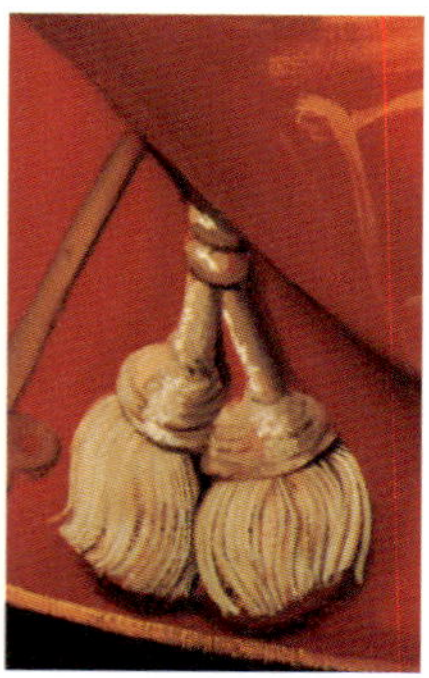

One of the most iconic images of the Jazz Age and perhaps de Lempicka's most frequently reproduced picture is the *Self-Portrait in the Green Bugatti* in de Lempicka's favourite "poison green", commissioned by the German Fashion magazine *Die Dame* in 1925. The tight driver's helmet that masks her permed blond hair and makes her look more like an aviator than a motorist and her cool impervious stare, characterise her as a thoroughly independent and self-confident modern woman. Like the sewing machine and the type-writer in the previous generation (that provided employment however humble inside and outside the home), the motor car contributed significantly to the emancipation of women, if only those at the upper end of the economic scale.

Portrait of His Imperial Highness
Grand Duke Gabriel

c. 1926
Oil on canvas, 116 x 65 cm
Private Collection

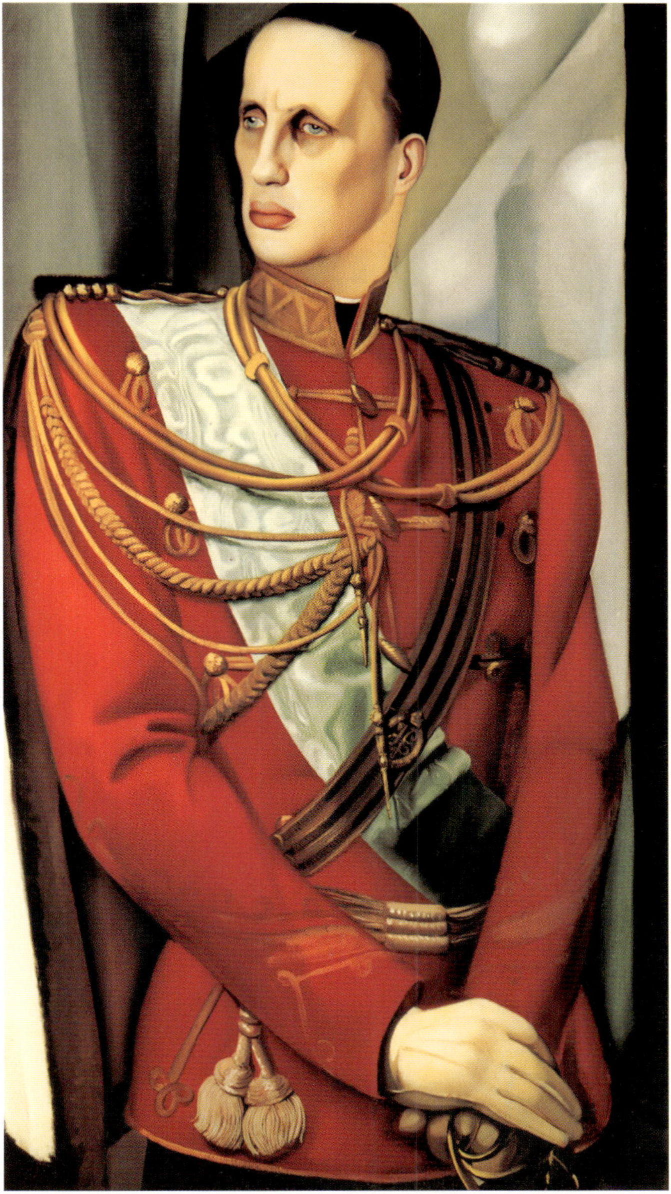

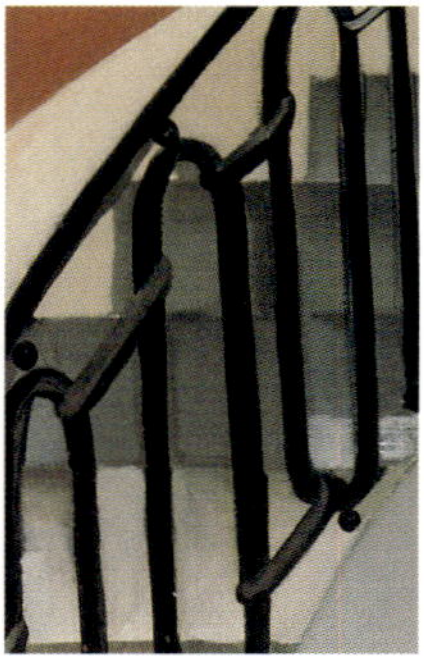

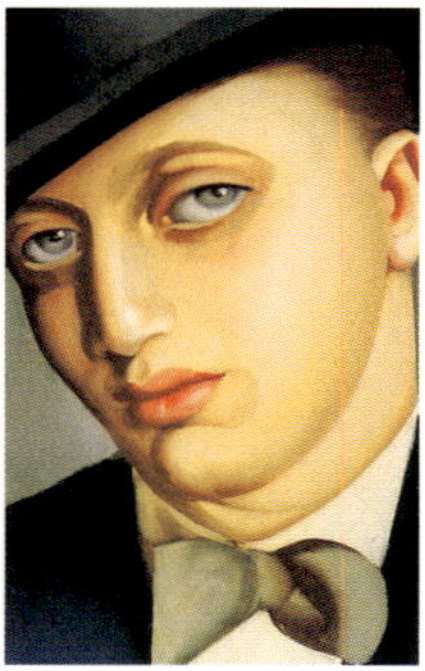

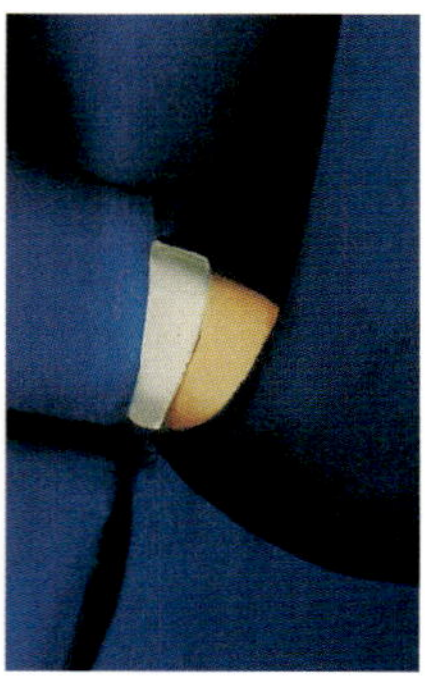

De Lempicka monogrammed this picture with her initials, looking like an industrial logo on the door of the car. Throughout the Art Deco period de Lempicka showed her allegiance to the machine aesthetic by signing her pictures in printed letters that look like industrial typeface in contrast to the flowing calligraphy favoured by the more painterly artists of the Belle Epoque.

As Arsène Alexandre suggested, de Lempicka's modernity also lay in her combination of coolness and sensuality and a certain ambiguity. Though he is too discreet to spell it out, this ambiguity was sexual.

Portrait of the Marquis d'Afflito
(On a Staircase)

1926
Oil on canvas, 116 x 73 cm
Private Collection

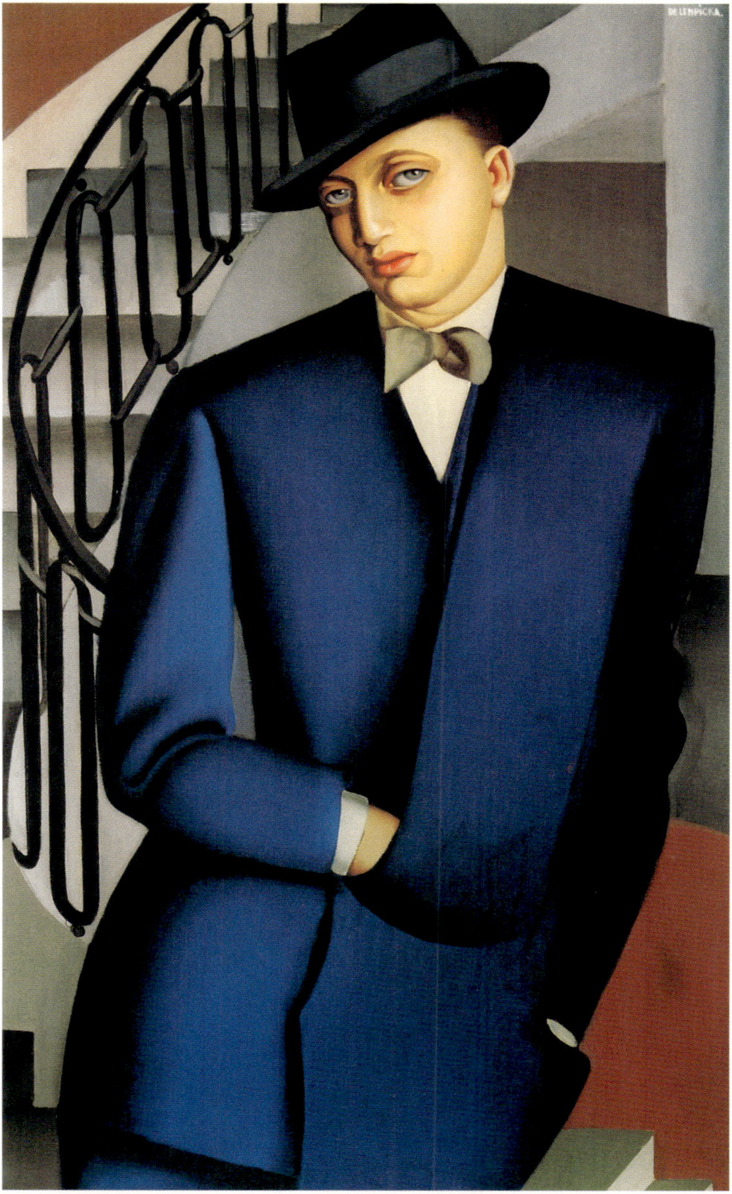
DE LEMPICKA.

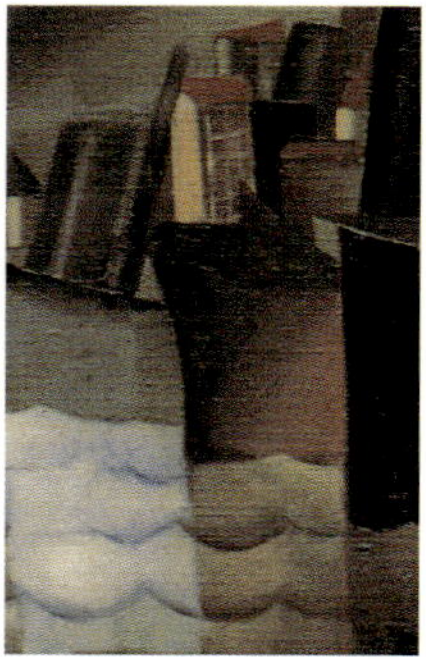

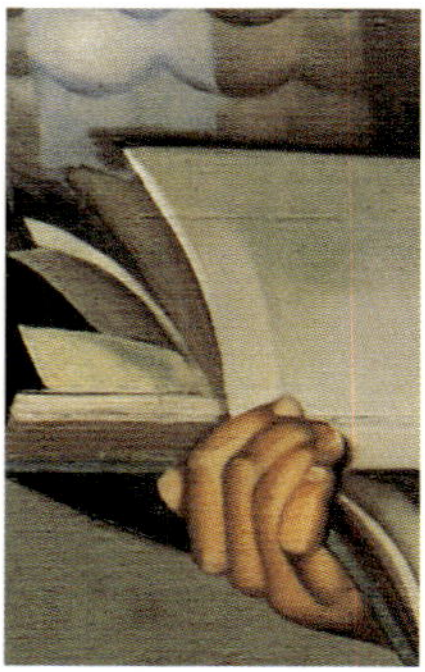

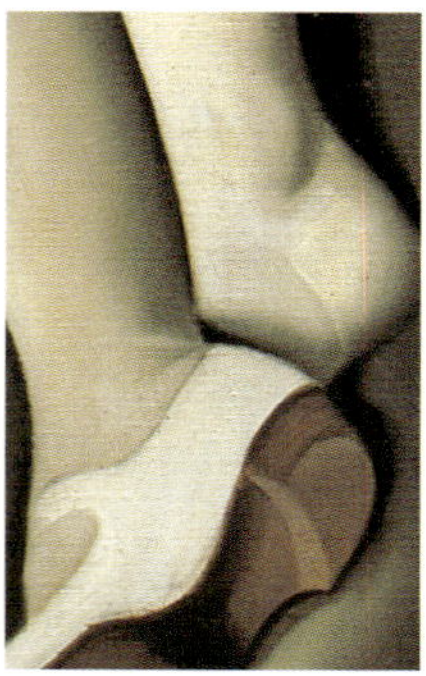

Amongst the value systems that had been thrown into question by the unparalleled catastrophe of the First World War were traditional concepts of gender. The 1920s in Paris might be termed a heroic age of Lesbianism. The war itself had much to do with this. When millions of young men departed for the slaughter of the Western Front, women were forced into new roles and many were released from domestic slavery. After the war there was no turning back. Changing roles were reflected in the changing appearance of women — bobbed hair and *la ligne à la mode* — boyish figures with flattened breasts and narrow hips. Young ladies proudly boasted that they were perverted. To be suspected of virginity at the age of sixteen would have been considered a disgrace in every school in Berlin". If Berlin was notorious for its transvestite balls, Paris was undoubtedly the lesbian capital of the world in the 1920s.

Kizette in Pink

---

c. 1926
Oil on canvas, 116 x 73 cm
Musée des Beaux-Arts de Nantes

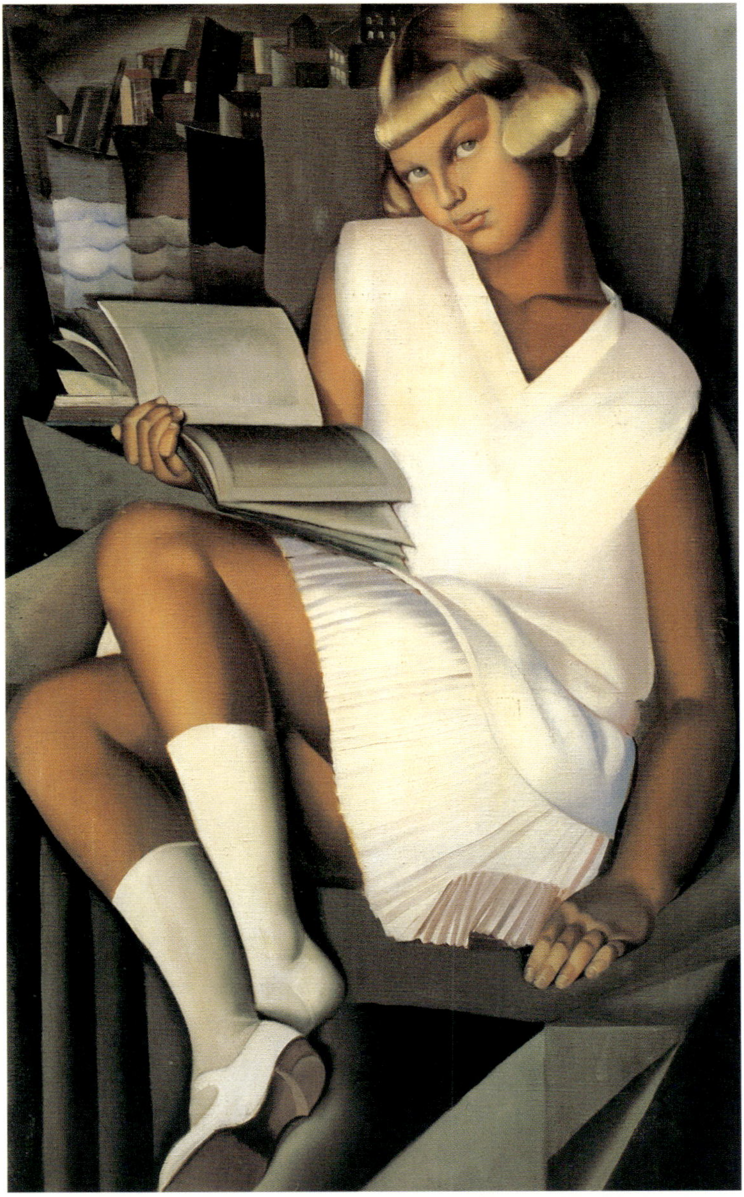

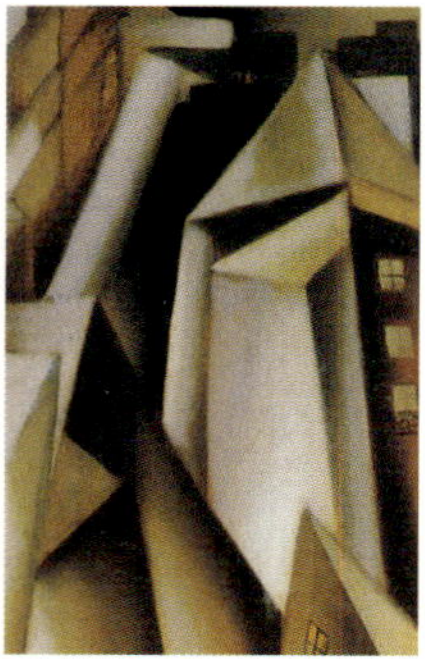
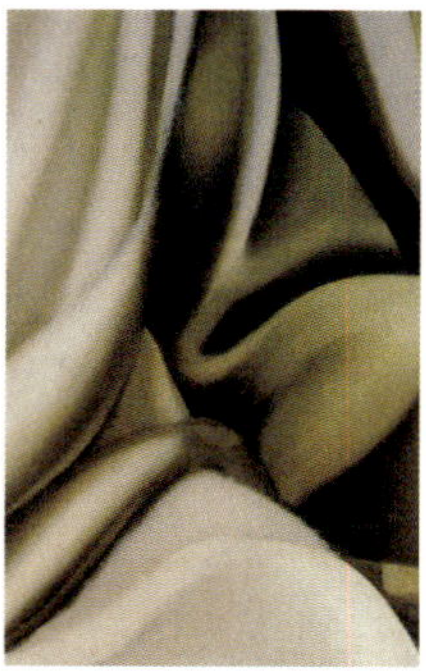
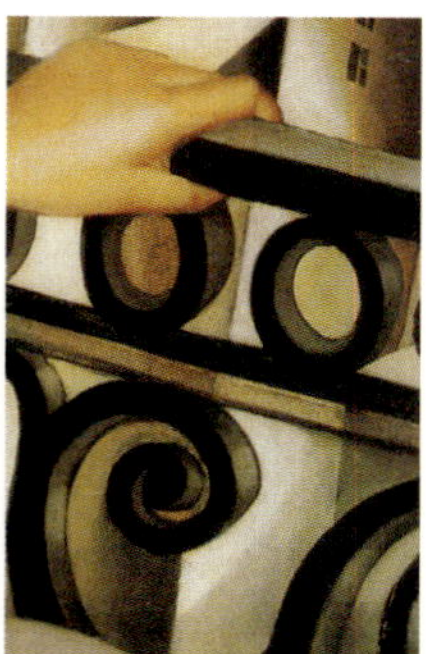

The relative acceptance of lesbianism in inter-war Paris allowed for the opening of well-known lesbian night spots such as *Le Monocle* and sympathetic and even glamorous representations of lesbians in French movies such as *Symphonie Pathétique* in 1928 and *La Garçonne* in 1936. This tolerance attracted to Paris creative and unconventional women from all over the world. Gertrude Stein and Alice B.Toklas and Nathalie Barney and Romaine Brooks, the best known Parisian lesbian couples had been in the city from before the war and they were joined there in the 1920s by the novelist Djuna Barnes, the journalist Janet Flanner, Sylvia Beach, proprietor of the famous English language bookshop *Shakespeare and Co.* De Lempicka dismissed Gertrude Stein and Ernest Hemingway as "boring people who wanted to be what they were not. He wanted to be a woman and she wanted to be a man."

Kizette on the Balcony

1927
Oil on canvas, 130 x 81 cm
Musée National d'Art Moderne, Paris

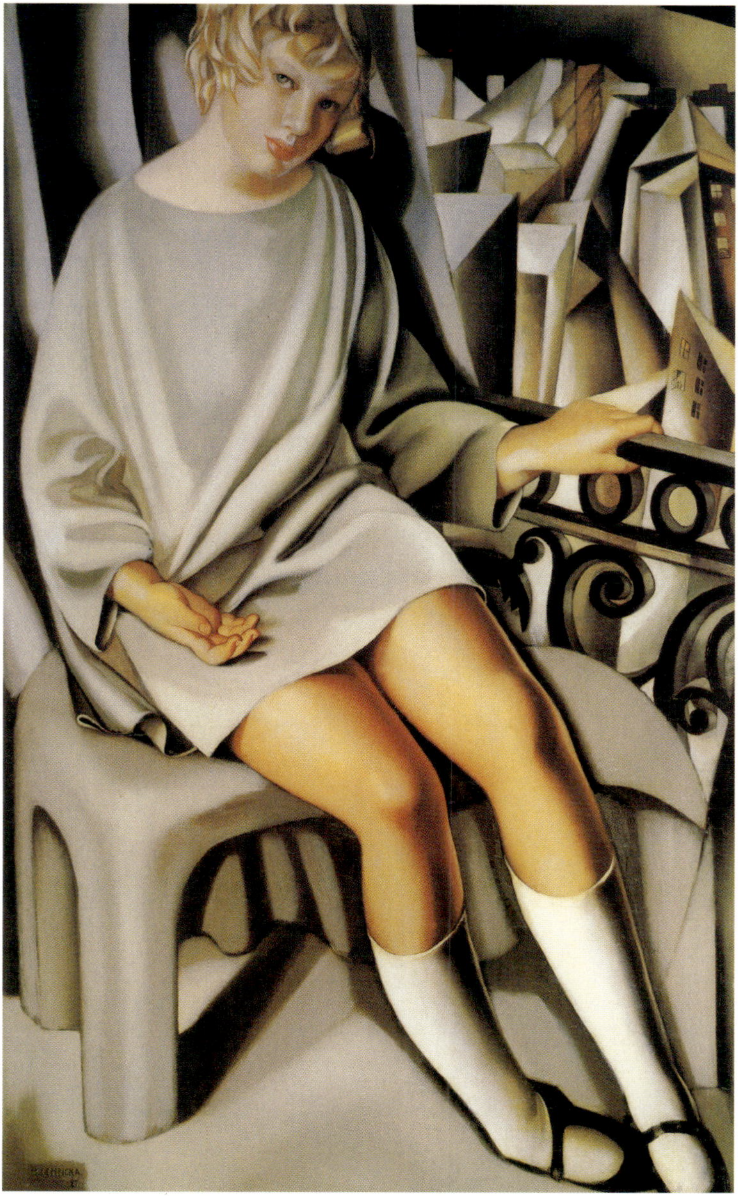

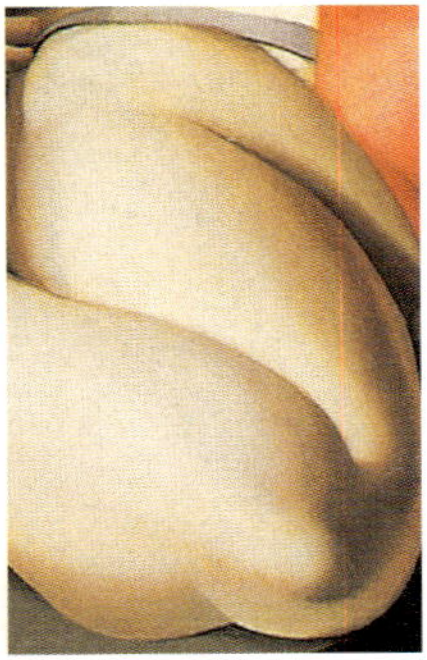

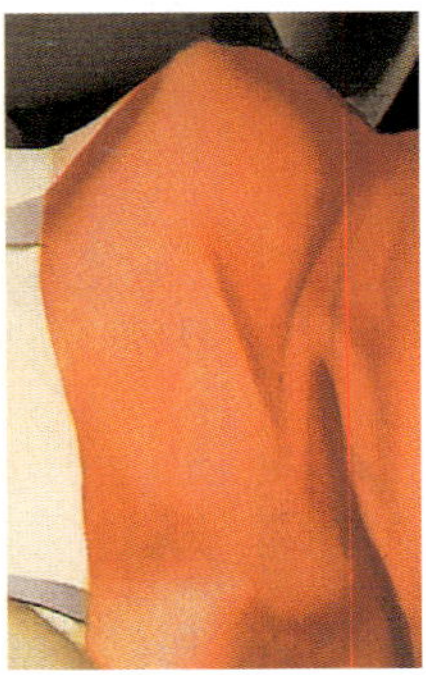

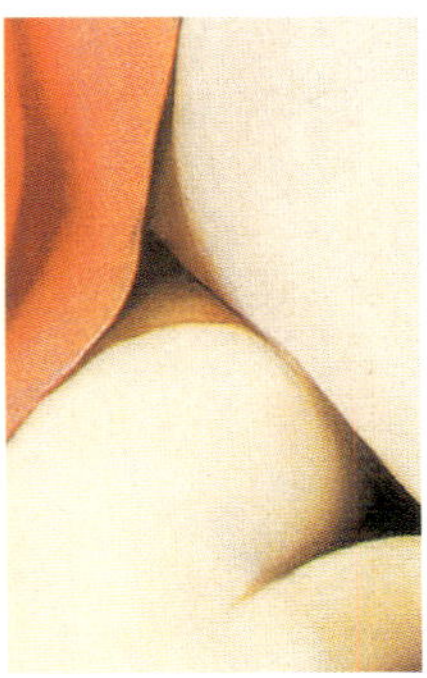

De Lempicka was never reticent about her sexual interest in her own sex. A photograph of her bedroom taken for publicity purposes in 1928 shows the portrait of the amazonian *Duchesse de La Salle* looming over her bed and the head board is decorated with a design made by de Lempicka herself showing two woman rapturously entwined with one another. The message could not have been louder or clearer.

De Lempicka began having sexual relationships with women early in her marriage. From 1922, she embarked on an affair with Ida Perrot that survived several tempestuous years, despite the multitude of de Lempicka's infidelities with both sexes.

The Pink Tunic

1927
Oil on canvas, 73 x 116 cm
Private Collection

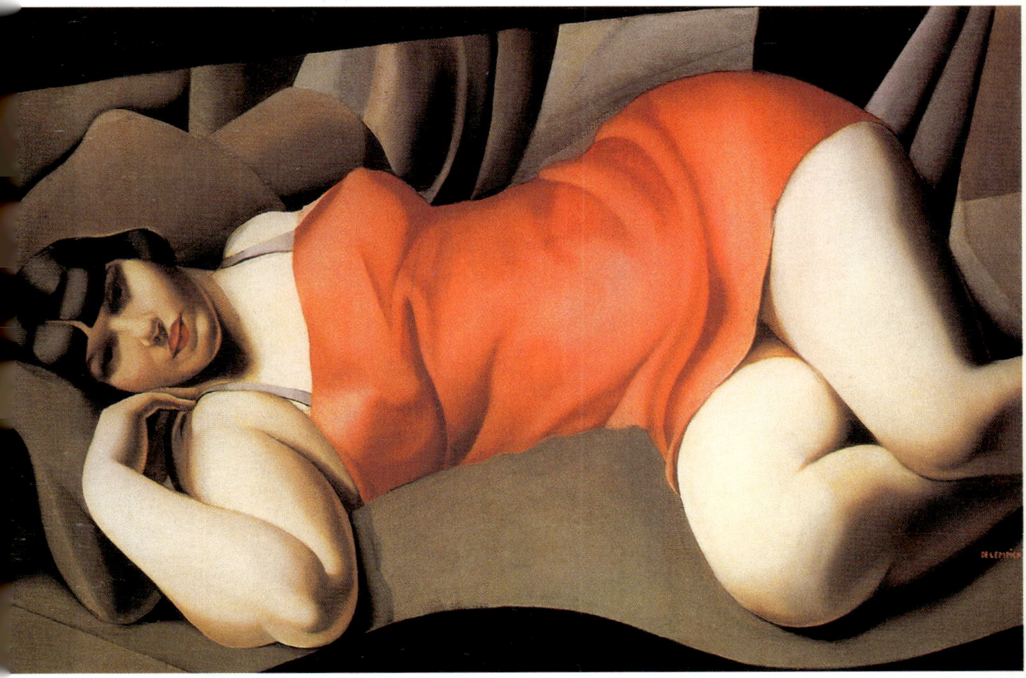

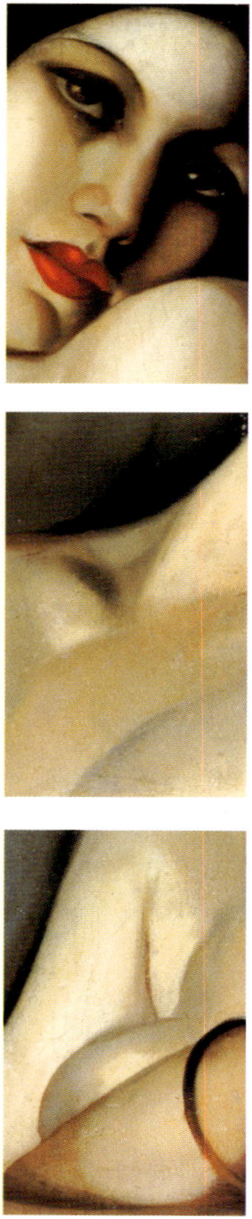

Ida Perrot posed for the first picture that de Lempicka exhibited at the Salon d'Automn and again for another portrait towards the end of their relationship in 1930. In this second portrait, the serpentine pose and the way de Lempicka fills the whole canvas from top to bottom with the twisting body of her lover, creates a sense of intimacy and oppressive voluptuousness. The erotic mood is reinforced by the bouquet of arum lilies clutched by the sitter. Like Georgia O'Keeffe, de Lempicka seems to have been fascinated by the suggestive form of the flowers and painted arum lilies on several occasions.

The Dream

1927
Oil on canvas, 81 x 60 cm
Mrs. Àntonia Schulman's Collection, New York

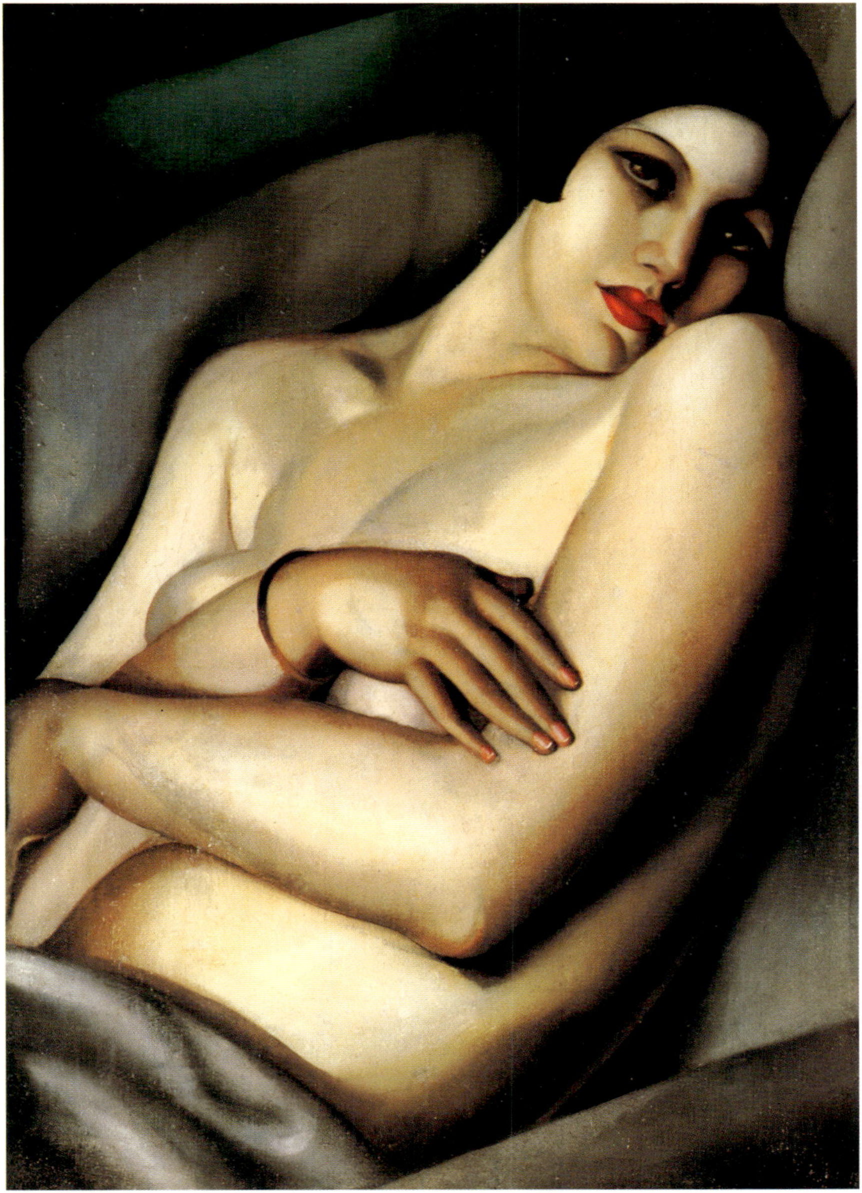

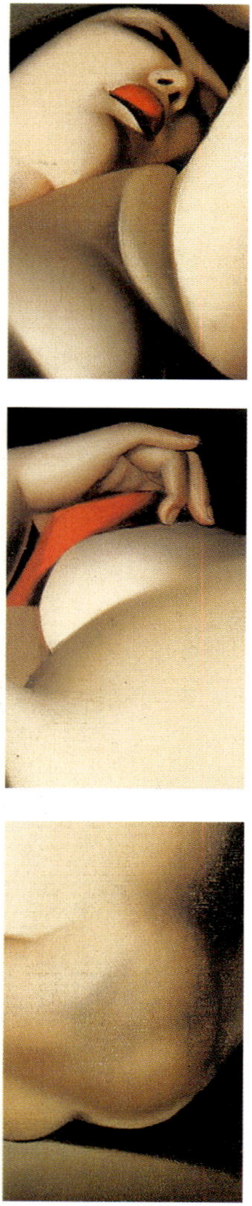

De Lempicka painted two portraits of well-known lesbians — *the Duchesse de La Salle* and the model and night club singer *Suzy Solidor*. The Duchesse is shown as an *amazone*, powerful and masculine. As she is painted against a cubist urban background, her black riding boots suggest the dominatrix rather than healthy outdoor pursuits. The half-length nude portrait of Suzy Solidor (also against a city background) is one of de Lempicka's least problematic female nudes with neither the eye-rolling pathos nor the oppressive passivity of most of the others. It is also exceptional amongst her portraits in being quite strongly individualised and actually looking like the sitter as we can tell from contemporary photographs. Every artist in Paris wanted to paint the tall, blond Solidor. Amongst the 225 portraits of herself that she collected were works by Foujita, Marie Laurencin, Kisling, Picabia and Van Dongen.

La Belle Rafaëla

1927
Oil on canvas, 65 x 92 cm
Private Collection

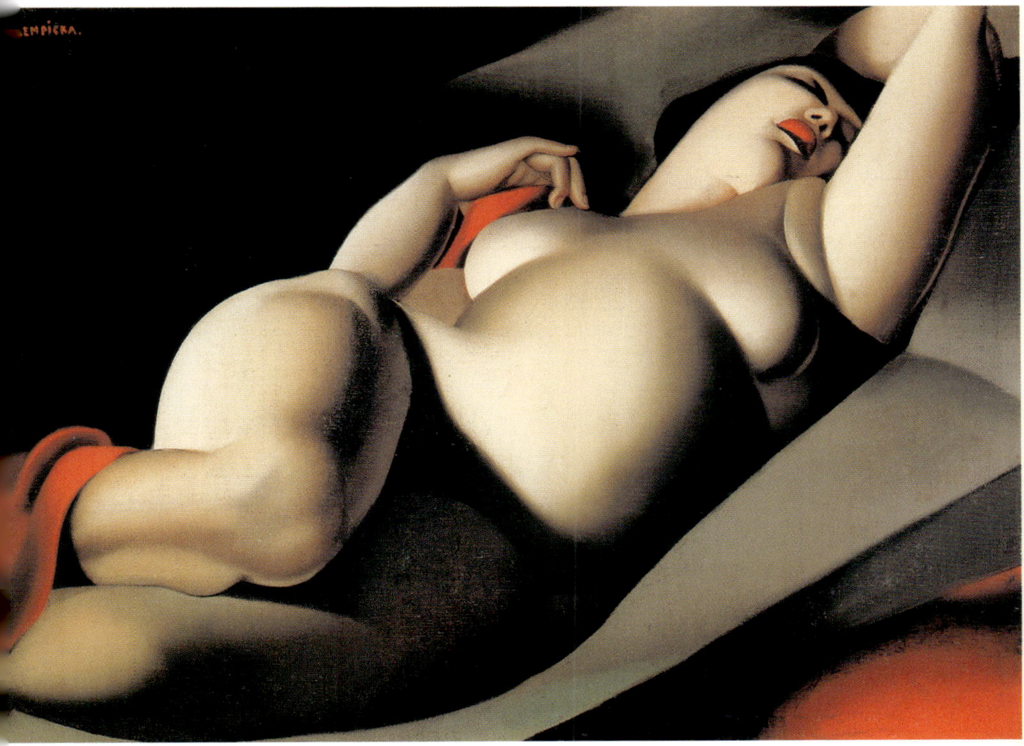
EMPICKA.

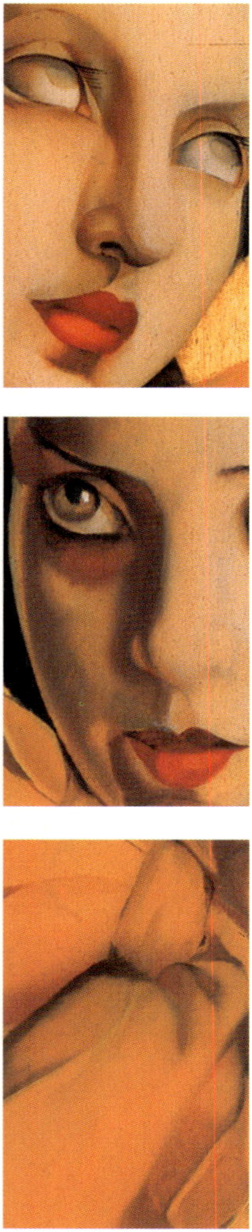

With all the predatory boldness of a man, de Lempicka would pick up women who attracted her in public places and proposition them to pose for her in the nude. One was propositioned at the Théâtre de Paris and another in the Bois de Boulogne. De Lempicka recalled the latter encounter 'Suddenly I became aware of a woman walking some distance in front of me. As she walks, everyone coming in the opposite direction stops and looks at her. They turn their heads as she passes by. I am curious. What is so extraordinary that they are doing this? I walk very quickly until I pass her, then I turn around and come back down the path in the opposite direction then I see why everyone stops. She is the most beautiful woman I have ever seen — huge black eyes, beautiful sensuous mouth, beautiful body. I stop her and say to her "Mademoiselle, I'm a painter and I would like you to pose for me. Would you do this?"

The Orange Scarf

1927
Oil on panel, 41 x 33 cm
Private Collection

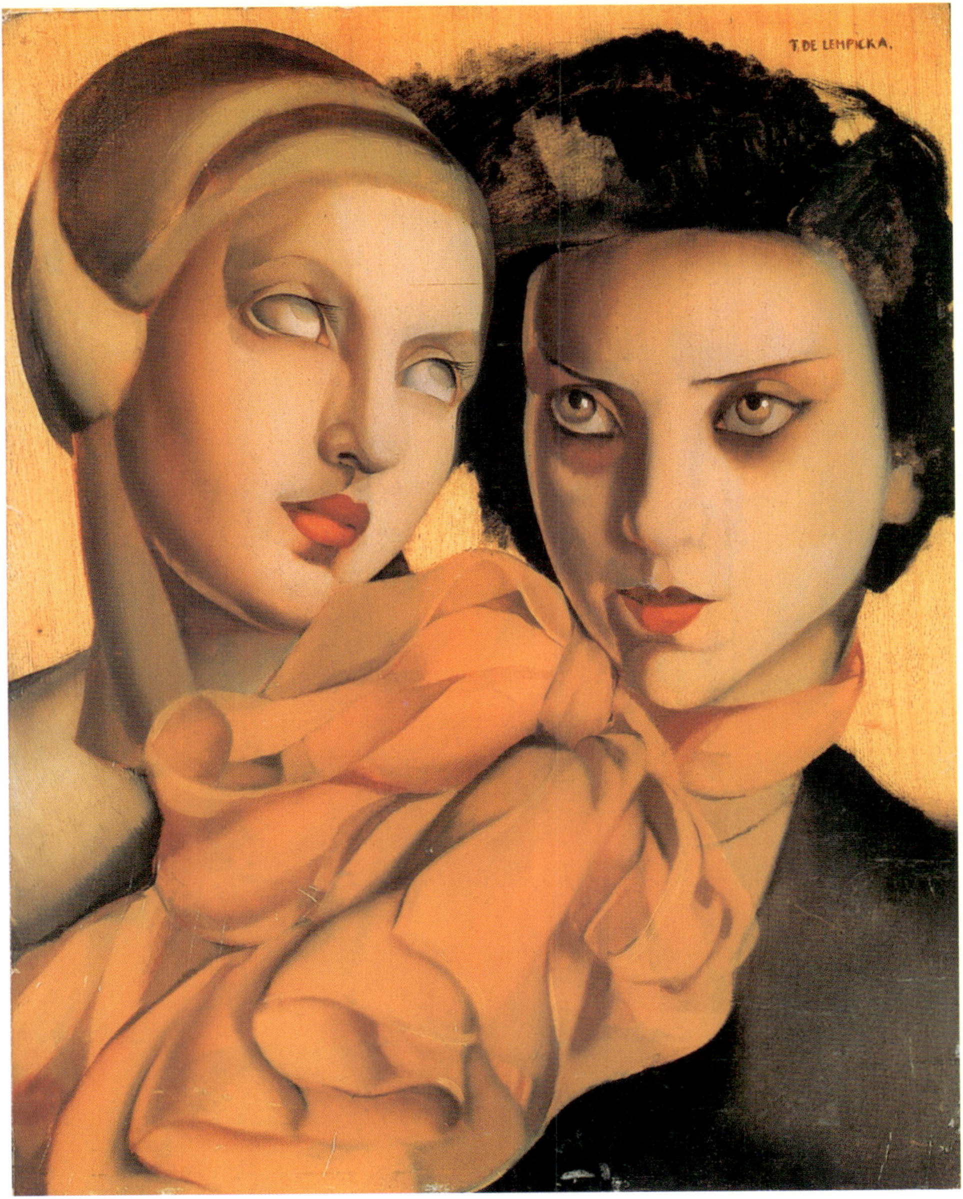
T. DE LEMPICKA.

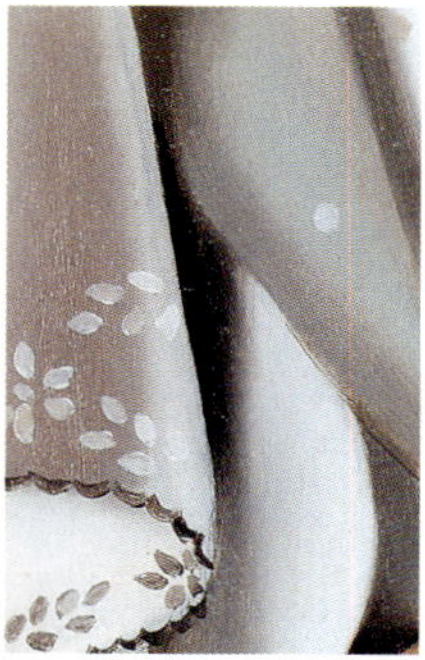

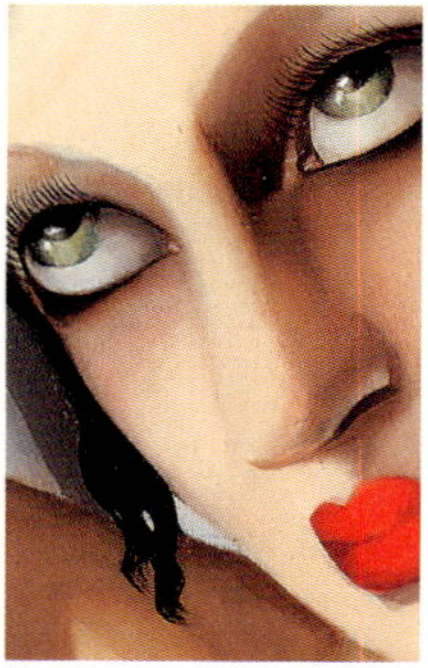

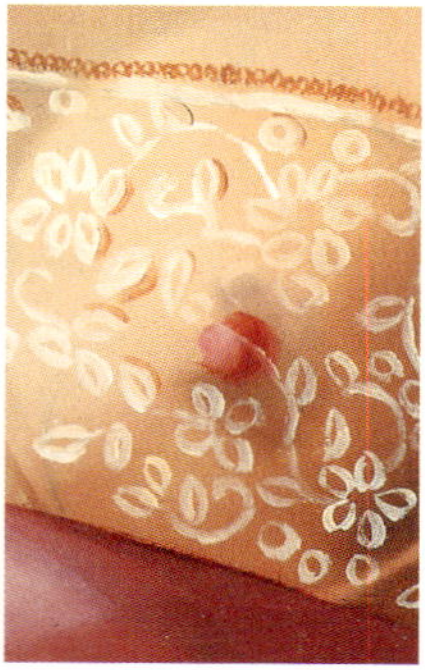

She says "Yes. Why not?" And I say "Yes come. My car is here." I took her home in my car, we had lunch and after lunch, in my studio, I said "undress, I want to paint you." She undressed without any shame. I said "Lay down on the sofa here." She lay. Every position was art — perfection and I started to paint her, and I painted her for over a year.' One of the resulting canvases was *La Belle Rafaela in Green* — amongst the most potently erotic works of de Lempicka in which the desire of the artist for the soft and curvaceous body of the model is palpable, De Lempicka understood, like any purveyor of soft-core pornography, that partial nudity can be more titillating than full nudity. She enjoyed painting her female models in expensive underwear and, as in the case of the soulful *Convalescent* with a nipple provocatively exposed.

The Pink Shirt I

c. 1927
Oil on panel, 41 x 33 cm
Private Collection

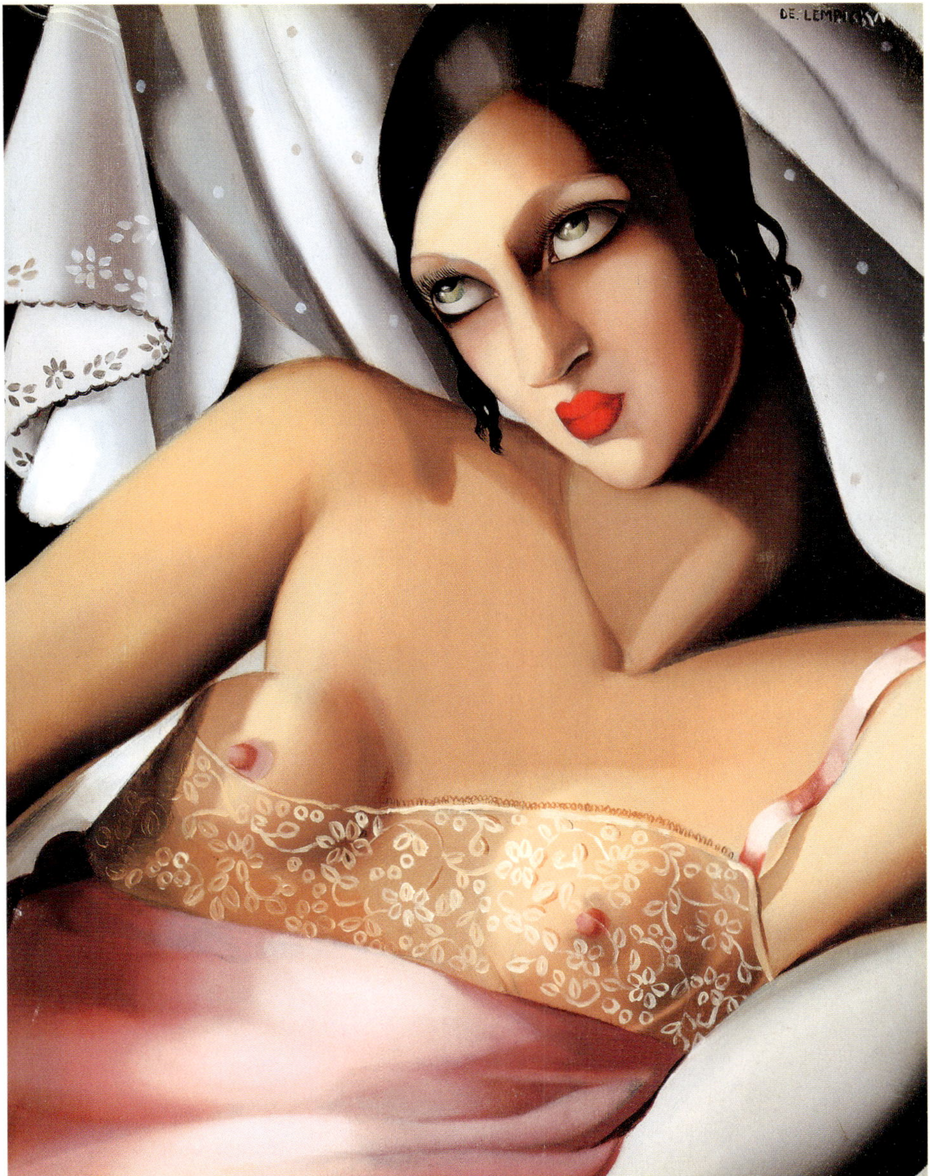
DE. LEMPICKA

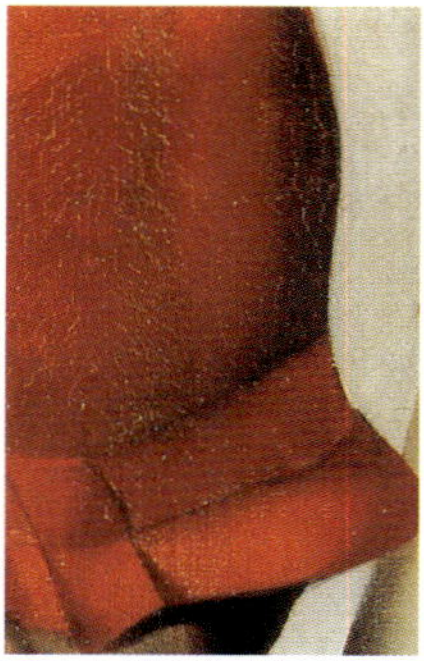

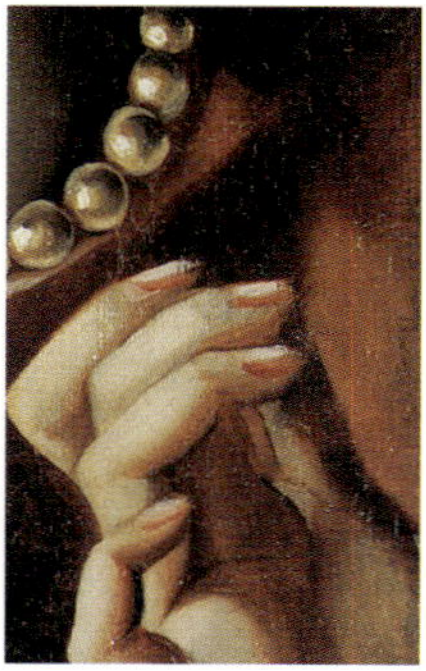

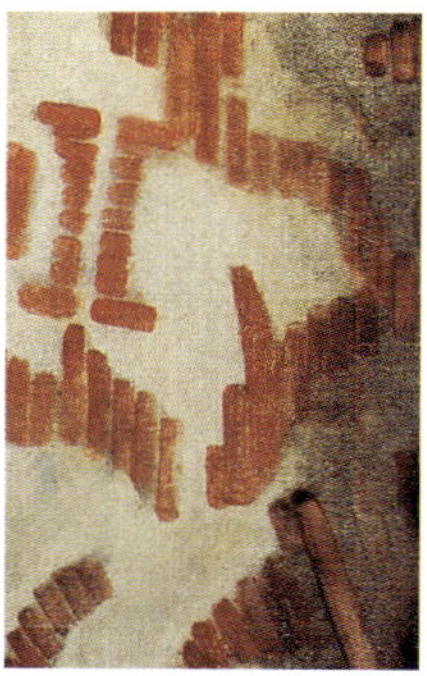

There is also a very special erotic tension in de Lempicka's portrayals of paired women. It was a motif she treated frequently including *The Orange Scarf* (1927), *The Bride* (1928), *Sharing Secrets* (1928), *The Green Turban* (1929), *The Girls* (c.1930) and *Spring* (1930).

Double 47, a depiction of two heads apparently painted from the same model, suggests a pair of rather masculine lesbians with short-cropped hair.

De Lempicka painted several canvases of passively and voluptuously posed groups of female nudes that recall the very male view of harem fantasy pictures by nineteenth century artists such as Ingres and Gerome.

Sharing Secrets

1928
Oil on canvas, 46 x 38 cm
Galleria Campo dei Fiori, Rome

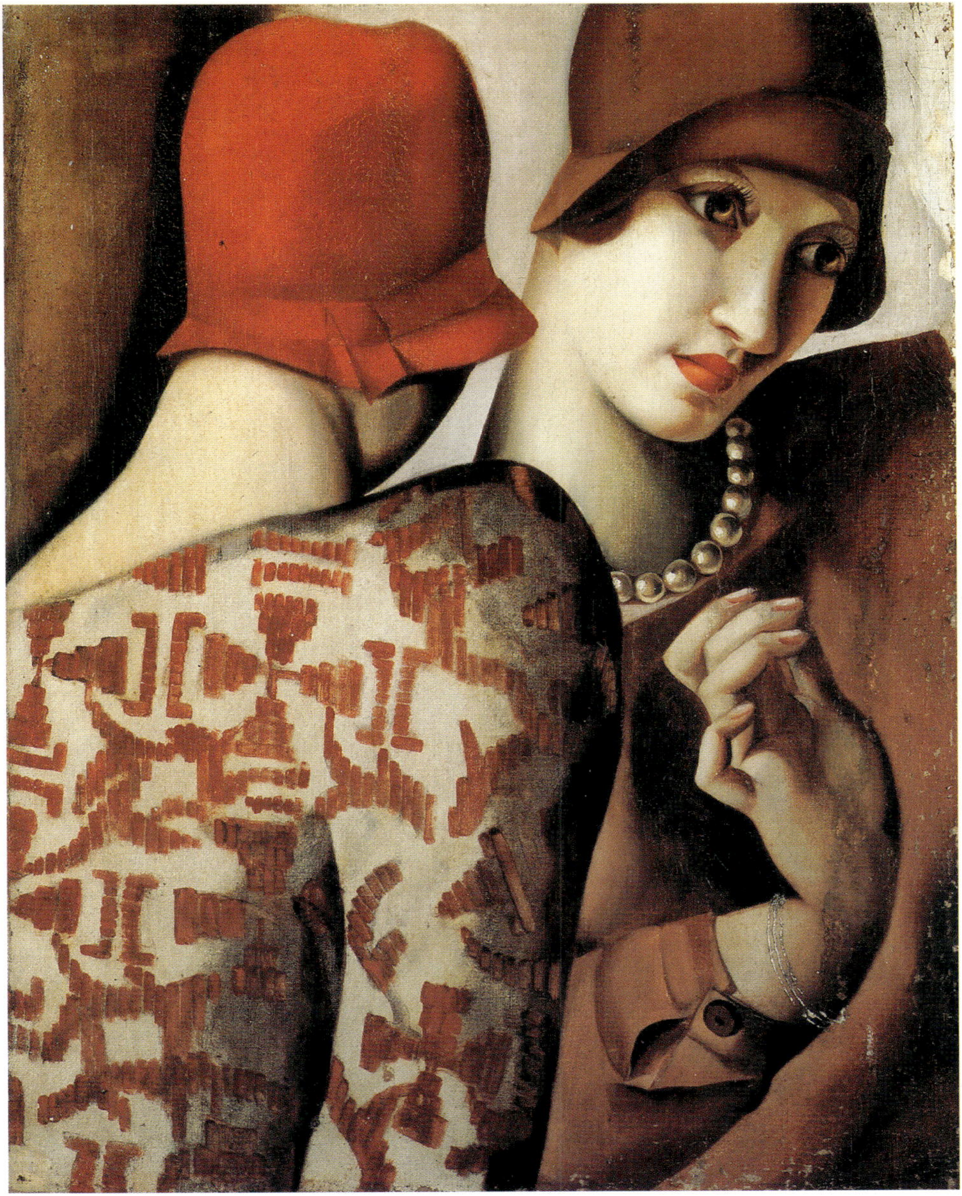

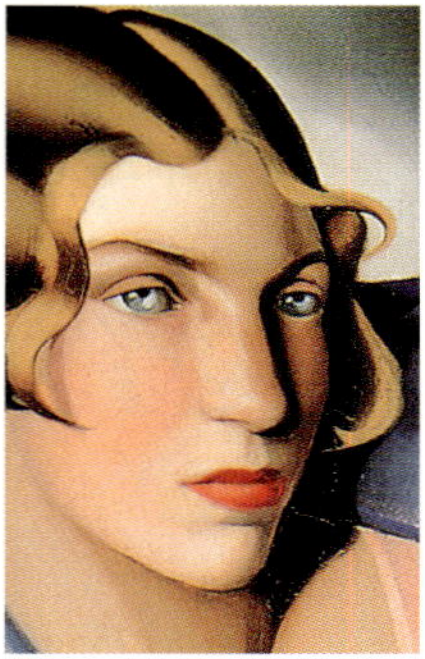
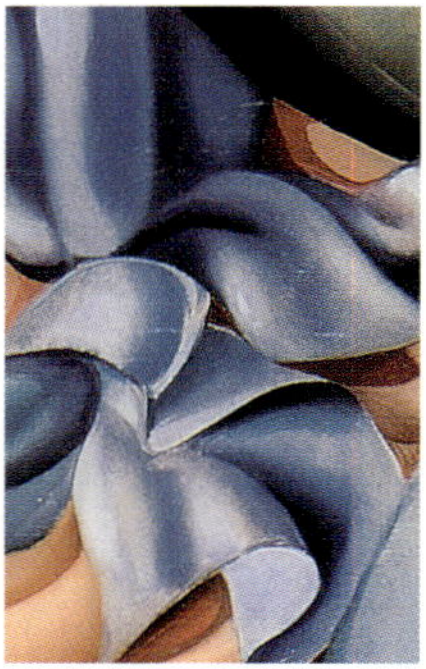
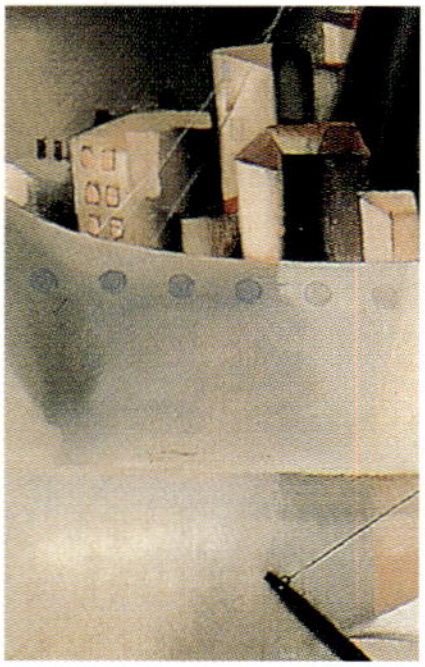

Perhaps the most disturbing paintings by de Lempicka to modern viewers are the portraits she made of young girls including those of her daughter Kizette. Once again these evoke the gaze of the male voyeur rather than that of a woman and a mother in the way they fixate on the young girl's legs and the often suggestive shadows between them. *Kizette in Pink* aged barely eight or nine, eyes up the viewer with a gaze as knowing as that of Tamara herself in the photo taken of her in Monte Carlo in 1911. As she freely admitted, de Lempicka picked up men in the same masculine and predatory way as she did women. "I refused myself nothing. I had always "Innamorato", always. For my inspiration, I liked to go out in the evenings and have a good-looking man tell me how beautiful I am or how great an artist I am — and he touches my hand…I loved it! I needed that. And I had many, many."

Portrait of Arlette Boucard

1928
Oil on canvas, 70 x 130 cm
Private Collection

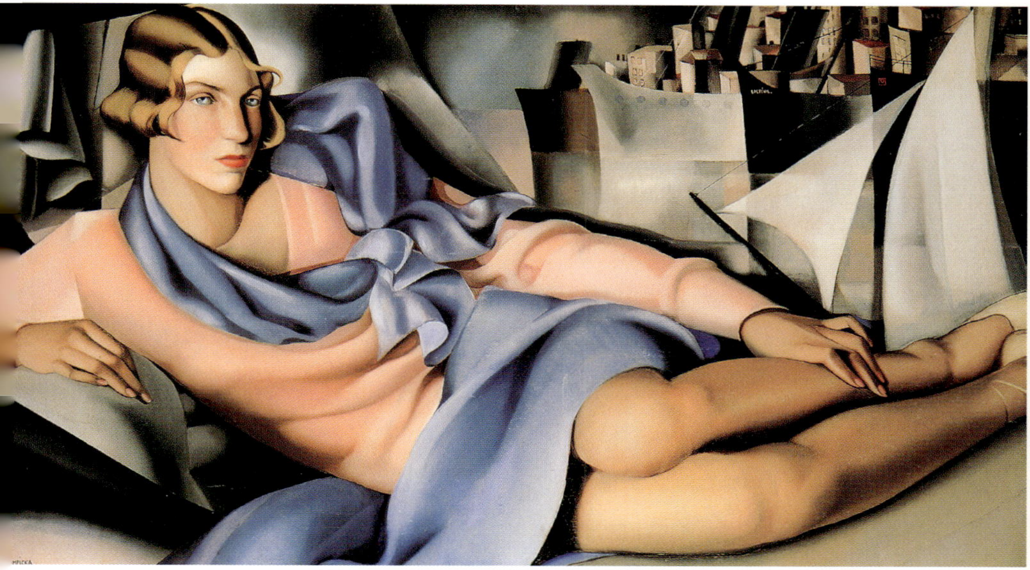

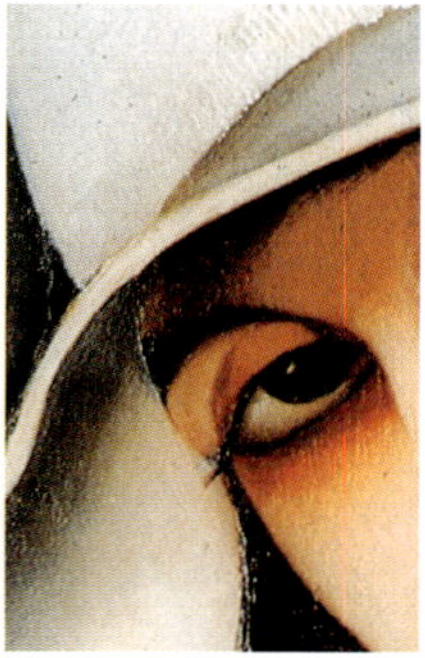

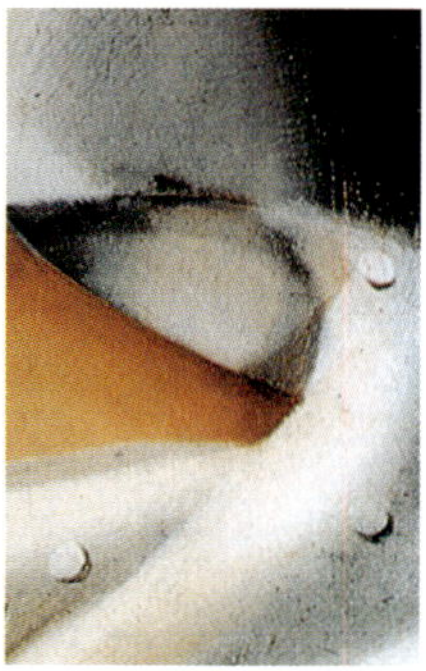

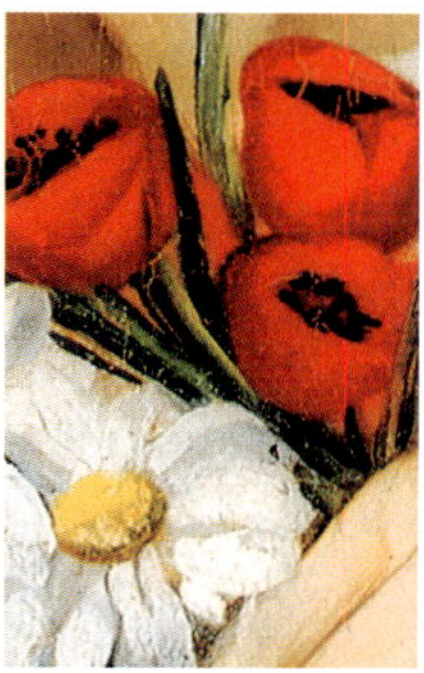

One of her rare male nudes, the superbly muscular figure, seen from the back in *Adam and Eve* was painted from a young policeman picked up on the streets of the Left Bank. 'When I finished the sketch (of the female model) I went out into the streets. This was the artist's quarter. I had before me the vision of Adam and Eve. In the street nearby I saw a gendarme, a policeman on his beat. He was young, he was handsome. I said to him: "Monsieur, I am an artist and I need a model for my painting. Would you pose for me?" And he said "Of course, Madame. I am myself an artist. At what time do you require me?" We made arrangements. He came to my studio after work and said; "How shall I pose?" "In the nude" He took off his things and folded them neatly on the chair, placing his big revolver on the top. I set him on the podium and then called my model. "You are Adam and here is your Eve" I said'.

High Summer

1928
Oil on panel, 35 x 27 cm
Private Collection

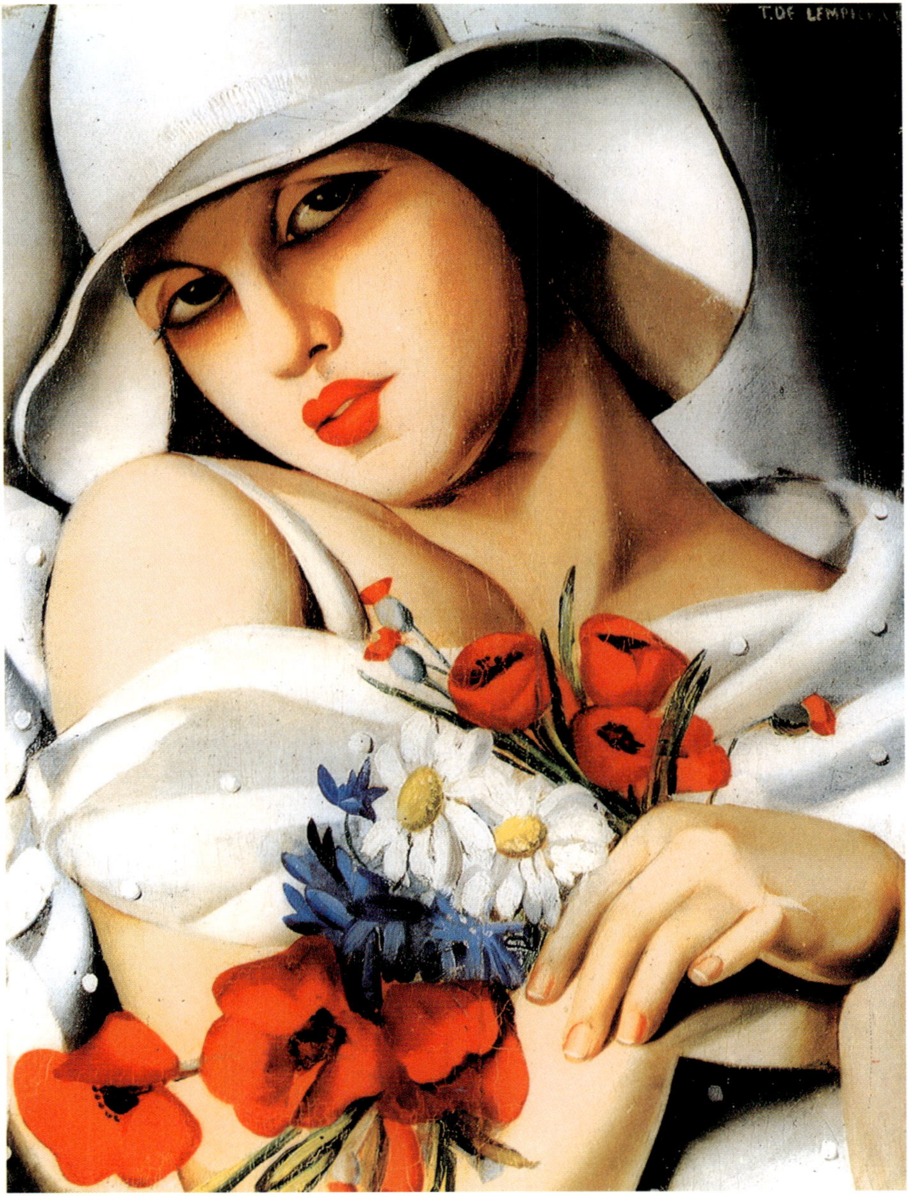

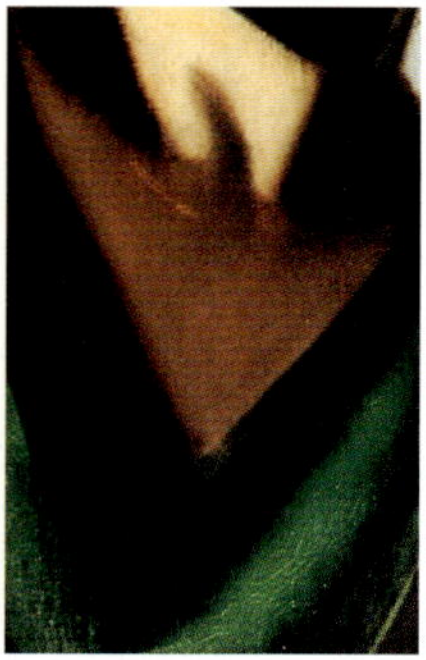
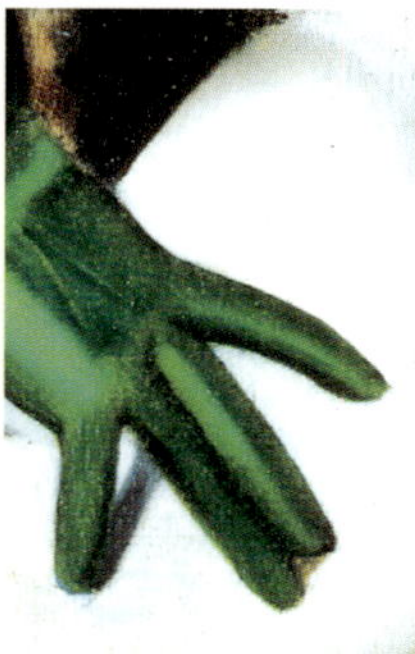
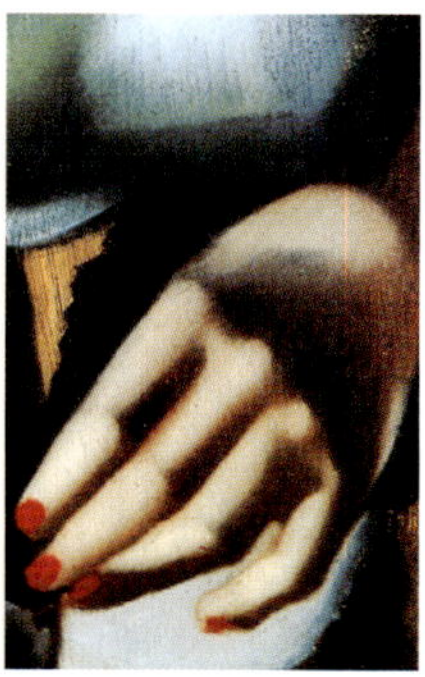

It is worth pausing at this point to compare de Lempicka with two other woman painters of the period with a specifically lesbian sensibility — the American Romaine Brooks and the German Jewish Lotte Laserstein. Both Brooks and de Lempicka possessed a solid basis of academic draughtsmanship and both combined elements of realism with decorative stylisation. The roots of Brooks' style are in the Belle Epoque and the Art Nouveau style rather than in the Jazz Age Moderne of de Lempicka. The most striking comparison between these two women artists is provided by Brook's portrait of Una, Lady Troubridge and de Lempicka's of the Marquise de La Salle — two icons of 1920s lesbianism painted within a year of one another in 1924 and 1925. The chunky Marquise and the pencil thin English lady are both in male attire and guiltless of the least hint of feminine curves.

Woman with a Green Glove

1928
Oil on plywood, 100 x 65 cm
Private Collection

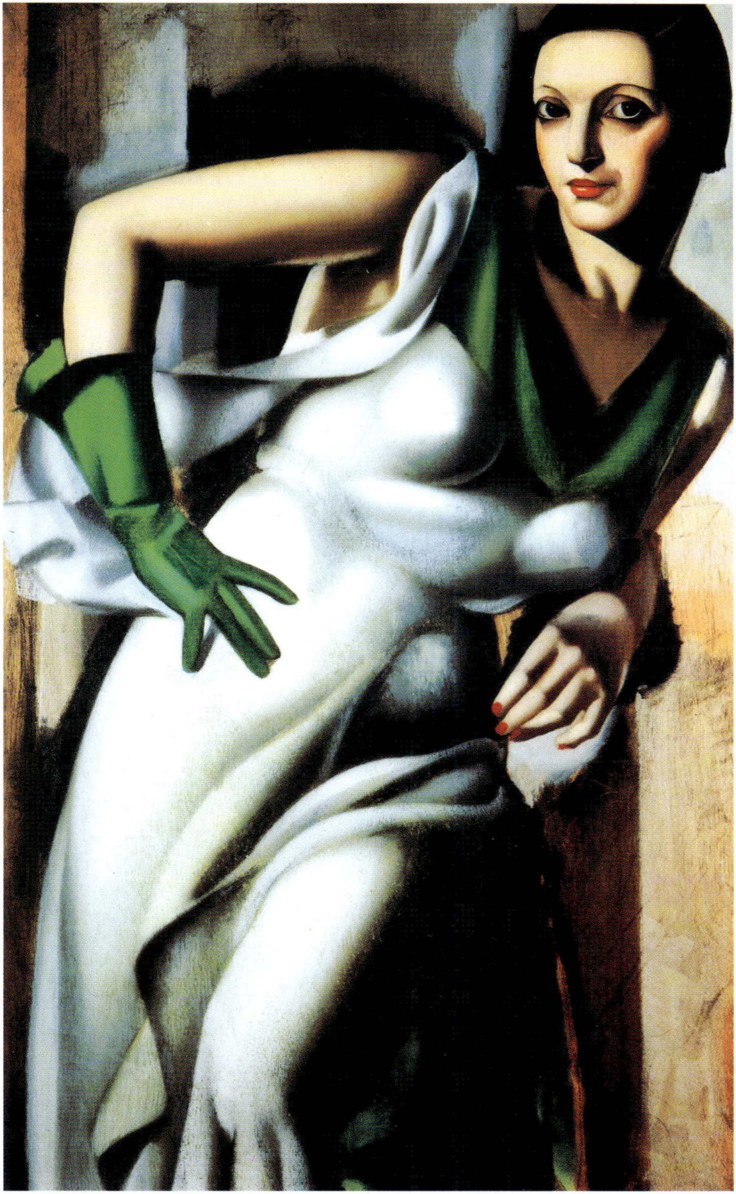

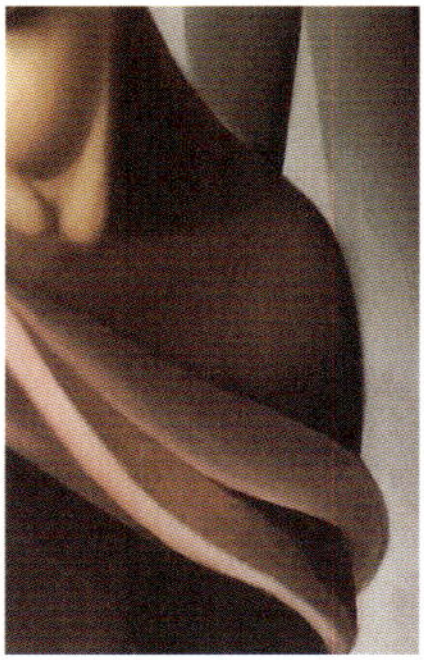
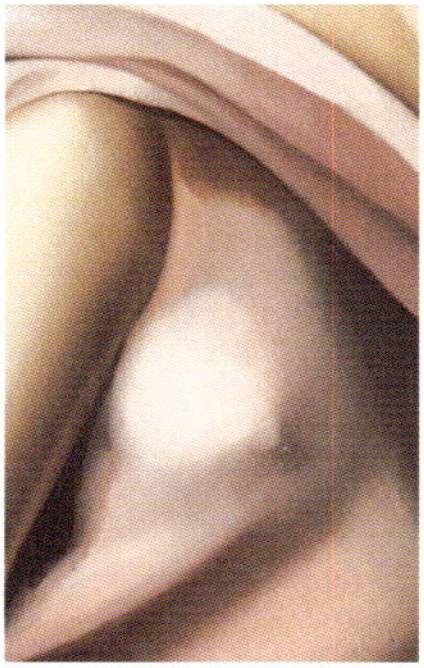
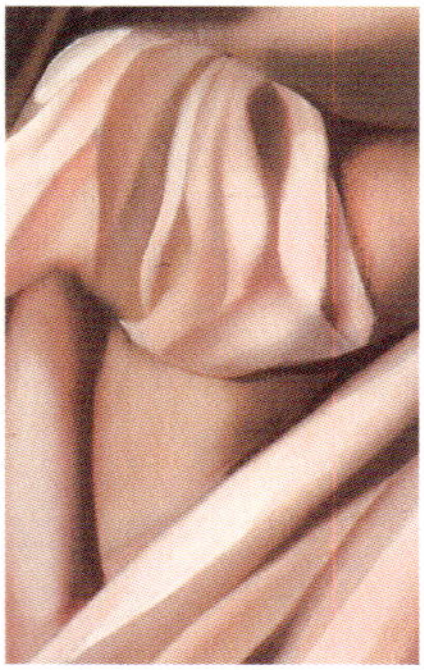

The masculinity of the Marquise is suggested by her heavy black riding boots while that of Lady Troubridge is conveyed by proxy through the pair of phallic dachshunds that seem to emerge from her hips. Each surveys the viewer challengingly. Lady Una sports that badge of inter-war lesbianism — a monocle.

Lotte Laserstein was an exact contemporary of de Lempicka, born in 1898 in a small East Prussian town now incorporated into Poland. In the 1920s Laserstein lived in Berlin, probably the only city more tolerant of deviance from sexual norms than Paris. The trajectory of Lasterstein's career went in tandem with that of de Lempicka — a period of brilliance from the mid 1920s to 1933 — exile in the late 30s followed by neglect and artistic decline and finally by belated discovery.

Portrait of Romana de La Salle

1928
Oil on canvas, 162 x 97 cm
Private Collection

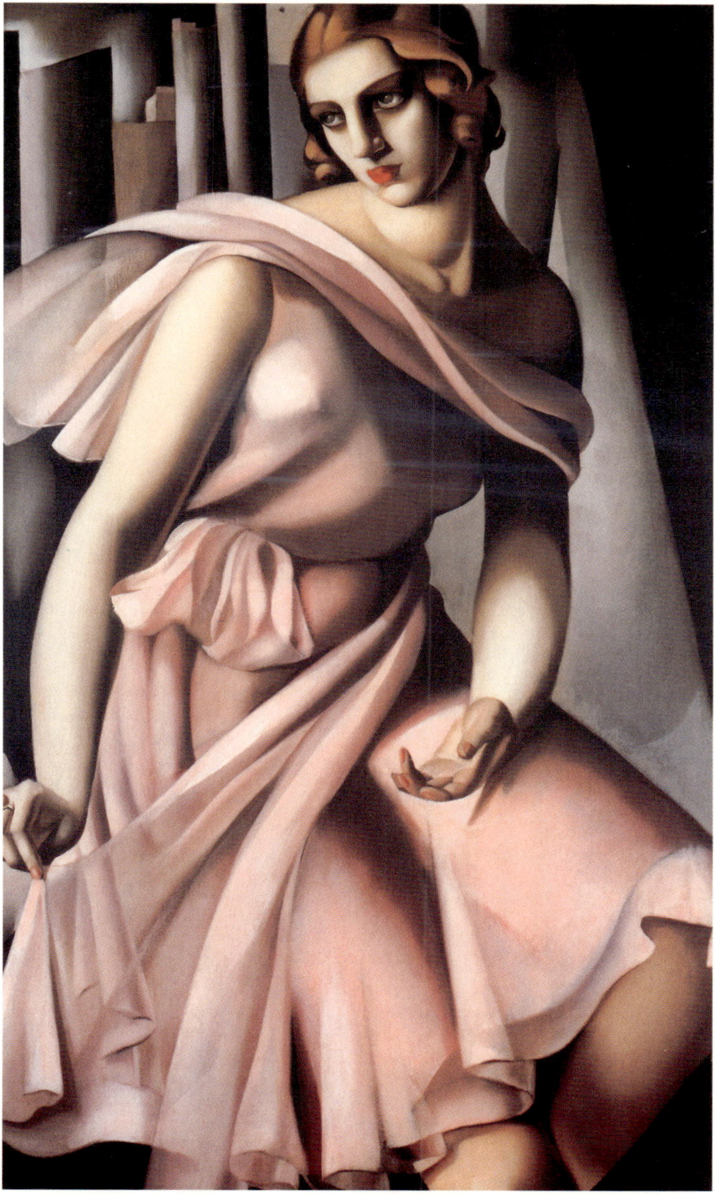

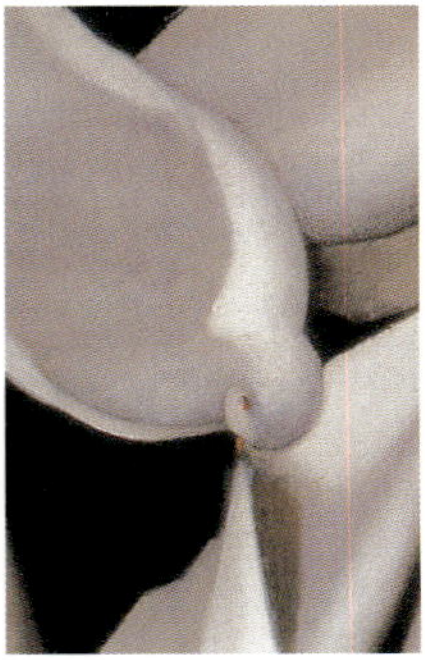

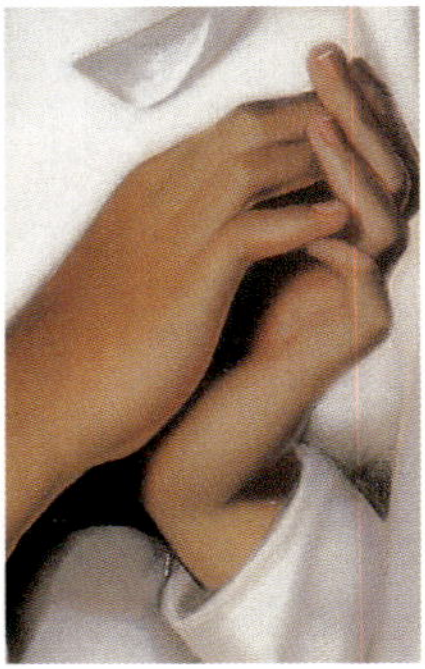

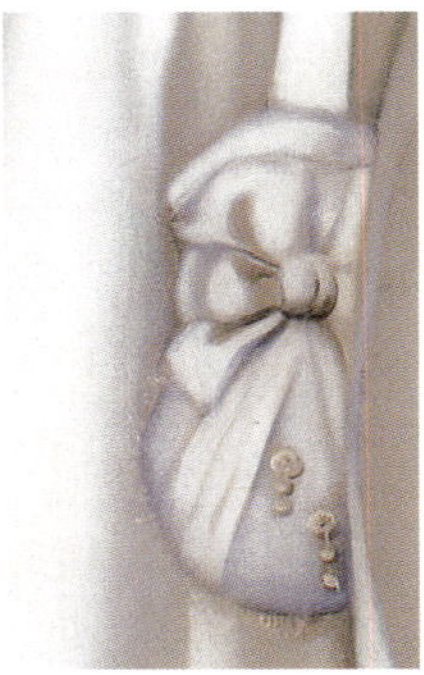

Laserstein's neo-realist style lacks the superficial trappings of modernism adopted by de Lempicka. Her sober and immaculate technique is closer to that of the nineteenth century realist Wilhelm Leibl than any of her avant garde Berlin contemporaries. Though the female nude was one of her principal subjects, her work lacks the obvious loucheness of de Lempicka and indeed of her fellow Berlin neo-realists Otto Dix and Christian Schad. Her modernity lies in a certain gritty truthfulness, far from the glossy glamour of de Lempicka's portraits and in a sensibility apparent particularly in her depictions of women. Her many images of paired women in which one depicts an emotional if not necessarily a sexual affinity between them, make an intriguing comparison with those of de Lempicka.

The Communicant

1928
Oil on canvas, 100 x 65 cm
Musée des Beaux-Arts de Roubaix

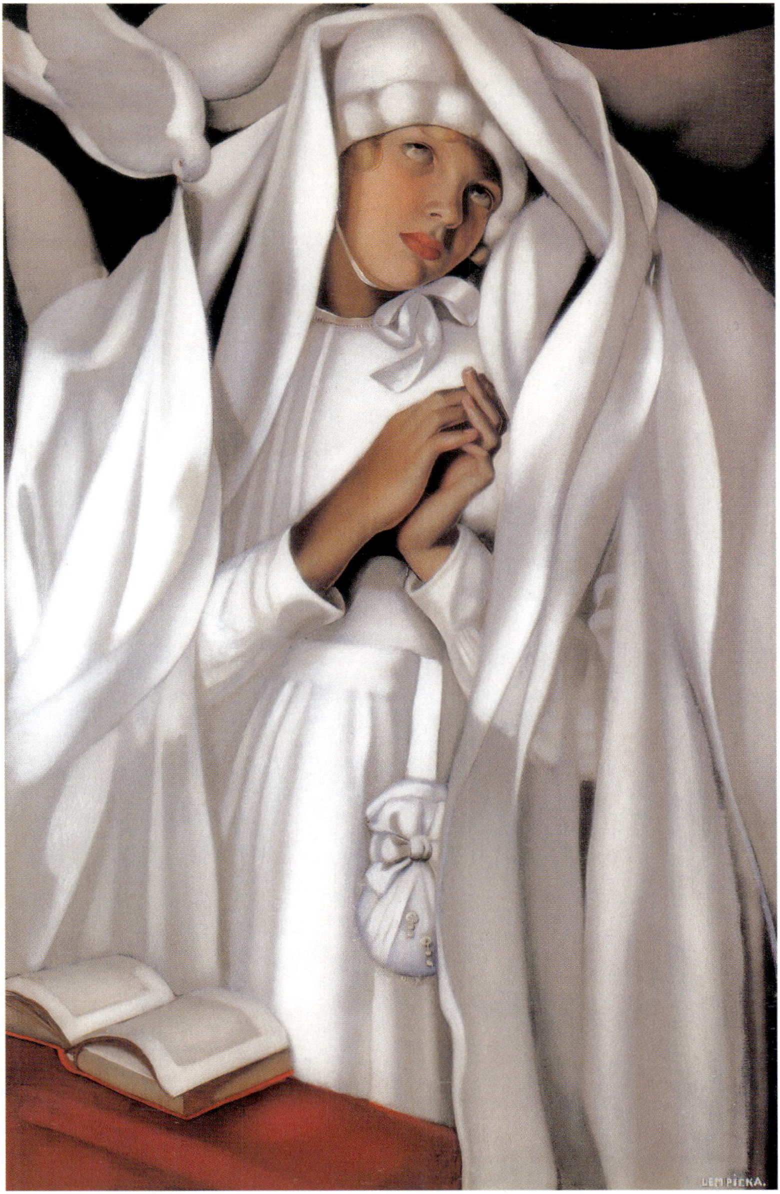
LEMPICKA.

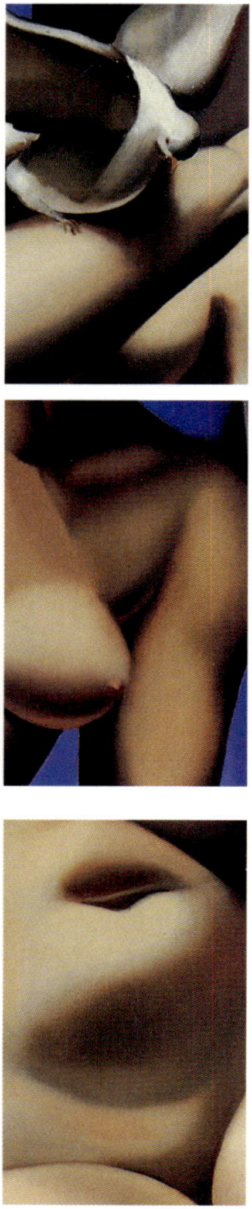

Both de Lempicka's work and that of Laserstein can be seen in the context of a widespread blossoming of more or less hard-edged neo-realism in the 1920s, from the Socialist Realism in Stalin's Russia to the work of Grant Wood and Edward Hopper in the United States and taking in such artists as Stanley Spencer, Dod Procter, Gluck, and Meredith Frampton in Britain, the so-called Neue-Sachlichkeit painters Otto Dix and Christian Schad in Berlin, the Novecento Group, Felice Casorati, Piero Marussig, Ubaldo Oppo in Italy, Josep Togores, Joaquim Sunyer, Francesc d'Assis Gali Feliu Elia Francesc Domingo in Spain, and Frida Kahlo and Diego Riviera in Mexico.

Nude with Dove

1928
Oil on canvas, 121.3 x 63.5 cm
Private Collection

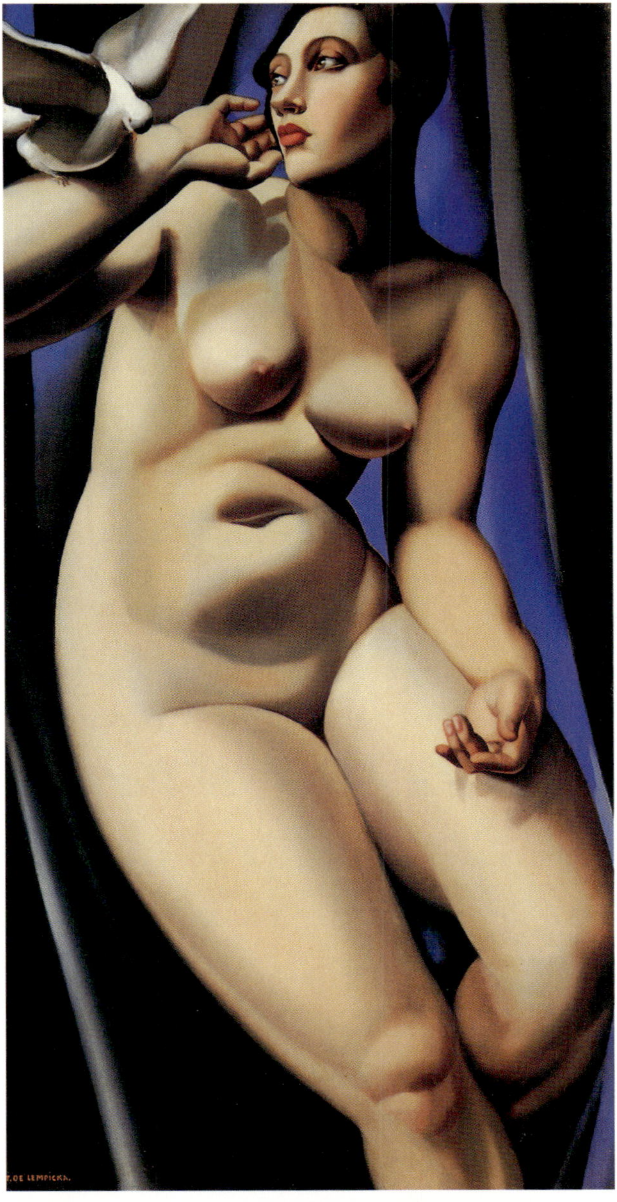
T. DE LEMPICKA.

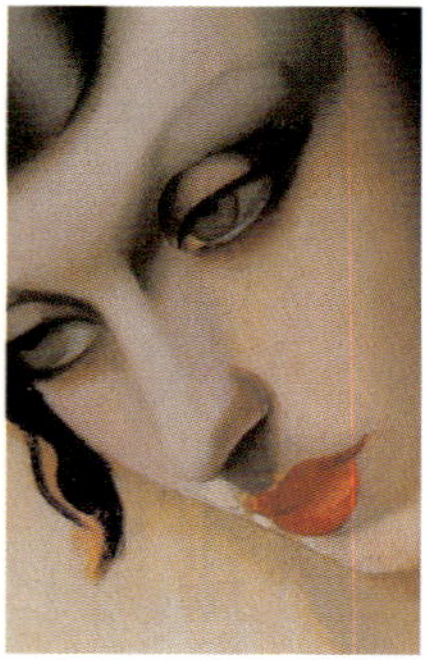
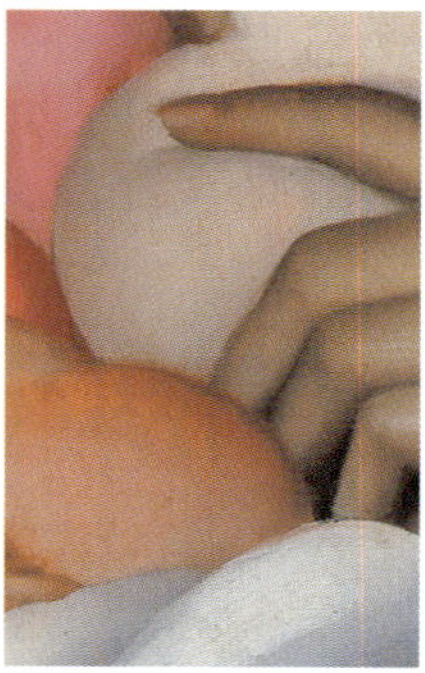
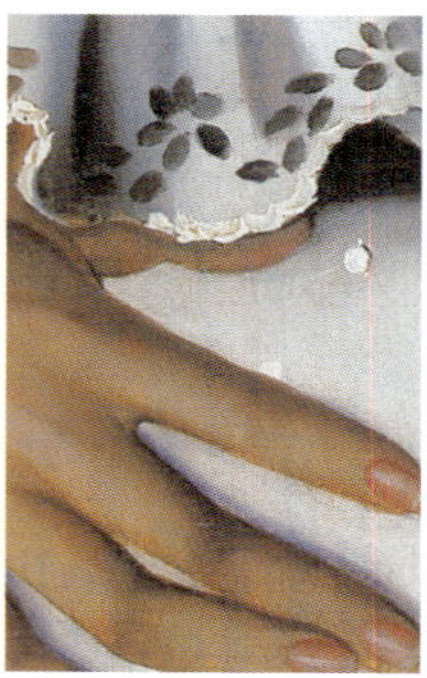

On the other side of the Atlantic, it was perhaps Georgia O'Keeffe who invites the most interesting comparisons with de Lempicka, both because of her methods of decorative abstraction and decoratively diluted cubism and because of her preoccupation with two motifs dear to de Lempicka — skyscrapers and lilies. O'Keeffe began to exhibit her stylised depictions of New York skyscrapers in 1926, three years ahead of de Lempicka's adoption of the New York townscape as an ubiquitous backdrop to her portraits. It is quite likely that de Lempicka would have come into contact with the work of the much praised and admired O'Keeffe during her New York sojourn of 1929 to 1930. She would certainly have been intrigued too by the way that O'Keeffe used the interiors of flowers to suggest the female sex.

Maternity

1928
Oil on panel, 35 x 27 cm
Private Collection

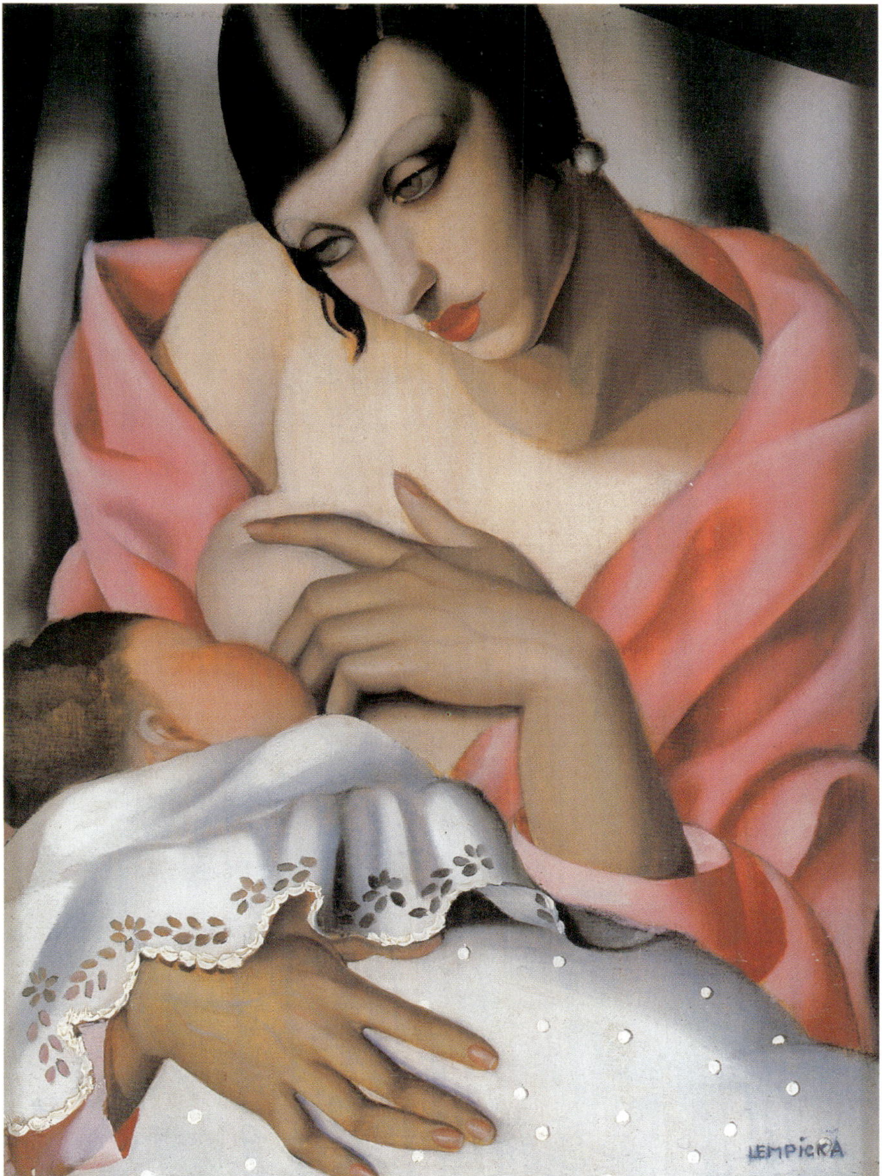
LEMPICKA

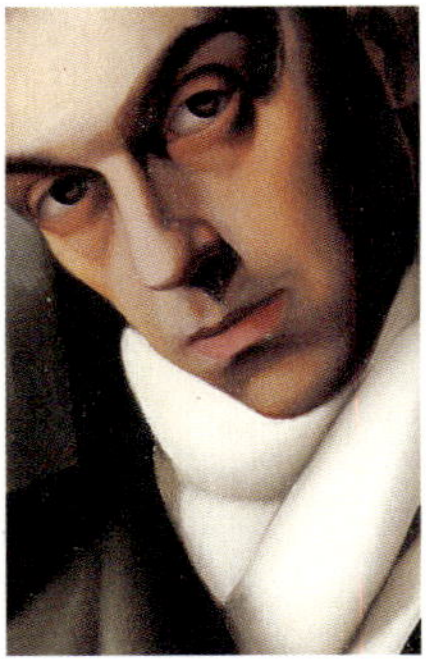

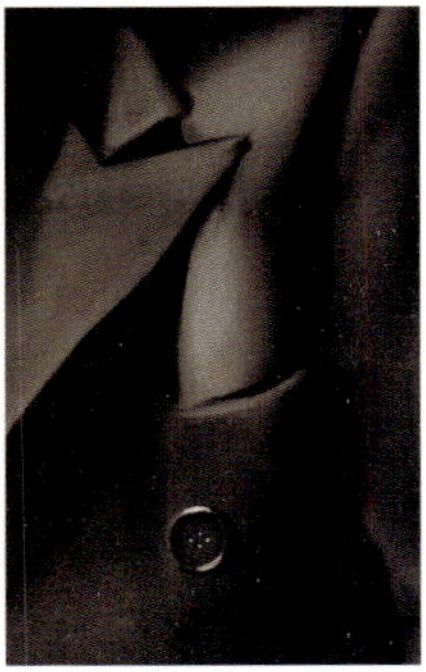

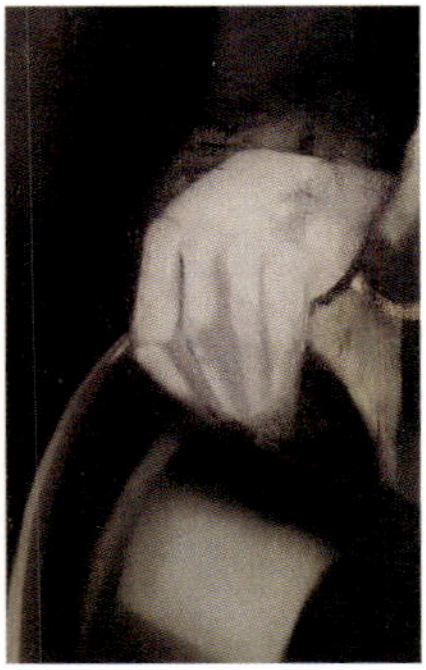

De Lempicka first exhibited at the prestigious Salon d'Automne in 1922 a mere two years after she had enrolled with Maurice Denis at the Academie Ranson and from 1923 she exhibited regularly at the Salon des Independents which in the past had shown such great masters as Georges Seurat and Henri Rousseau. Her breakthrough came in 1925 with a one woman show at the Bottega di Poesia in Milan. De Lempicka's timing was perfect. 1925 saw the triumph of the Art Deco style at the great exhibition of decorative arts in Paris. This show marked not only the highpoint of the style but also the moment of transition from the earlier more florid and heavily decorated version of the style to the sleeker more streamlined version of the style that flourished until the Second World War.

Portrait of a Man or Mr. Tadeusz de Lempicki

1928
Oil on canvas, 130 x 81 cm
Musée National d'Art Moderne, Paris, stored at
the Musée des Années Trente, Boulogne-Billancourt

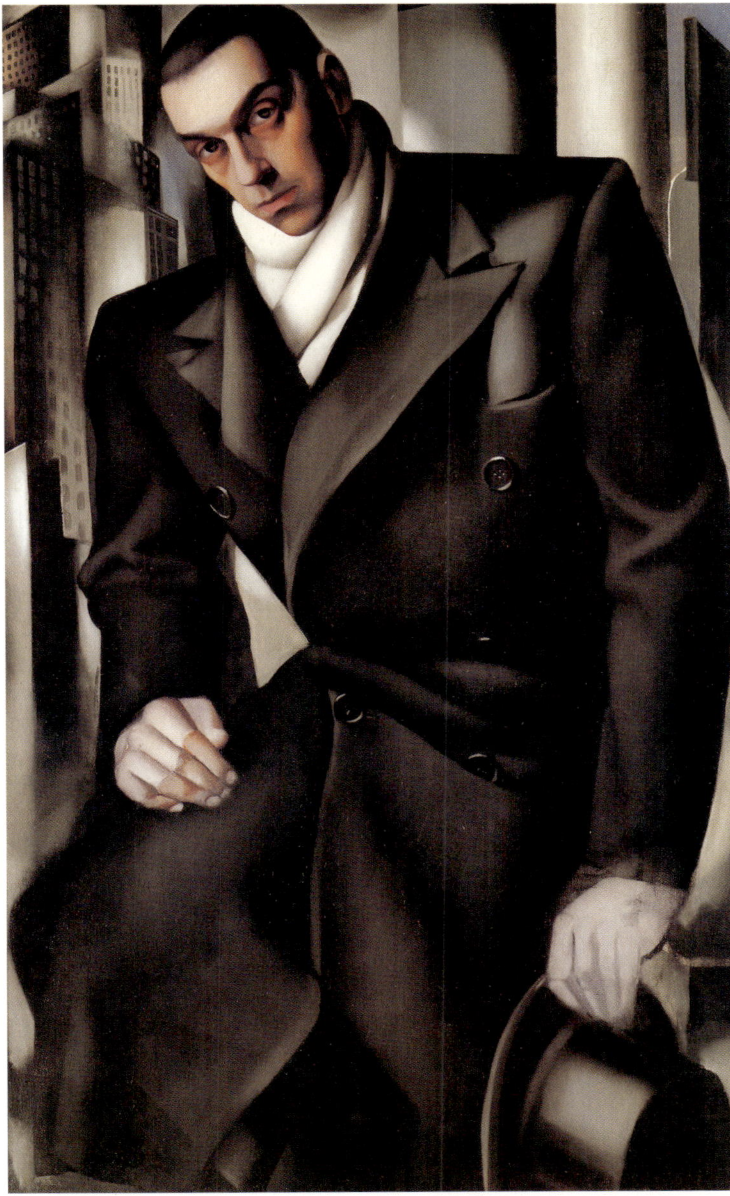

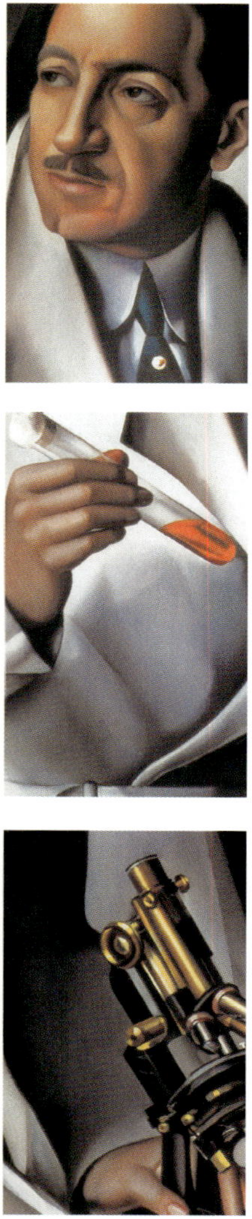

Though she was in fact exhibiting elsewhere at the time, de Lempicka will forever be associated with the moment of the 1925 Paris exhibition. For the best part of a decade she rode the crest of a wave as perhaps the most representative of the later version of the Art Deco style.

Apart from the headboard of her bed adorned with lesbian lovers frolicking in a stylised jungle, there is little trace either in her work or in the design of her apartment of the kind of geometricised floral decoration so evident in the 1925 Paris exhibition.

Portrait of Doctor Boucard

1928
Oil on canvas, 135 x 75 cm
Private Collection

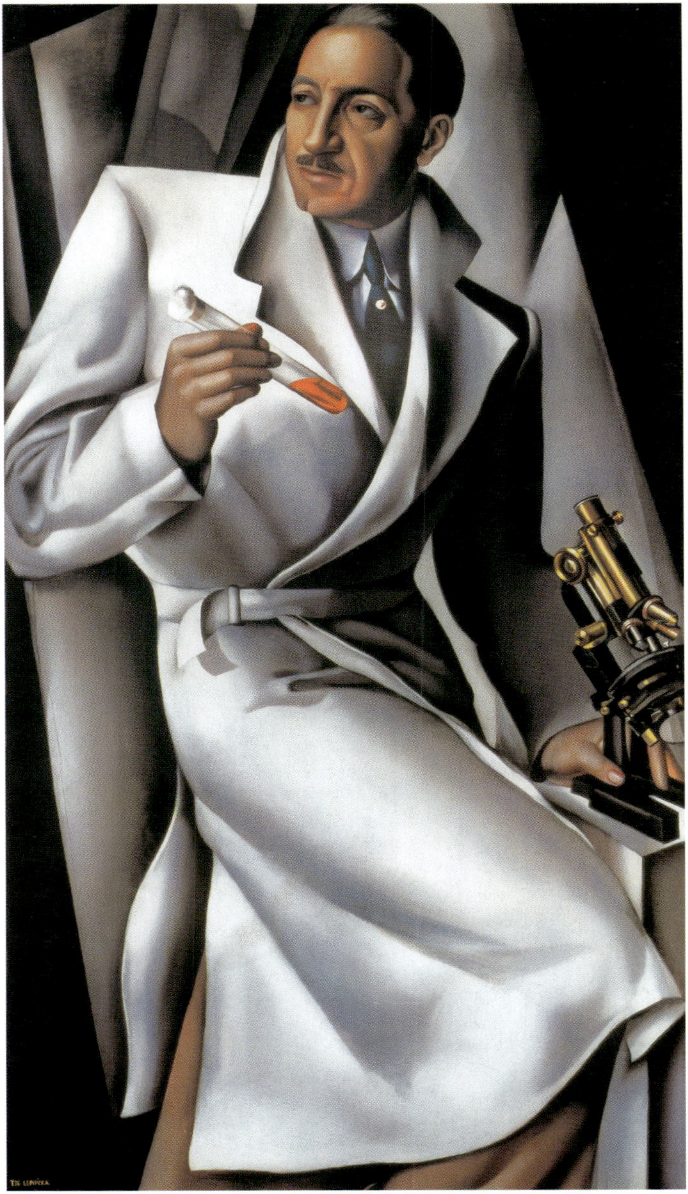

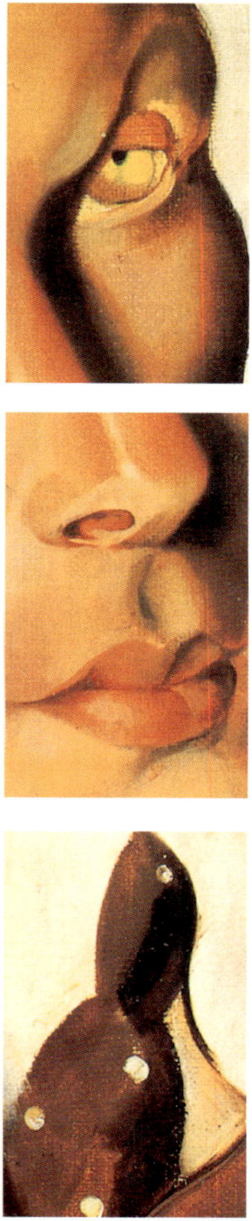

Nevertheless de Lempicka's art perfectly fulfils most of the criteria listed by Charlotte and Tim Benton in their attempt at an inclusive definition of the Art Deco style in their introduction to the catalogue of the Art Deco exhibition at the Victoria and Albert Museum in 2003. "We can try to identify some of the features that link the apparently antithetical works ascribed to Art Deco. They often refer to historic styles, whether Western or non-Western, but are not literally dependent on them, though they are often respectful of them. They are often influenced by avant-garde art and design yet, unlike these, they make no claim to being disinterested and are, in fact, thoroughly contingent and engaged with the commercial world.

Portrait of the Count of Fürstenberg-Herdringen

1928
Oil on canvas, 41 x 27 cm
Private Collection

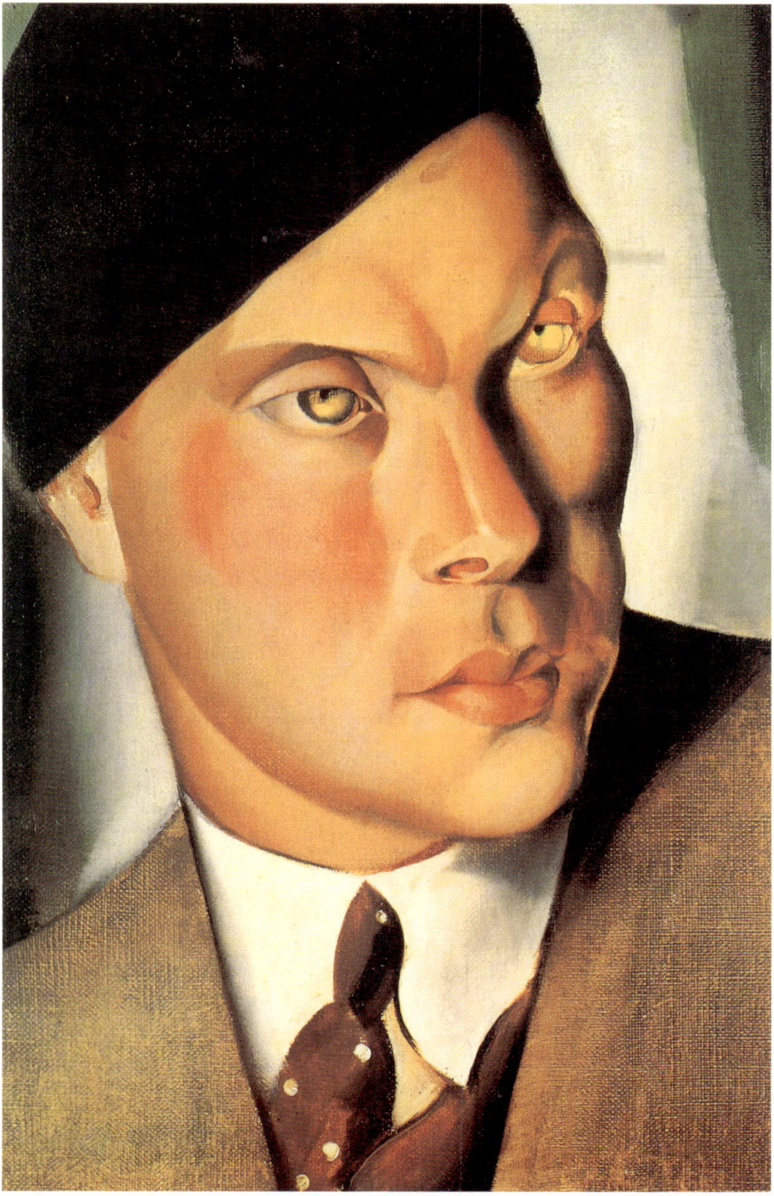

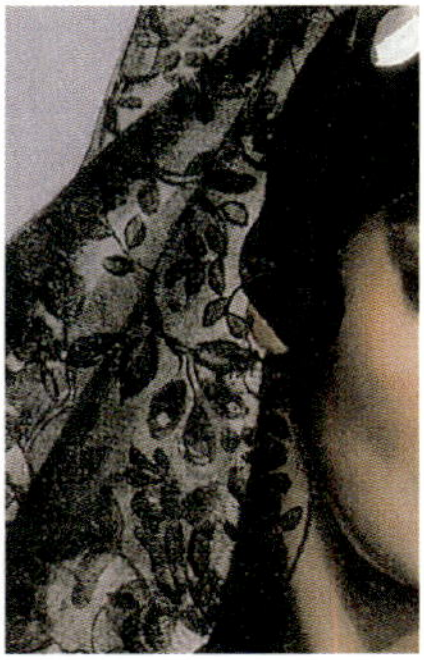

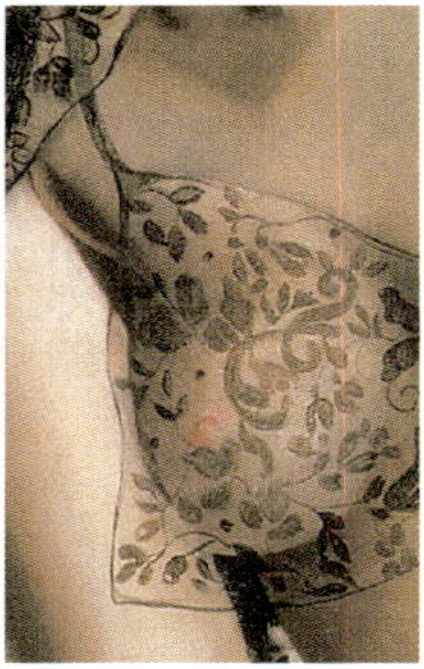

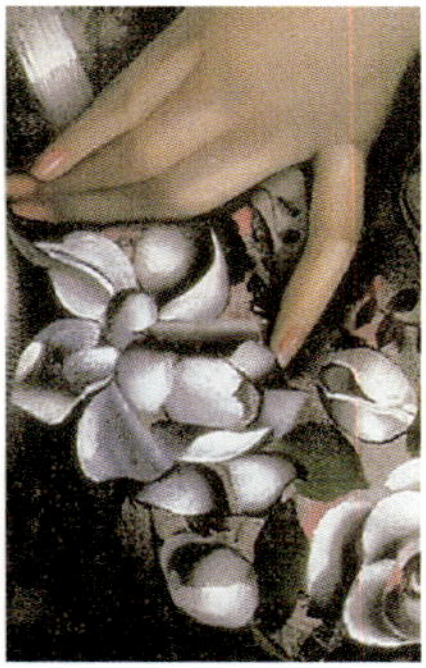

But whether inspired by traditional or by avant-garde sources, they have a tendency to simplified form and an absence of three-dimensional, applied ornament. They are "decorative" even when they do not employ ornament; and they frequently stress "surface" values or effects. They are often novel or innovative — but not radical or revolutionary. They frequently employ new technologies even when their forms and methods also reference tradition. They often refer, overtly or symbolically, to "Modern" themes, such as youth, liberated sexuality and aspects of contemporary mechanical culture, through a recurrent visual repertoire of frozen fountains, sunbursts, electrification, mechanisation and transportation."

Nana de Herrera

1928-1829
Oil on canvas, 121 x 64 cm
Private Collection

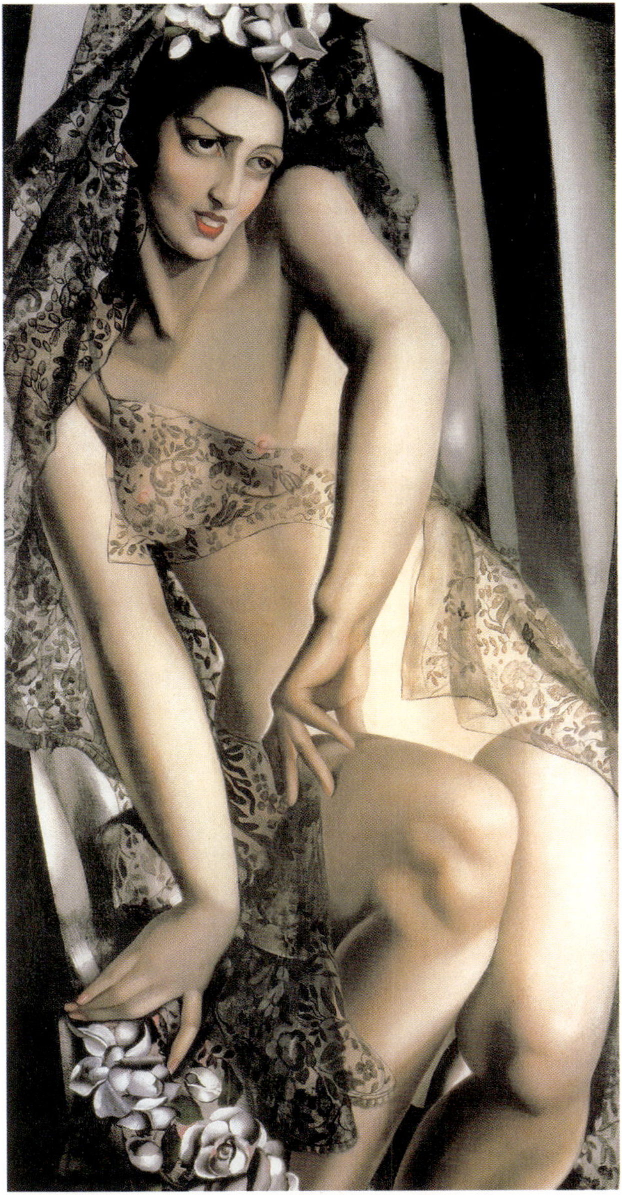

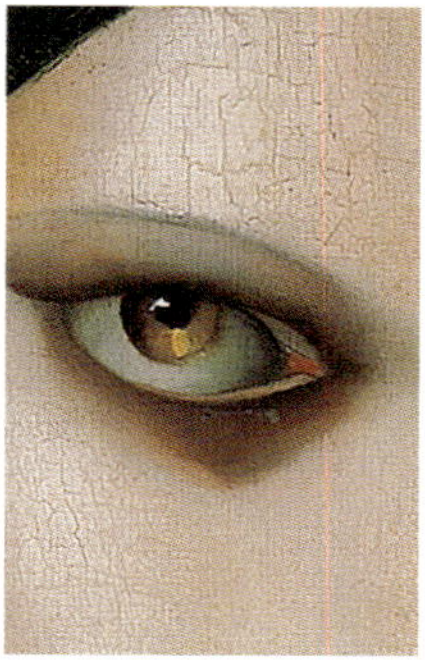

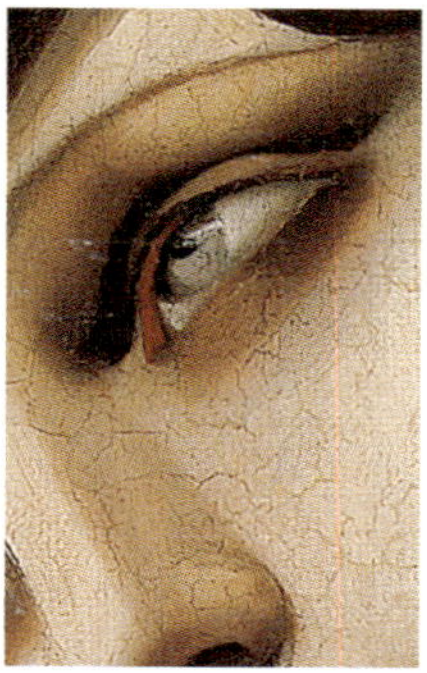

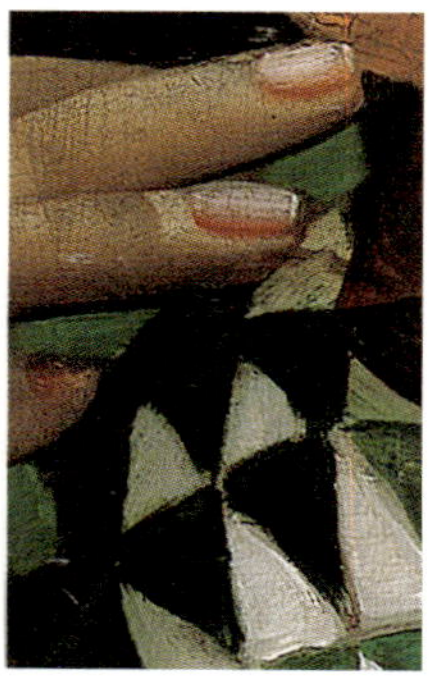

The commercialism of de Lempicka's work is apparent in its striking similarity with fashion illustration. Like de Lempicka, the fashion illustrators of the twenties and early thirties absorbed elements from avant-garde art movements, notably cubism and futurism, to create a style that was modern and at the same time decorative and accessible to a wider public. In the pages of *Vogue* and *Harper's Bazaar* we find many of the same motifs that we see in the paintings of de Lempicka — the abstracted, metallic forms and surfaces, the Manhatten back-drops and naturally the fashionable clothes and accessories.

The Green Turban

1929
Oil on panel, 41 x 33 cm
Private Collection

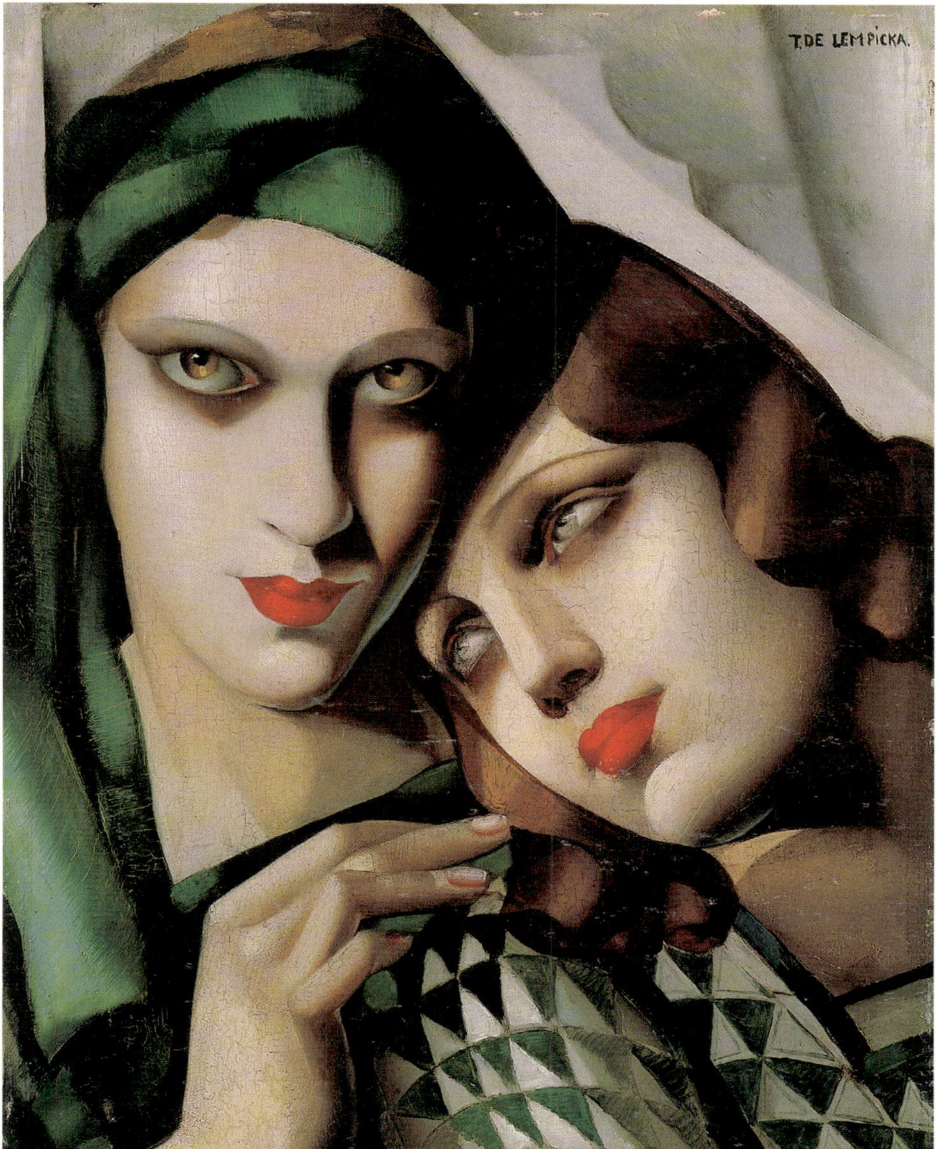
T. DE LEMPICKA.

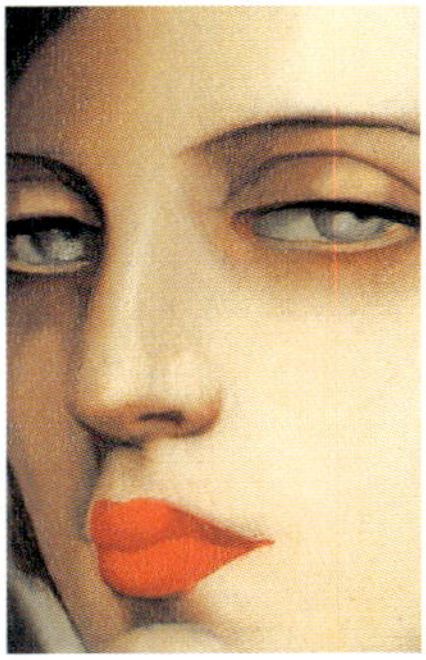

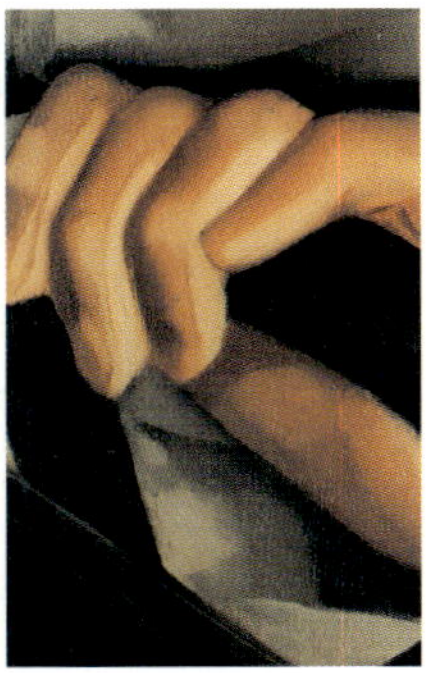

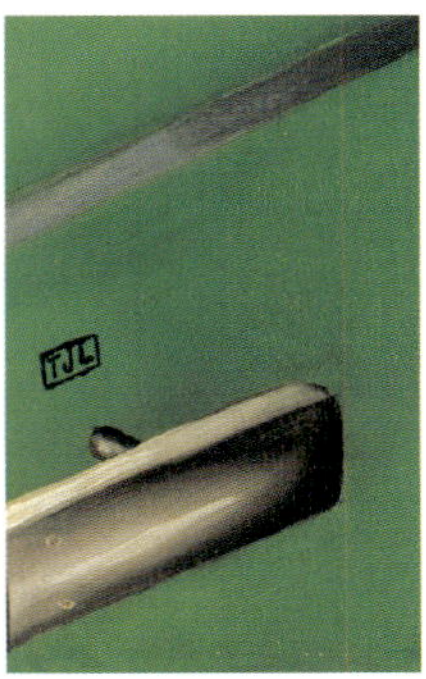

As well as stealing from the fine artists, the fashion magazines sometimes invited them to design covers too. Leon Bakst, Marie Laurencin, Pavel Tchelitchew, Raoul Dufy, Pierre Roy and Salvador Dali all contributed to *Vogue*. So happily does de Lempicka's art fit in with the world of fashion magazines that it seems surprising that she designed covers for neither the American nor the French versions of *Vogue*. However she was invited to create several cover designs for the leading German fashion magazine *Die Dame*. Amongst these was the 1925 Bugatti self-portrait that has become her most famous and frequently reproduced image.

Seft-Portrait in the Green Bugatti

1929
Oil on panel, 35 x 27 cm
Private Collection

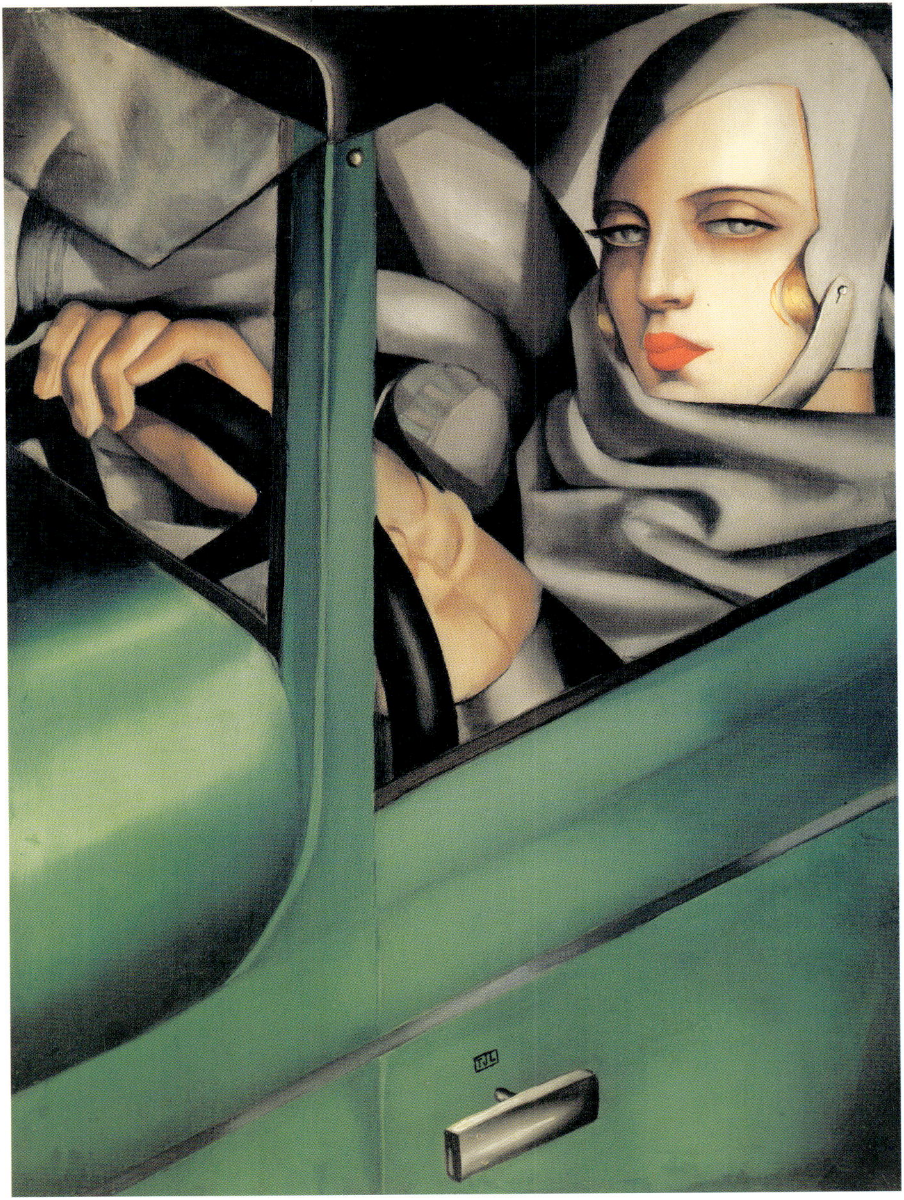
TJL

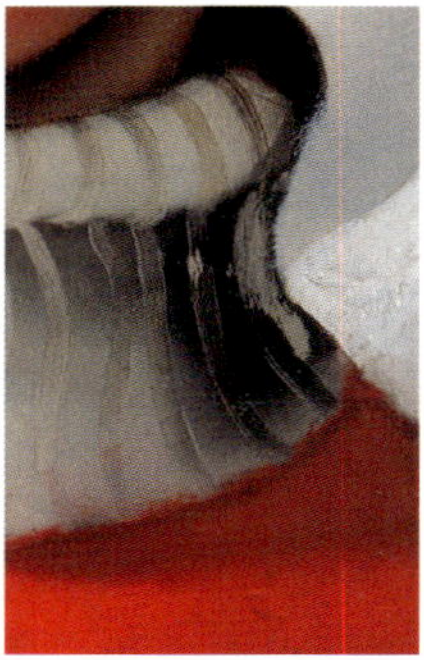

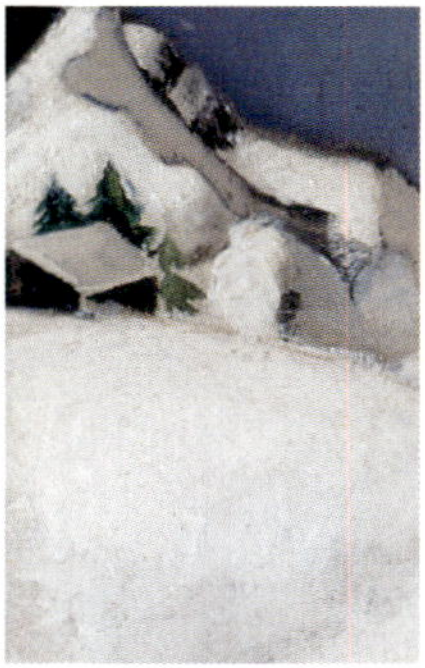

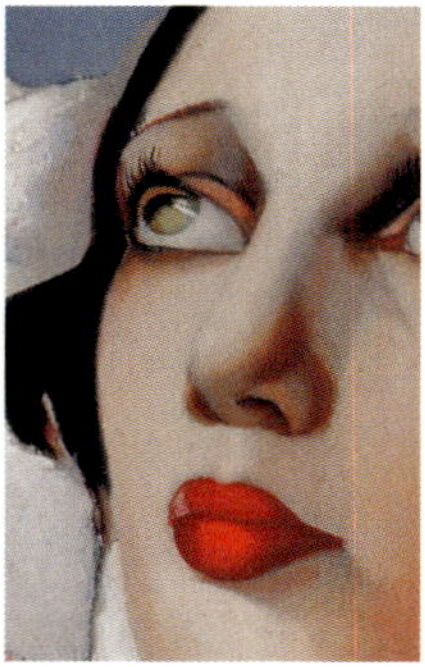

De Lempicka's commissioned portraits all date from the relatively short period between her triumphant 1925 exhibition in Milan and 1933 when the Depression began to bite in France and changes in economic circumstances as well as changes in taste which caused the flow of commissions to dry up. Collectively these commissioned portraits form a portrait of a class and period that is perhaps de Lempicka's greatest achievement. By and large de Lempicka paints men more as individuals, however glamorised, and women more as types. There was nothing new in this. Most professional portraitists have been men and male artists have tended to relate to their male sitters on a more human level while objectifying their female sitters. Lely, Kneller, Reynolds and Ingres are all examples of artists whose male portraits are far more sharply characterised than their female ones.

Saint Moritz

1929
Oil on panel, 35 x 27 cm
Musée des Beaux-Arts d'Orléans

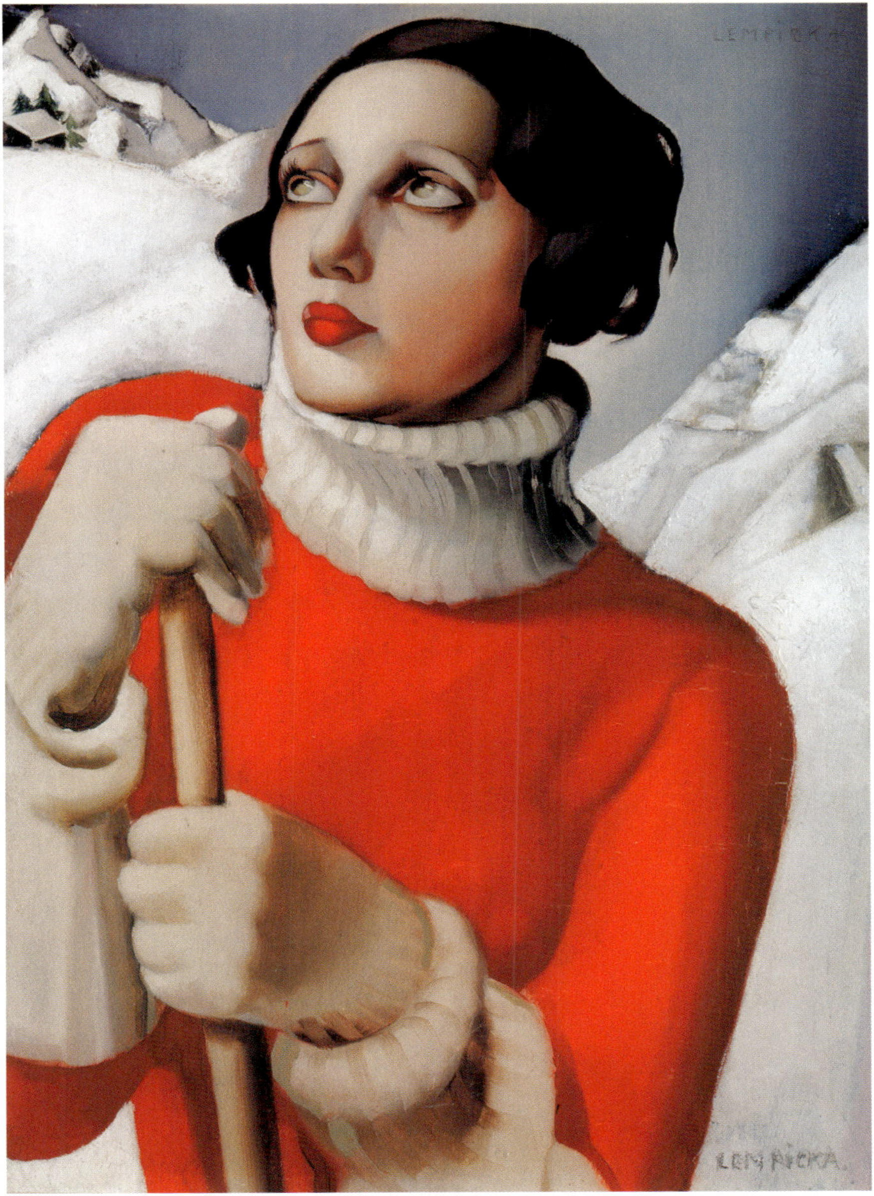
LEMPICKA

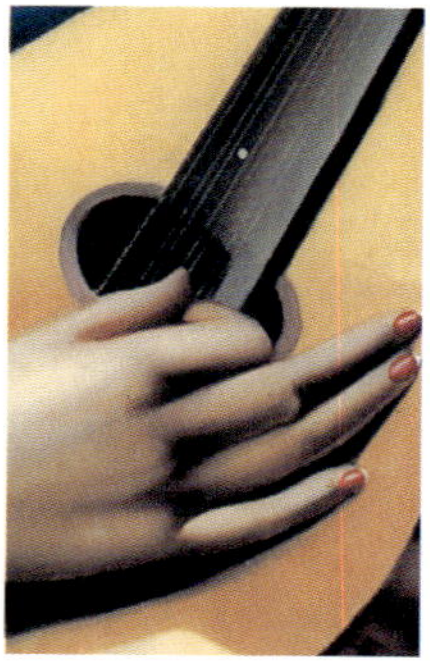

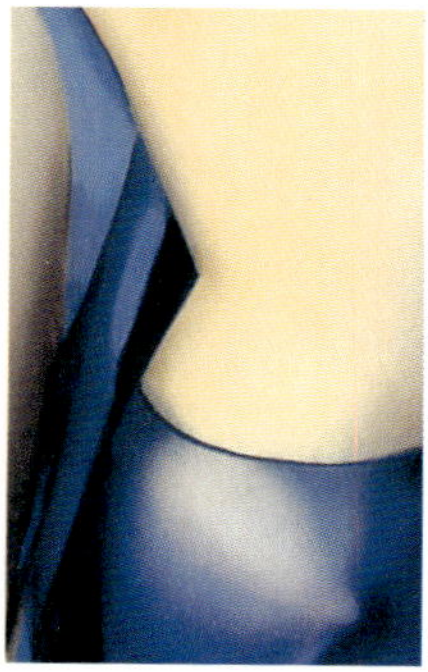

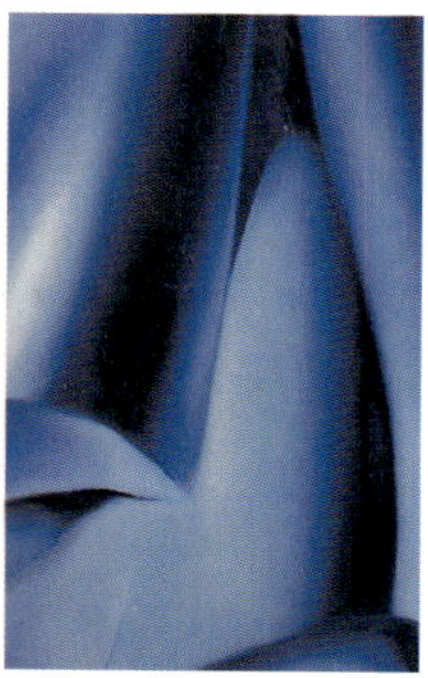

De Lempicka's male portraits can seem critical or even faintly mocking of their subjects, the portrait of the notoriously decadent Grand Duke Gabriel Constantinovitch verges upon the caricatural with his arrogant expression and a uniform that looks like a cast-off from a Ruritanian operetta production. Perhaps the most complex and telling of all her male portraits is that of her husband Tadeusz de Lempicki painted in 1928. Humiliated beyond endurance by Tamara's flagrant infidelities, as well no doubt by her social and artistic successes, de Lempicka announced that he was leaving his wife for another woman while this portrait was being painted. De Lempicka captures an expression of shiftiness and wary suspicion on the face of this handsome man whom she had once loved but no longer respected.

The Musician

1929
Oil on canvas, 116 x 73 cm
Barry Friedman Ltd, New York

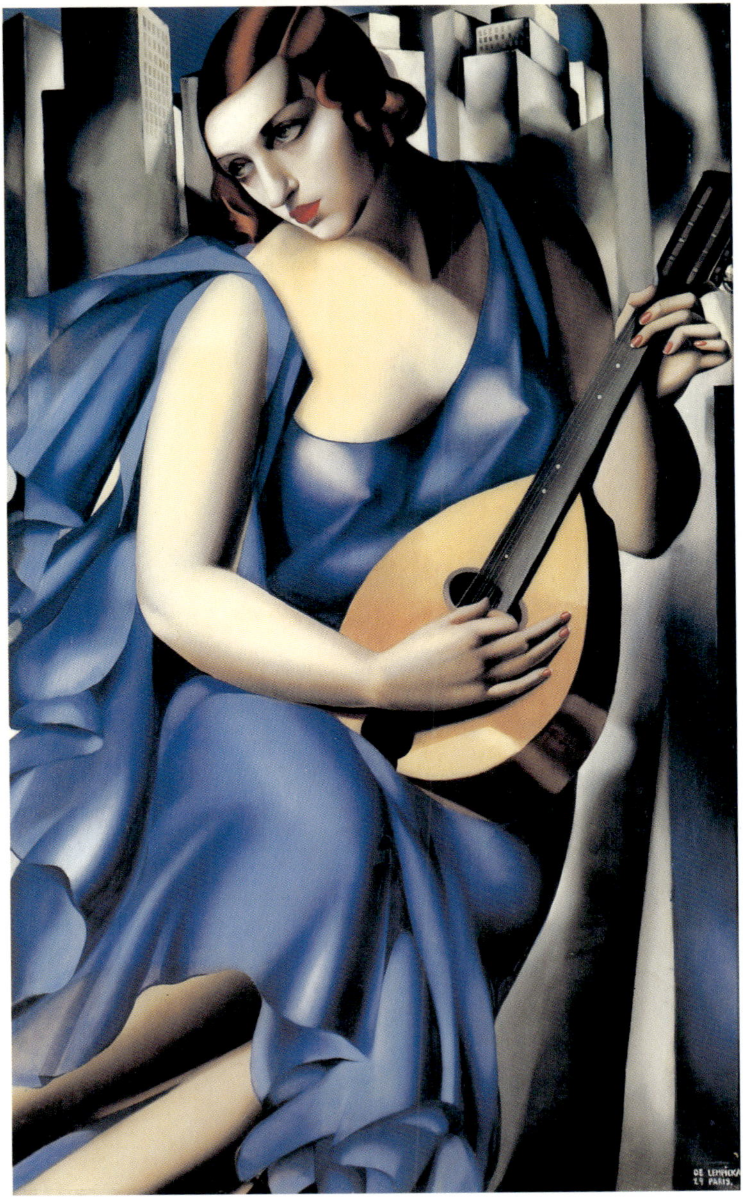
DE LEMPICKA
29 PARIS.

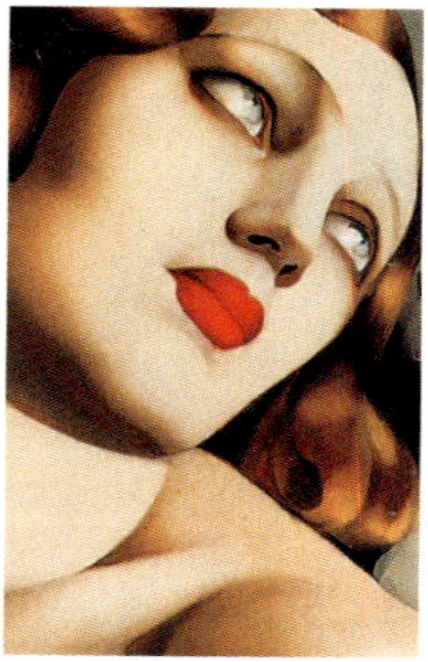

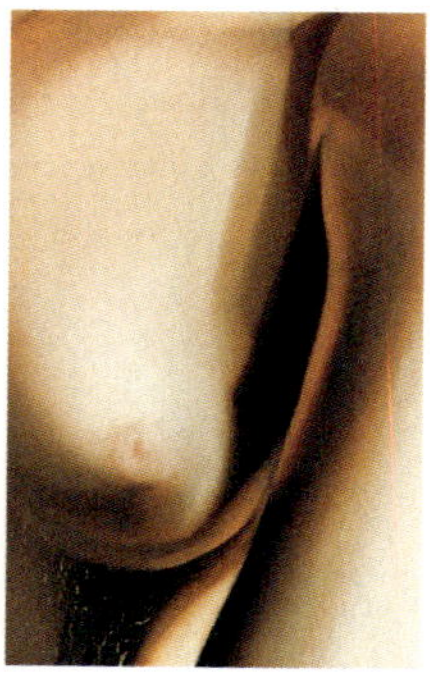

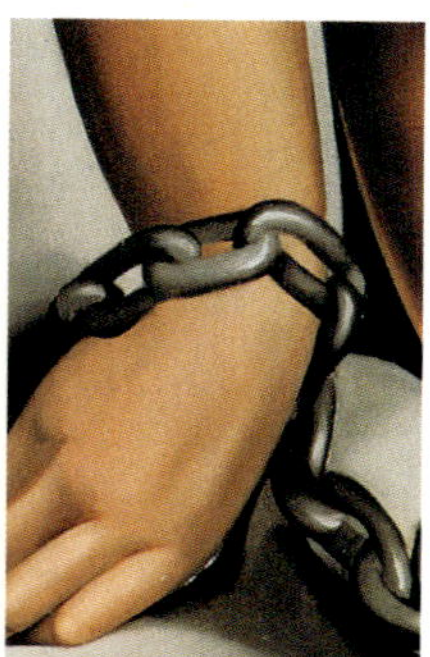

Furious at being deserted for another woman, de Lempicka left the right hand unfinished and exhibited the picture under the ambiguous title *Unfinished Portrait of Tadeusz de Lempicki.* The wariness of de Lempicki contrasts with the impression of confident dynamism made by Dr. Boucard in the portrait he commissioned in 1928. The wealthy doctor, inventor of the patent medicine lacteol, paid handsomely for the portraits of himself, his wife and his daughter Arlette. His investment paid off in the striking portrait that immortalises him as a scientist dandy with white coat and a pearl tie pin. His dynamism is suggested by his coiled pose and also by the angular planes of the background that are reminiscent of an expressionist movie. Altogether Dr. Boucard looks like an actor playing the part of a brilliant doctor in a film.

The Slave

1929
Oil on canvas, 100 x 65 cm
Private Collection

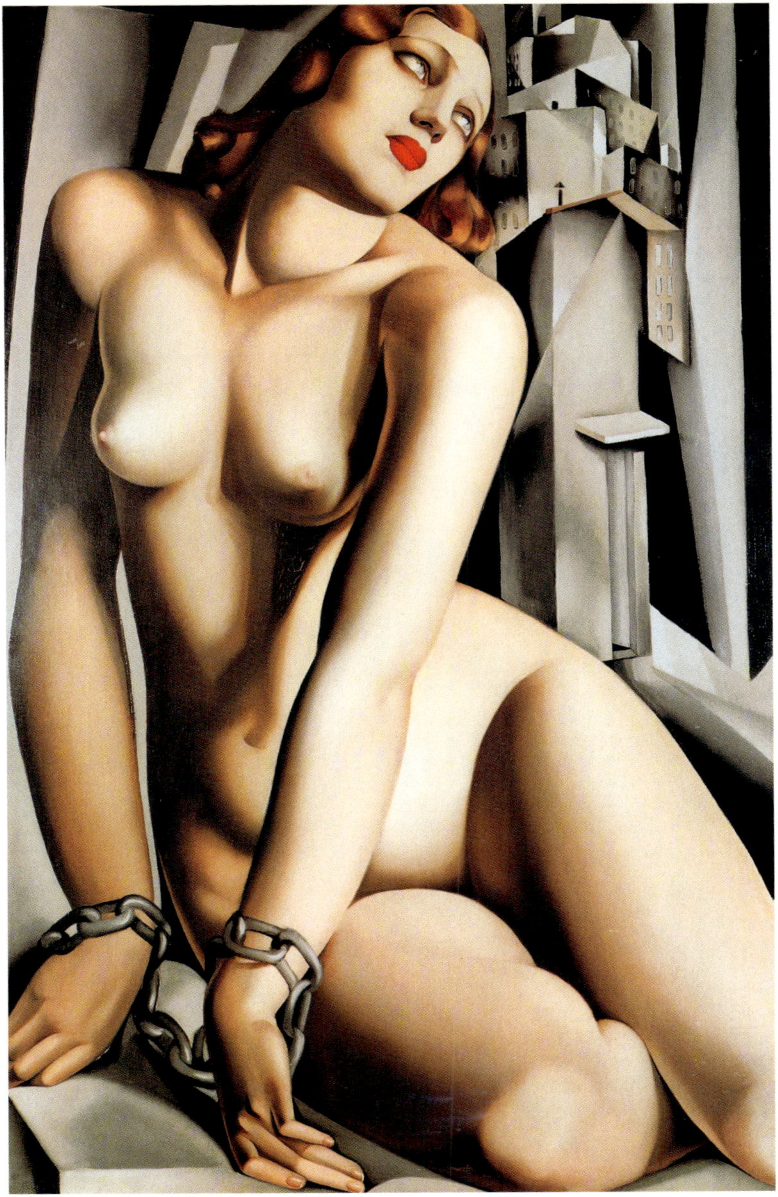

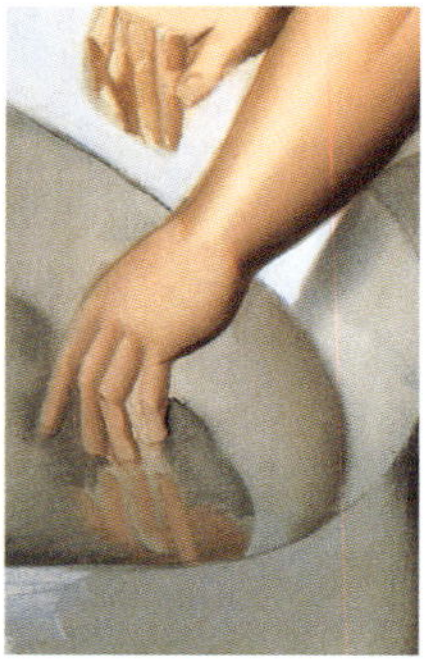

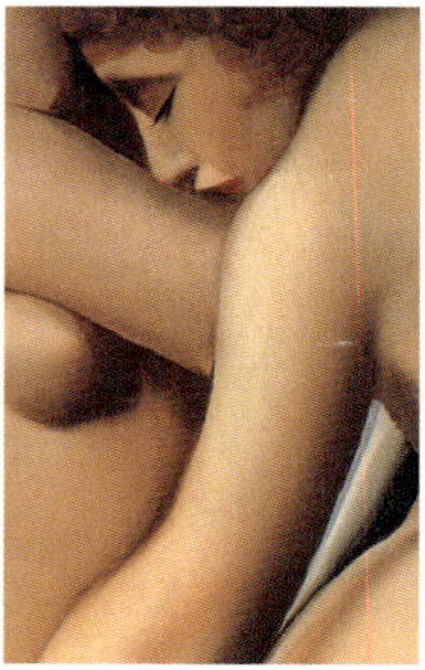

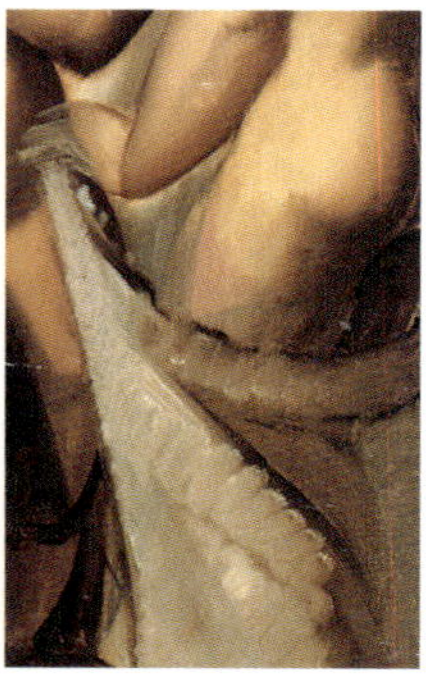

The gleaming microscope and test tube are used like the attributes in a Renaissance portrait to intimate his scientific interests. The commissions for de Lempicka's female portraits usually came from their wealthy husbands. What she offers is a series of spectacular images of "trophy" wives. The first of these was Mrs. Rufus Bush. In the spring of 1929 Rufus Bush, whose family owned the Bush Terminal in New York, turned up at de Lempicka's studio with a request to paint his fiancée. Impressed with the beauty of the girl and with the young man's air of wealth, de Lempicka agreed to follow the couple to New York for sittings, having quadrupled her original asking price. Travelling on the luxury liner *Paris* (surely the perfect setting for this artist who was the living embodiment of Art Deco) de Lempicka arrived in New York in September 1929.

Women Bathing

1929
Oil on canvas, 89 x 99 cm
Private Collection

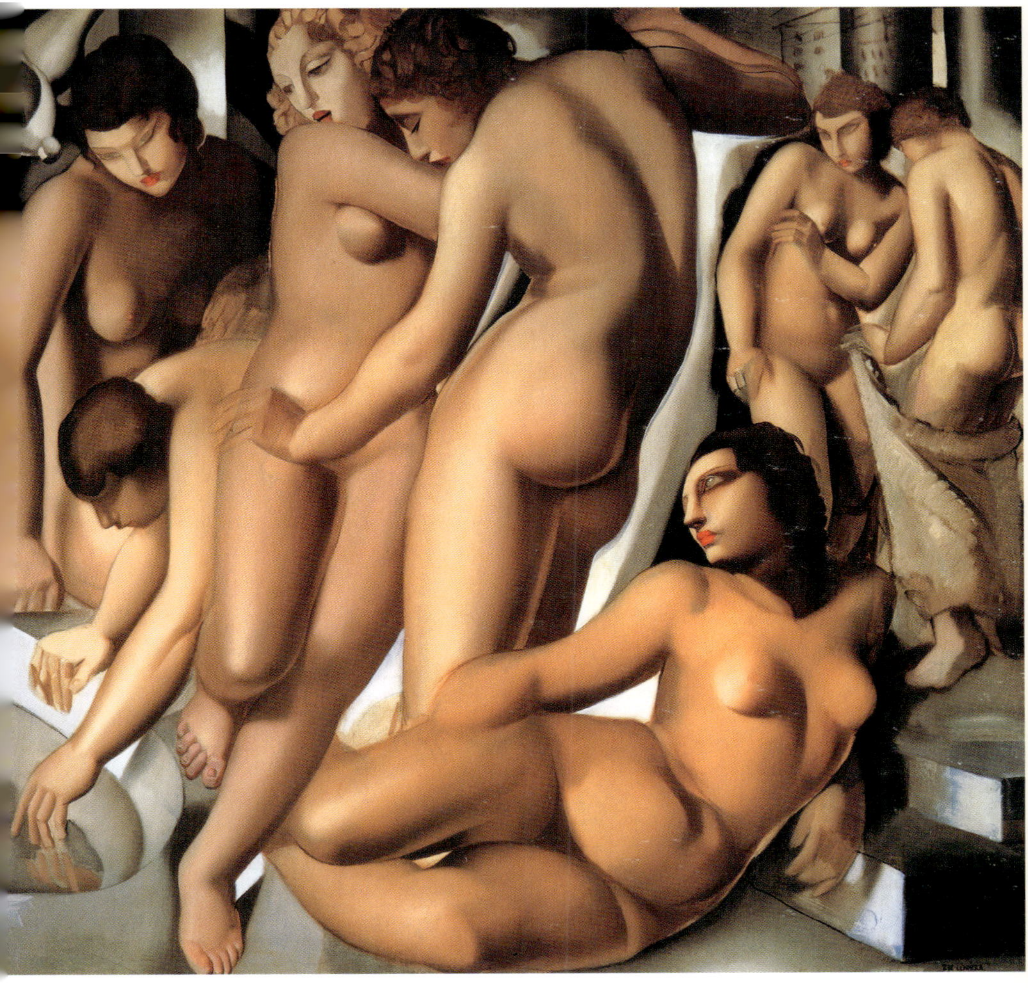

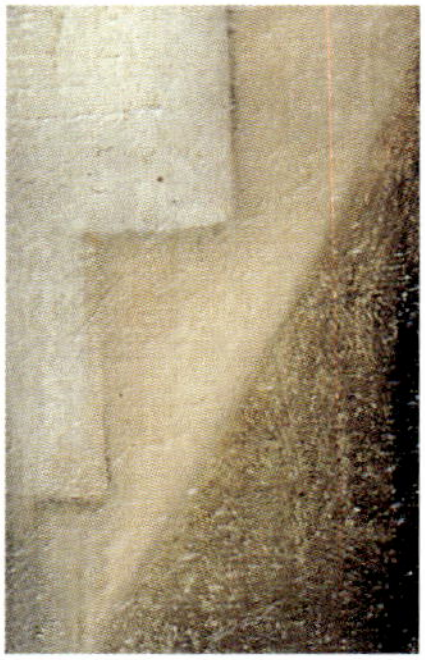

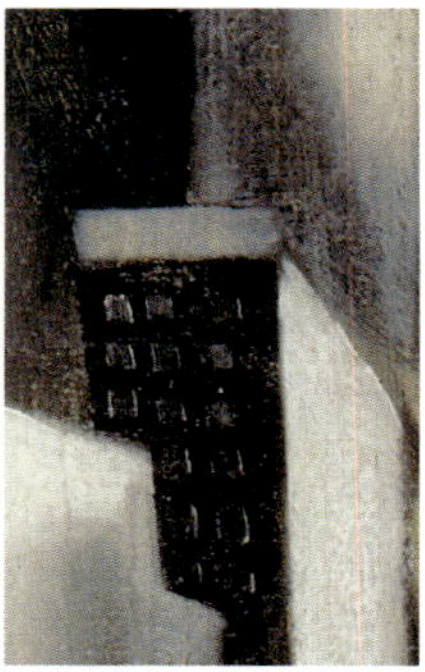

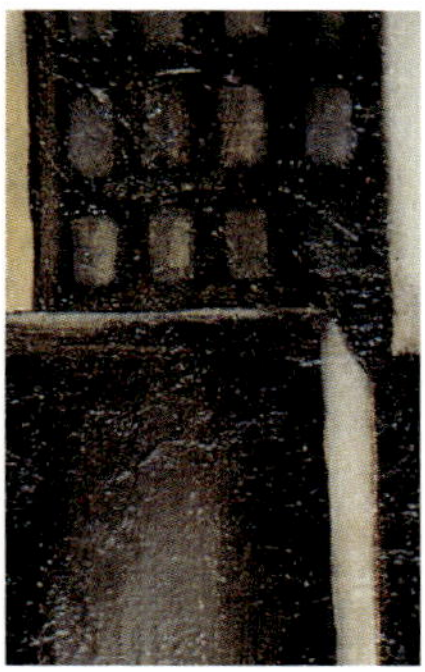

Like so many visitors to New York in this period de Lempicka instantly fell in love with New York's skyline, which like countless other tourists and émigrés she would have first seen from the decks of the approaching liner. From this moment a stylised version of Manhattan becomes the standard backdrop to her portraits, even those painted in Paris, when she wanted to give her sitters an air of modernity and urban sophistication. Mrs Bush is shown against just such a background in a simple red tailored jacket and black skirt picked out with much care by de Lempicka herself. She is coltishly androgynous — more *garconne* than *amazone* and not obviously suited to the role of "trophy wife". In fact the marriage was of very short duration and the portrait disappeared from view until after the revival of de Lempicka's reputation.

New York

c. 1929
Oil on canvas, 46 x 38 cm
Private Collection

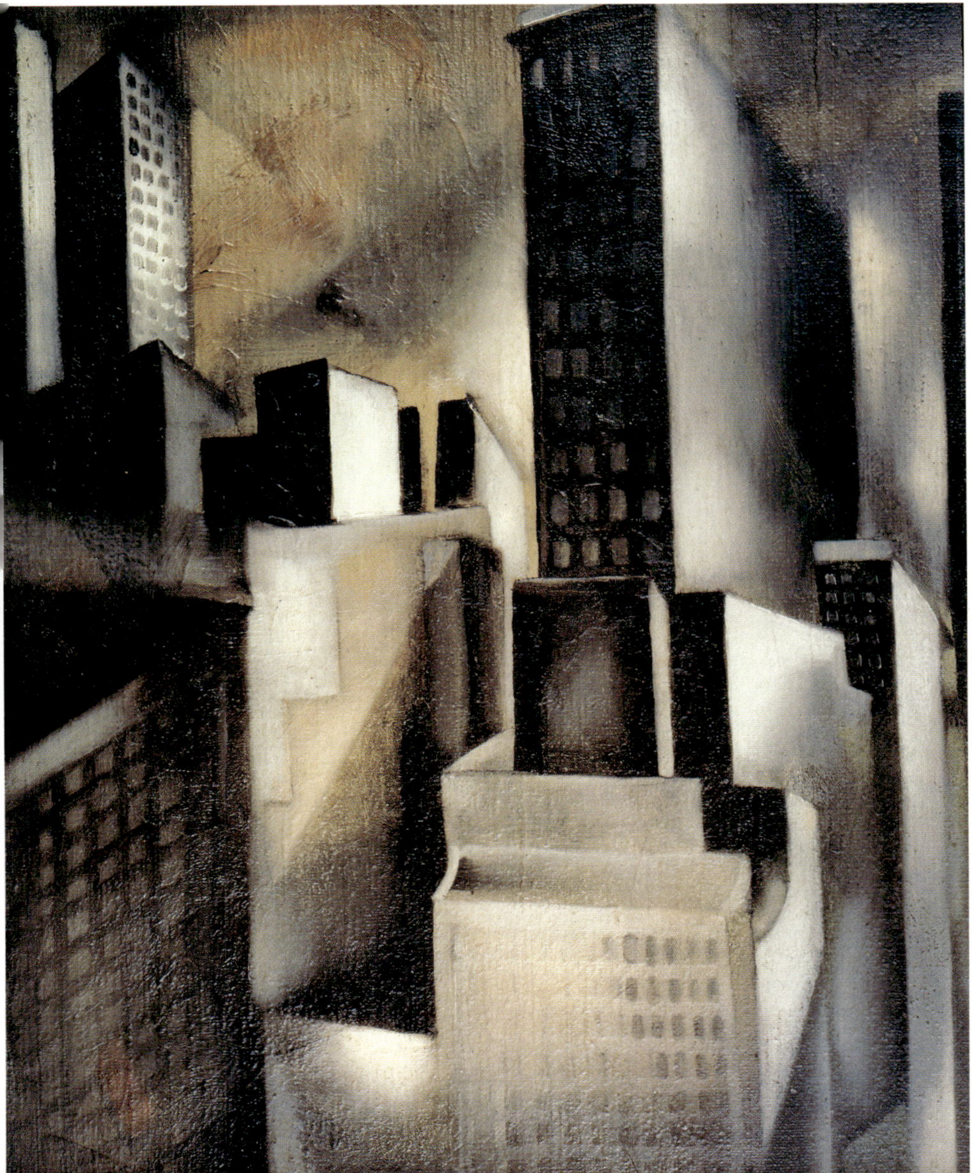

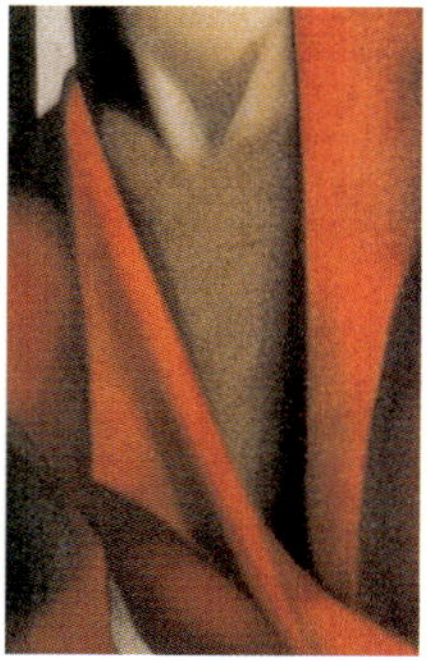

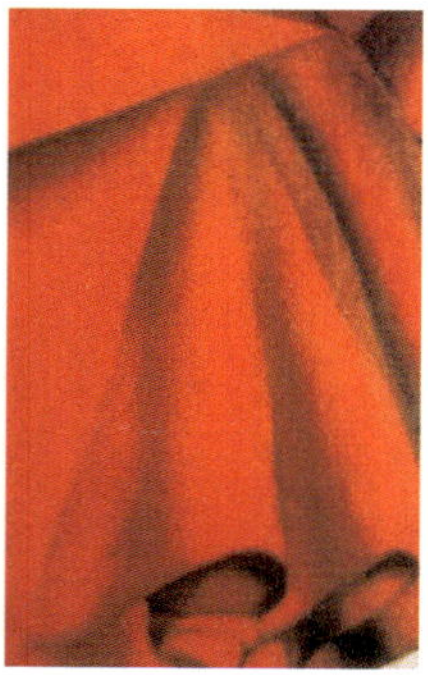

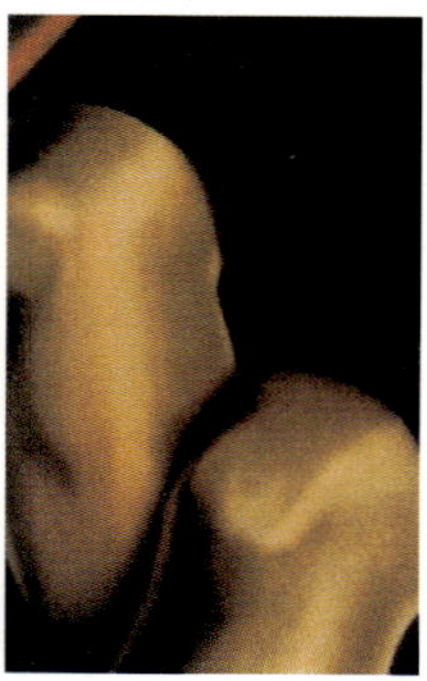

By contrast with Mrs Bush, Mrs. Alan Bott looks every inch the luxury wife. Her height is emphasised by the vertical format of the canvas and the skyscrapers behind her. Her body forms a graceful curve from top left to bottom right of the canvas with the top of her head and elegantly shoed left foot cut off at top and bottom. She provocatively lifts the hem of her skirt to expose her knees. So flimsy and transparent is her lacy dress, under which she appears to wear no underwear that she need not have bothered as every detail of her anatomy from her nipples to her thighs is clearly visible. The exquisite but minimal dress contrasts piquantly with the chunky luxuriousness of the Cartier style diamond and emerald bracelet and the sumptuous fur collared and silk lined coat that she trails negligently beneath her.

Portrait of Mrs. Bush

1929
Oil on canvas, 122 x 66 cm
Private Collection

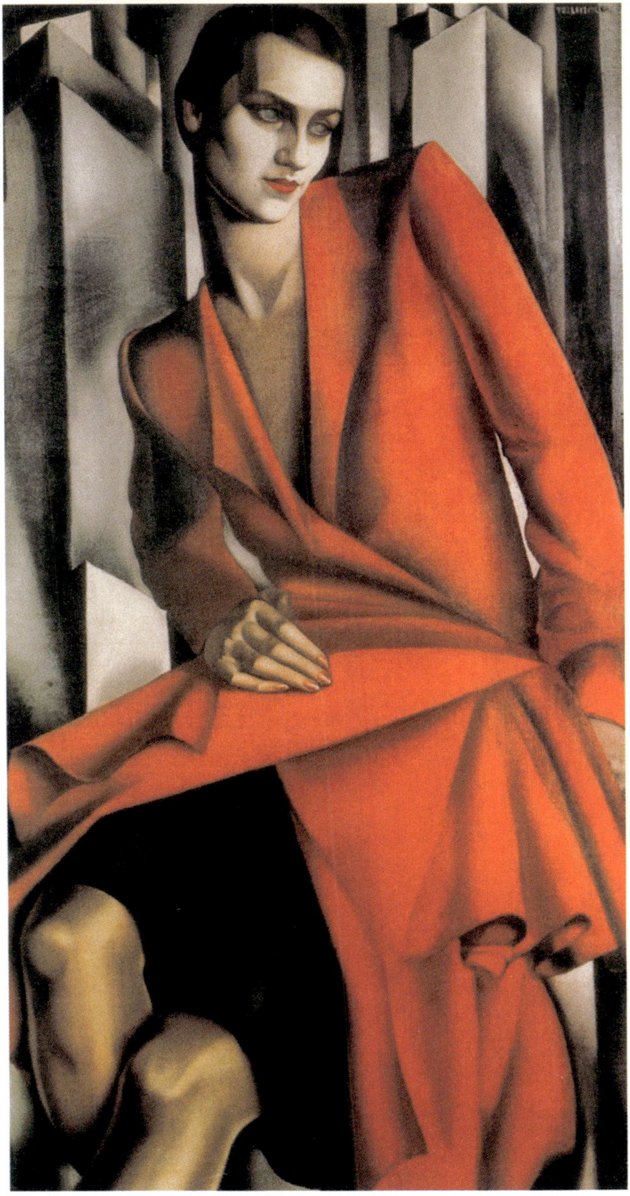

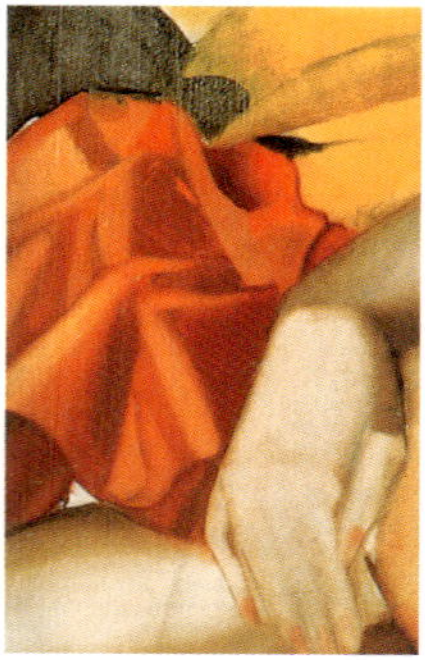
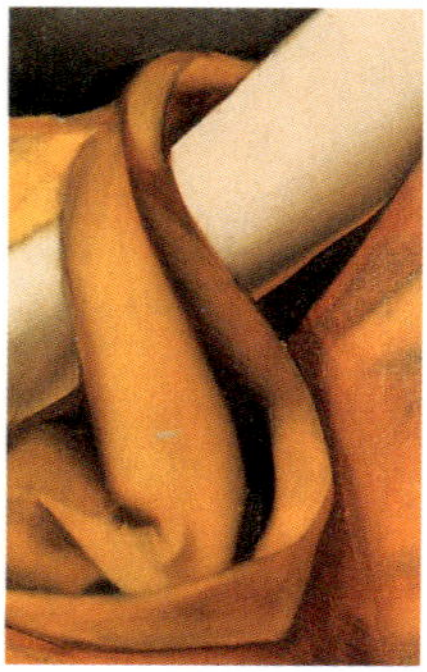
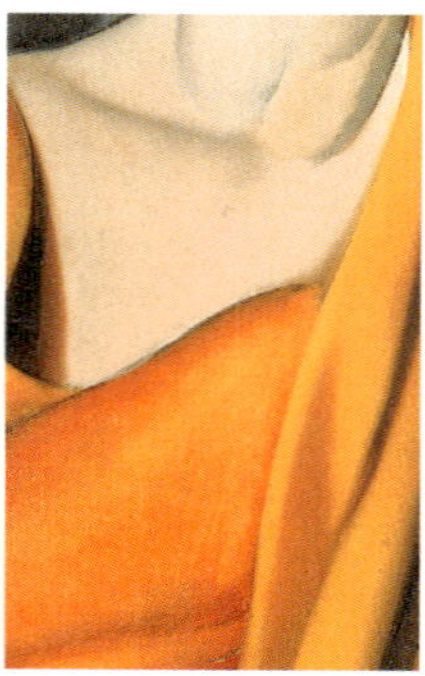

The "jungle red" of her painted fingernails and lurid lips and the bruised languor of her eyes give her a sinister allure. Despite her tender years she looks as if she has lived for centuries.

It was not till after her delayed return from New York that de Lempicka was able to fulfil her commission from Dr. Boucard by painting his wife. The Juno-esque Madame Boucard is older than most of de Lempicka's other female portraits but is just a more mature version of the luxury wife. The Parisian Madame Boucard is given the generic New York backdrop. Her serpentine pose spirals from bottom left to close to the top of the picture. She seems to have shopped at the same luxury stores as Mrs. Bott, and though, as is appropriate to her age, her dress is somewhat more discreet, her cone-like breasts and erect nipples project clearly through the metallic sheen of her white dress.

Woman in a Yellow Dress

1929
Oil on canvas, 78 x 118 cm
Private Collection

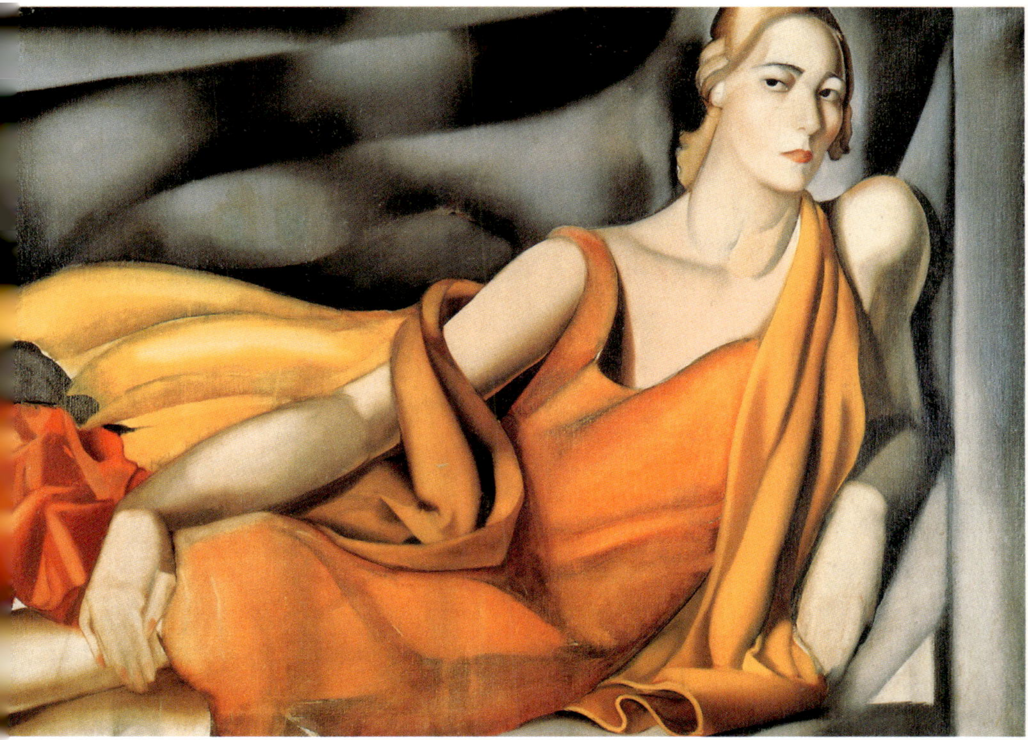

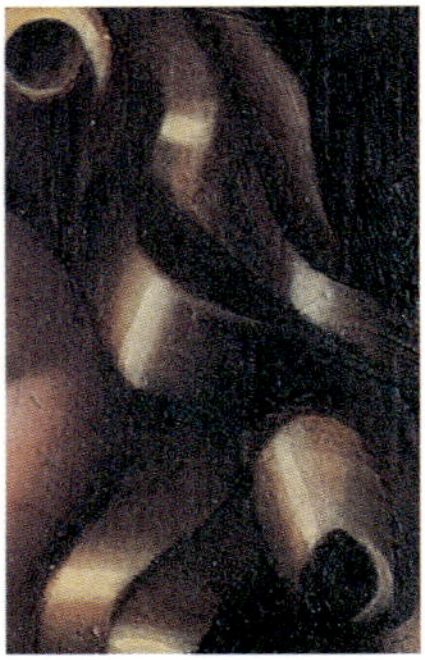

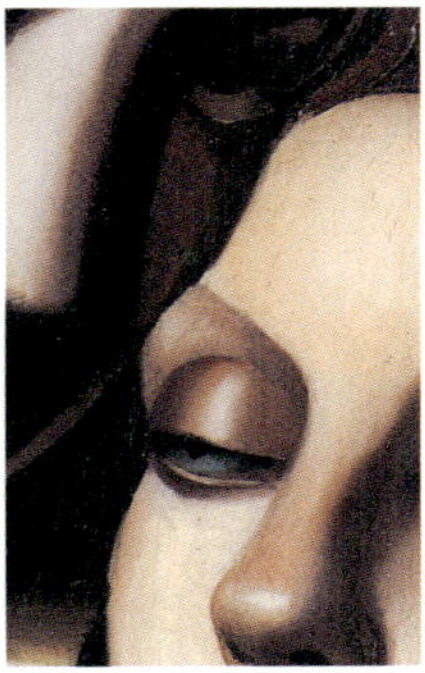

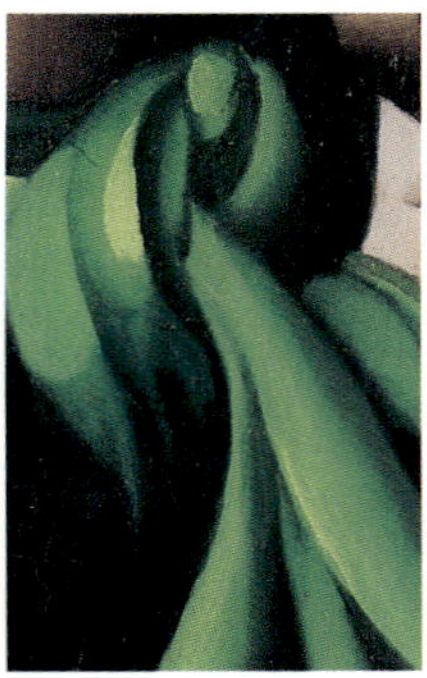

Amongst the last commissioned portraits of de Lempicka's Art Deco phase is the alarming 1933 *Portrait of Miss Poum Rachou*. De Lempicka takes a low viewpoint and fills the narrow vertical canvas from top to bottom with the little girl's figure, making her loom large, rather as the Hulsenbeck children do in Philip Otto Runge's famous portrait of them. This is certainly no sentimental image of fragile childhood. Miss Poum Rachou's metallic locks, icily unfocussed eyes, rouged lips and her exposed legs make her seem disturbingly adult and sexual, despite the rather fierce looking teddy that she clutches.

The Girls

c. 1930
Oil on panel, 35 x 27 cm
Private Collection

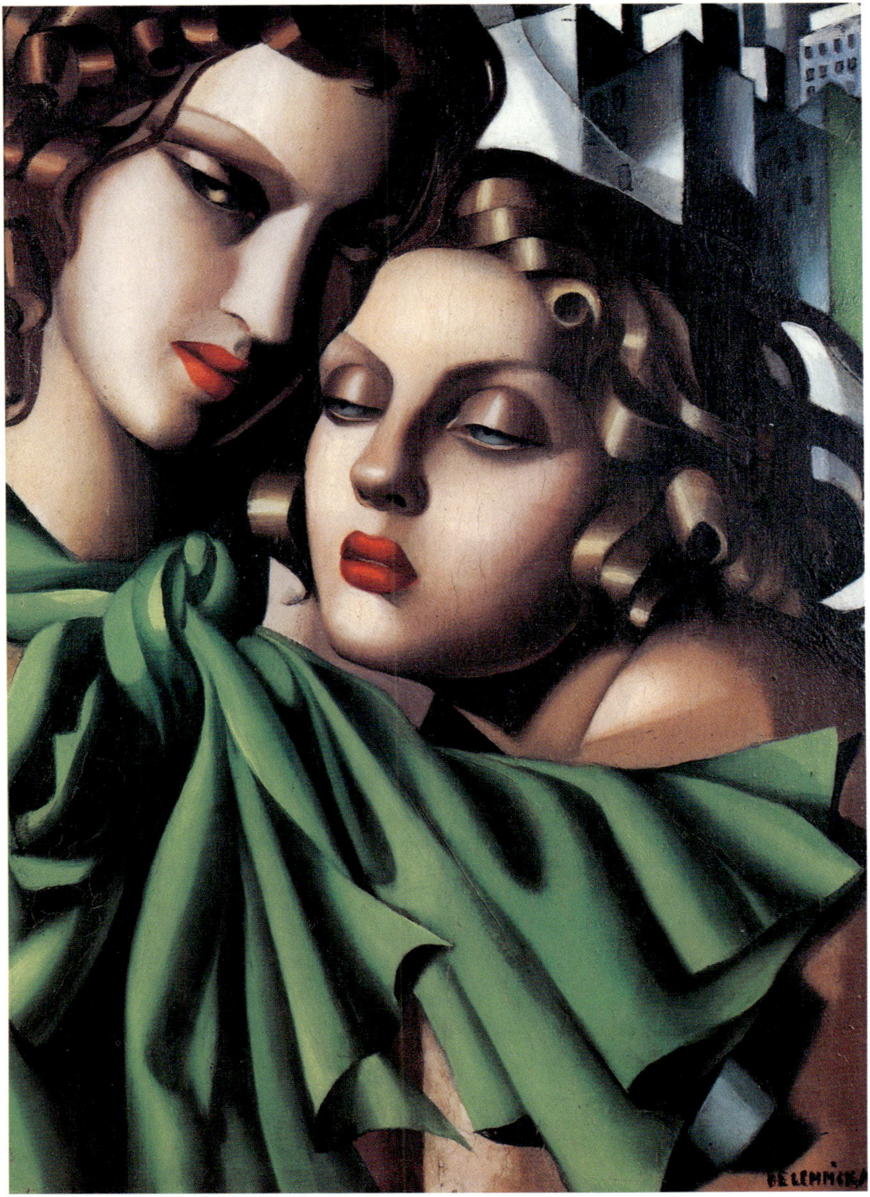

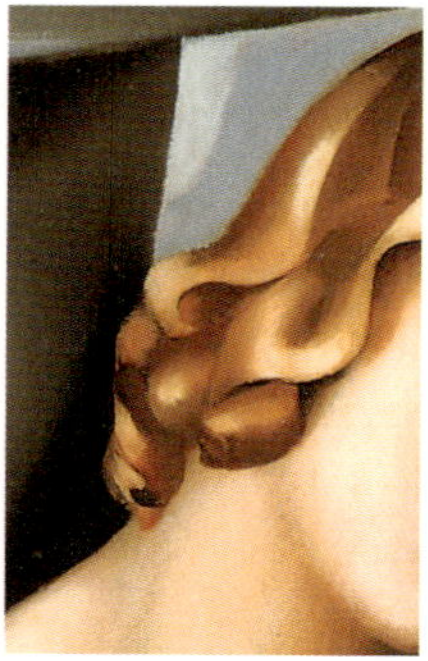

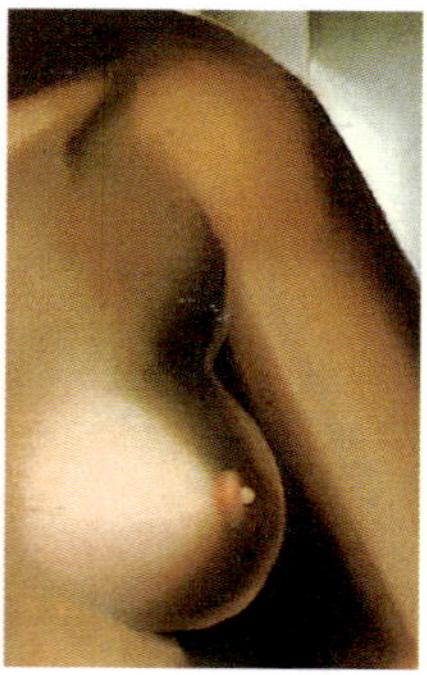

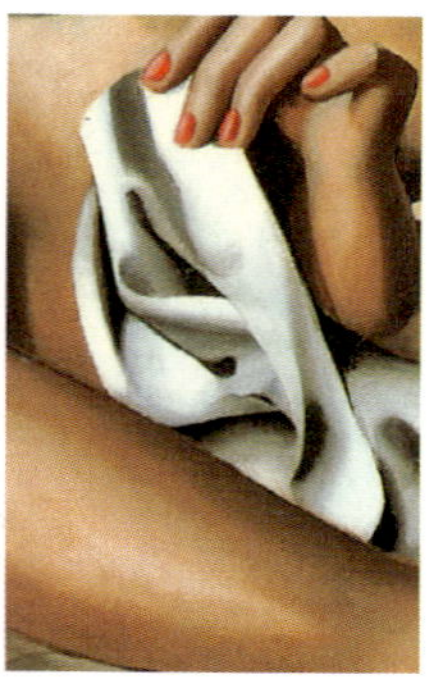

Amongst de Lempicka's commissioned portraits of women, that of the Spanish dancer Nana de Herrera is exceptional in that it was commissioned not by a husband but by a lover. Nana de Herrera's carnivorously vampish sensuality is exaggerated to the point of parody.

The portraits of Marjorie Ferry and of *Mrs. M.* both dating from 1932 are remarkable for the way the hands are posed with self-conscious and mannered elegance as though to display the scarlet nail varnish and enormous pearl rings. Hands have always presented a problem to portraitists. The depiction of hands cruelly exposes weaknesses in draughtsmanship as we see in the portraits of Gainsborough and Reynolds and even in a few early portraits by Rembrandt.

Nude with Buildings

1930
Oil on canvas, 92 x 73 cm
Private Collection

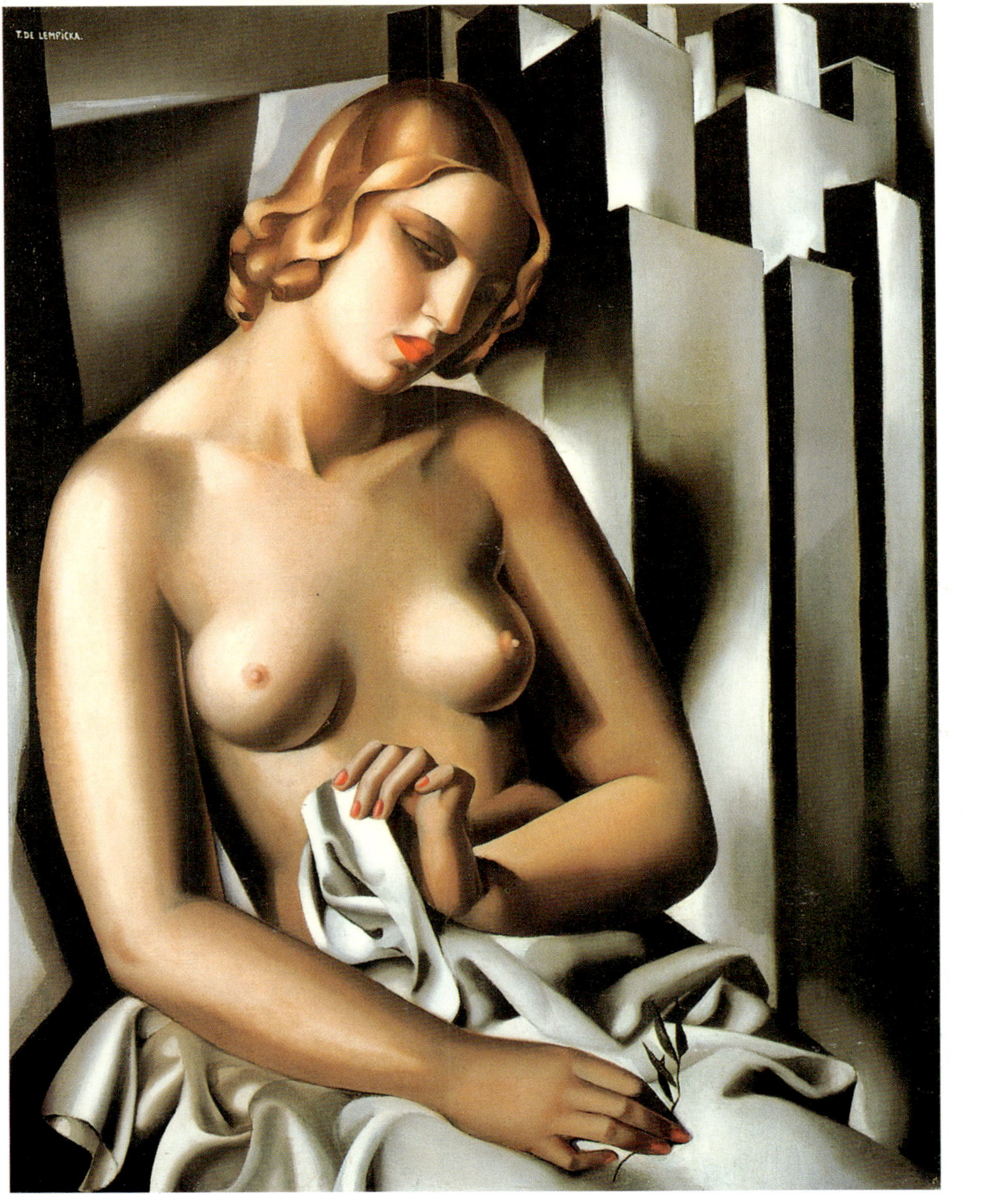
T. DE LEMPICKA.

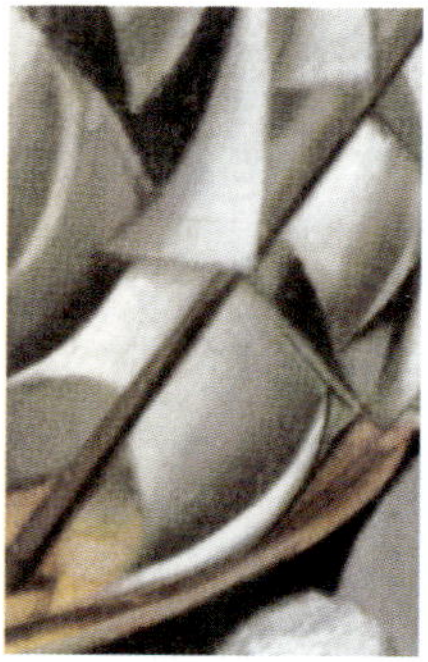

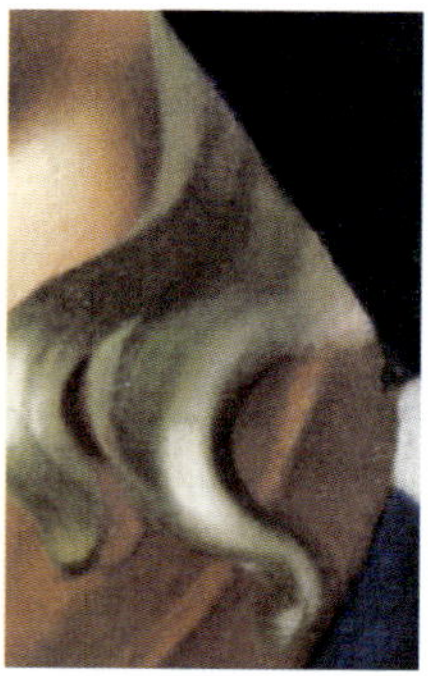

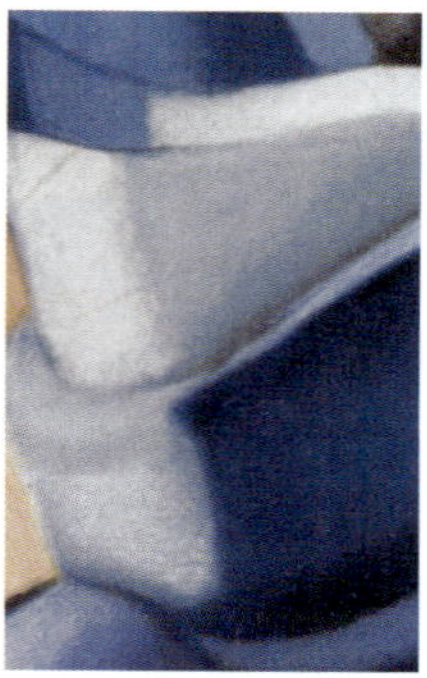

Whether dressed or nude, de Lempicka's women have perfectly manicured fingernails painted in the kind of gaudy, carnivorous "Jungle red" nail polish that played such a pivotal role in the plot of George Cukor's 1939 movie *The Women*. Mrs. M's white dress and the sheet with which Marjorie Ferry covers her nudity seem to be cut from the same material. In both cases it is crumpled into complex folds. De Lempicka was well aware of the role that drapery had played in Western art since the Renaissance or indeed since classical Greece. Though she enjoys painting female flesh through lace and transparent materials and the sheen on silks and satins, de Lempicka does not greatly differentiate between the textures of different fabrics.

The Blue Scarf

1930
Oil on panel, 35 x 27 cm
Private Collection

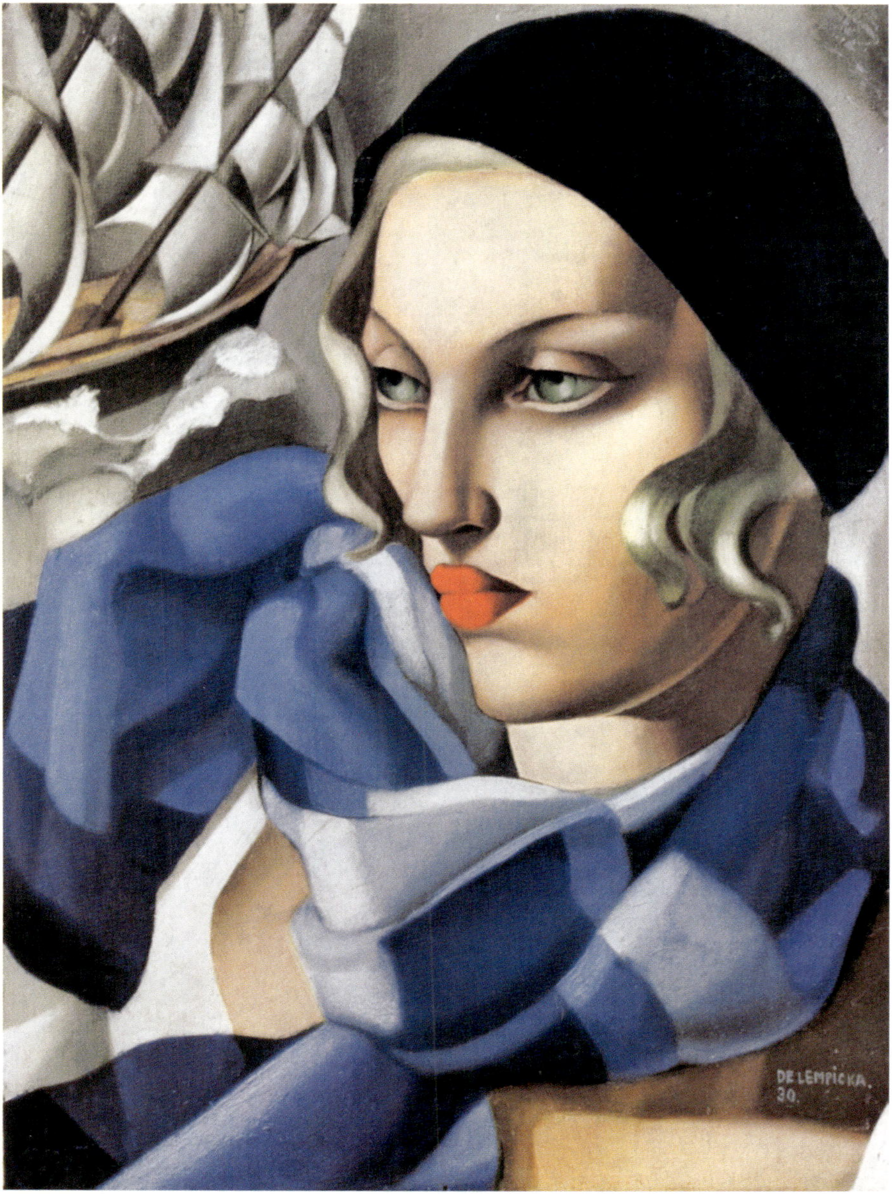
DE LEMPICKA.
30.

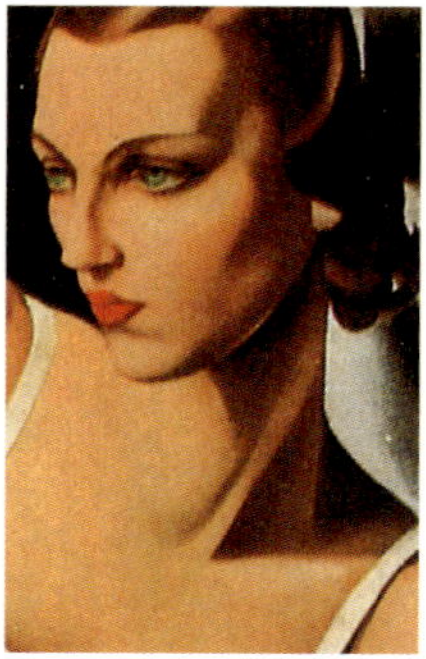

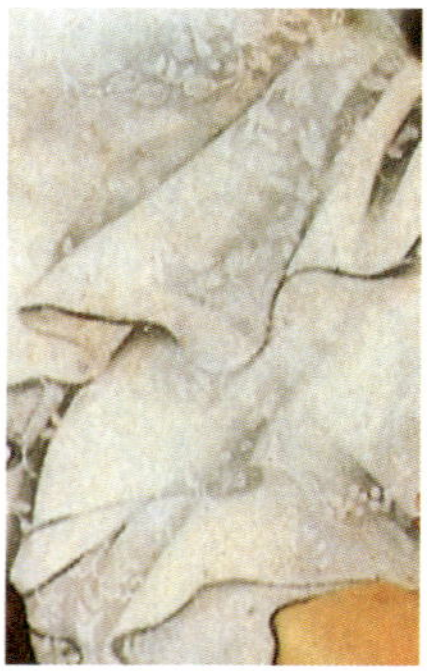

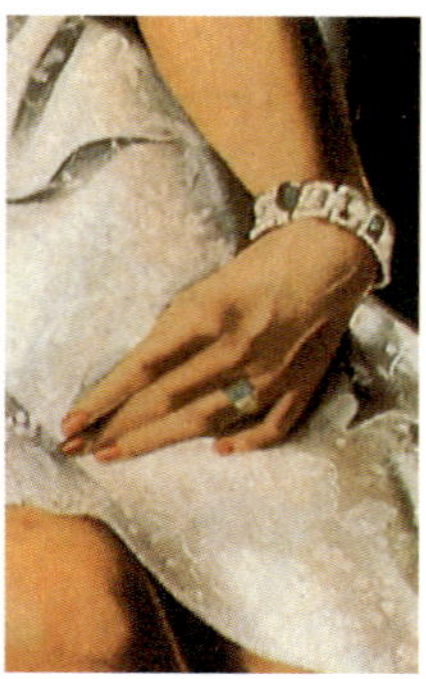

In this she follows the academic doctrines of Sir Joshua Reynolds who maintained in his *Discourses* that it was the mark of higher art to generalise rather to specify the precise qualities of materials. Like the masters of the Renaissance and the Baroque, de Lempicka often used drapery to fill space and for compositional purposes. Mrs. M.'s blue stole blooms like a flower behind her left shoulder to fill the upper right corner of her portrait. The complex folds of Ida Perrot's orange stole, billowing out behind her, as though lifted like Marilyn Munroe's skirts in *Seven Year Itch* by the updraft of an air vent, look as though they have been drawn from a length of material carefully arranged on the floor.

Portrait of Mrs. Allan Bott

1930
Oil on canvas, 162 x 97 cm
Private Collection

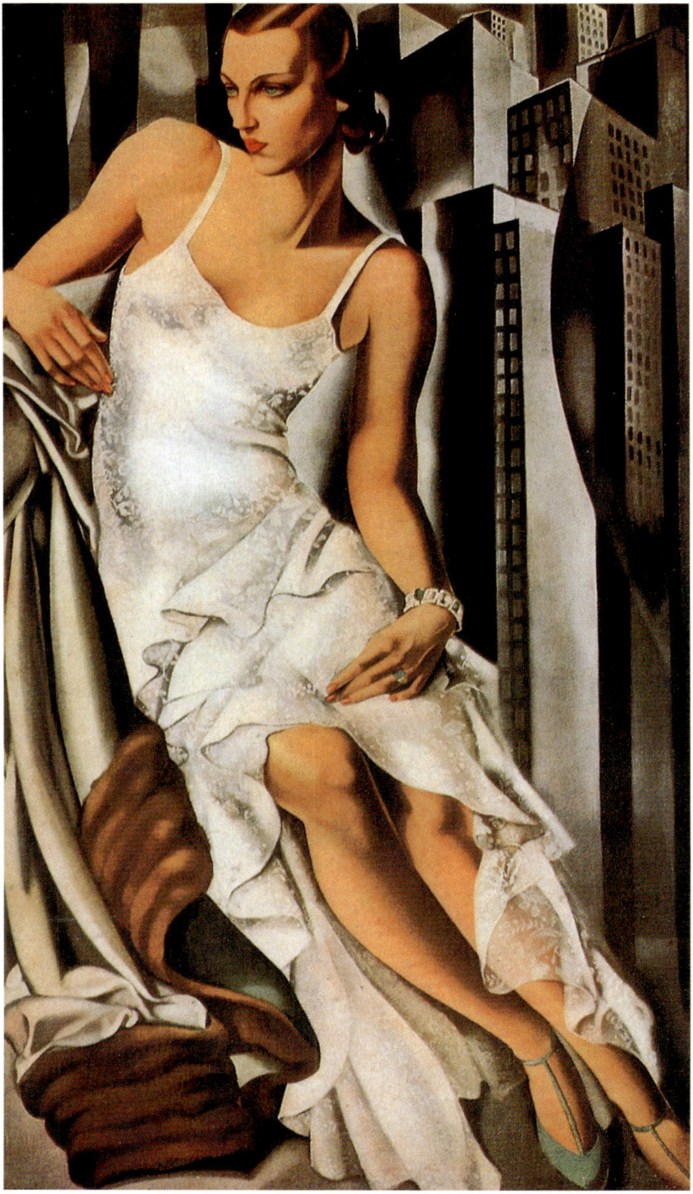

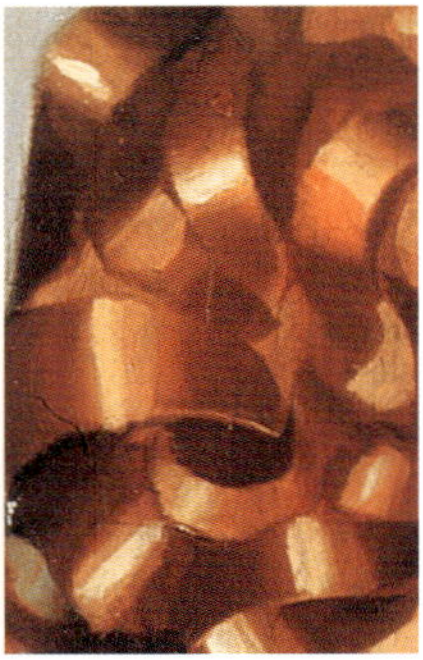

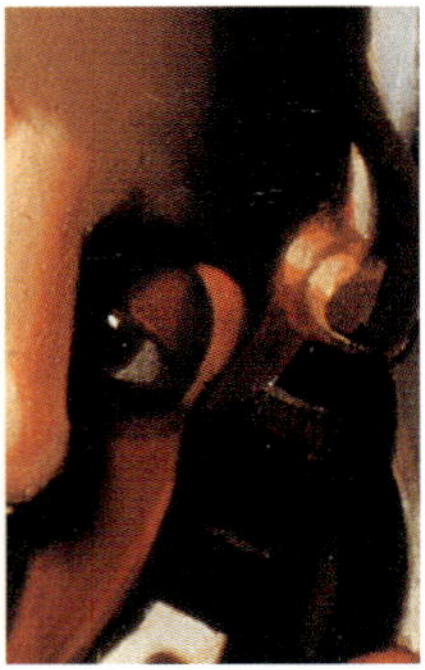

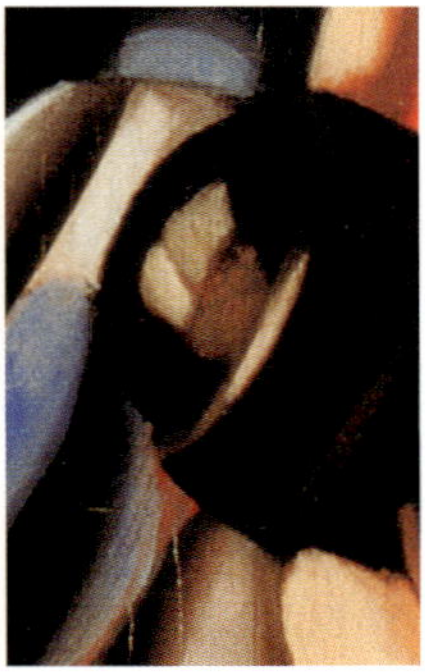

In each case these brightly coloured scarves offer a strong accent of pure unmodulated colour. De Lempicka was never a particularly subtle or expressive colourist. In her best period, she uses a relatively limited range of bright, clear colours with the crude and simple effectiveness of a poster designer. A bright pure red is used for lips and fingernails. Brick red and a strong pure blue are often used for fabrics in contrast with whites or creams. An acidic "poison" green, sometimes shaded to blue is also used by de Lempicka to great effect. There is never any attempt to analyse or explore the colour of shadows that are painted quite simply brown or black.

The Telephone II

1930
Oil on panel, 35 x 27 cm
Private Collection

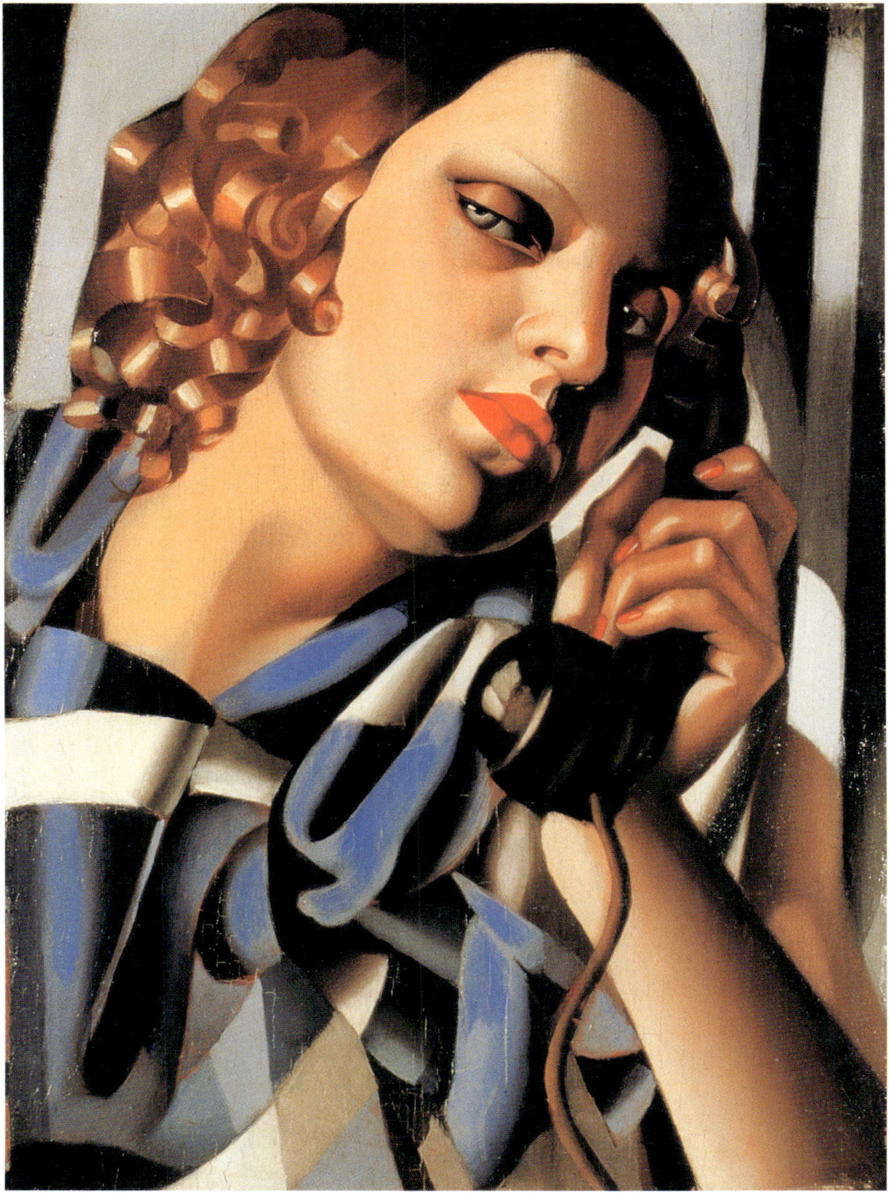

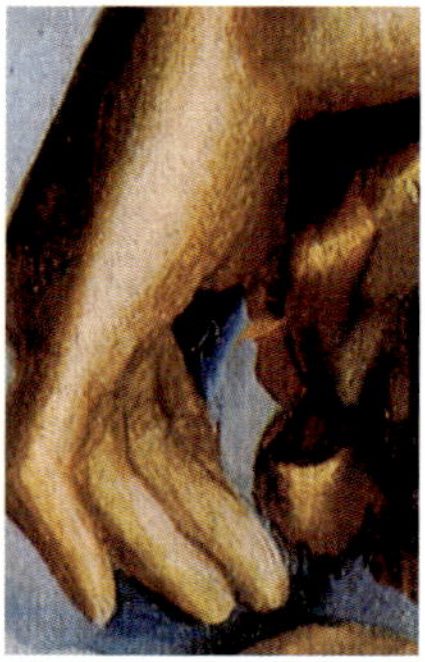

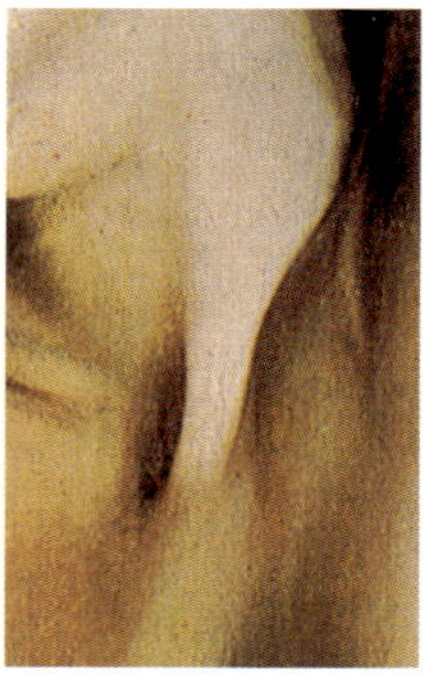

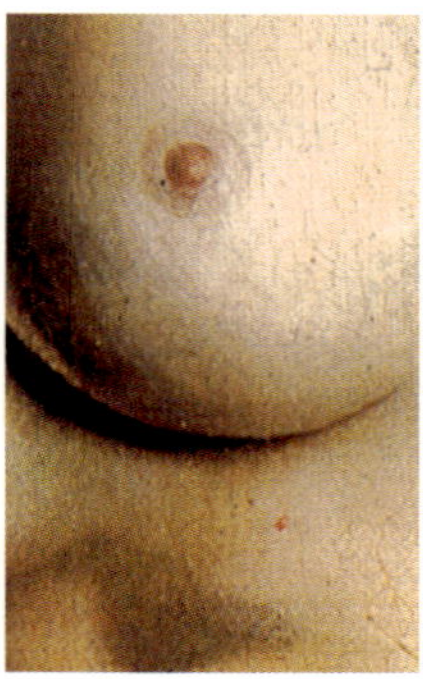

Probably the grandest of de Lempicka's commissions during her short heyday as a fashionable portraitist were from Queen Elizabeth of Greece and the recently deposed King Alfonso of Spain. Though France was the first European country to get rid of its monarchy and in bloody fashion, it was the playground of international royalty and the first port of call for deposed or abdicated monarchs such as Edward VIII of Britain who arrived there on his honeymoon with Wallis Simpson. De Lempicka got on well with Alfonso though she found his constant talking and lack of concentration rather tiresome during sittings and peremptorily ordered him to keep quiet. She liked to recall that when the ex-King protested "We are not accustomed to being addressed in such a manner" she answered that she was "not used to models who talk so much."

Sleeping Girl

c. 1930
Oil on panel, 35 x 27 cm
Daniel Fischel and Sylvia Neil's Collection

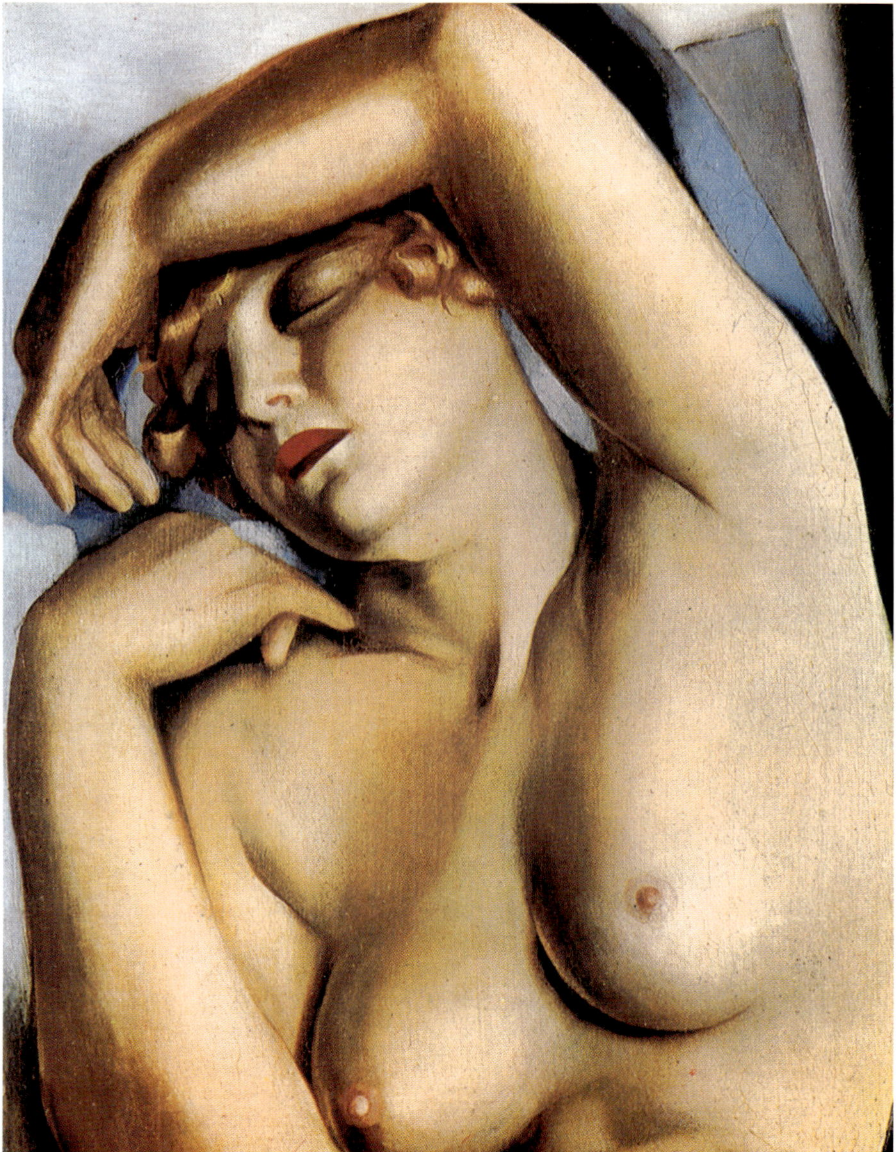
DE LEMPICKA.

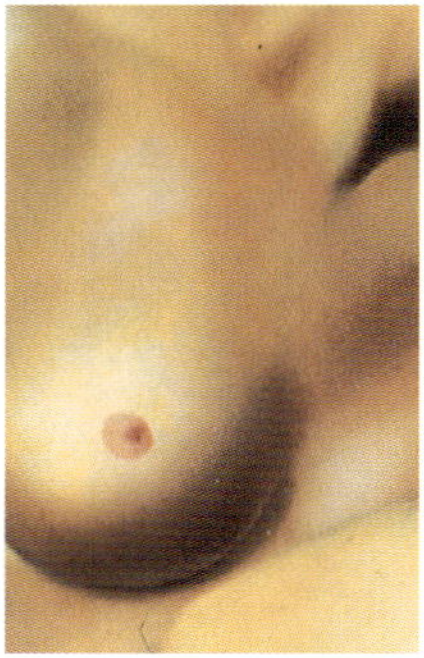

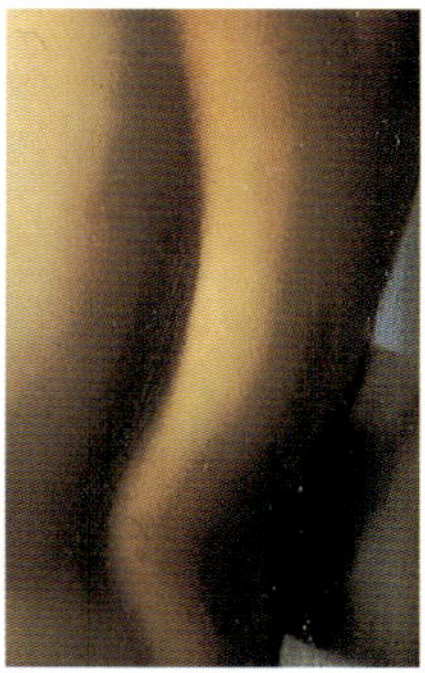

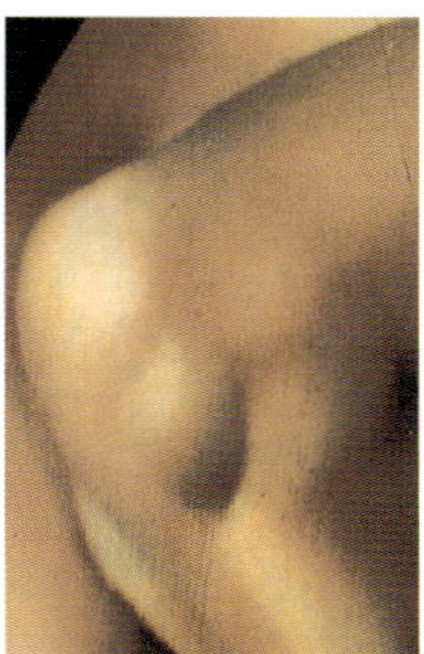

The triumphant success of de Lempicka's 1925 show in Milan led to a number of portrait commissions resulting in some of her best and most characteristic works. The two portraits of the Marquis d'Afflitto are particularly memorable for their disturbing characterisations. For the first portrait de Lempicka chose a reclining pose that is highly unusual in male portraits. The Marquis has what Stefan Zweig would have termed an "artificial waistline" and looks like a gigolo. In the second he has the louche air of an upmarket *spiv*.

Tamara's new Italian aristocratic contacts brought her to the attention of Gabriele d'Annunzio and led to the most colourful and notorious incident in her life — her attempted seduction by the aging poet. For once this is an episode that is documented not only by her own somewhat unreliable reminiscences but by the diary of d'Annunzio's long time house-keeper and mistress Aelis Mazoyer.

The Two Girlfriends

1930
Oil on panel, 73 x 38 cm
Private Collection

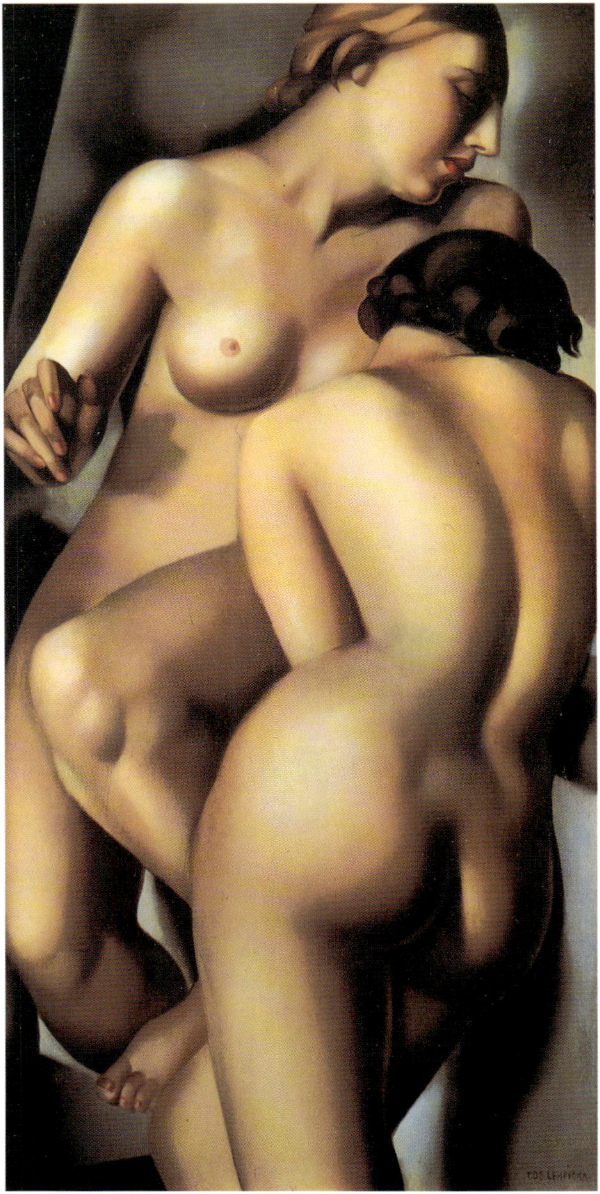

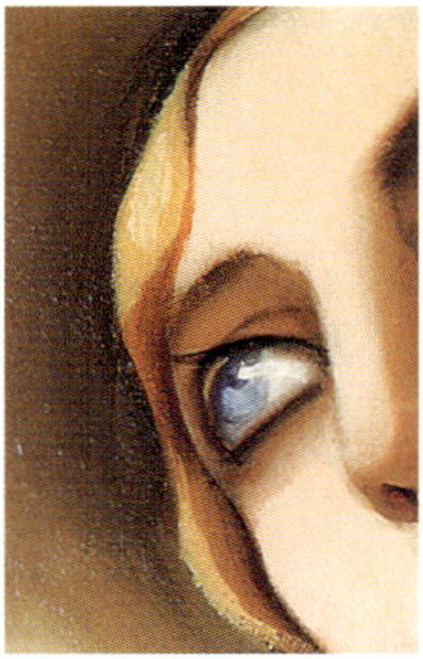
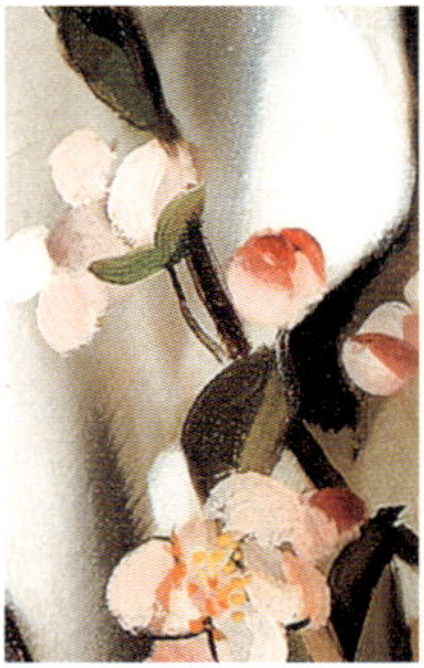
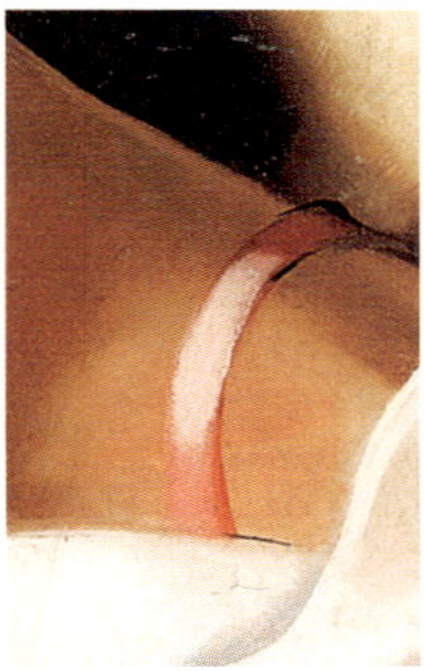

In his youth and with his abundant curly locks still in tact, d'Annunzio had been a young man of stunning if somewhat androgynous beauty. At sixty-three he was of bullet-headed baldness, wizened and prematurely aged. De Lempicka herself called him "an old dwarf in uniform". Nevertheless she can hardly have been less than flattered by his attentions. Today he is chiefly remembered as a historical phenomenon.

The attempted seduction took place against the spectacular backdrop of d'Annunzio's villa on the shores of Lake Garda. The details recorded by Aelis Mazoyer and complemented by de Lempicka's own reminiscences read more like a pornographic fantasy than a romantic novel. D'Annunzio made his first clumsy attempt to make love to de Lempicka on the first night of her visit.

The Straw Hat

1930
Oil on panel, 35 x 27 cm
Private Collection

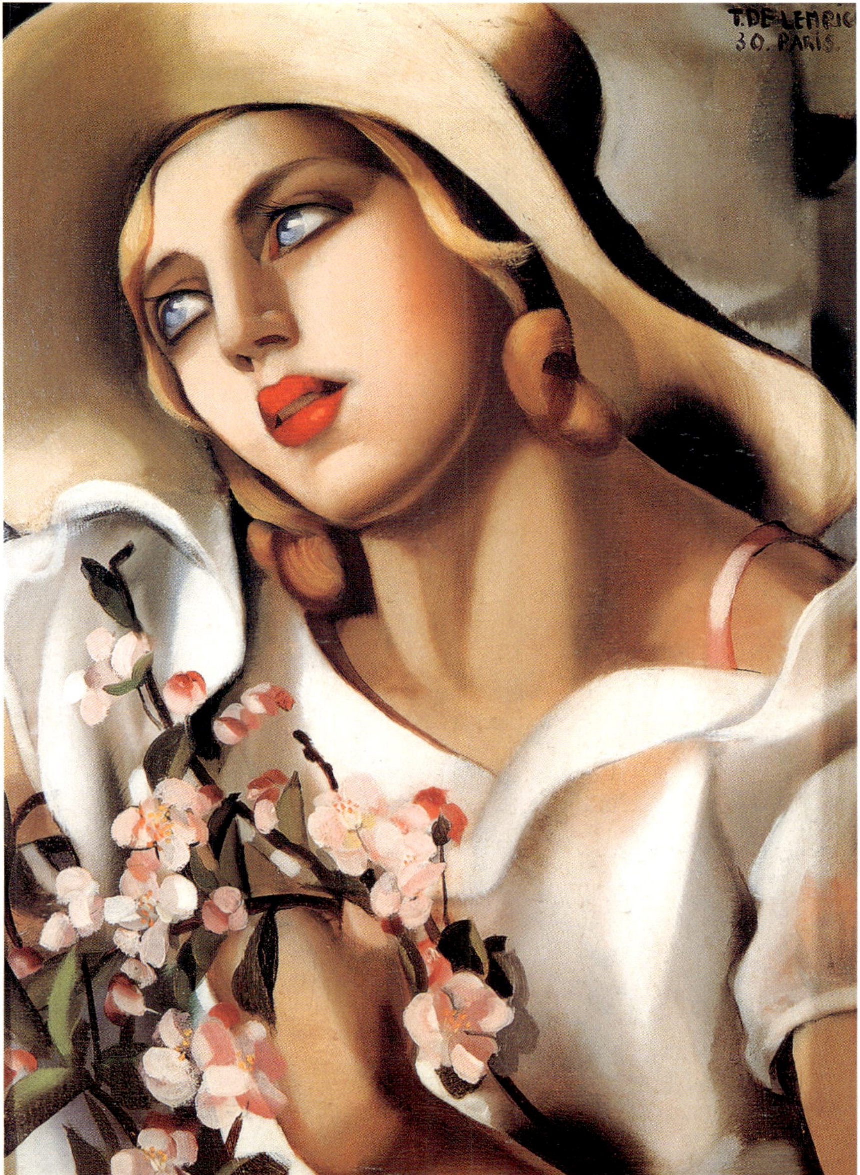
T. DE LEMPICKA
30. PARIS.

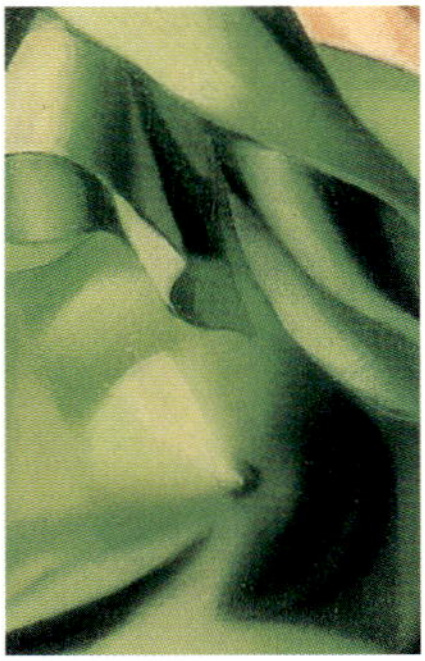

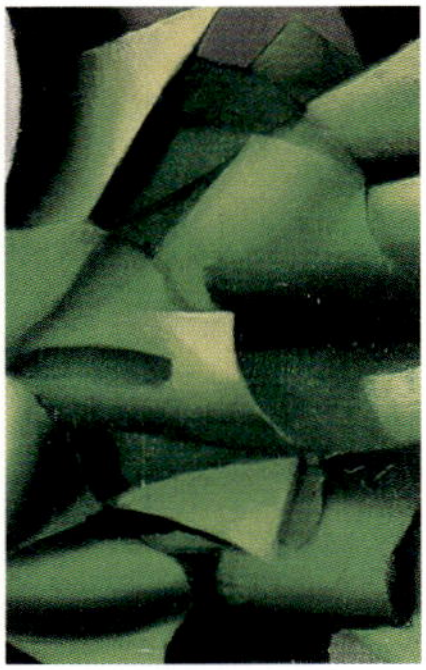

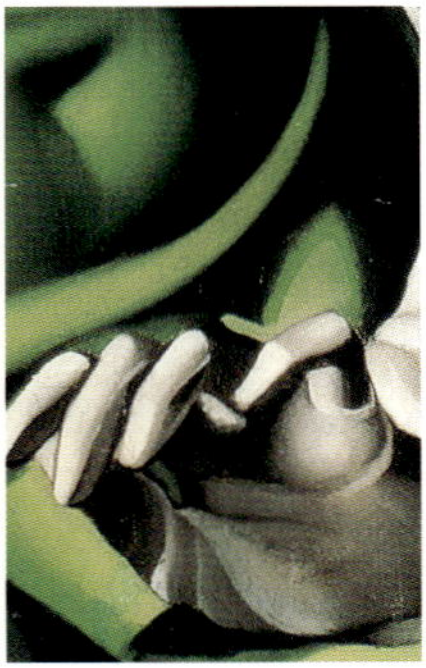

She managed to fend him off as she did the following day when he renewed his advances during the first portrait sitting. Her excuse was that she feared to contract syphilis from a man who had enjoyed the favours of so many women. That night the housekeeper assured d'Annunzio that only a "professional" would use such an excuse and the two made love in the doorway of Tamara's bedroom. Over the ten days of de Lempicka's stay at *Il Vittoriale* the poet and the painter played a game of sexual "cat and mouse" with one another, with de Lempicka allowing d'Annunzio ever greater intimacy but never giving in completely. Finally she called a taxi in the middle of the night and without saying goodbye left for a hotel in the nearby city of Brescia. The games were not yet over. De Lempicka hung around in Brescia for some time, waiting for d'Annunzio to make a move.

Young Lady with Gloves

1930
Oil on plywood, 61 x 46 cm
Fonds national d'art contemporain

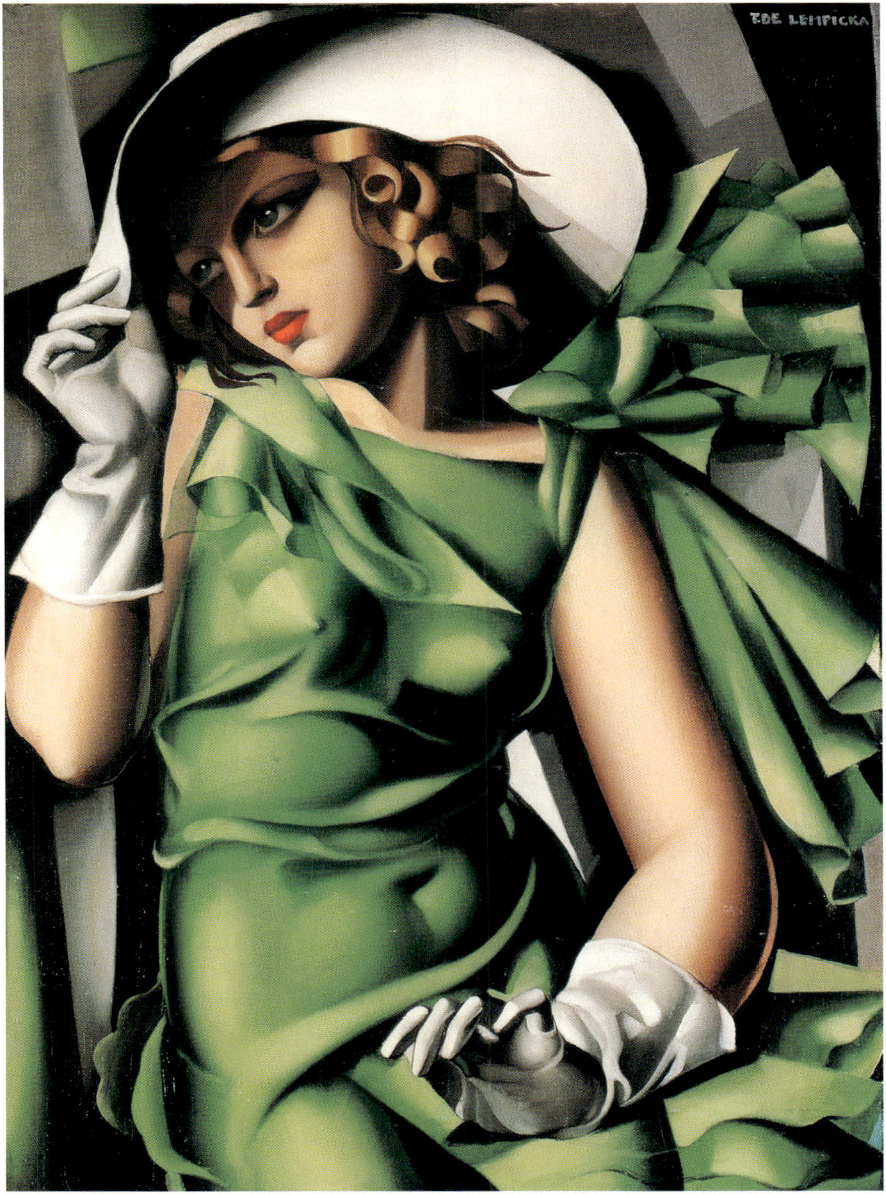
T. DE LEMPICKA

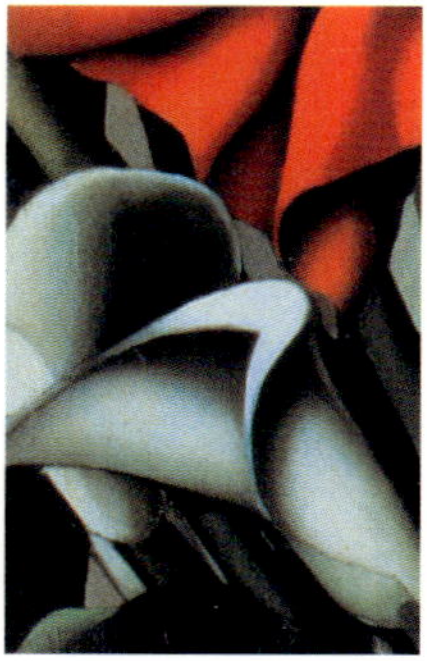

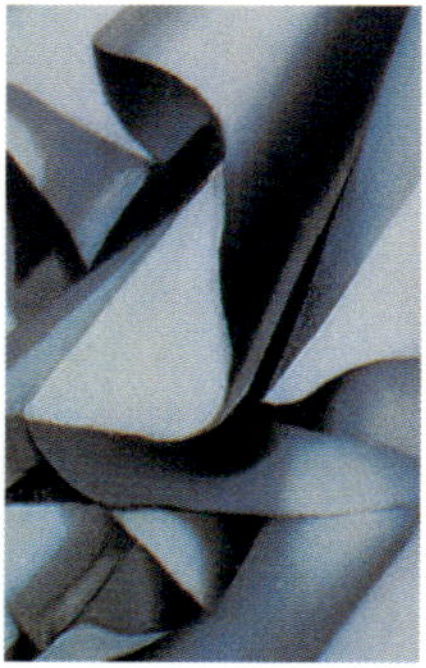

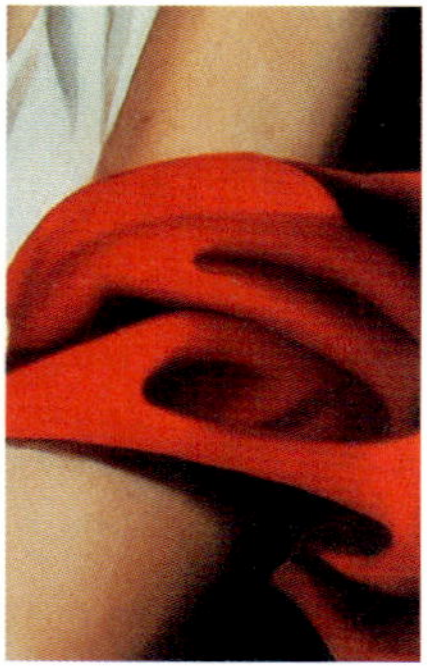

In a splendid gesture d'Annunzio sent a messenger on a white horse to her hotel bearing a poem addressed to *la Donna d'Oro* and a magnificent topaz ring. On the way back to Paris de Lempicka sent d'Annunzio a letter that suggests a genuine ambivalence in her feelings towards him but also shows how frustrating her hot and cold tactics must have been for the amorous poet.

"Everything passes, everything fades...and the fire, so burning and painful, of these last few days, perhaps it, too will pass, like everything else... Brescia, city of suffering! I had to stop there, but I knew it was only an excuse I was inventing to delay my departure — once again... but what was I waiting for? A telephone call? You perhaps? Oh, how endless the hours seem when one is waiting!

Portrait of Ira P

1930
Oil on panel, 99 x 65 cm
Private Collection

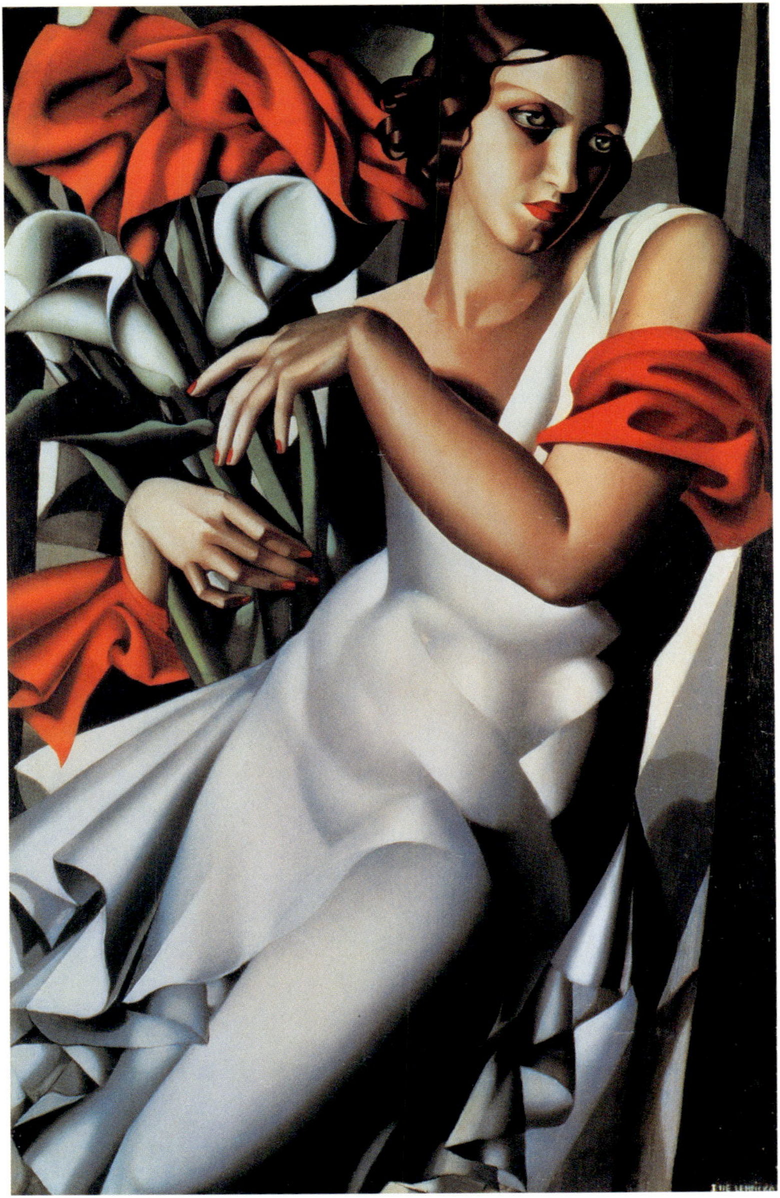

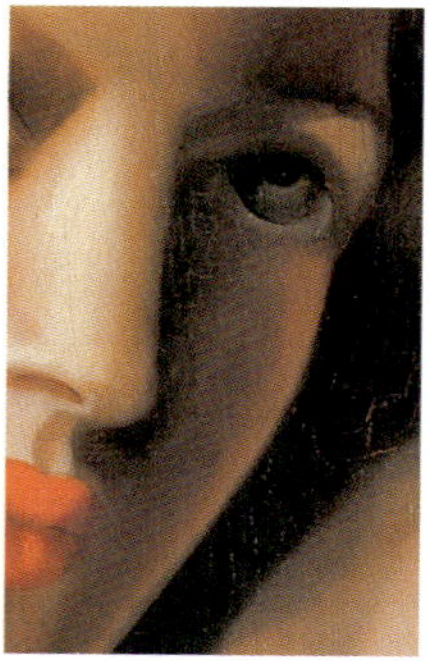
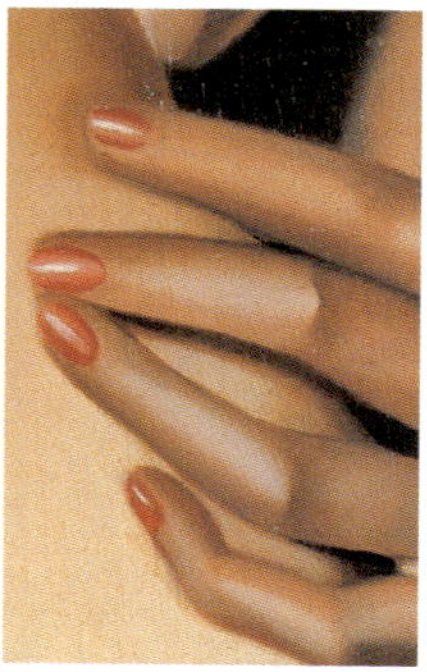
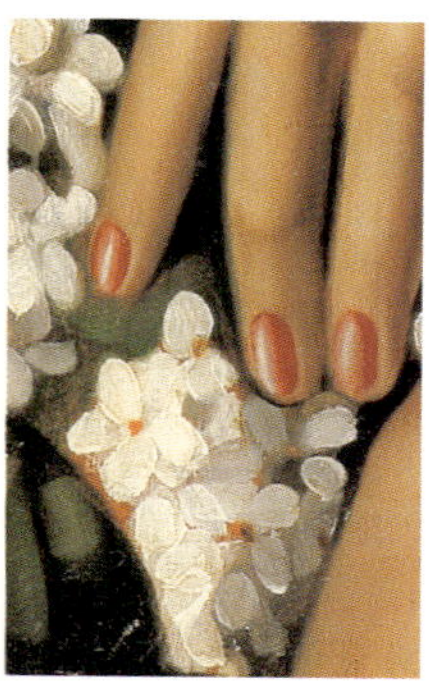

And that night when I heard a knocking at the door, I didn't have the courage to move. What was I waiting for ? What did I want? I didn't even know myself. But my only wish was to see you again. Next day... I couldn't stand it anymore, between the four walls of that miserable hotel room. I was consumed by fever and anxiety. I was suffocating. I needed air, air. I got up and started running, straight ahead like a madwoman, with no destination in mind. For how long I kept running I don't know but finally, I regained my sang froid and realised I was on the road to Gardone...And I. Who have never been yours! The sin of my betrayal has never felt so heavy. The interminable hours of the journey. The haunting idea that I'm going away, at each bend in the road, a little farther, always farther, forever....Still I've found the courage to write to you this letter of confession!"

Spring

1930
Oil on panel, 41 x 33 cm
Private Collection

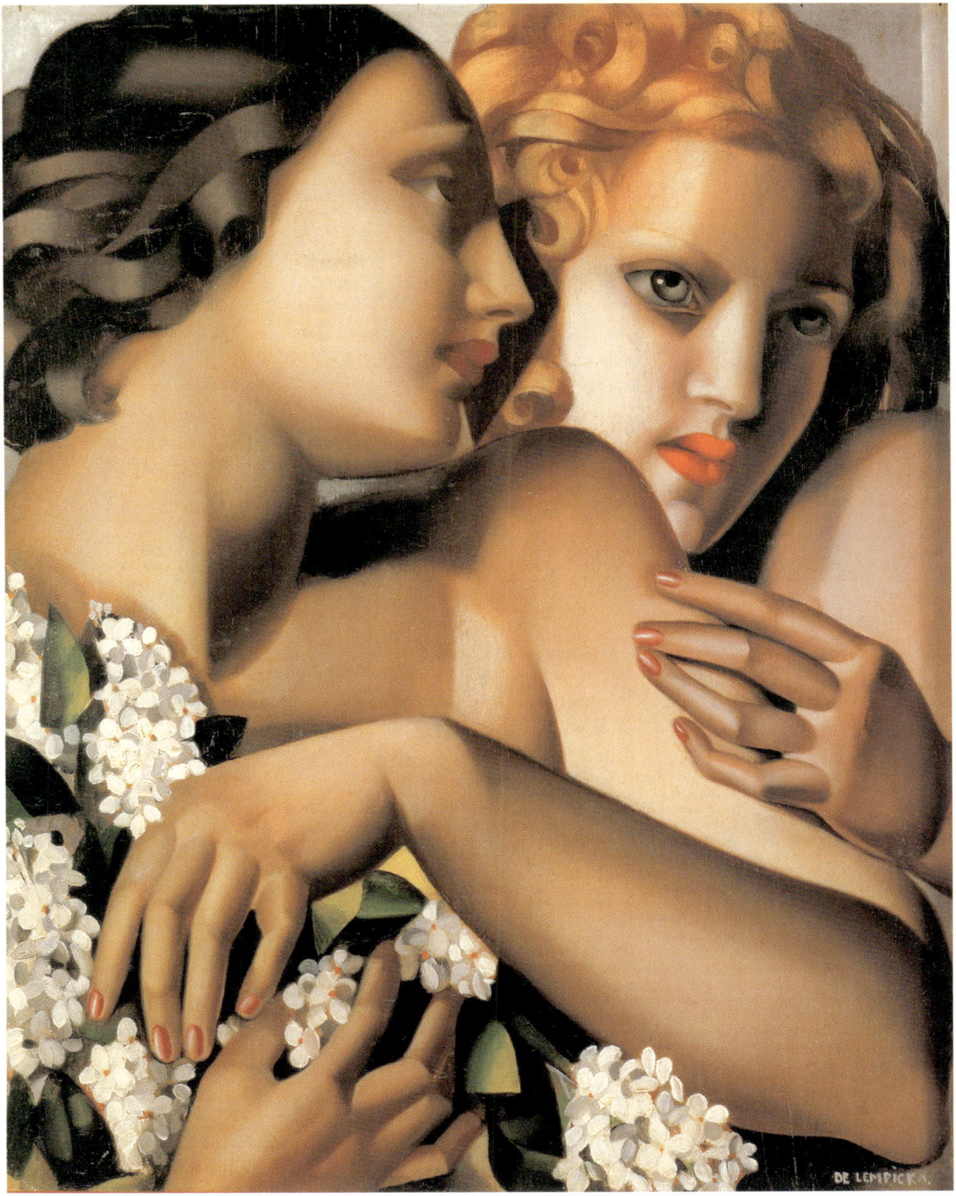

DE LEMPICKA.

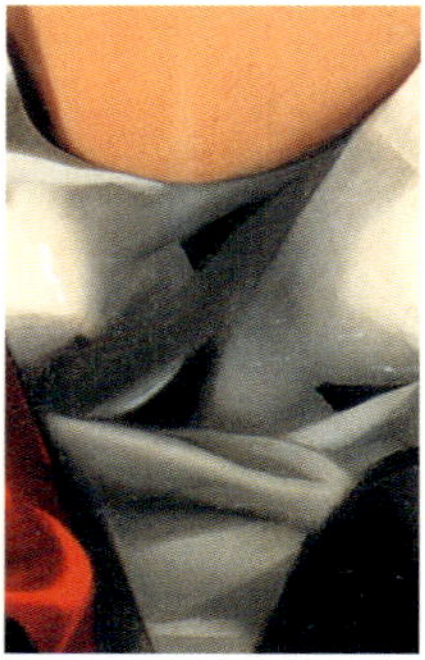
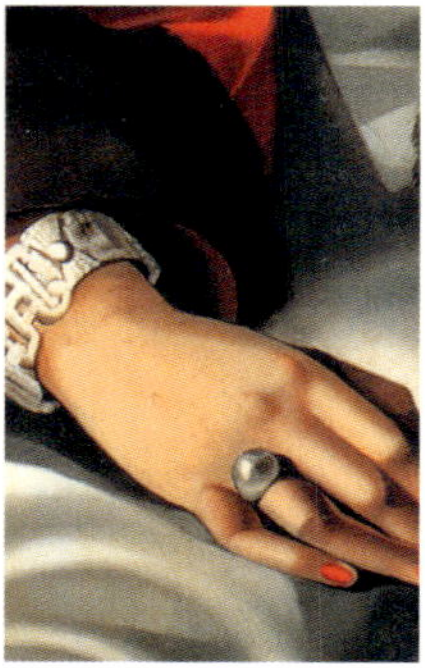
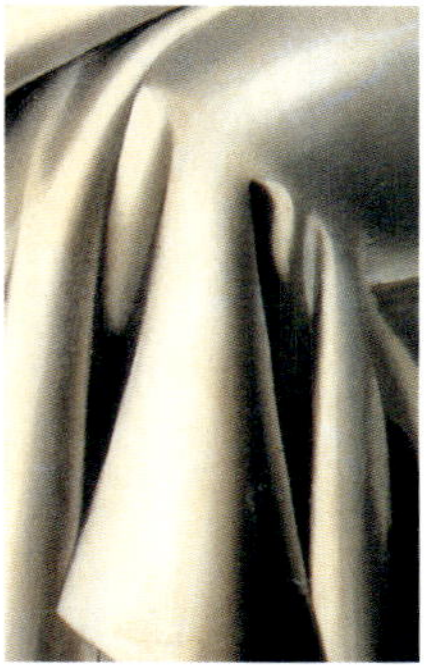

De Lempicka's demeanour throughout this somewhat grotesque episode was that of a silent movie heroine. Film seems to have played an inordinately important role in both the life and the art of de Lempicka. The immense popularity of de Lempicka's work, starting in the 1970s, was fuelled by nostalgia for the movies of the inter war period. If the women she painted often had the eye-rolling allure of silent film stars, the style of the paintings also reminded people of the gleaming, streamlined sets of musicals and screwball comedies. There is no doubt that de Lempicka herself was profoundly influenced by the burgeoning art form of the cinema. In the 1920s as she formed her style, the great Hollywood studios of M.G.M., Paramount, Columbia, Universal and R.K.O. began what has been termed *the golden age* of Hollywood and their domination of world entertainment.

Portrait of Mrs. Boucard

1931
Oil on canvas, 135 x 75 cm
Private Collection

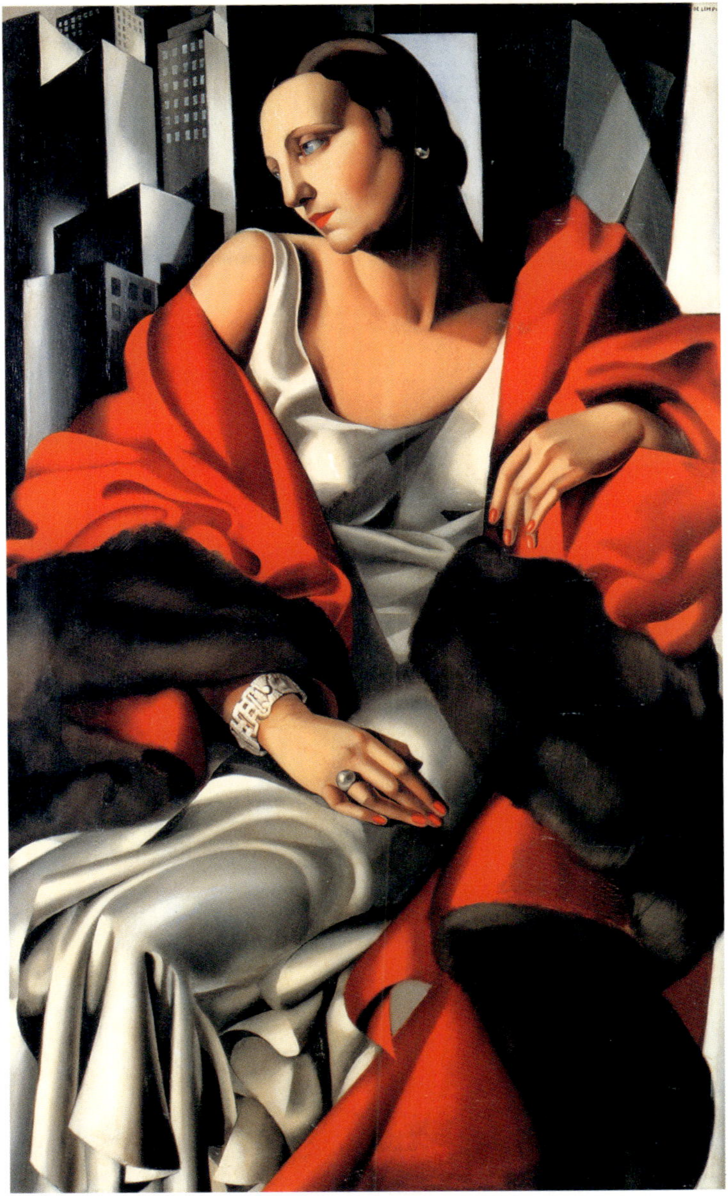

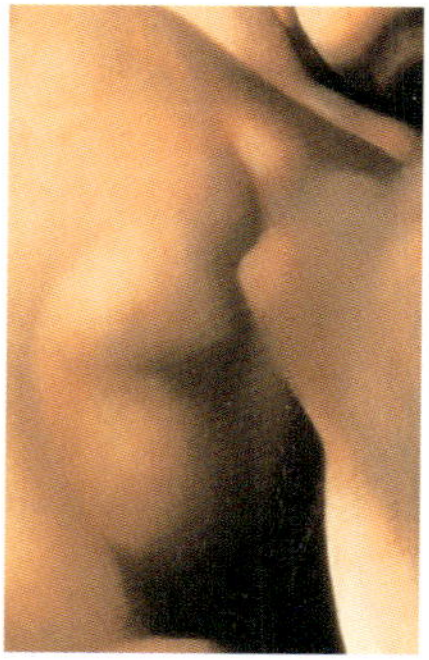

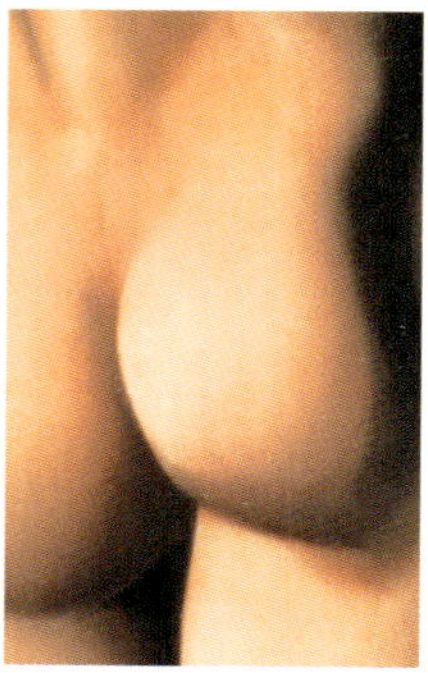

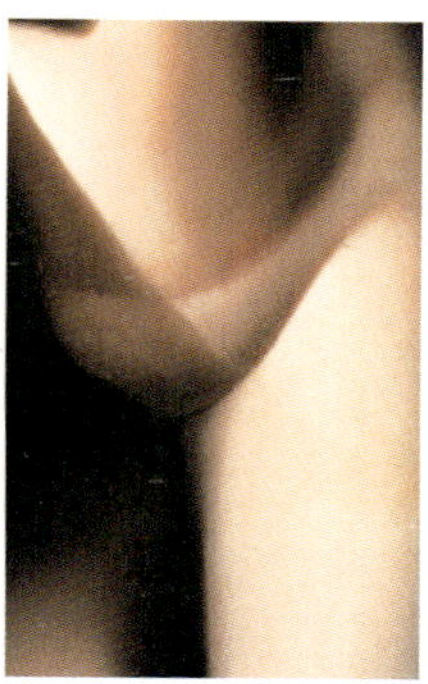

The French and German film industries also enjoyed a golden age of creativity, turning out many of the twentieth century's finest films in these years. The ubiquity of movies began to influence the way people looked and behaved. De Lempicka's female subjects with their heavy makeup, perfectly coiffed hair and their theatrical poses and facial expressions full of artificial pathos could have stepped out of the silver screen.

De Lempicka herself with her striking beauty gave herself the airs of a film star. In the late 20s and early 30s, de Lempicka repeatedly had herself photographed in images similar to the stills of glamorous stars issued by the film studio publicity departments, using the same techniques of soft focus, dramatic chiaroscuro, the essential accessories of clunky Art Deco jewellery, casually draped furs and the elegantly wielded cigarette.

Adam and Eve

1931
Oil on panel, 116 x 73 cm
Private Collection

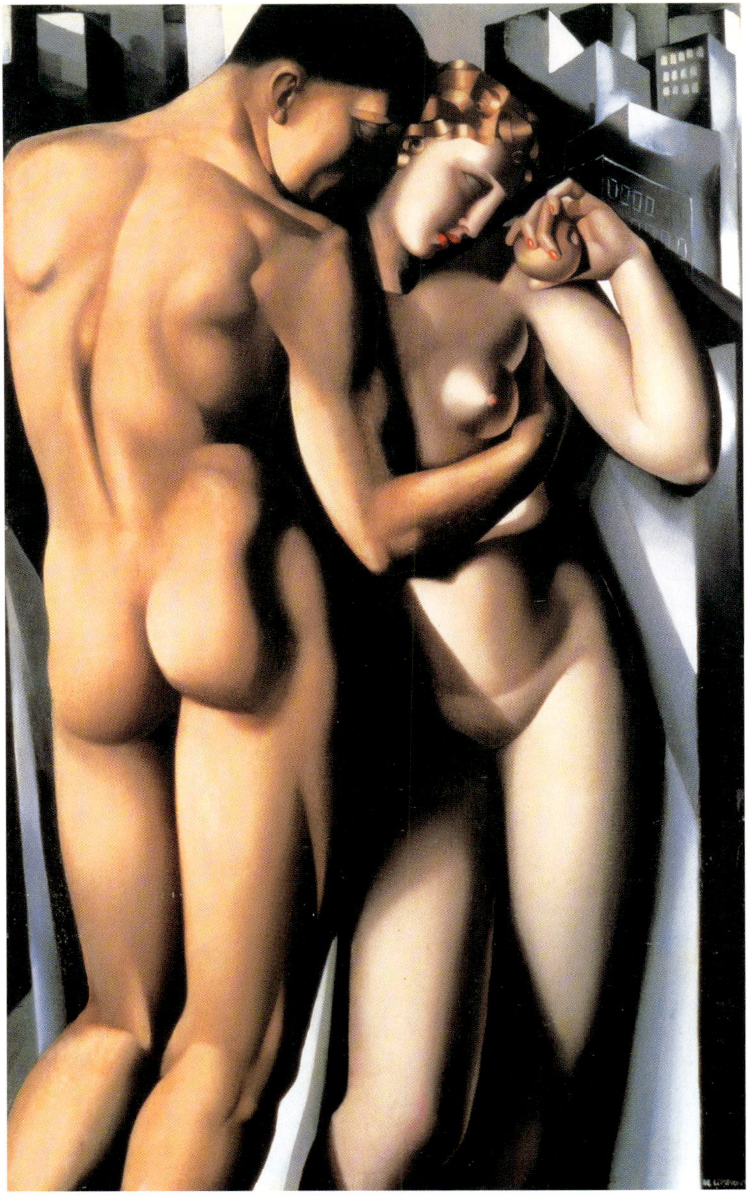

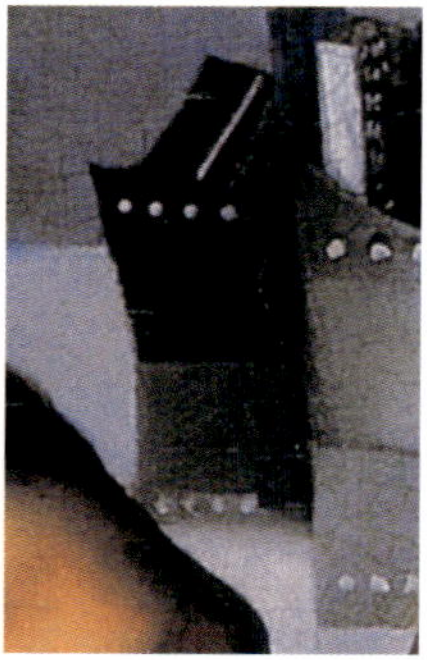

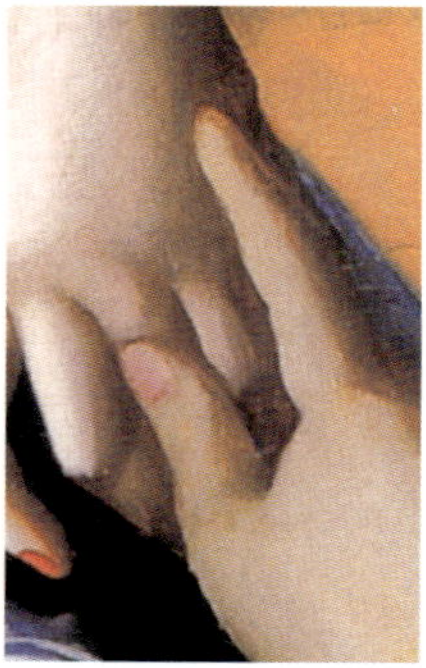

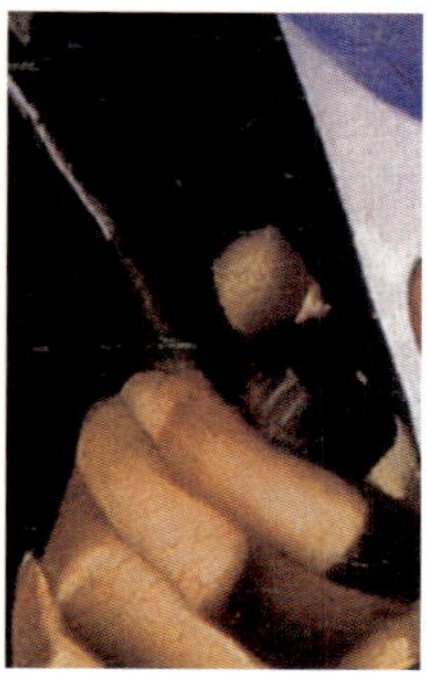

In 1932 the French film company Pathe shot footage of de Lempicka descending a staircase with cigarette holder in hand — the classic star entrance and one particularly associated in Paris with the great star of the *varietes, Mistinguett.* In the late 20s and 30s, de Lempicka had not only herself photographed but also the interiors of her Paris apartments as part of an ambitious plan of self-promotion. These interiors with their uncluttered, streamlined elegance do not look lived in. There is certainly never any evidence of the existence of her daughter Kizette. Instead, these rooms are intended to showcase the artist and her glamorous life-style. With an erotic design on the headboard of the spacious double bed and an easel with a large preparatory study for the portrait of Dr. Boucard placed at the foot of the bed, de Lempicka's bedroom in the Rue Guy de Maupassant is a shrine to art and love.

Idyll

1931
Oil on panel, 41 x 32.5 cm
Private Collection

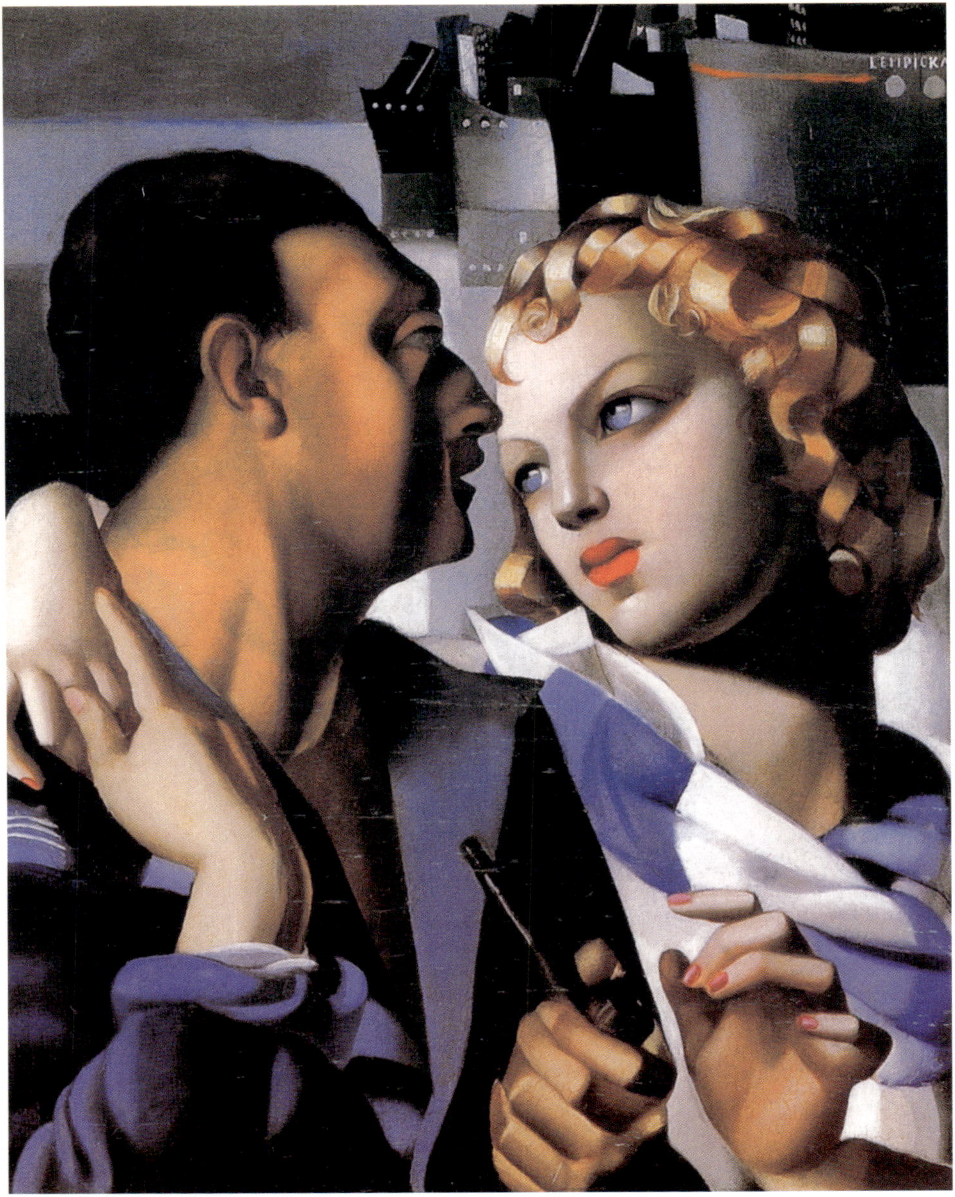
LEMPICKA

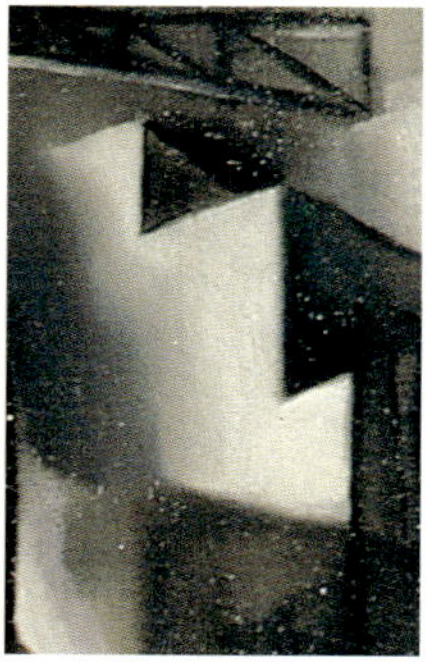

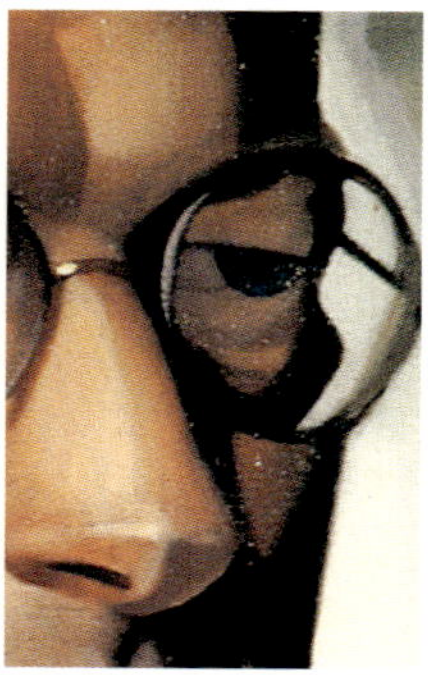

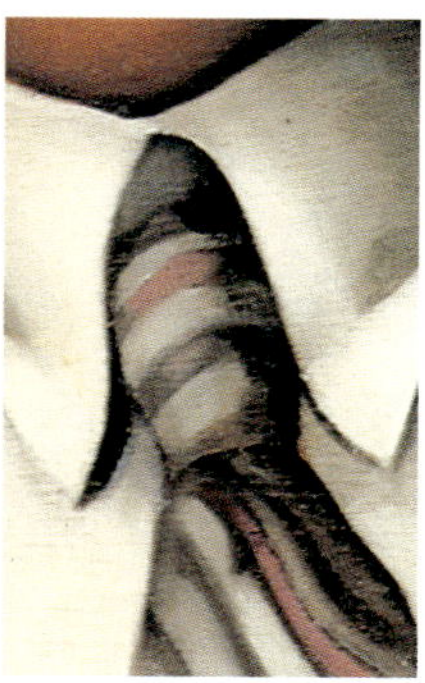

In 1928 de Lempicka moved into a spacious two-floored apartment in a new block on the rue Mechain designed by the fashionable architect Robert Mallet-Stevens.

For Parisian journalists, the exotically beautiful Polish artist in the elegant surroundings of her rue Mechain apartment was good copy. She was described breathlessly as "tall, soft. Harmonious in her movements...glowing with life, her face illuminated by large rather artificial eyes, and with an easily smiling mouth reddened by costly Parisian lip-rouge." On one occasion as she received a journalist, she was wearing a "white satin evening gown with a dark red sash and short sable jacket". On another occasion she wore "a beige, yellow, whipcord coat, trimmed in black, designed by Creed." The apparently casual mention of the name of the couturier responsible for the beige yellow coat would have been no accident.

Portrait of Pierre de Montaut

1931
Oil on panel, 41 x 27 cm
Barry Friedman Ltd, New York

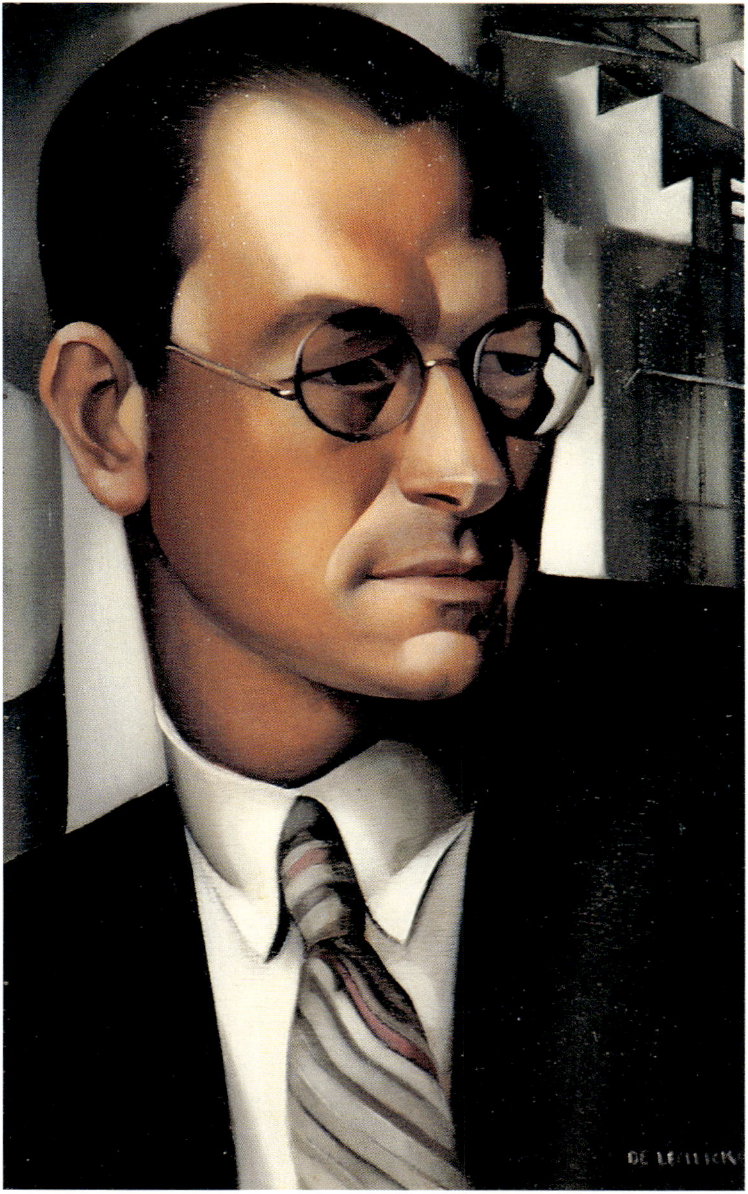

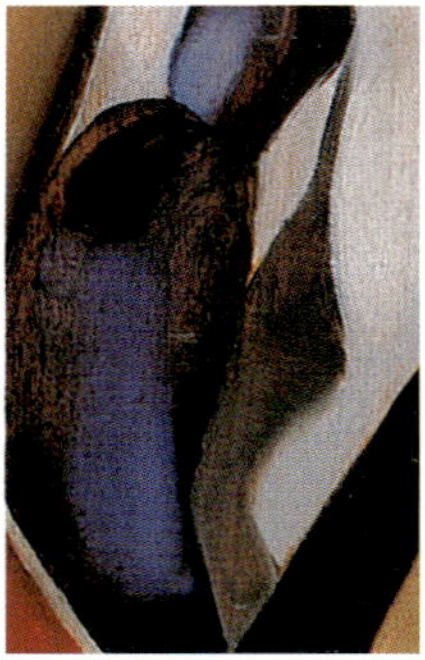

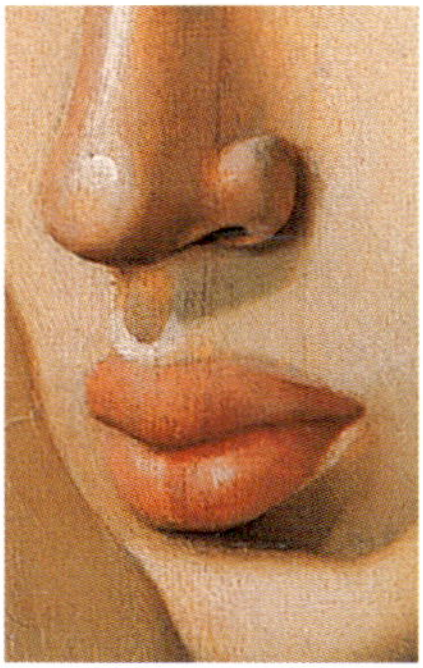

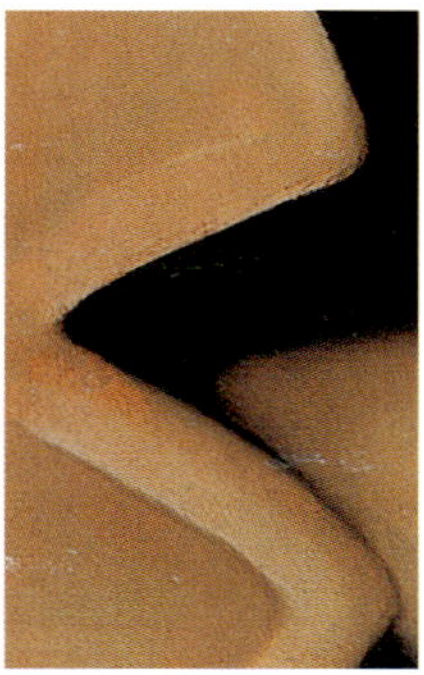

It was the custom for Parisian couturiers to dress glamorous women in the public eye gratis in return for the publicity they generated. It was a great age of celebrity endorsement. One of de Lempicka's favourite watering holes was the bar *Le Bœuf sur Le Toit* named after the ballet devised by Jean Cocteau to the pulsating music of Darius Milhaud. The stage designer Jean Hugo, another habitue of *Le Bœuf sur Le Toit* remembered it as "the crossroad of destinies, the cradle of loves, the matrix of disputes, the navel of Paris". With its undertone of bisexual intrigue, it was the perfect setting for de Lempicka. There she could run into Cocteau surrounded by his musical acolytes Darius Milhaud, Georges Auric and Francis Poulenc. Musical entertainment for the guests at *Le Bœuf sur Le Toit* was provided by the pianist Jean Wiener who was also a great promoter of the music of *Les Six* as well as of American Jazz.

Portrait of a Man with His Collar Turned Up

c. 1931
Oil on panel, 41 x 33 cm
Private Collection

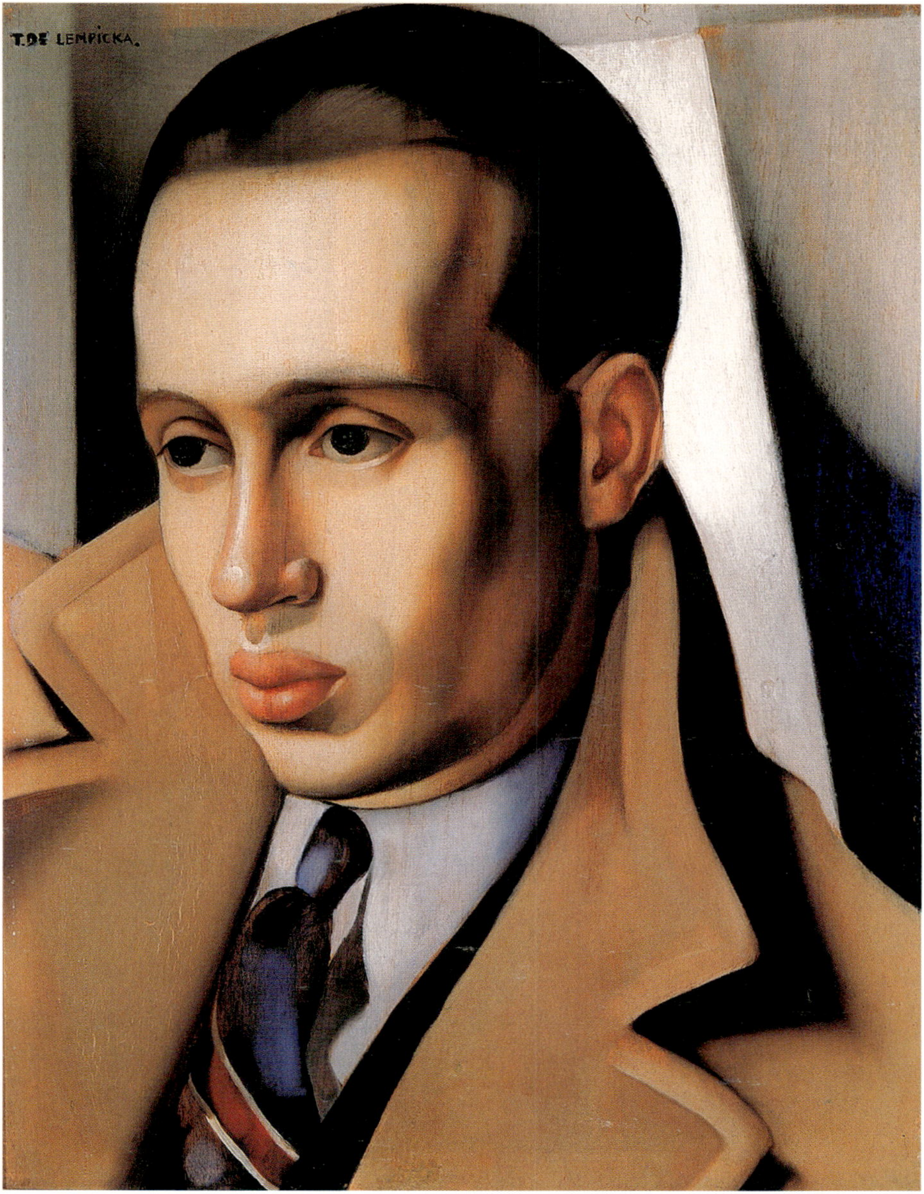
T.DE LEMPICKA.

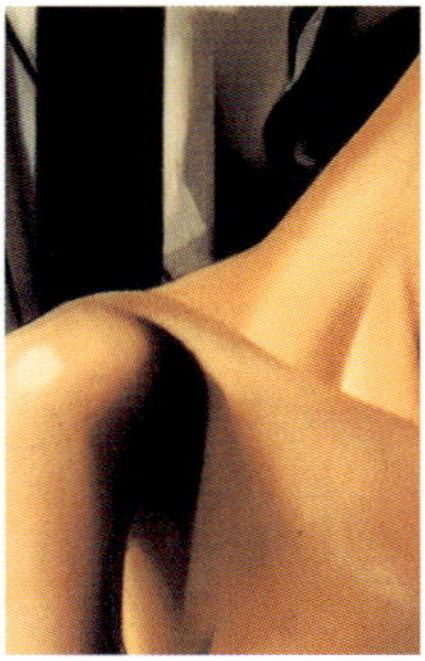

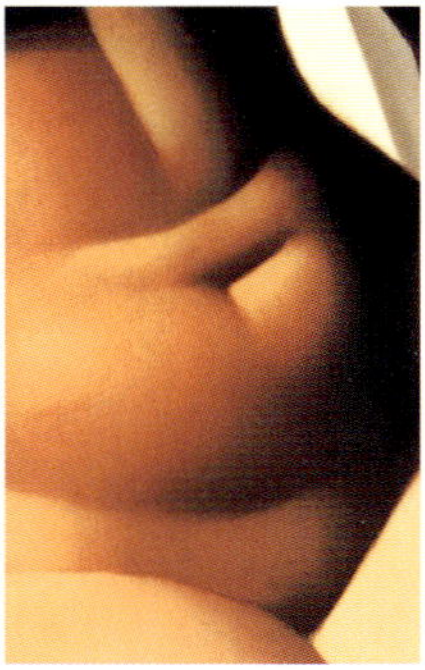

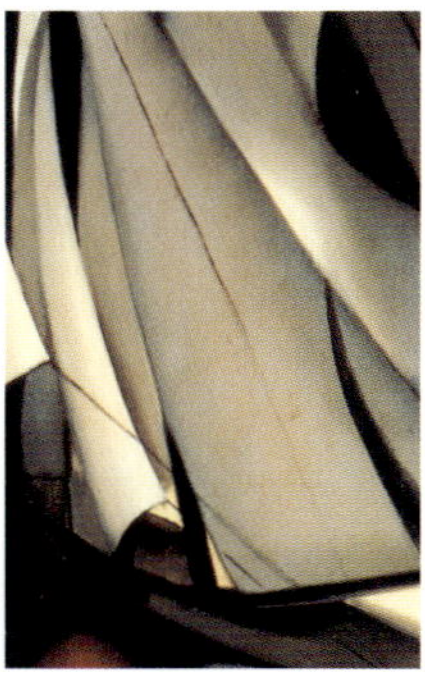

Tamara was not long in finding a new husband after she was deserted by Tadeusz — one who may not have been as handsome as Tadeusz but who was wealthy enough to keep her in the style to which she had become accustomed who could give her a title and the kind of social cache that she craved and who would remain devoted to her for the rest of his life. This was Baron Raoul Kuffner or *Rollie* as Tamara liked to call him. Kuffner was the possessor of a considerable fortune and extensive landed properties throughout the former Austro-Hungarian Empire. Kuffner had been an enthusiastic collector of de Lempicka's work from the very beginning.

Nude with Sailboats

1931
Oil on canvas, 113 x 56.5 cm
Bruce R. Lewin Gallery, New York

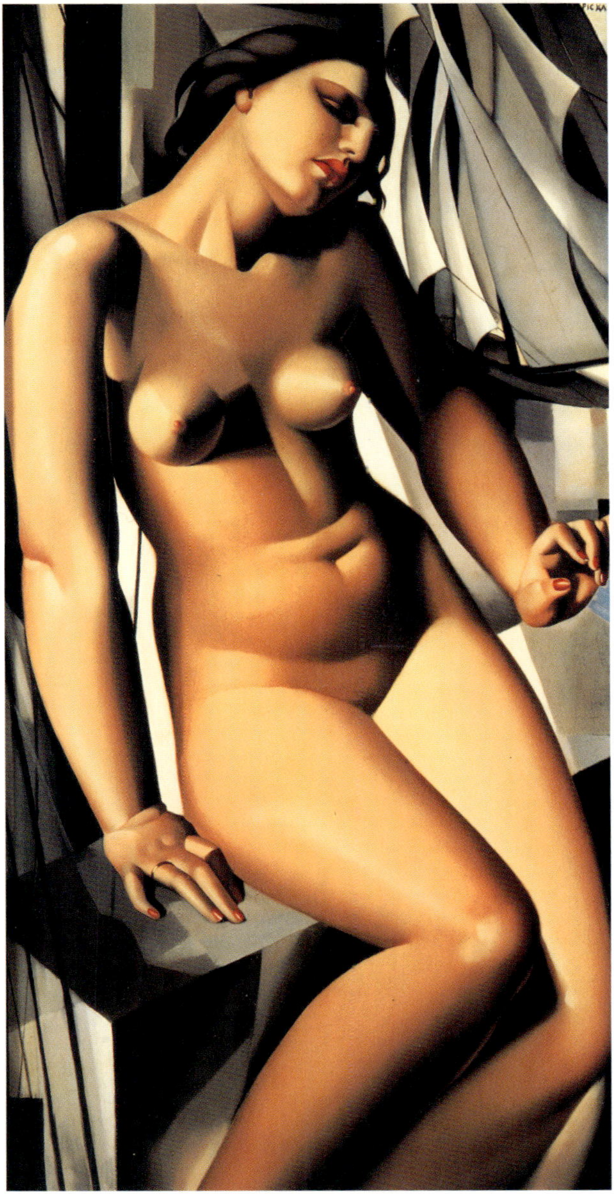

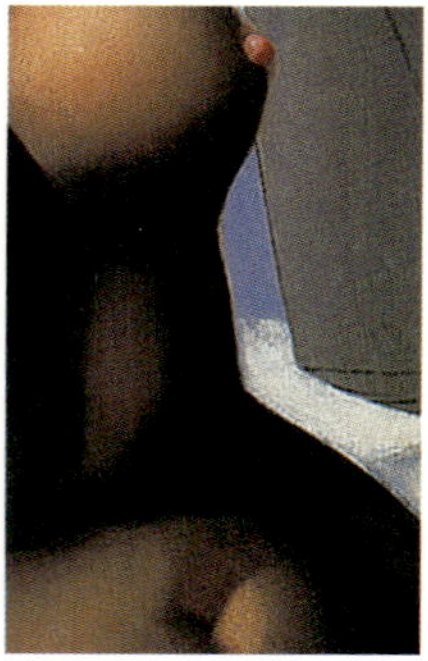

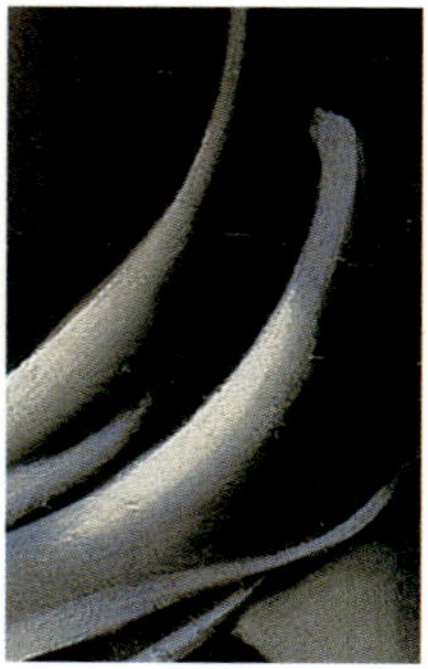

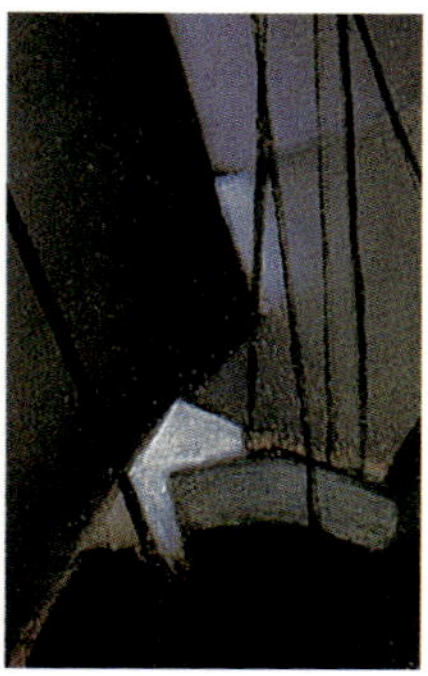

They had probably been lovers from the time he commissioned her to paint the portrait of Nana de Herrera in 1928 but it was not until 1933 when his first wife died that Kuffner was in a position to propose marriage to de Lempicka. It was far from a love match on her part and there was considerable hesitation before she accepted his offer. Nevertheless it turned out to be a highly successful arrangement that allowed her to continue her career and her independent life style. After a honeymoon spent in Egypt Kuffner took an apartment in the same block as de Lempicka's studio and continued to live mainly in a suite at the Westminster Hotel. Baron Kuffner was more tolerant than Tadeusz de Lempicki had been of his wife's infidelities with men and women and of her thirst for sexual adventure that did not end with her second marriage.

The Blue Hour

1931
Oil on canvas, 55 x 38 cm
Private Collection

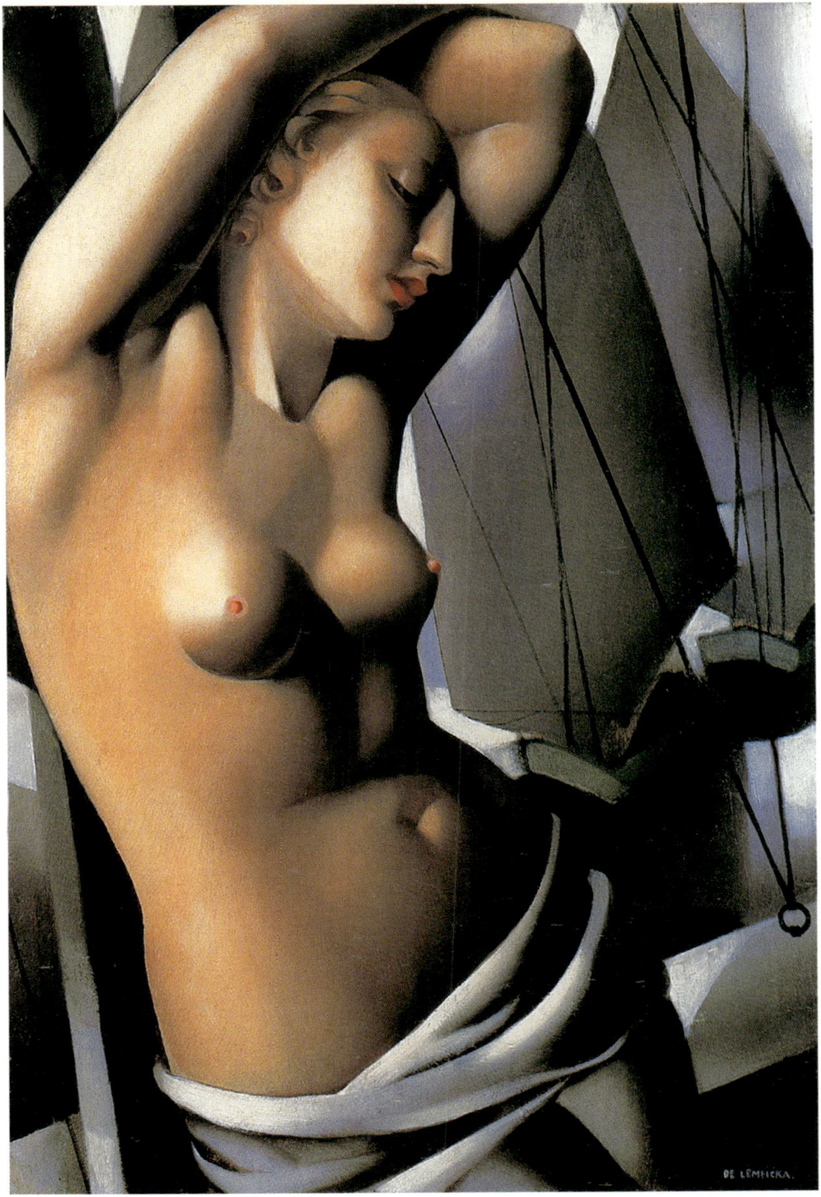
DE LEMPICKA.

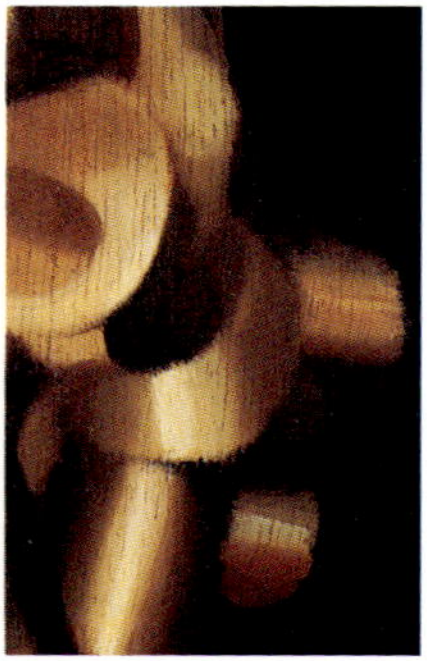

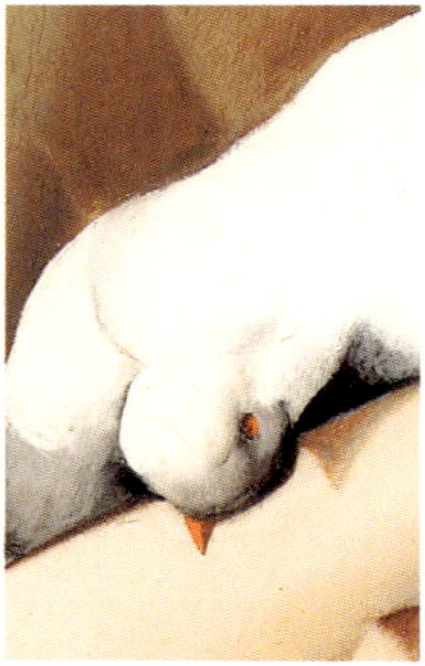

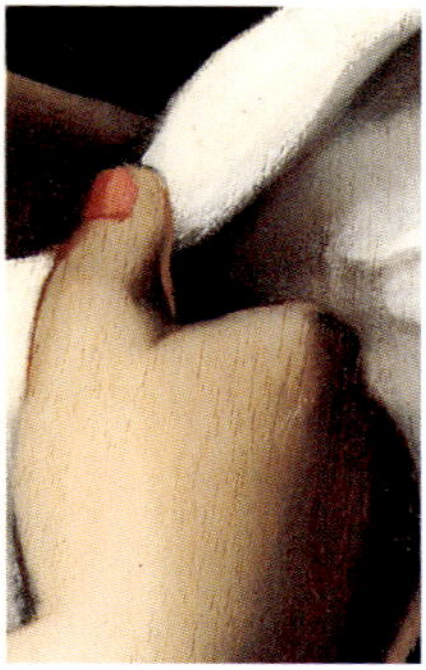

The French art critic Michel Georges-Michel confided in Tamara's biographer Charles Phillips how he first met her at around this time when "he walked into a sordid little bar in one of the dirtiest streets in Cannes where one encountered only the tough faces of sailors, women with a look in their eyes wilder than the men, and pale young homosexuals dressed in pink shirts and exchanging acid glances. The owner of the place, whose red and purple face matched his wines, sat at the door like a prison guard. In the darkest corner reclined a barefoot, nearly bare-breasted woman, betopped by an outrageous donkey hat. Her hair was pulled through the holes reserved for the donkey's ears, and her huge eyes glimmered in the dimness.

Woman with Dove

1931
Oil on panel, 37 x 28 cm
Private Collection

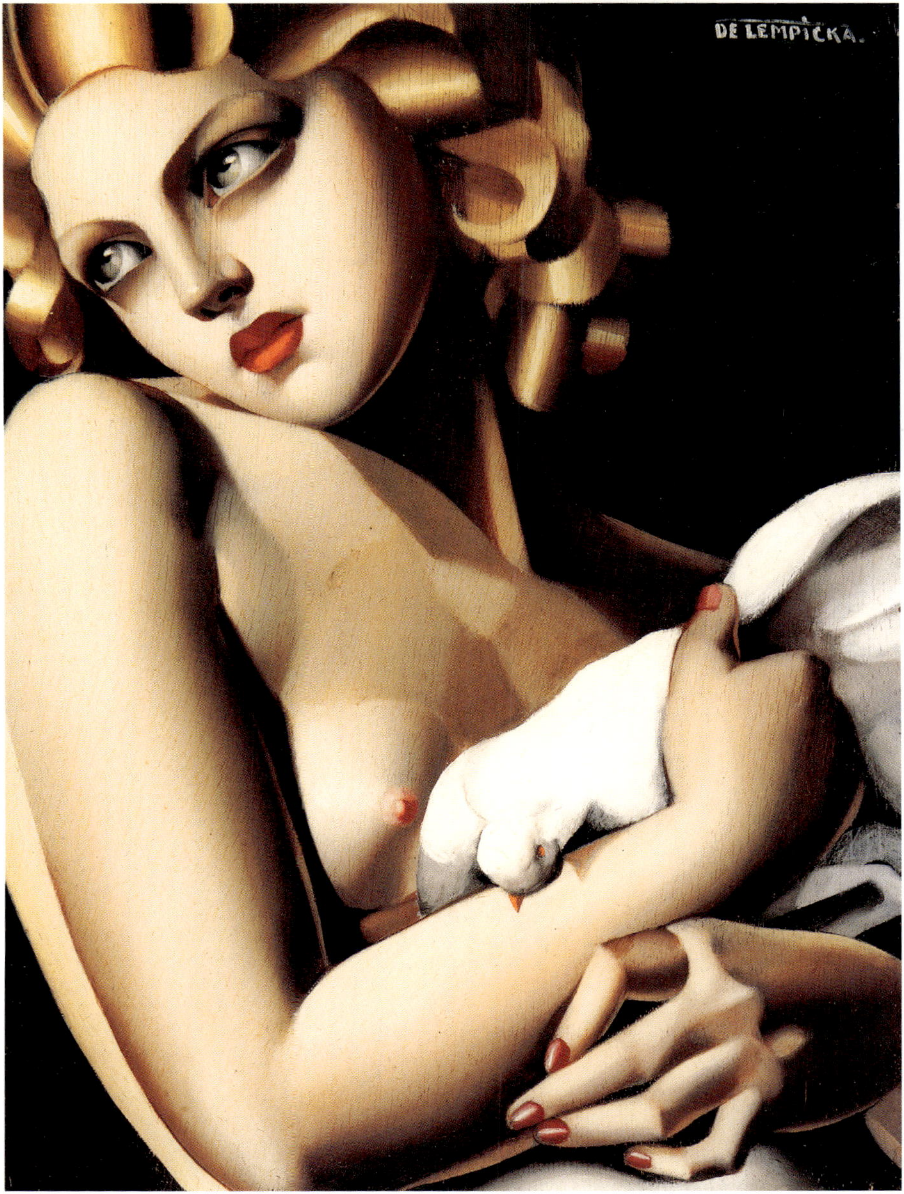
DE LEMPICKA.

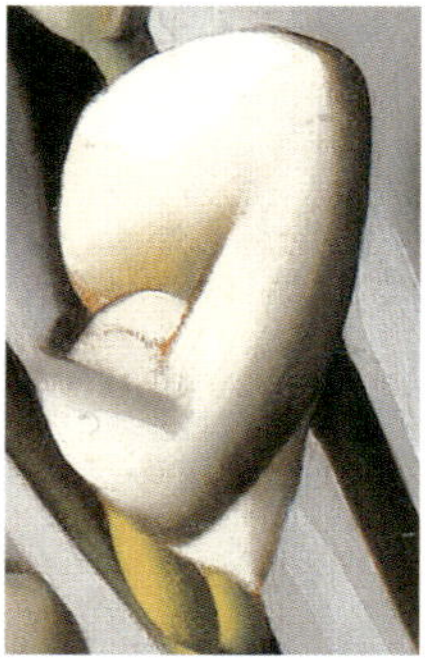

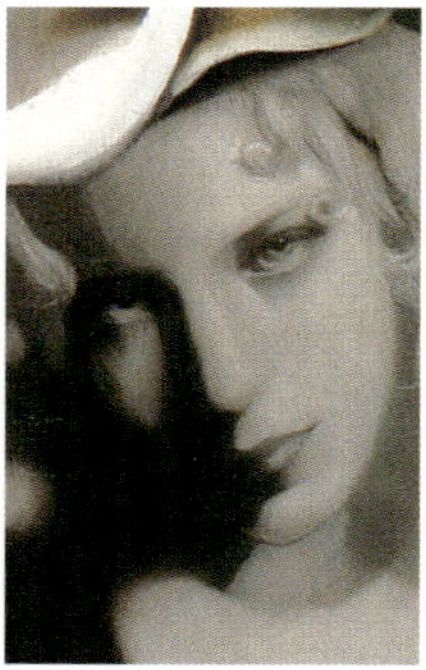

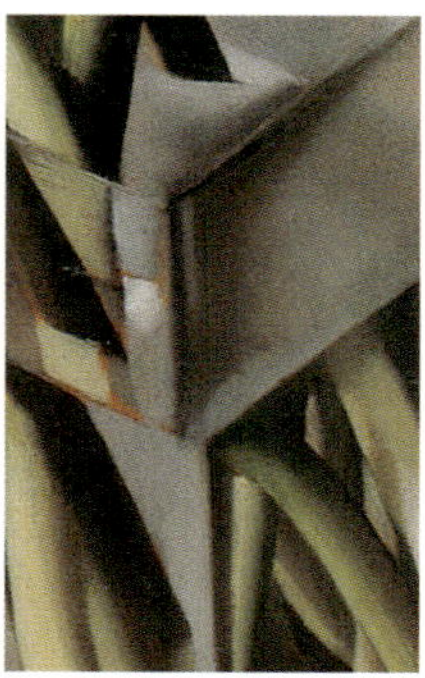

He stared at her. She shrugged her shoulders and turned her back, a magnificent back, naked to the loins. That night he was invited to a plush and elegant party at one of Cannes' more respectable addresses. As he amused himself with private observations about the lavish display of food and the decorous behaviour of the guests, he felt a slap on his shoulder and heard a woman say in a husky voice. "Well you certainly were in a strange place this morning." He turned around to see the woman from the bar, this time sparkling with jewelry from the tip of her shoes to the top of her tiara, which sat like a halo on her golden head." It was of course Tamara.

Arlette Boucard with Arums

1931
Oil on plywood, 91 x 55.5 cm
Private Collection

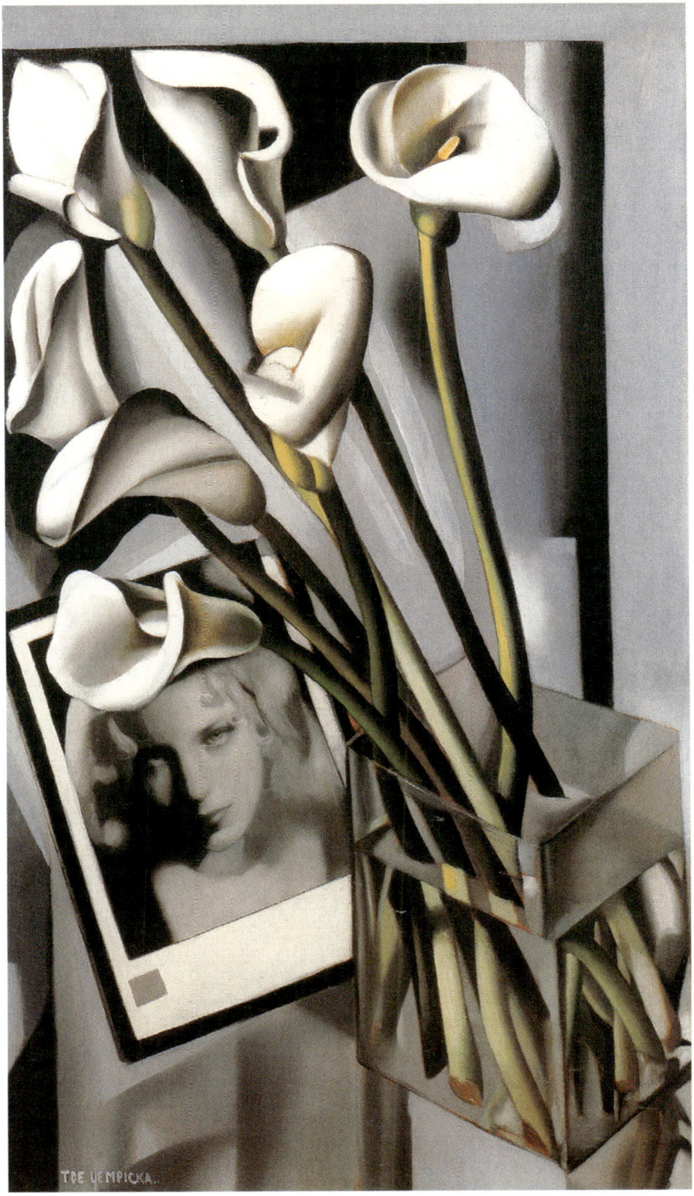
TDE LEMPICKA.

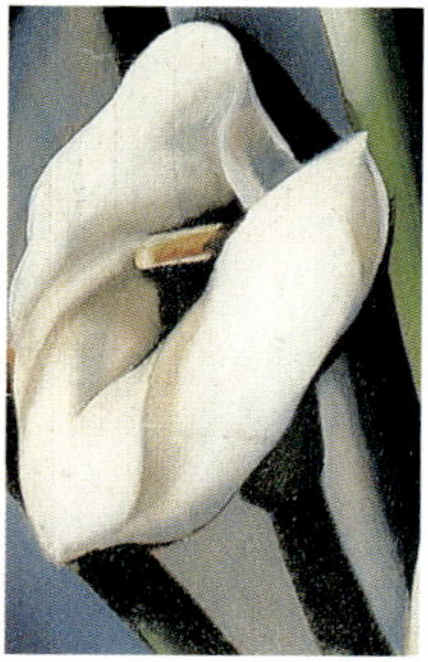

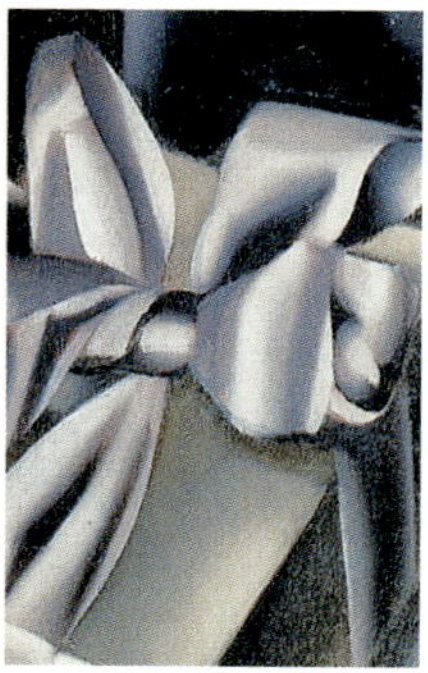

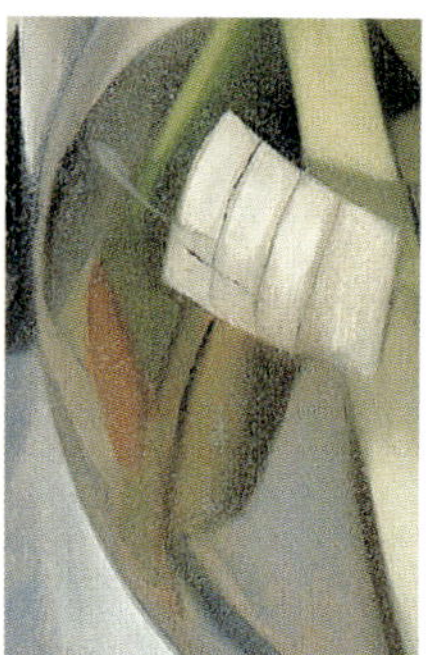

1933, the year that Tamara remarried was also the year in which Hitler came to power, triggering a new wave of intellectual and artistic émigrés towards Paris. It was also a turning point in the life and career of de Lempicka. Though she would not perhaps fully realise it for several years, the period of her greatest creativity had passed. The portrait commissions dried up almost immediately. This may have been in part because there was no urgent need for her to earn money after she married. It was also a sign of the times. The effects of the Wall St. Crash and the Depression finally filtered through to the wealthier classes in Paris who had provided de Lempicka with her clientele. This corresponded with changes in taste, with the kind of jazzy Art Deco that de Lempicka had so perfectly represented, going out of fashion.

Arums

c. 1931
Oil on panel, 92 x 60 cm
James and Patricia Cayne's Collection

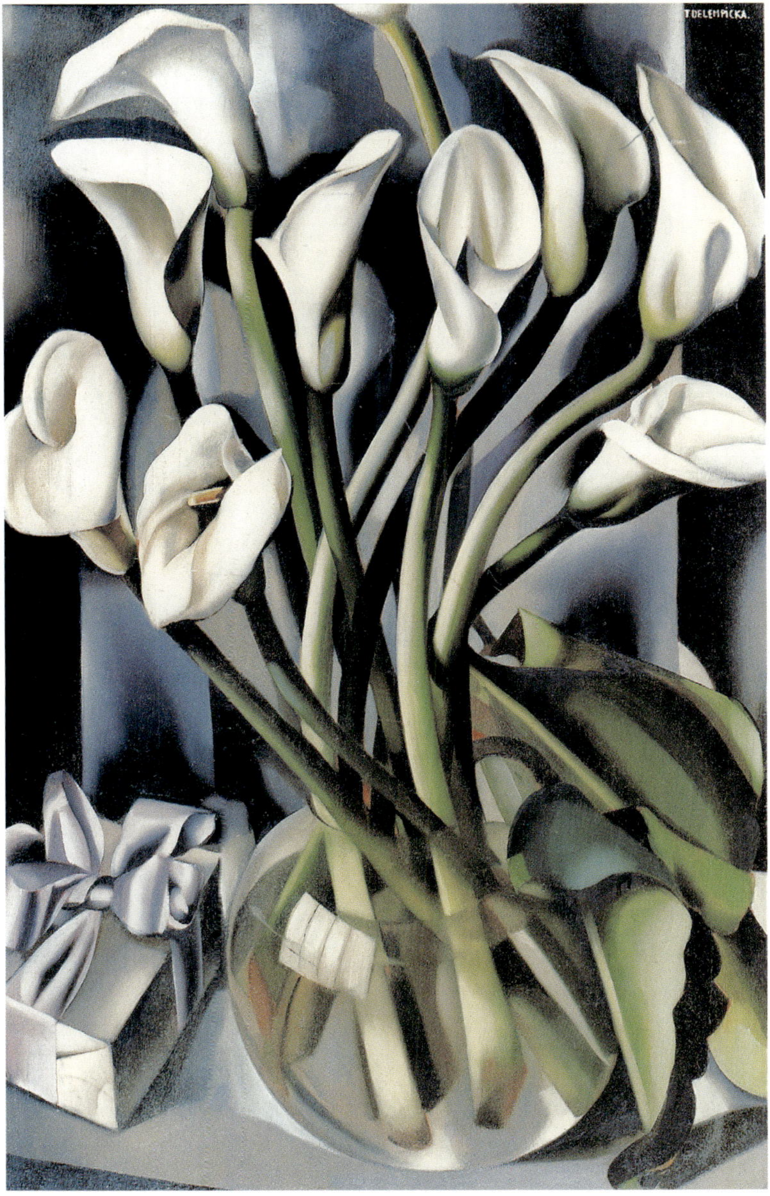
T DE LEMPICKA.

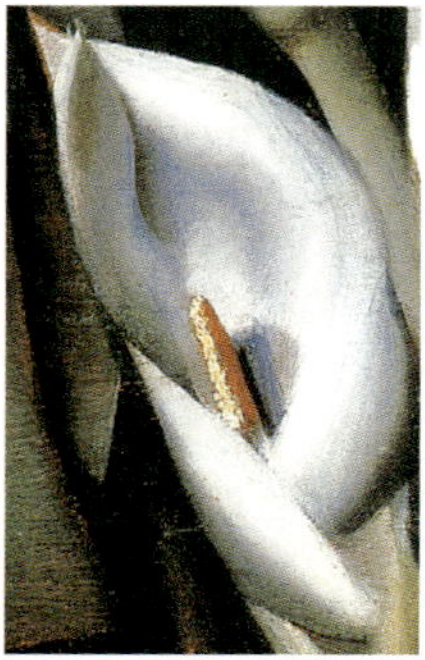

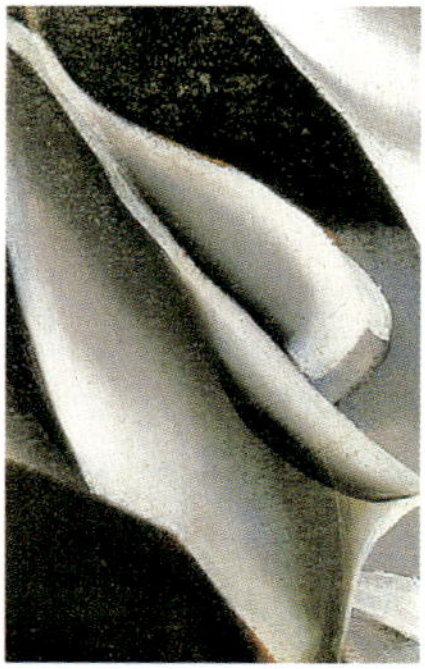

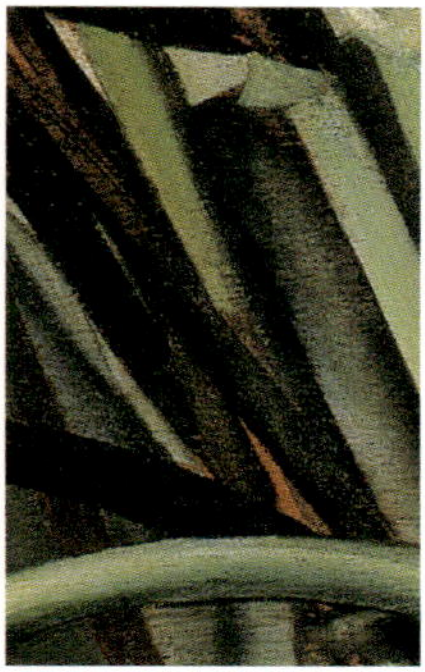

There was no immediate or radical change in de Lempicka's style, though there is less of the jazzy quasi cubist element that had characterised her work in the late 20s and early 30s. This move towards sobriety and away from modernity seems to be the result of a considerable psychological and spiritual crisis that overwhelmed de Lempicka in the years after her marriage. A painting entitled *The Refugees* dating from as early as 1931 anticipates the new phase. It shows a care-worn mother with her few possessions wrapped in a scarf and her arm around her sad-eyed child. The brittle hedonism of the Jazz Age has been replaced by a tear-jerking pathos that sits uneasily with the glossiness of Tamara's technique.

Arums

1931
Oil on panel, 55 x 33 cm
Private Collection

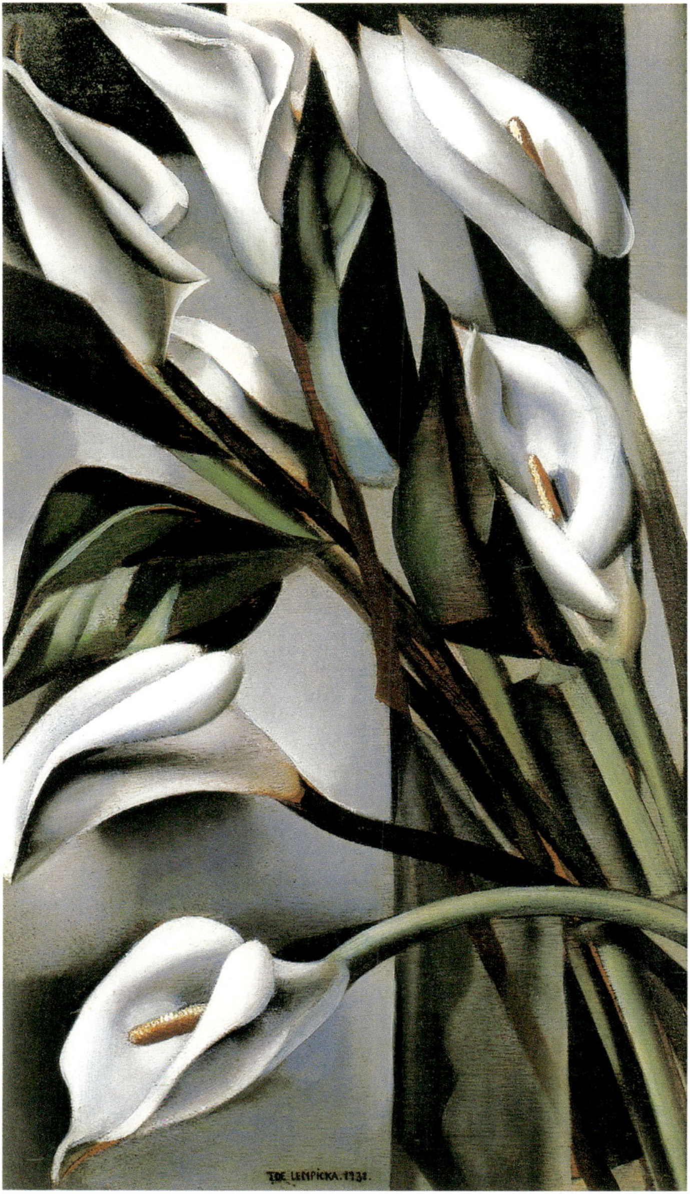
T. DE LEMPICKA. 1938.

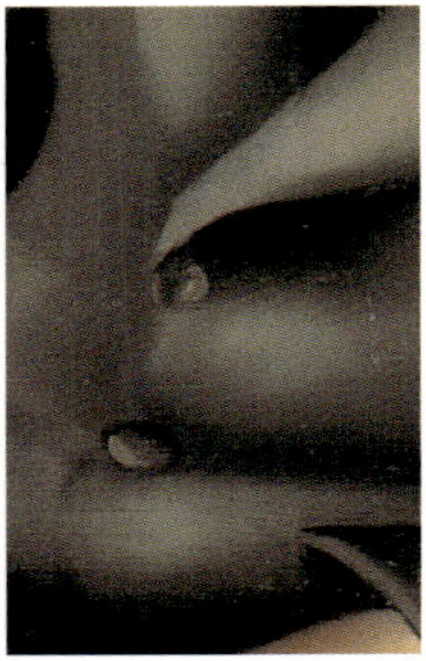

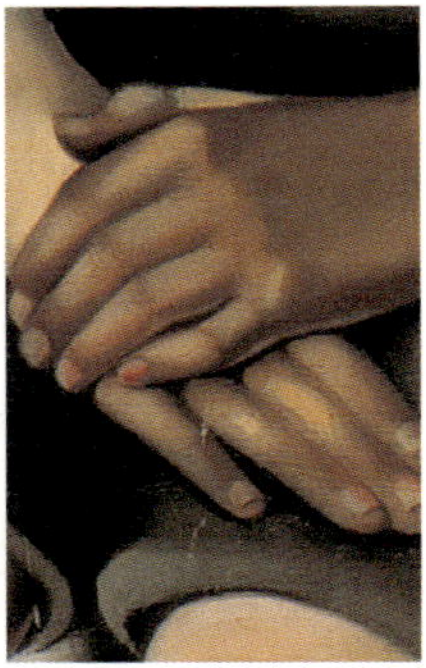

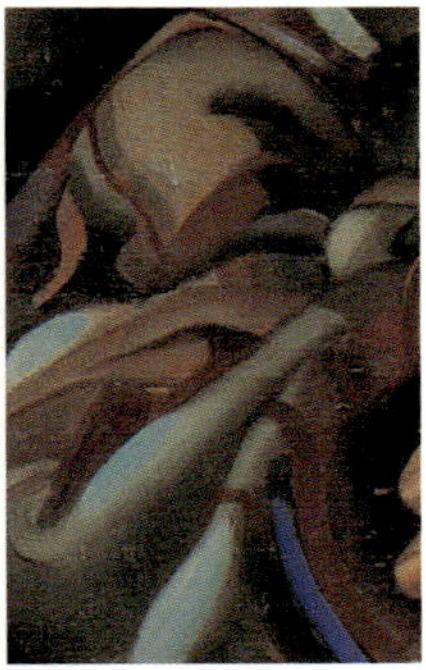

In 1936 de Lempicka began seeing a psychiatrist whom she painted as St. Anthony. De Lempicka was nearing 40 and like many fast living women whose beauty has begun to fade, she turned to religion for comfort. It was at this point that she painted her extraordinary *Mother Superior*. De Lempicka explained the origins of this picture "When you create, create, create, and put out so much of yourself, you become drained and depressed. I had gone to study in Italy to deal with the depression, and to enter a convent and just paint simple things. I went to a convent near Parma and rang the bell. A lovely nun answered, and I asked to see the Mother Superior. "Sit down, my child," she says. I sit on the hard bench and wait. I do not know how long.

The Refugees

1931
Oil on panel, 51 x 53 cm
Musée d'Art et d'Histoire de St Denis

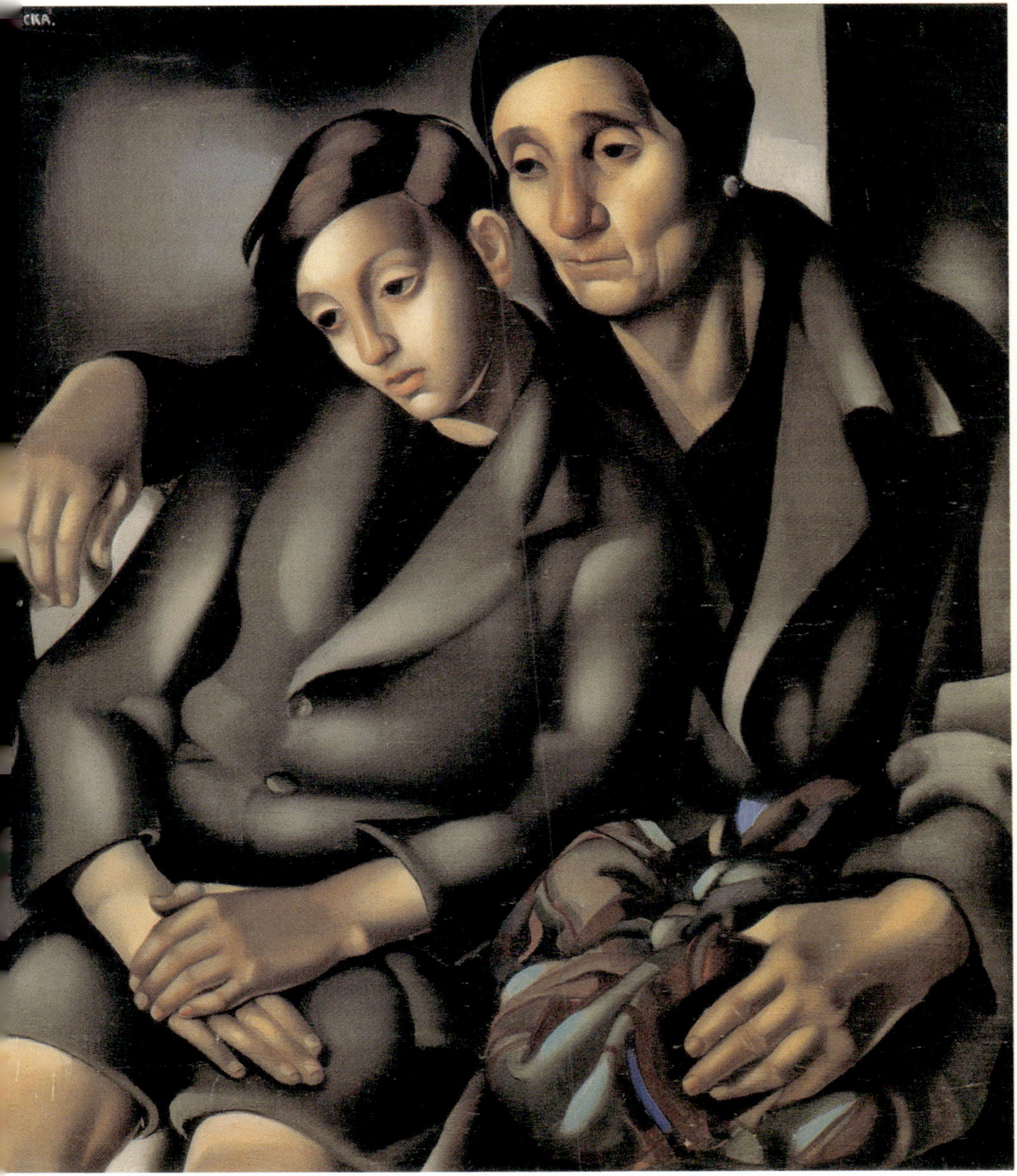
CKA.

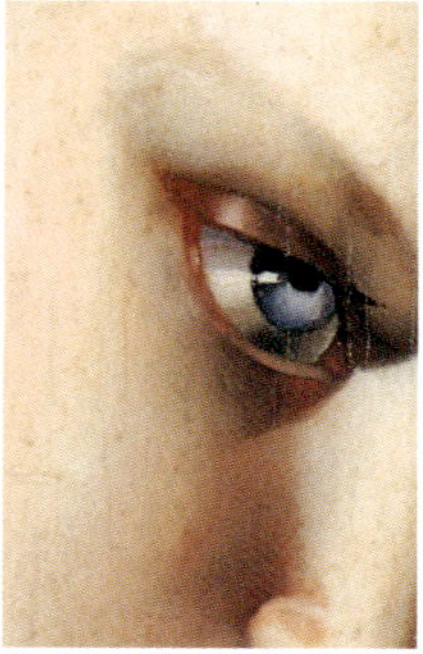

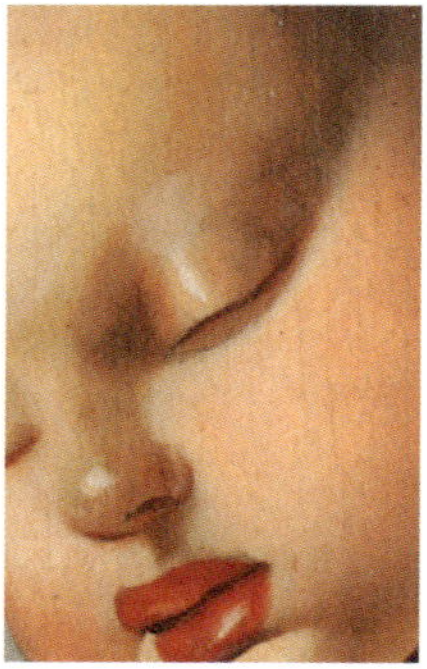

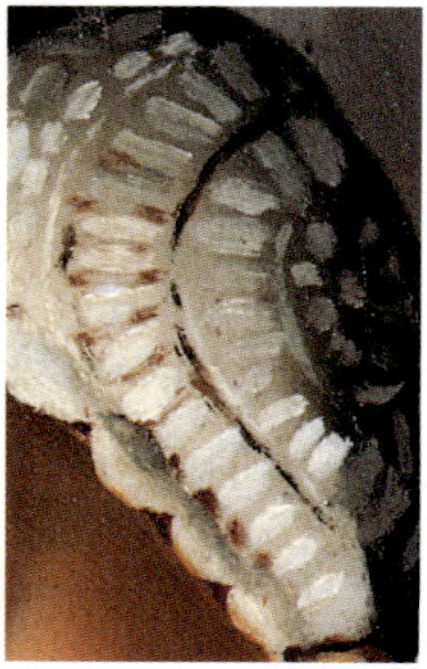

Then I go into a wonderful Renaissance room with the ceiling and the columns and there was the Mother Superior, and on her face was the suffering of the world, so terrible to look at, so sad, and I rushed out of the room. I forgot what was there for. I knew only that I must have canvas and brush and paint her, her face."

De Lempicka's malaise and fragile state of mind in the late 1930s may also reflect the anxious political and cultural mood in Europe at the time. With civil war in Spain to the West, Mussolini's Italy eyeing up France's North African colonies to the South and the rise of Hitler to the East, the mood was either one of justified foreboding or else of wilful escapism.

Mother and Child

1931
Oil on panel, 33 x 24 cm
Musée départemental de l'Oise, Beauvais

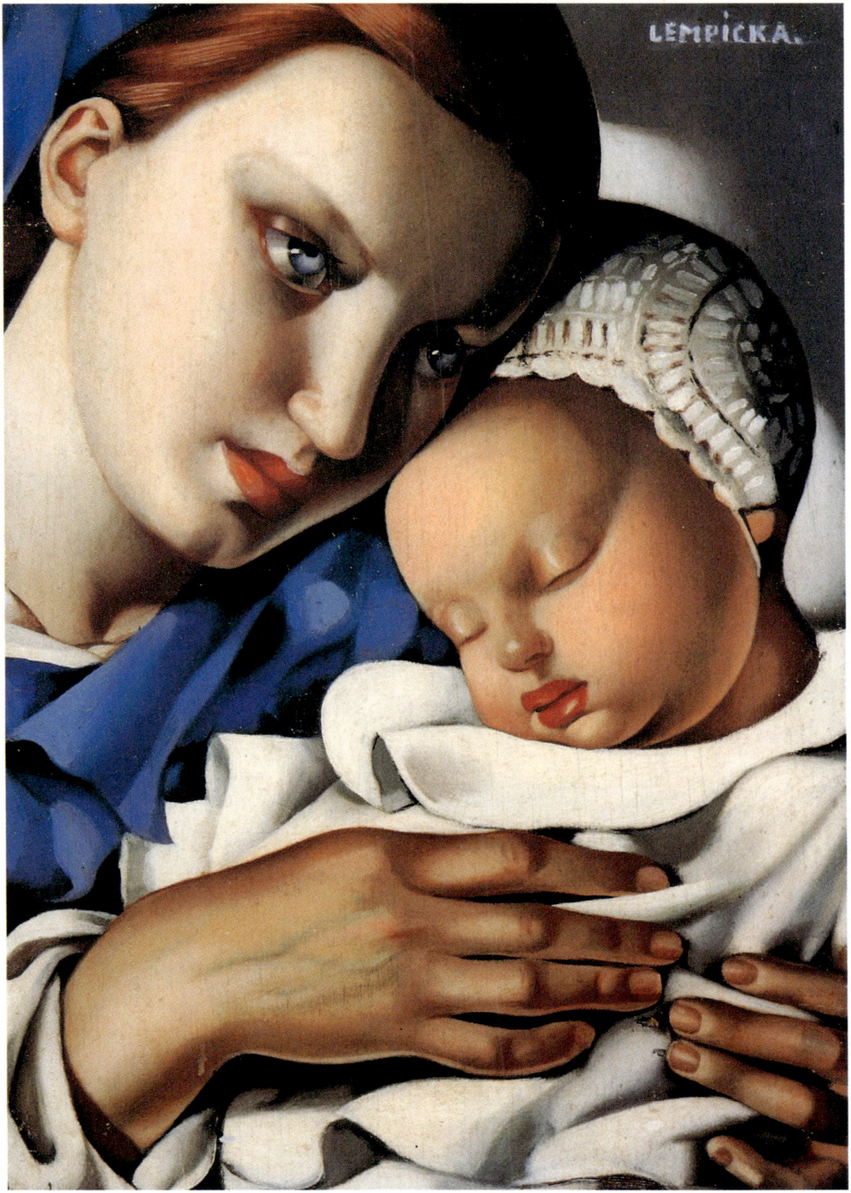
LEMPICKA.

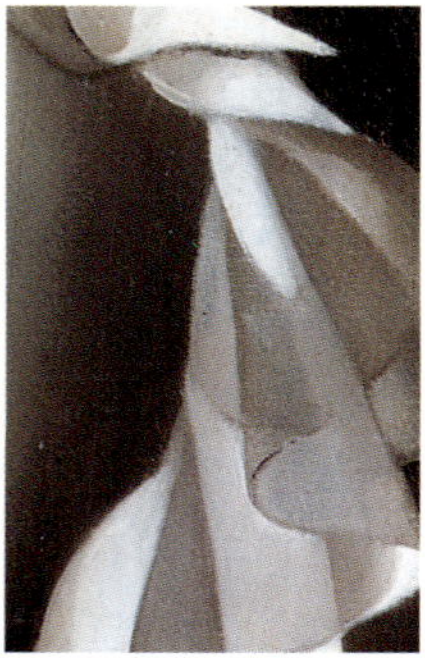

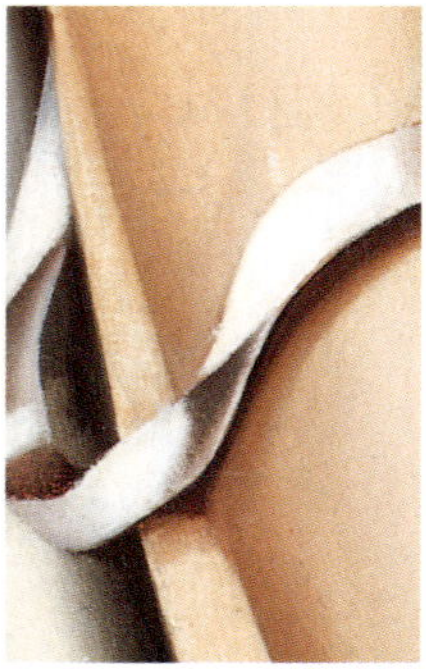

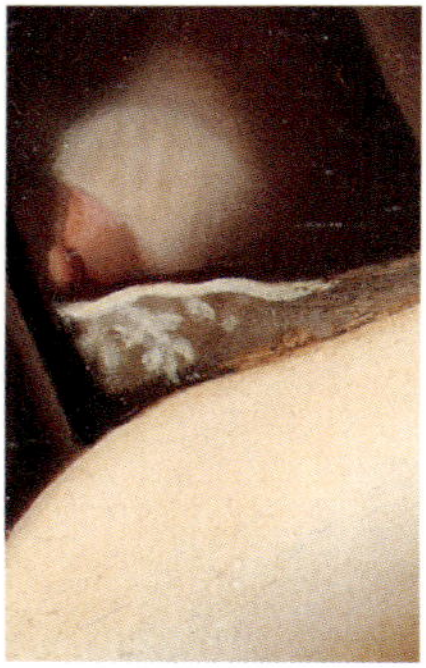

De Lempicka claimed to have seen the writing on the wall when she saw a group of Hitler youths singing in the street, while she was on holiday with her husband in the Austrian Alps. From that moment, apparently she attempted to persuade Baron Kuffner to sell up and leave Europe. For whatever reason and with remarkable prescience Kuffner sold most of his Central European properties, placed his possessions in storage in Switzerland and boarded the SS Paris on February 24 1939, well ahead of the outbreak of war. Over the next year or so artists flooded into the United States as refugees from the European conflict. Very few arrived in the comfort and style of the Kuffners, especially those who left it till after the collapse of France in 1940.

The Convalescent

1932
Oil on panel, 56 x 42 cm
Private Collection

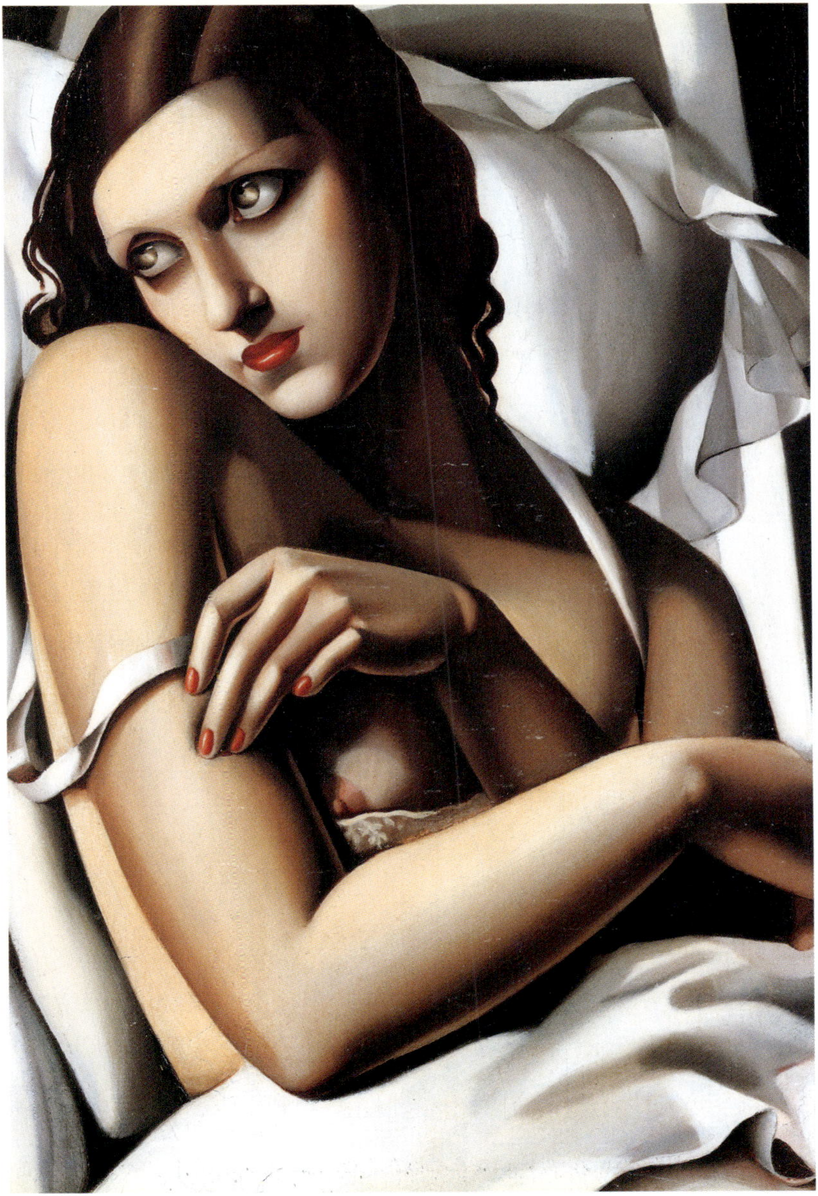

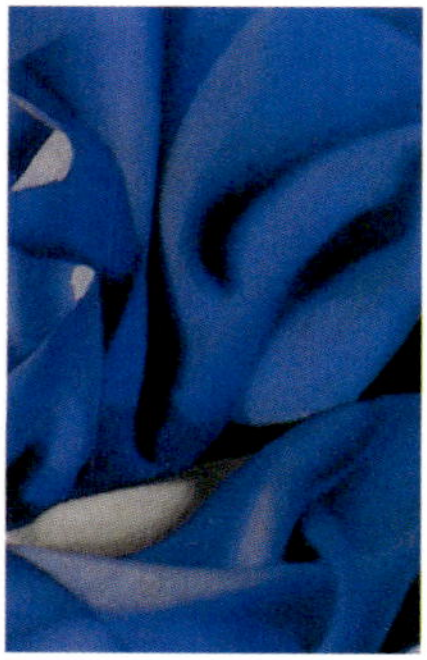

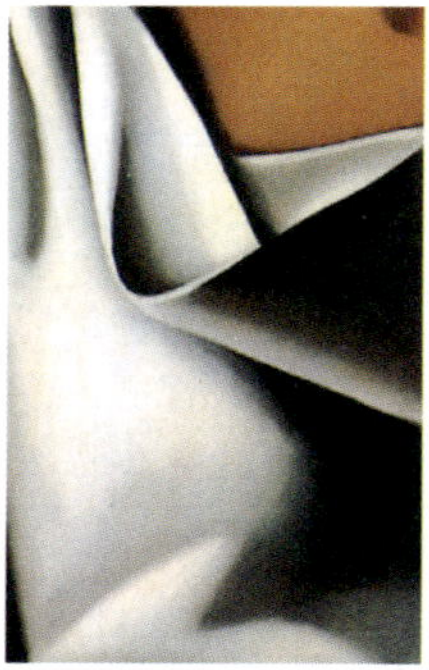

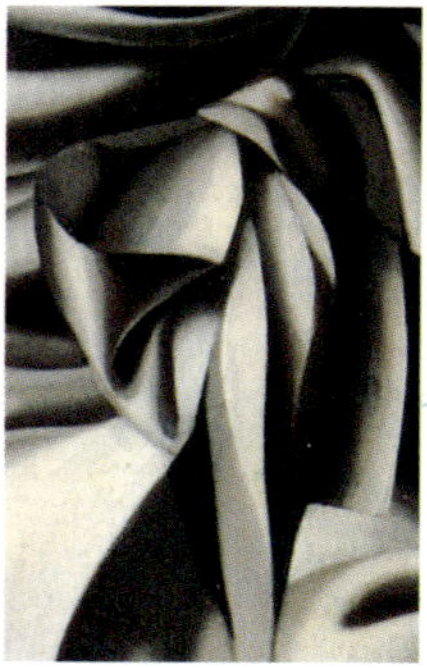

Hitler's hatred of all aspects of modern art had been clear from as early as the 1934 Nuremberg Rally, when he had denounced the "artistic and cultural stuttering of cubists, futurists and Dadaists" in the shrieking , hysterical tones of a madman. It was not necessary to be Jewish or communist to be in danger and with a few notable exceptions (Picasso, Braque and Matisse) those amongst the avant-garde who could escape to the United States did so. Varian Fry set up his *Emergency Rescue Committee* which between June 1940 and the Autumn of 1941 rescued the reluctant Marc Chagall (who needed to be reassured that there were indeed trees and cows in the United States) Max Ernst, André Breton, André Masson, Tristan Tzara and Jacques Lipchitz amongst many others.

Portrait of Mrs. M

1932
Oil on canvas, 100 x 65 cm
Private Collection

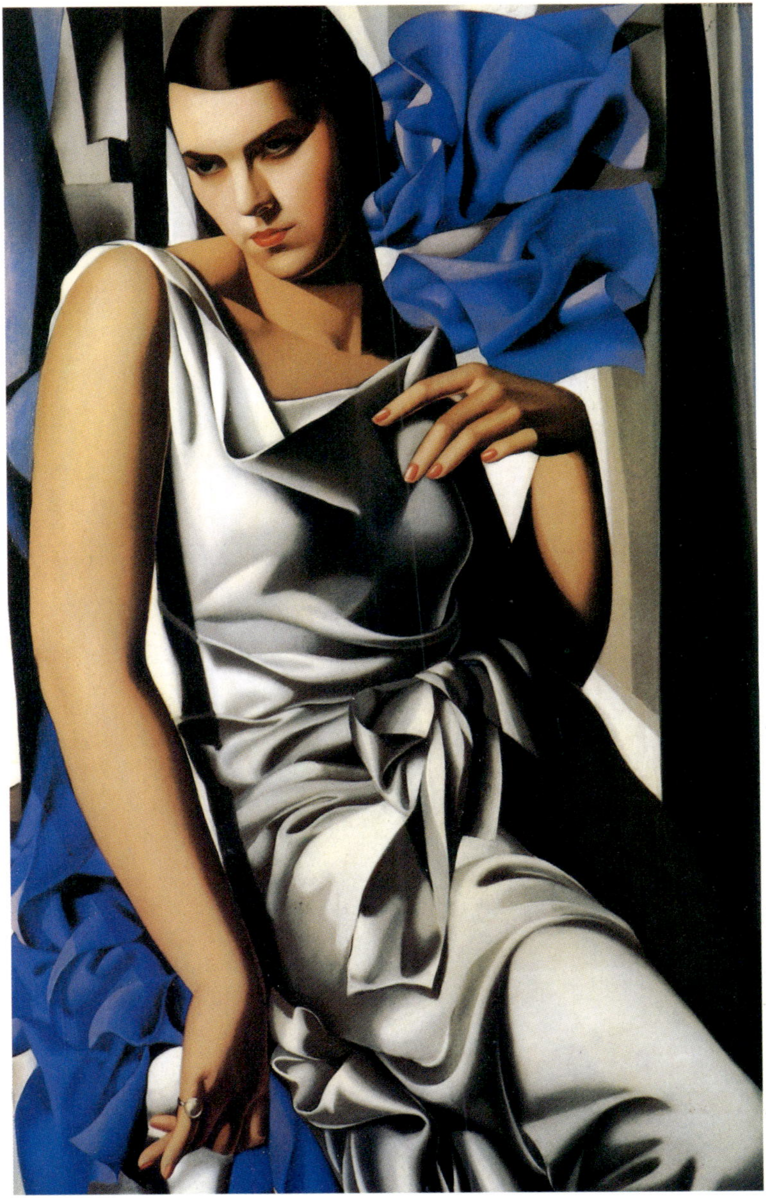

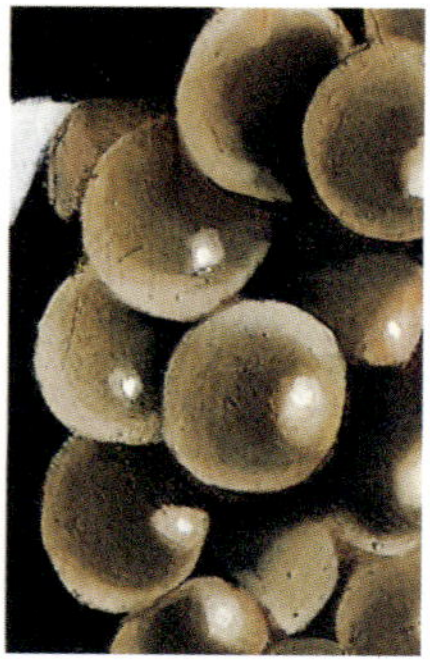

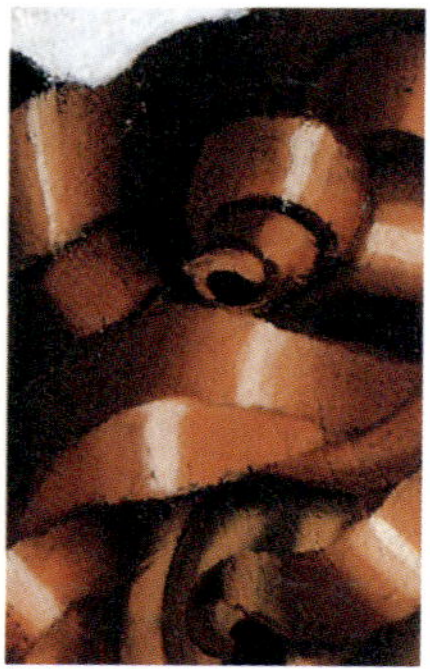

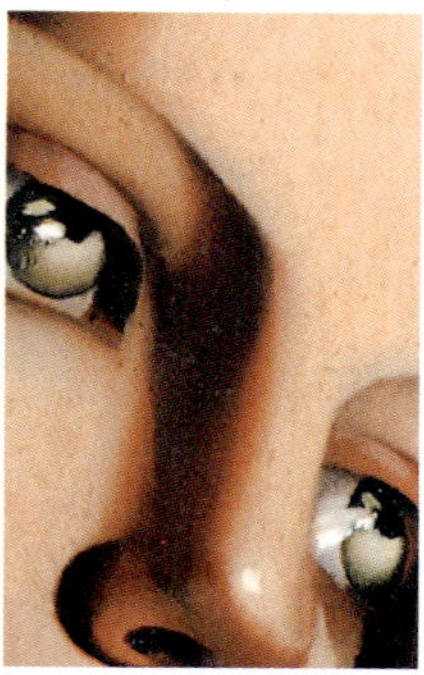

Chagall later wrote a poignant letter to the artists left behind. "I suffered for having to leave you that terrible year. It was not my destiny to sacrifice my life to Paris. The enemy was preparing a degrading death for me somewhere in Poland. I took the hospitable hand offered me by America." When the German armies arrived in Paris in June 1940, the critic Harold Rosenberg wrote "The laboratory of the twentieth century has been shut down" Now it was the turn of New York. The presence of Mondrian, Leger, André Breton and so many artists associated with the Surrealist movement triggered a cultural ferment and helped kick start the New York School. For de Lempicka though, it was the wrong place and the wrong time. She had brought a large quantity of her paintings over with her on the SS Paris. She was able to stage an exhibition at the Paul Reinhardt Gallery as early as May 1939.

The Brilliance

c. 1932
Oil on panel, 35 x 27 cm
Private Collection

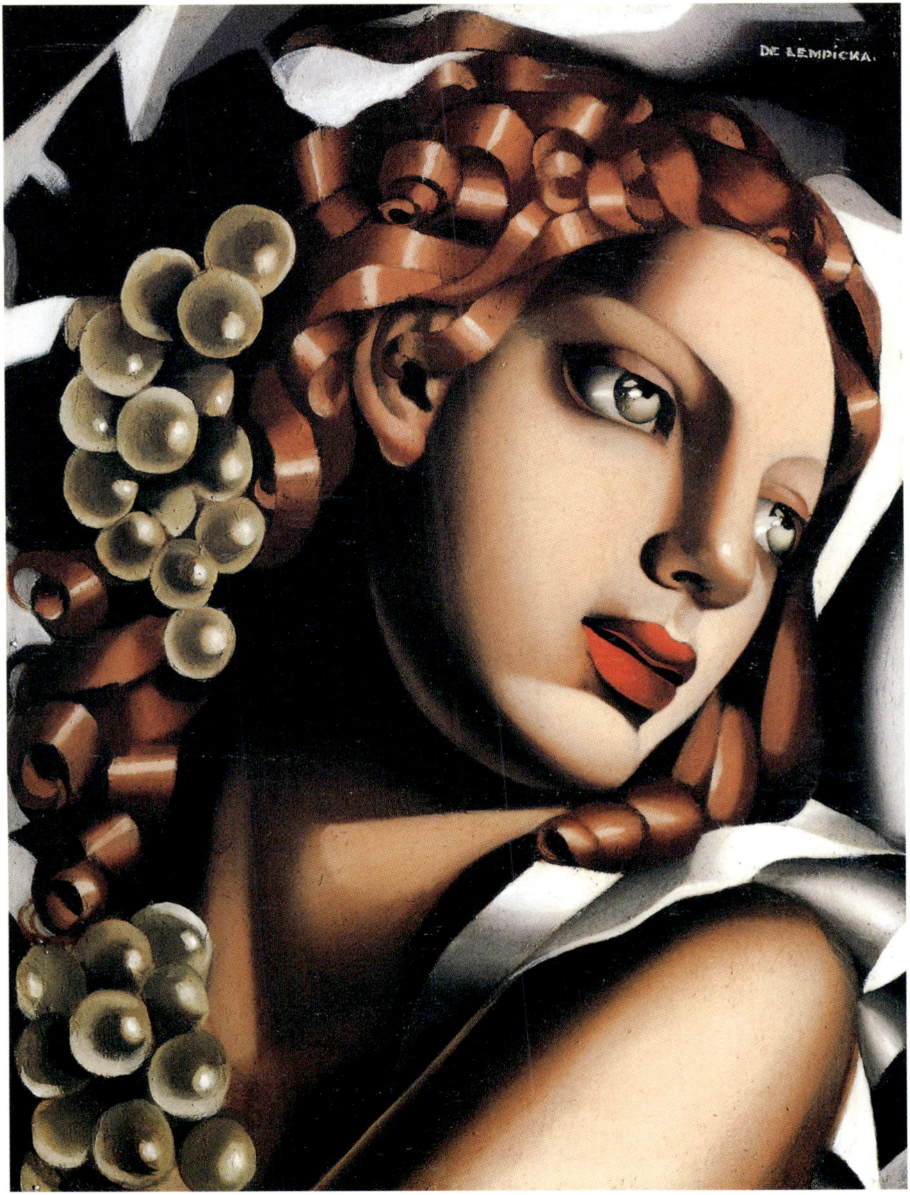
DE LEMPICKA.

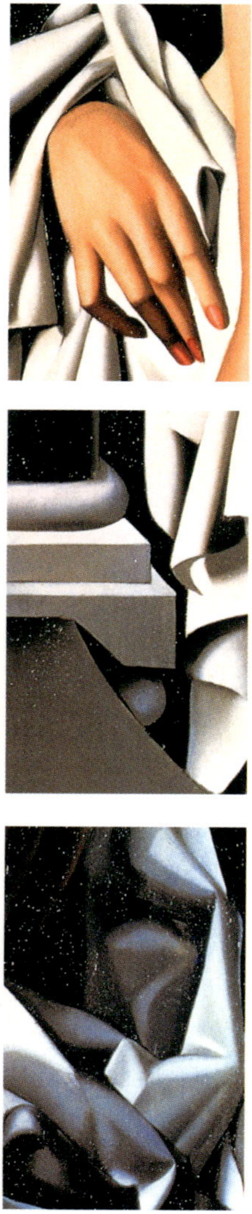

This was followed in April 1941 by a show at the Julien Levy Gallery that travelled to Los Angeles the next year. A photograph of Tamara at the opening of her 1939 exhibition shows her looking more stylish than ever with a jauntily perched fur hat and padded shoulders bigger than Joan Crawford's. The art itself though, must have seemed stale to the New York art lovers who were used to the more cutting edge shows of émigré artists put on by Pierre Matisse and Peggy Guggenheim. Though the New York shows included works from her best period, these would already have looked dated and it has to be admitted that her more recent work, though technically accomplished, lacked de Lempicka's more attractive qualities as an artist.

Portrait of Marjorie Ferry

1932
Oil on canvas, 100 x 65 cm
Private Collection

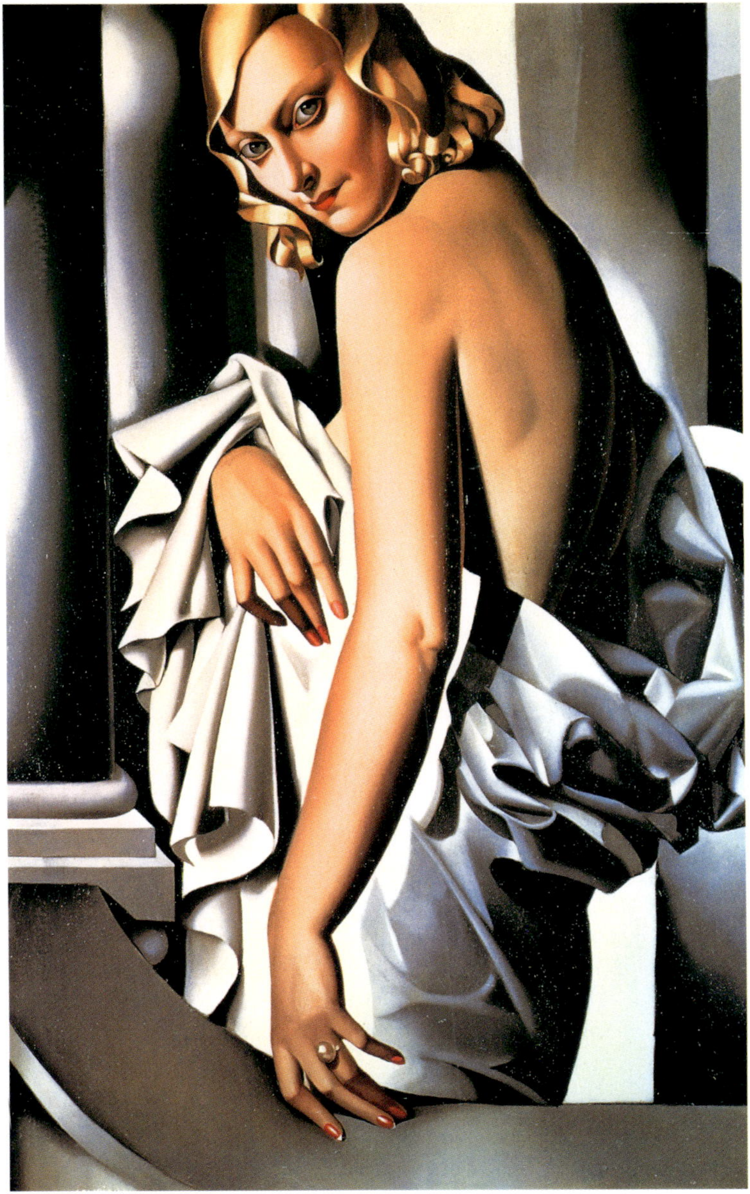

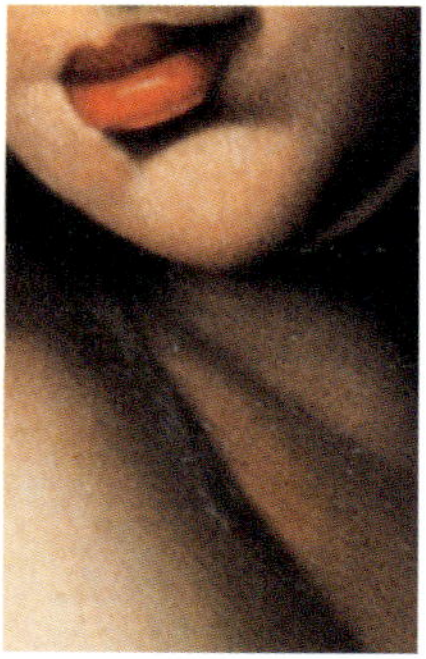

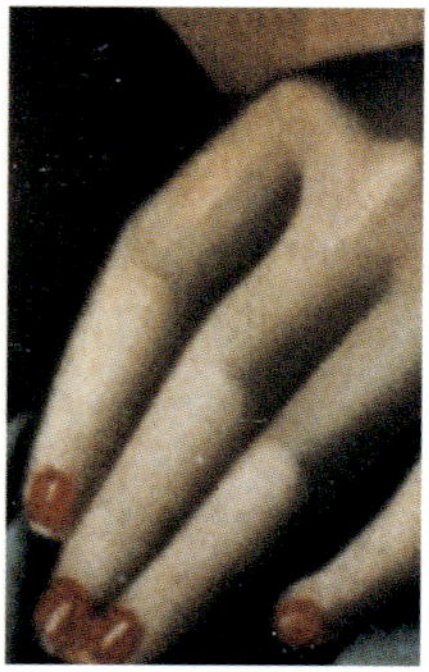

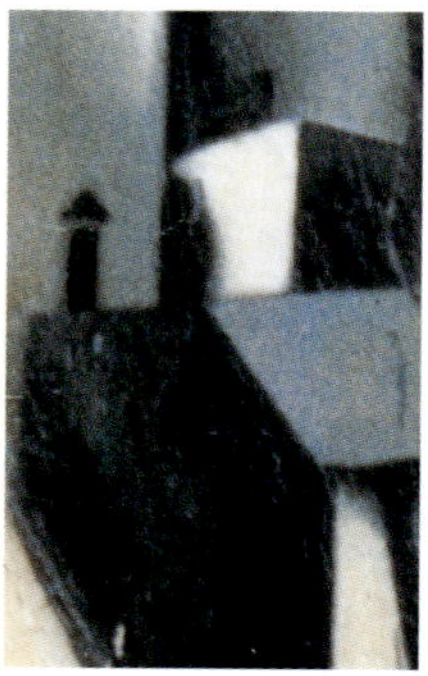

De Lempicka maintained the glossy smoothness of her Art Deco manner until the end of the 1940s but abandoned the trappings of modernity that had characterised her best work. Instead she turned to a variety of old master and nineteenth century sources to bolster her flagging inspiration. De Lempicka's painting *At the Opera* of 1941 recalls nineteenth century painters such as Renoir, Degas and Cassatt in its subject of an elegantly dressed woman in an opera box. Instead of the streamlined rectilinearity of the Art Deco phase we find the curling lines of a rather lumpen neo-Baroque. The disagreeable effect of this picture is heightened by de Lempicka's use of hot saturated colours reminiscent of an early technicolour movie.

Portrait of Suzy Solidor

1933
Oil on panel, 46 x 38 cm
Château Musée de Cagnes

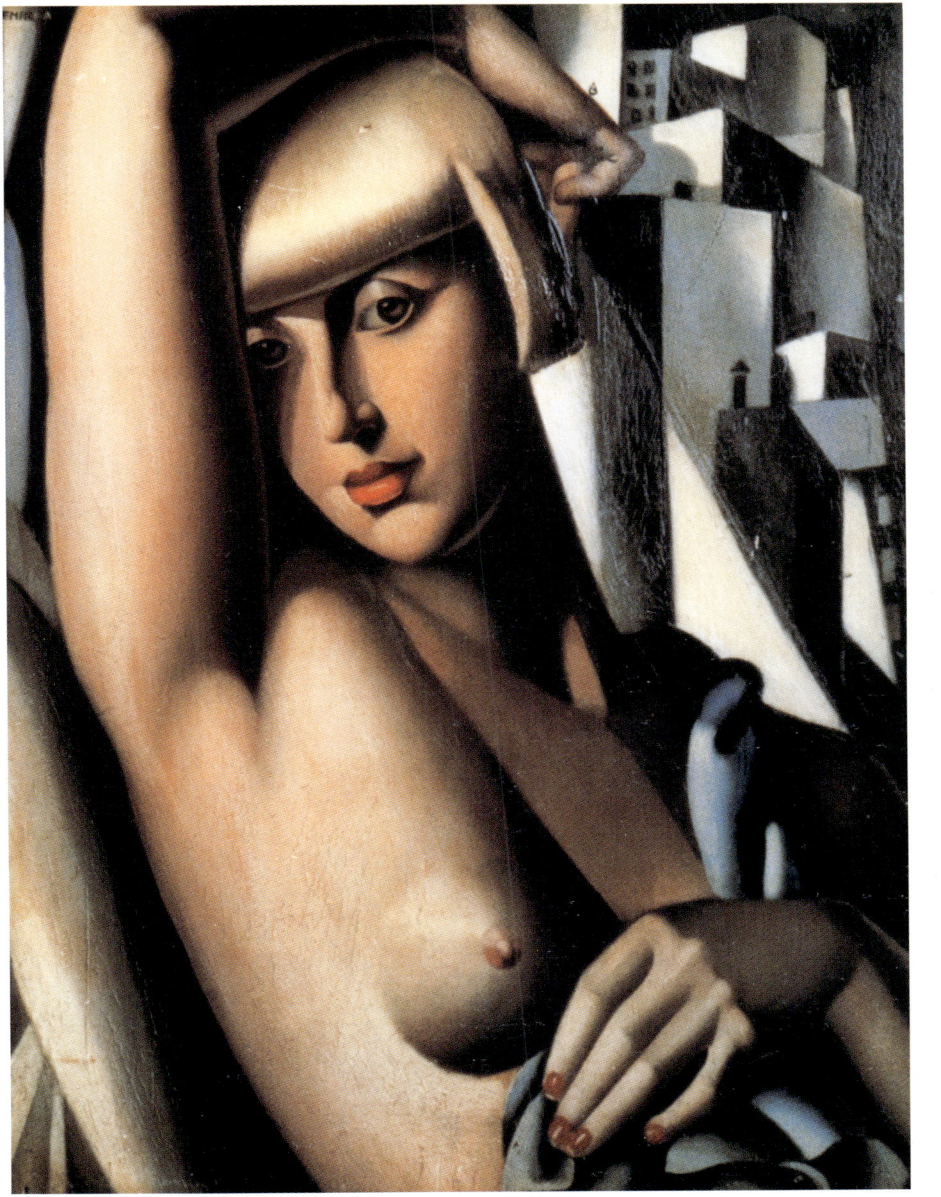

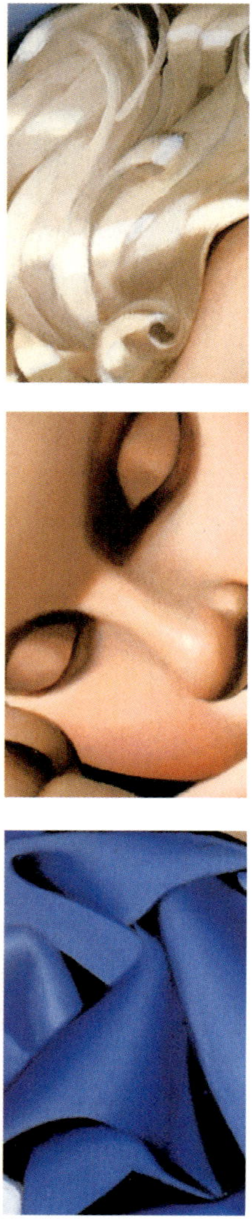

Probably de Lempicka's best works of the 1940s are her still-lives such as *Succulent and Flask* of c.1941 or *The Key* of 1946. These pictures benefit from a certain surreal strangeness. The references here, especially the post card of what seems to be a Rubens portrait pinned against the wall, indicate a new found interest in the Baroque. *The Key* with its illusionistic tricks and complex wrinkled forms looks back to Dutch still life painting, though de Lempicka's lack of interest in differentiating between surface textures is quite unlike any Dutch painting. Two works derived from that most cliched of Old Master sources Raphael's *Madonna della Sedia*, *The Orange Turban* of 1945 and *La Madonne ronde* of 1948 show just how thin de Lempicka's inspiration was running as the decade progressed.

The Sleeping Girl (Kizette) I

c. 1933
Oil on panel, 30.8 x 40.6 cm
Private Collection

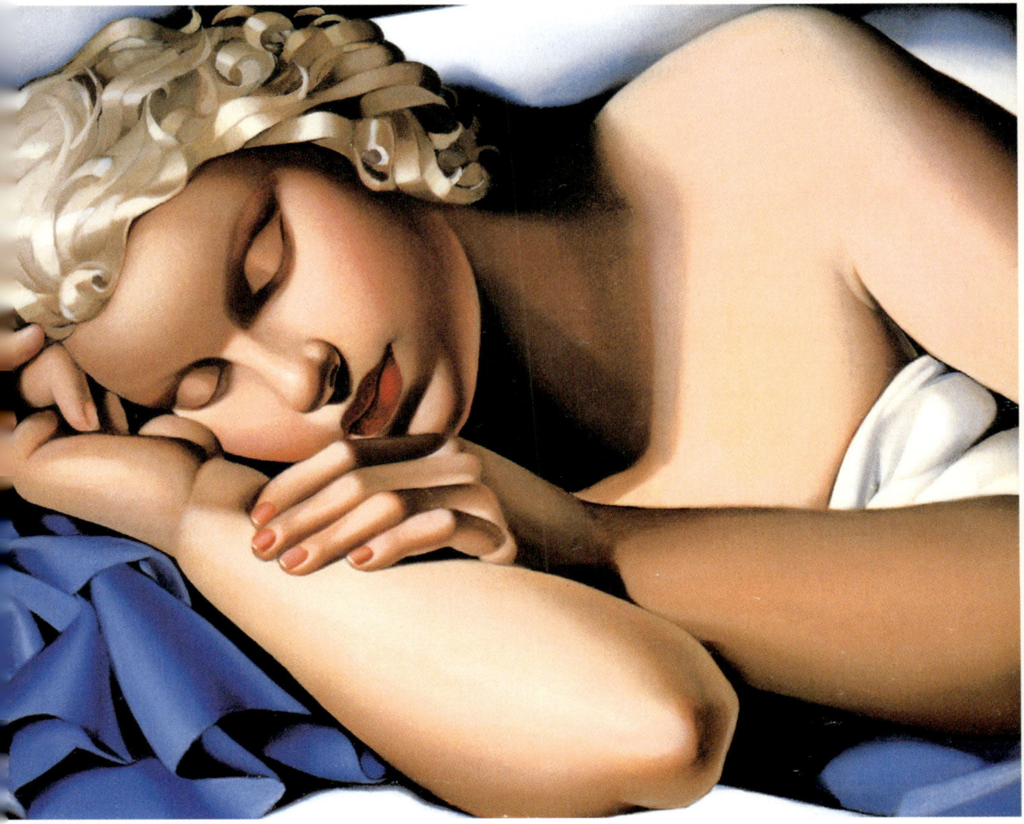

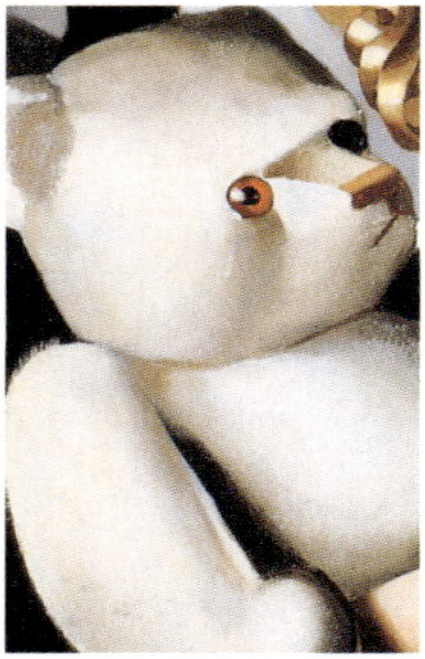

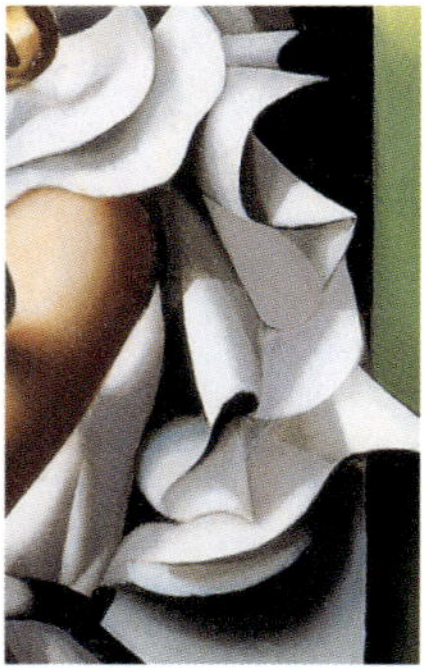

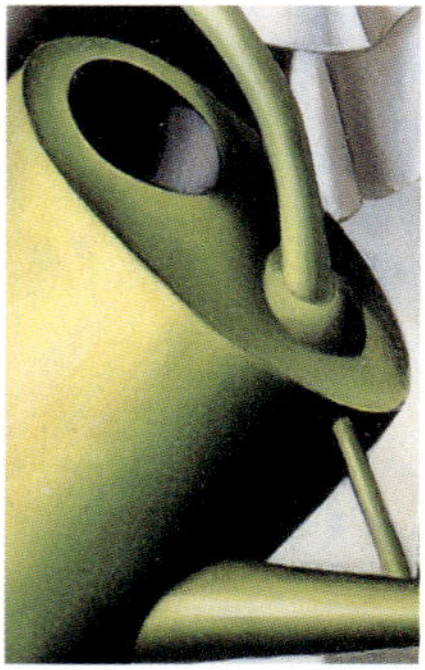

With her love of glamour and celebrity it was inevitable that de Lempicka would have been attracted to Hollywood. In 1940 the Kuffners moved there for an extended stay. An obviously posed photograph shows de Lempicka boarding the Union Pacific train for Los Angeles and sporting a gardenia, a fur coat thrown nonchalantly over her shoulder and an outrageously fashionable hat. She has the distant, unfocussed expression of a star in a publicity still. De Lempicka was still a strikingly beautiful woman and may have hoped for some new kind of career in Hollywood, even for roles on screen.

Portrait of Miss Poum Rachou

1933
Oil on canvas, 92 x 46 cm
Private Collection

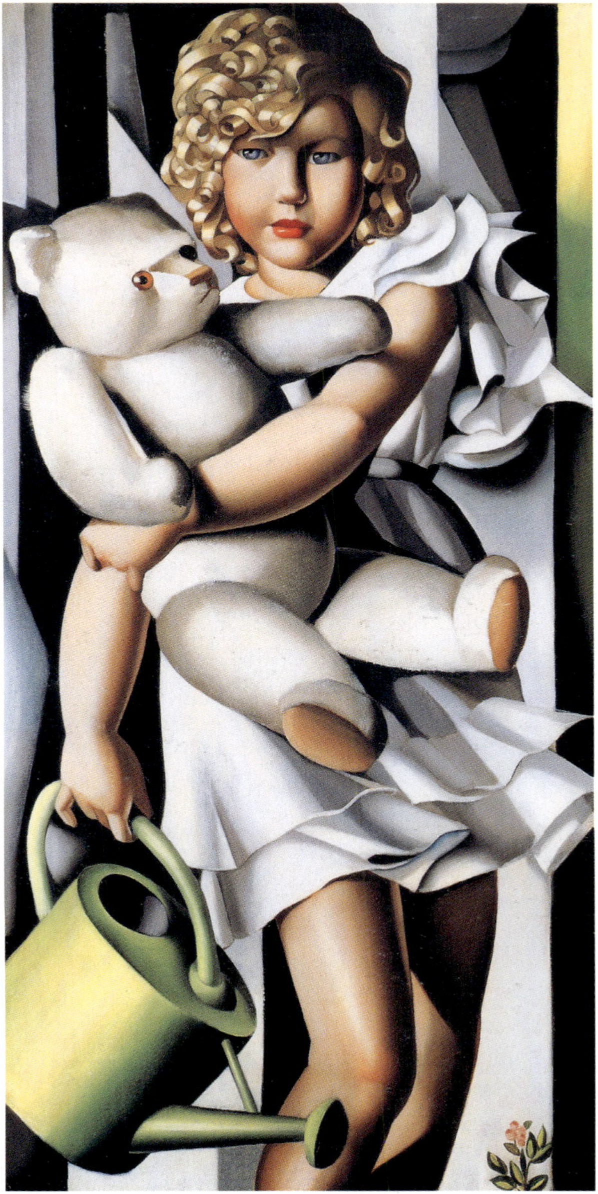

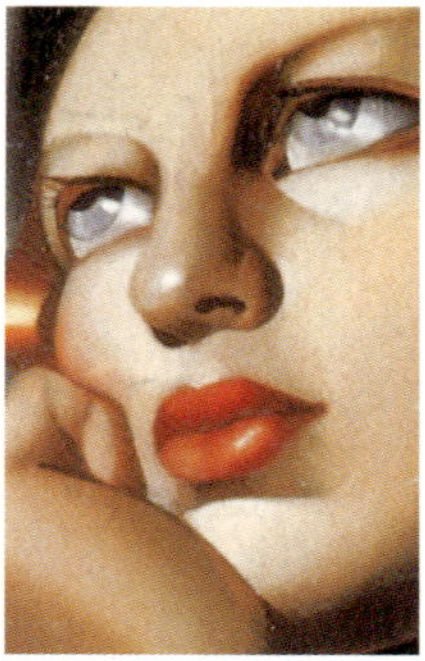
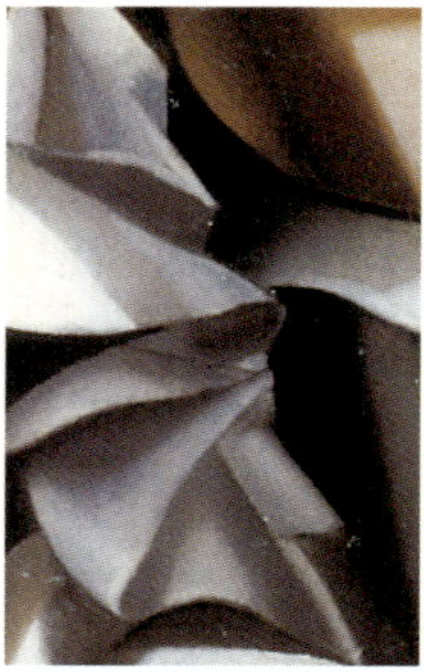
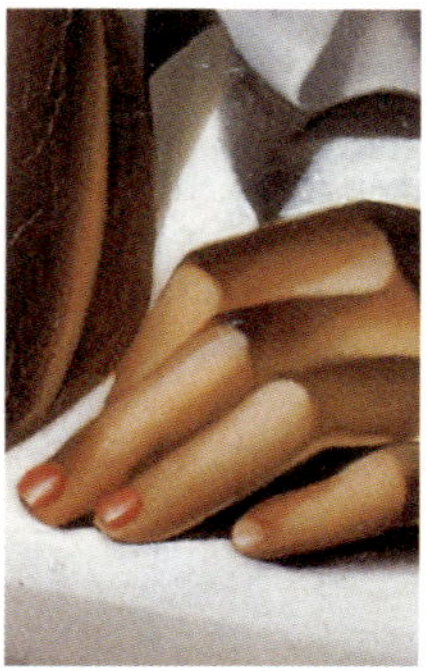

With their central and eastern European backgrounds, the Kuffners may have felt more at home in Hollywood than on the East Coast. The Hollywood film industry itself had been the creation of entrepreneurial Russian and Hungarian Jews in the period before and after the First World War. Even before the rise of Hitler, Hollywood had depended upon a constant flow of talent from Europe. Trading on her title as well as her good looks, Tamara slipped easily into the upper echelons of the Los Angeles social world, getting a great deal of press coverage as *The Baroness with the Brush* and receiving such stars as Greta Garbo, Tyrone Power and Dolores del Rio in her studio.

Wide Brimmed Hat

1933
Oil on panel, 46 x 38 cm
Private Collection

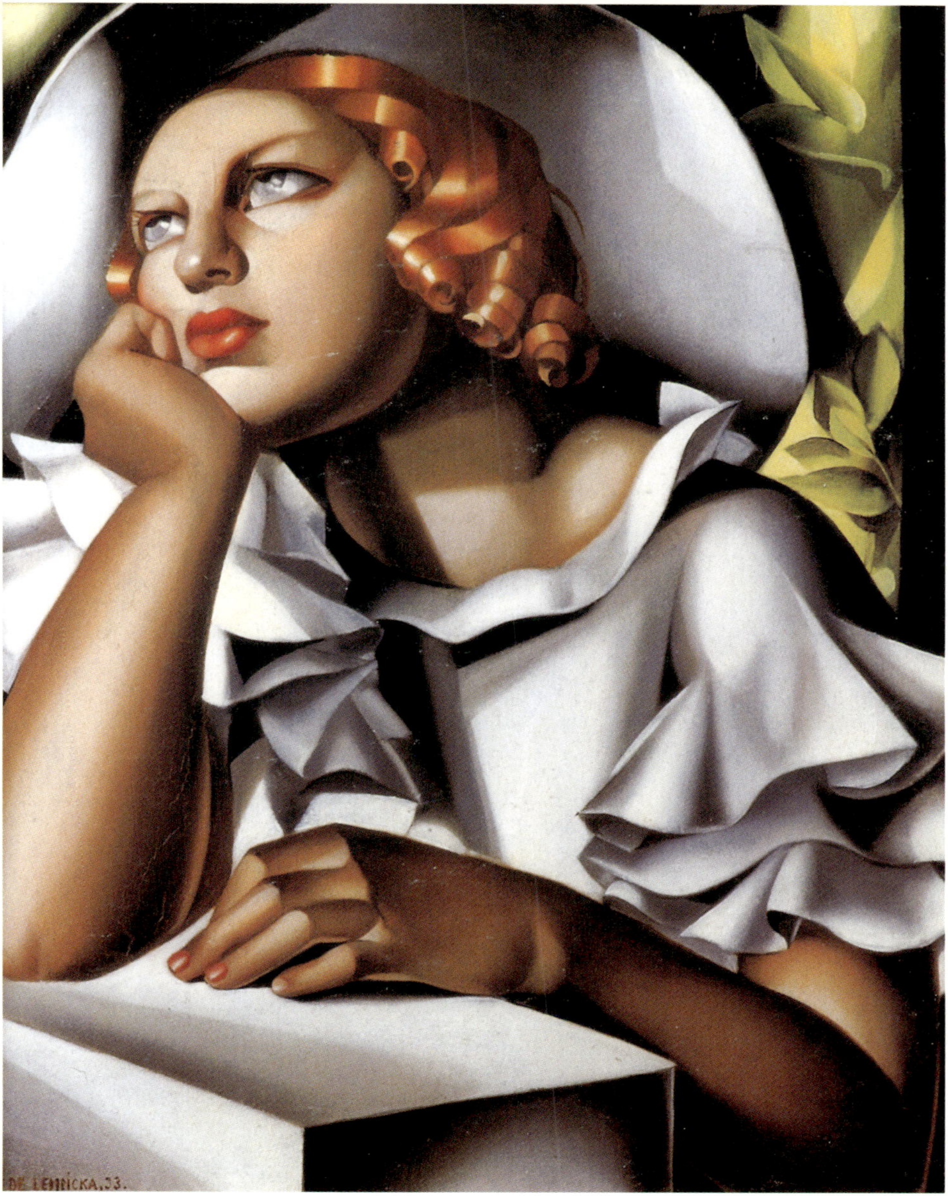
DE LEMPICKA.33.

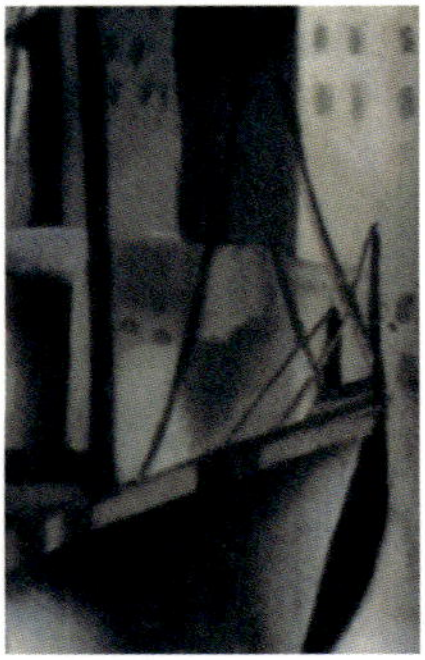

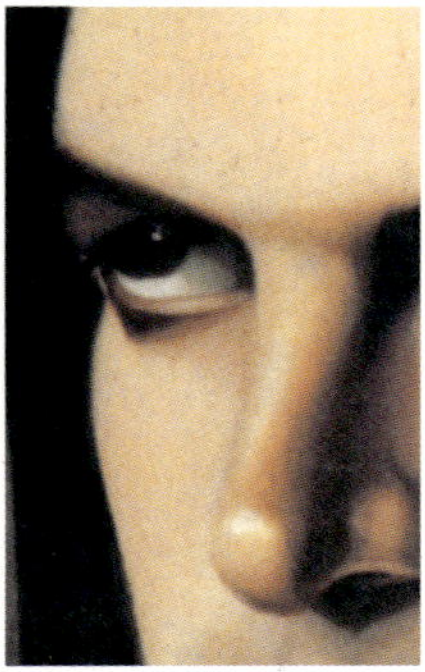

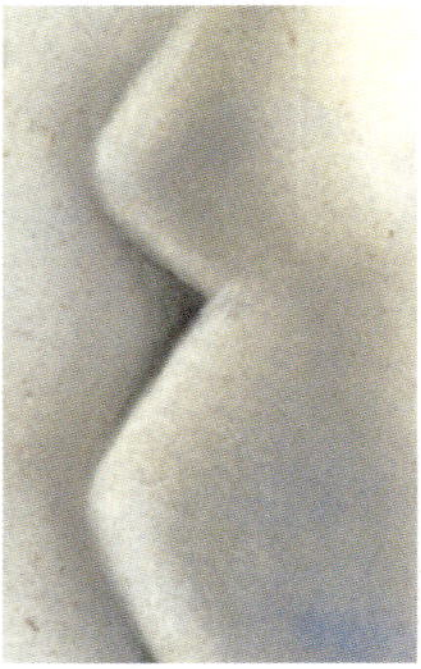

In 1940, the year she arrived in Hollywood, de Lempicka pulled a stunt worthy of a Hollywood publicity department or the story line of a Preston Sturges comedy when she announced to the female students of U.C.L.A. that she was looking for a nude model for a painting of *Susannah and the Elders.* Tamara had the pleasure of "auditioning" over a hundred young women who came to her studio to take their clothes off.

Somewhat belatedly at this time de Lempicka also remembered her Polishness, working for the Paderewski Fund, amongst other war relief causes.

Portrait of Count Vettor Marcello

c. 1933
Oil on panel, 35 x 27 cm
Private Collection

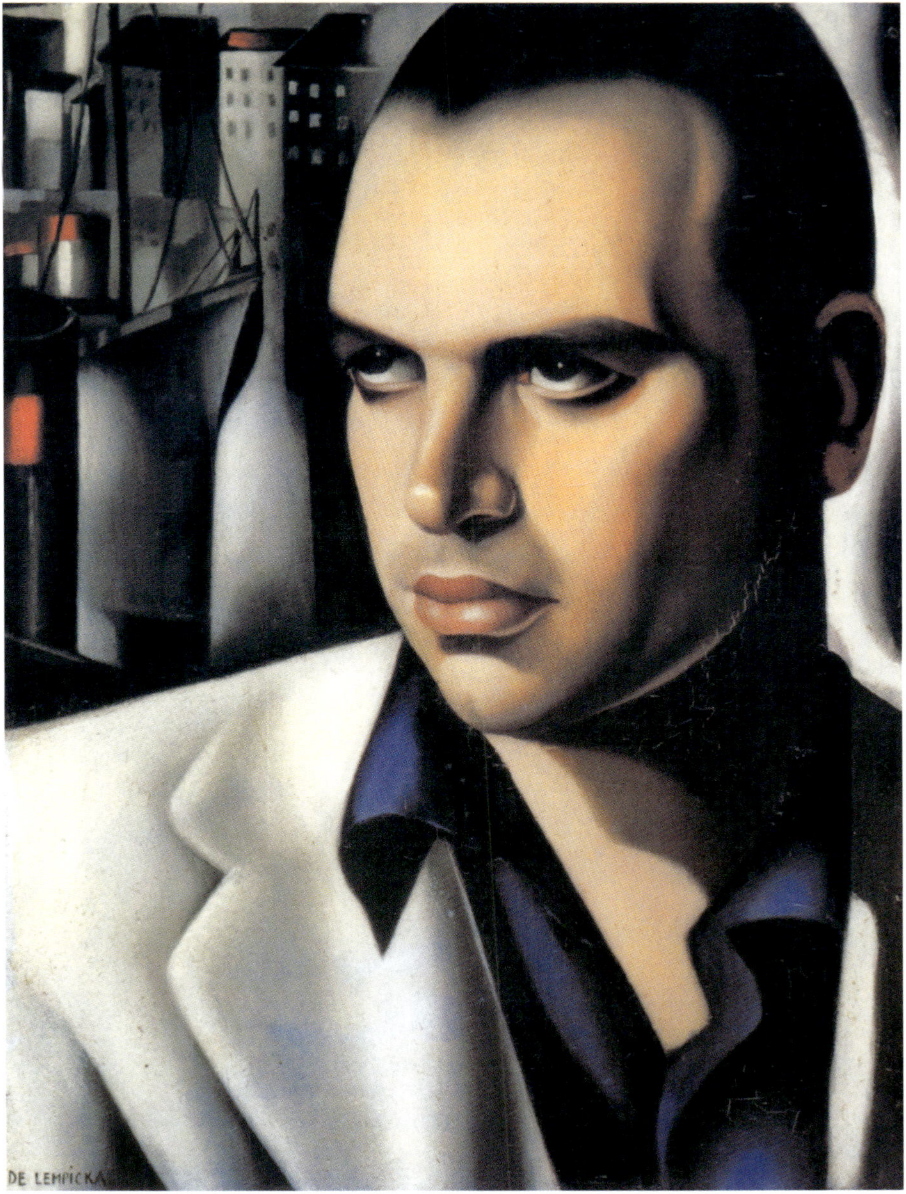
DE LEMPICKA

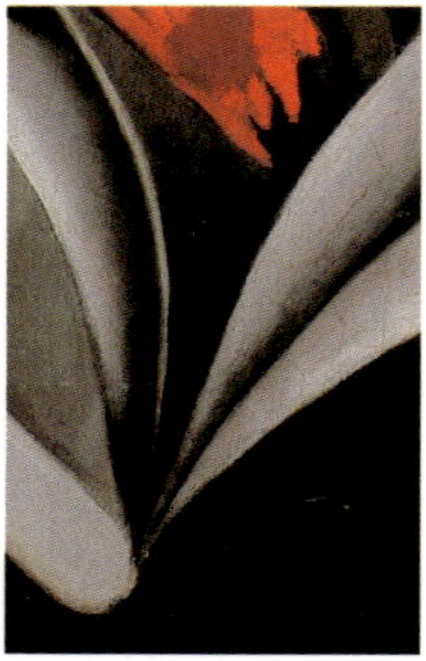

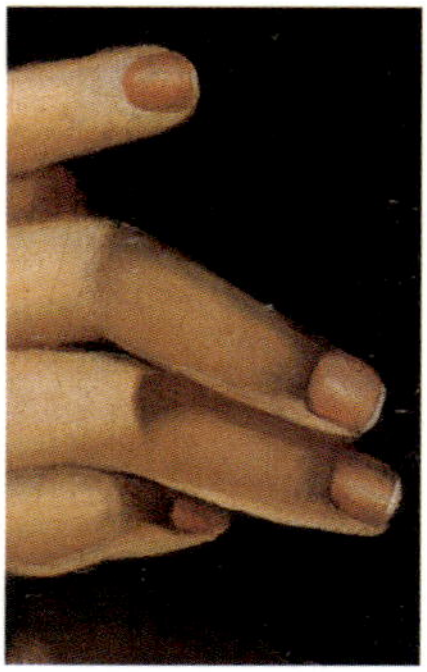

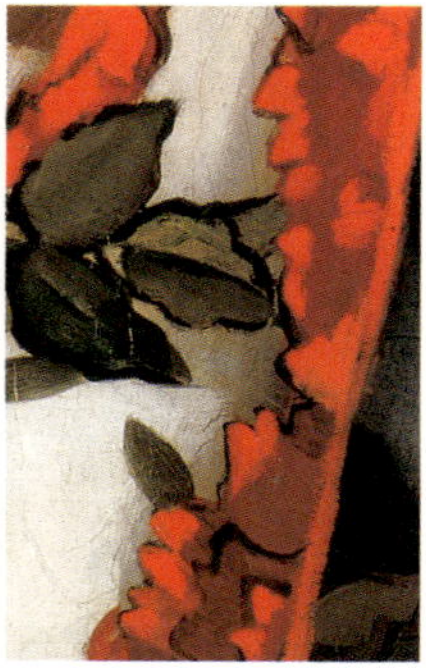

In 1942 Baron Kuffner finally tired of their life in Hollywood and insisted upon returning to New York. They bought a spacious apartment in the best part of town at 322 East 57th Street where they remained based until the Baron's death. Post war photographs of the interiors of this apartment show them looking somewhat like film sets. There are none of de Lempicka's own paintings visible. Instead the apartment was decorated with art works and heavy antique furniture retrieved from the Baron's central European estates. Though de Lempicka continued her painting in a somewhat desultory fashion, her energies seem to have been devoted mainly to her life as a New York socialite.

The Polish Girl

1933
Oil on panel, 35 x 27 cm
Private Collection

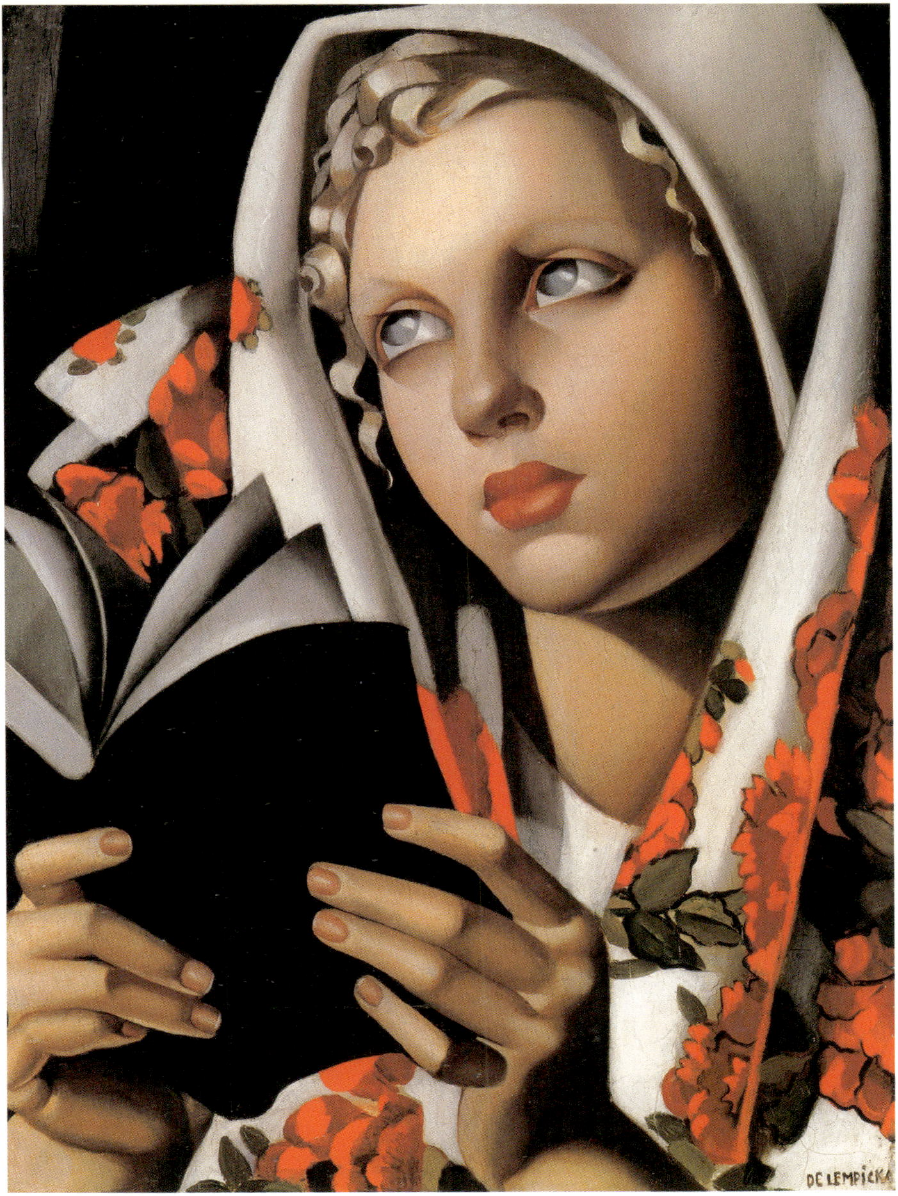
DE LEMPICKA

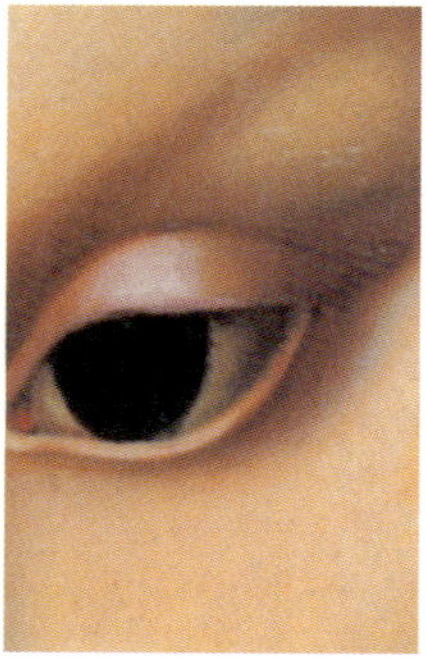

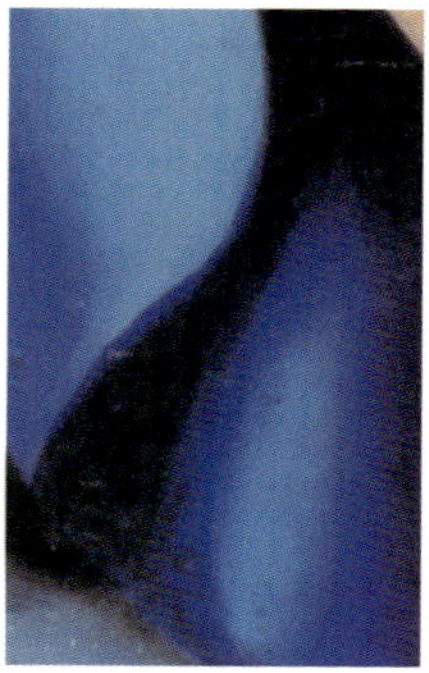

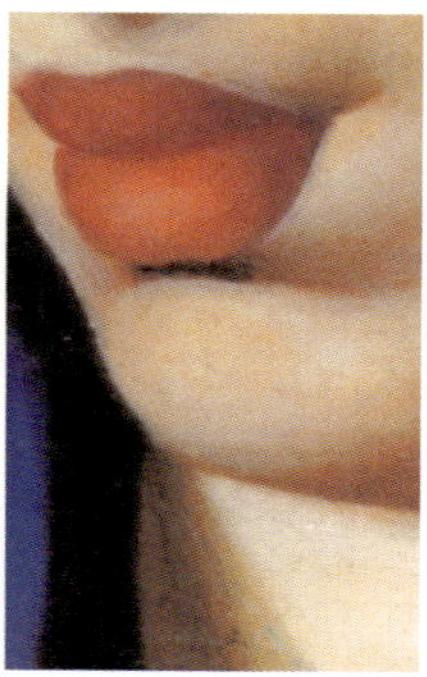

The truly terrible *Mexican Woman* painted in the late 1940s shows de Lempicka's Art Deco style at its most debased and exhausted. With the patronising attitude of a bored socialite de Lempicka paints the picturesque and nubile peasant in a style so bland and kitschy that it reminds the viewer of the crude and lurid reproductions of paintings of Oriental women that sold in vast numbers in chain stores in the 1950s. De Lempicka's art could sink no lower and it was time for radical change.

Madonina

c. 1934
Oil on copper, 18 x 12.8 cm
Private Collection

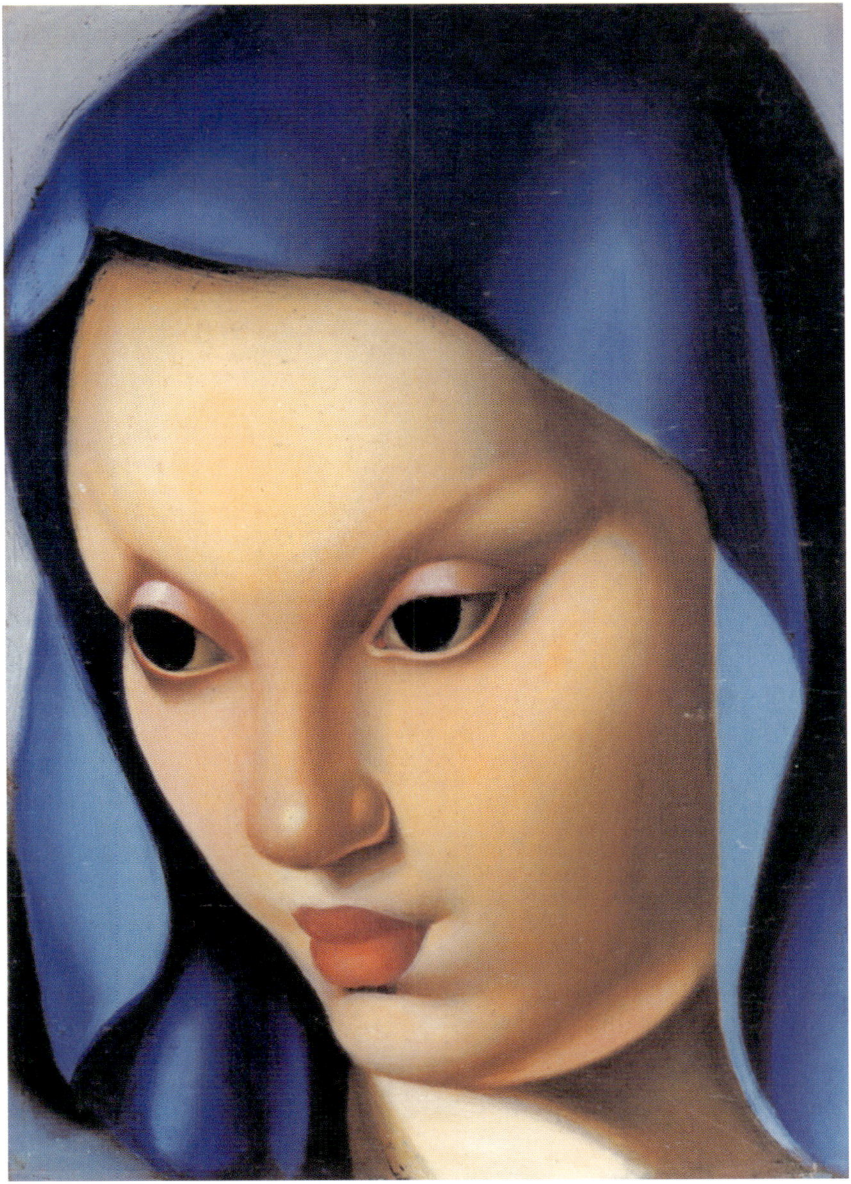

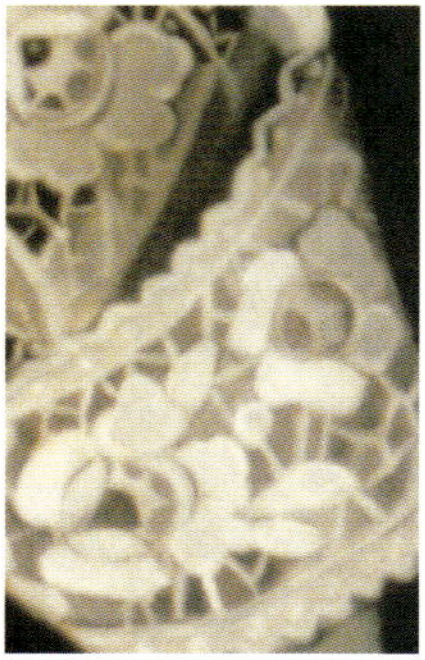

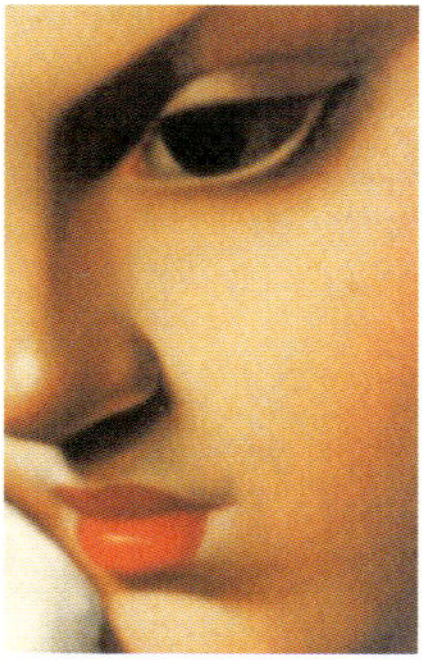

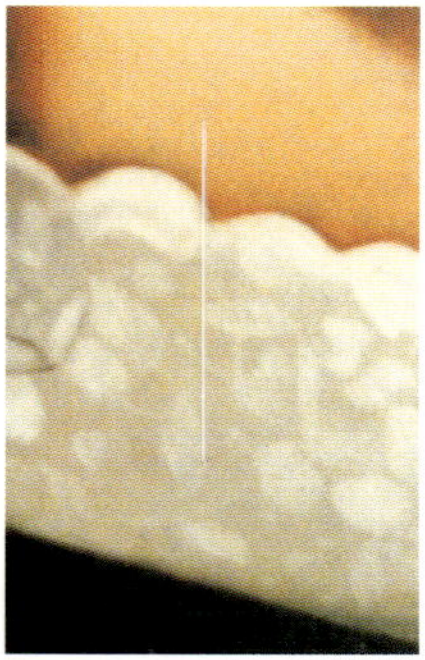

From 1949 de Lempicka travelled again in Europe. A photograph taken around this time shows her once again installed in her rue Mechain studio. The Art Deco interior is still intact but enriched by a large plaster cast of a classical head. De Lempicka wears a full-skirted New Look evening dress with bare shoulders and appears to work on what is very evidently a pre-war picture but with the 1940 painting *Escape* beside her.

The late 1940s saw the triumph of Abstract Expressionism. For many critics figuration was a thing of the past. It took considerable courage and conviction to swim against the tide and continue with figuration as did Balthus, Edward Hopper, Stanley Spencer and Lucian Freud. Other artists such as Victor Passmore and de Lempicka herself gave up the unequal struggle and jumped on the bandwagon of abstraction.

The Breton Girl

1934
Oil on panel, 31 x 29 cm
Private Collection

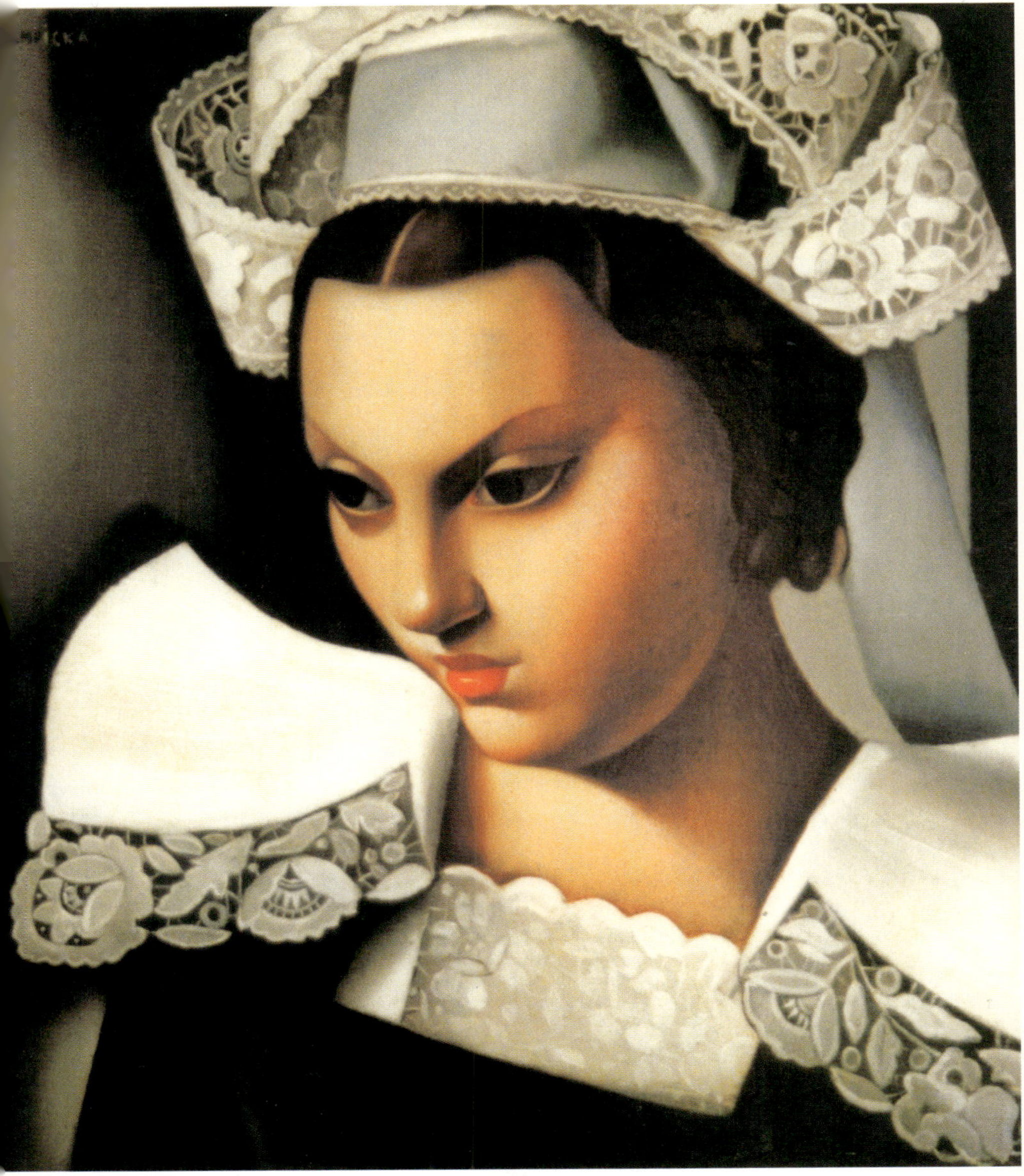

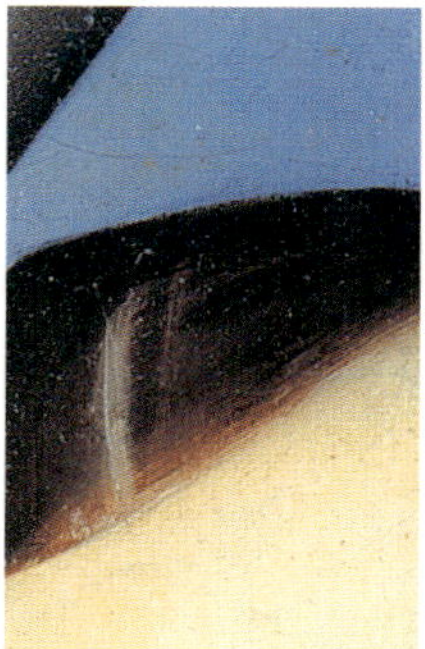

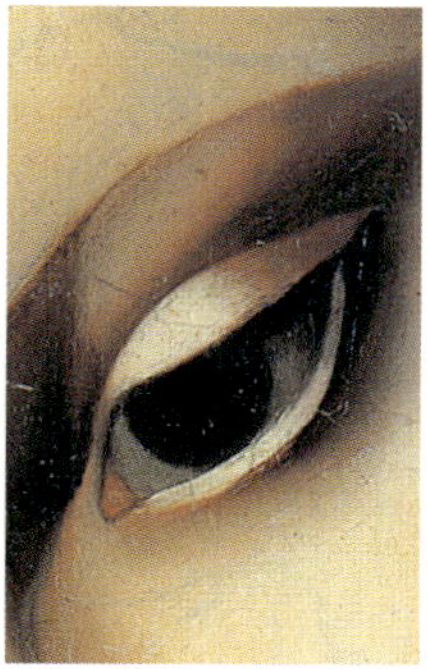

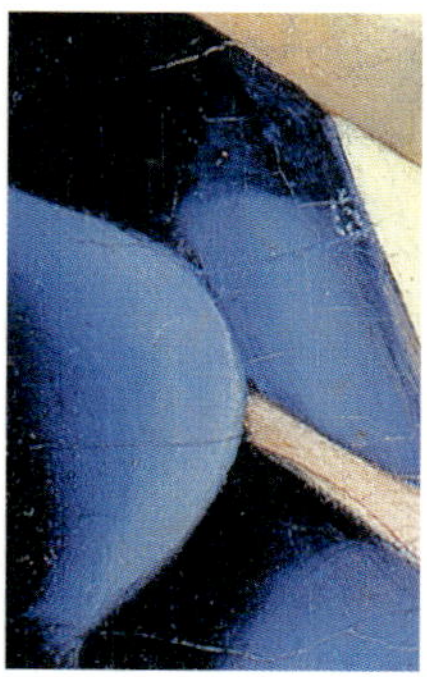

Starting in 1953 de Lempicka painted abstractions in a smooth hard edged style that had more to do with 1920s Purist Abstraction than with the gestural, painterly abstraction of 1950s New York. These paintings recapture some of the dynamism and "modern" feel of her work of the late 20s and early 30s and are mercifully free of the mawkish sentimentality that had marred her work since the late 1930s. But by the 1950s de Lempicka's "modern" already looked antique. A series of exhibitions between 1955 and 1961 in Paris, Milan and New York failed to attract any interest.

The Blue Virgin

1934
Oil on panel, 20 x 13.5 cm
Private Collection

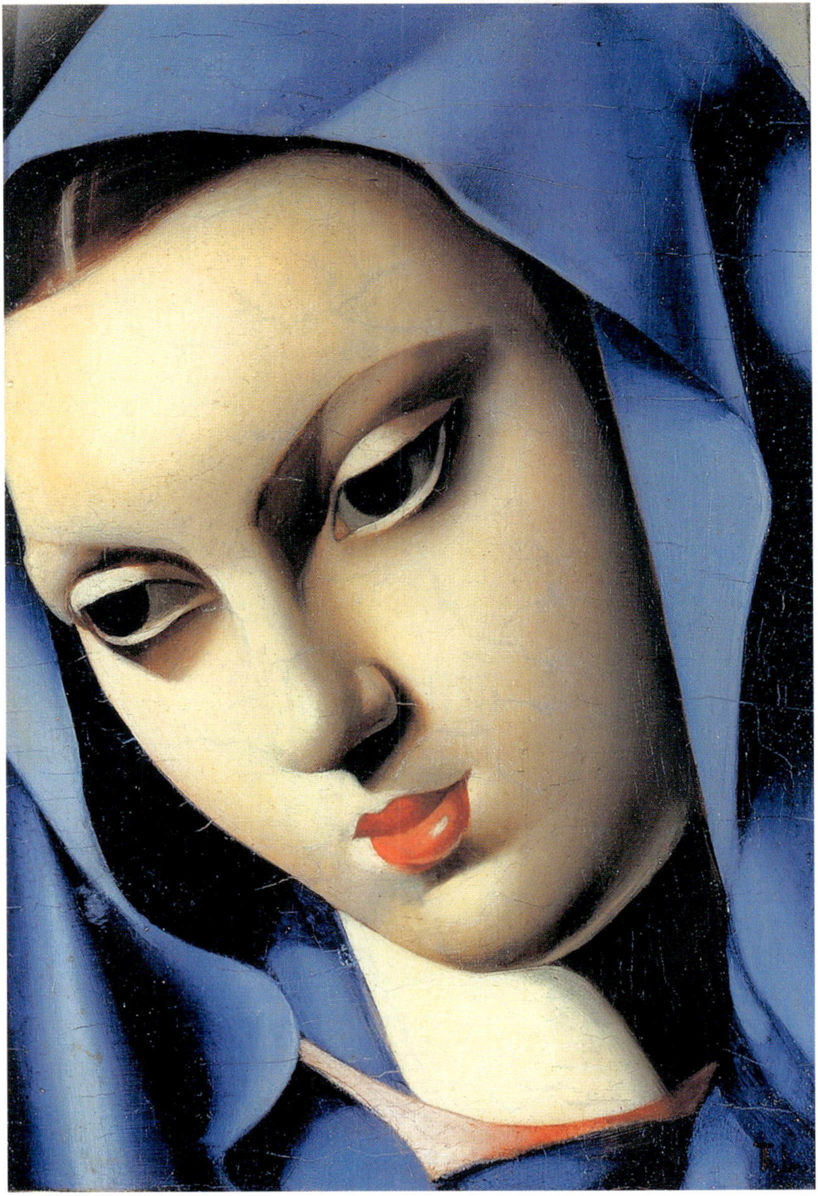

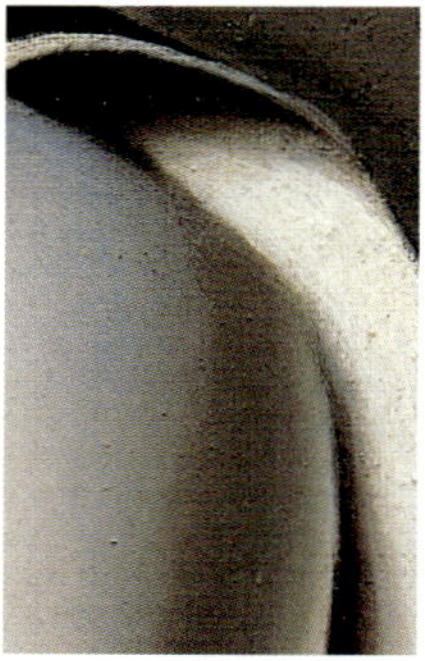

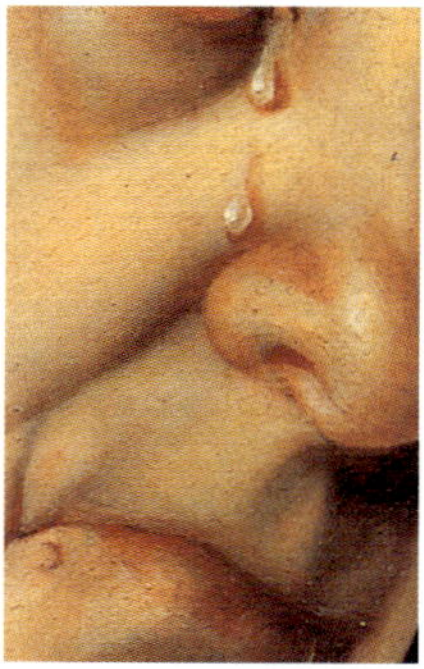

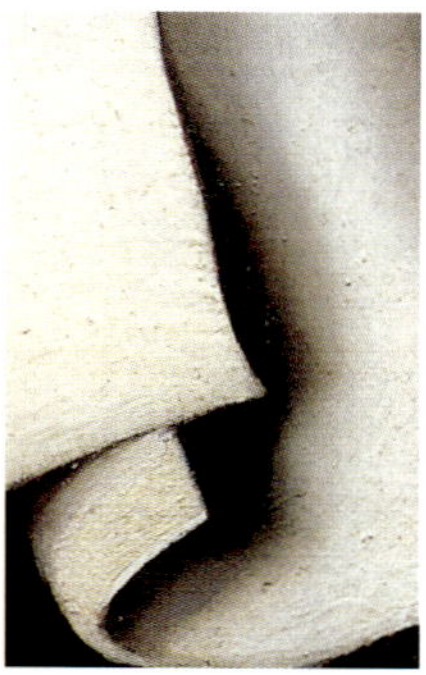

Another radical change of direction in the 1960s failed to bring any dividends either. De Lempicka returned to figurative painting. Working in a pale, pinkish palette and applying the paint with a palette knife, she arrived at a painterly technique for which she had absolutely no aptitude. These works of the 60s seem to be the negation of everything that had characterised her best work. A view of Venice in the rain painted in the 1960s has all the banality of a cheap tourist souvenir or a greetings card. Still worse were her attempts to repaint some of her old themes in the new style, such as the *Girl with Guitar* of 1963.

The Mother Superior

1935
Oil on canvas, laid down, 30 x 20 cm
Musée des beaux-Arts de Nantes

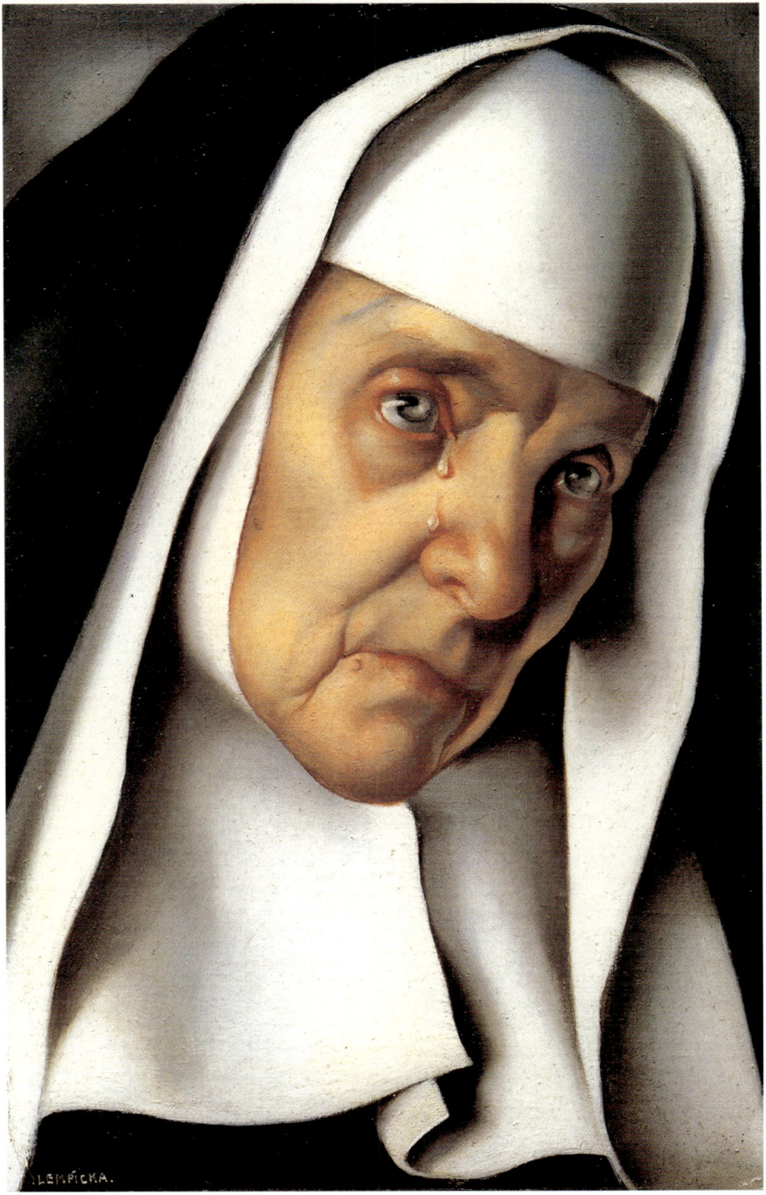
LEMPICKA.

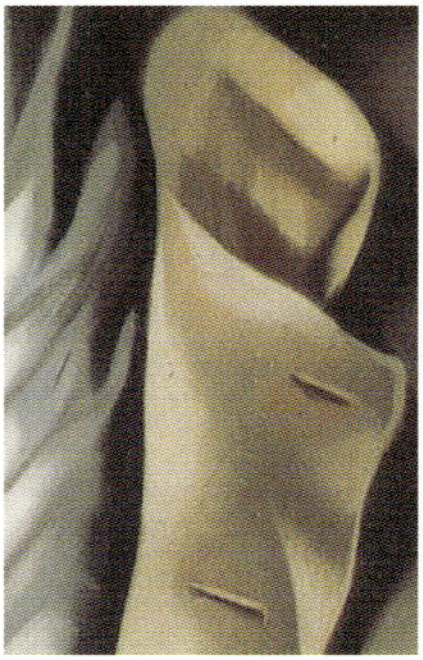

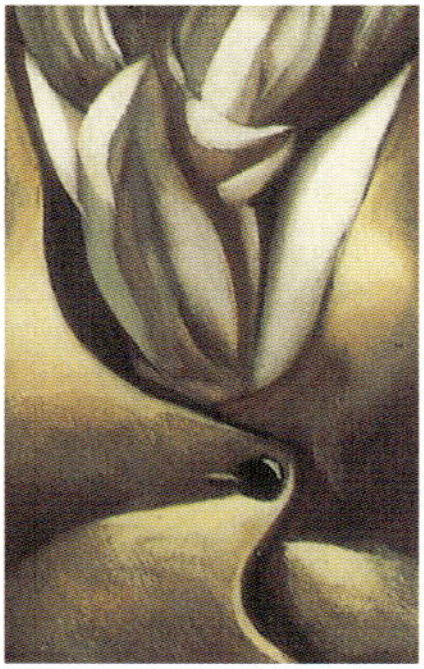

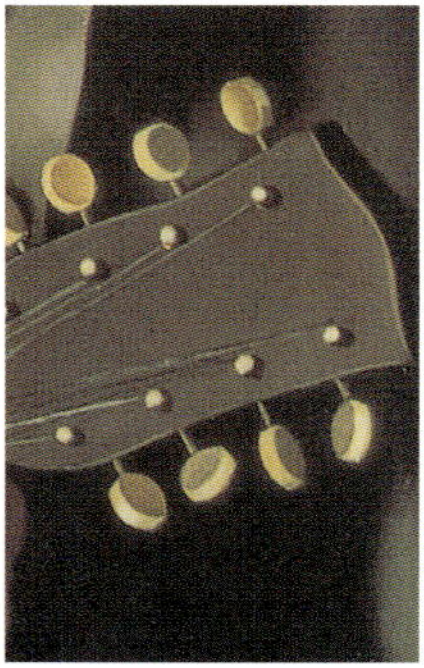

The 1960s marked the lowest ebb in de Lempicka's life as well as her art. In 1961 Baron Kuffner who had given Tamara unstinting love and protection for over thirty years died on a return voyage across the Atlantic. After the failure of several exhibitions, de Lempicka ceased to exhibit altogether.

After Kuffner's death, Tamara set off on three world voyages, one after another and after selling up her New York apartment descended upon Houston to be near her daughter who had married a geologist named Harold Foxhall (nicknamed *Foxy*) who worked for the firm of Dow Chemical. From this point Kizette was forced to take over the role of her deceased step-father as protector, secretary and general factotum to her imperious mother.

Beggar with Mandolin

1935
Oil on canvas, 67 x 51 cm
Musée départemental de l'Oise, Beauvais

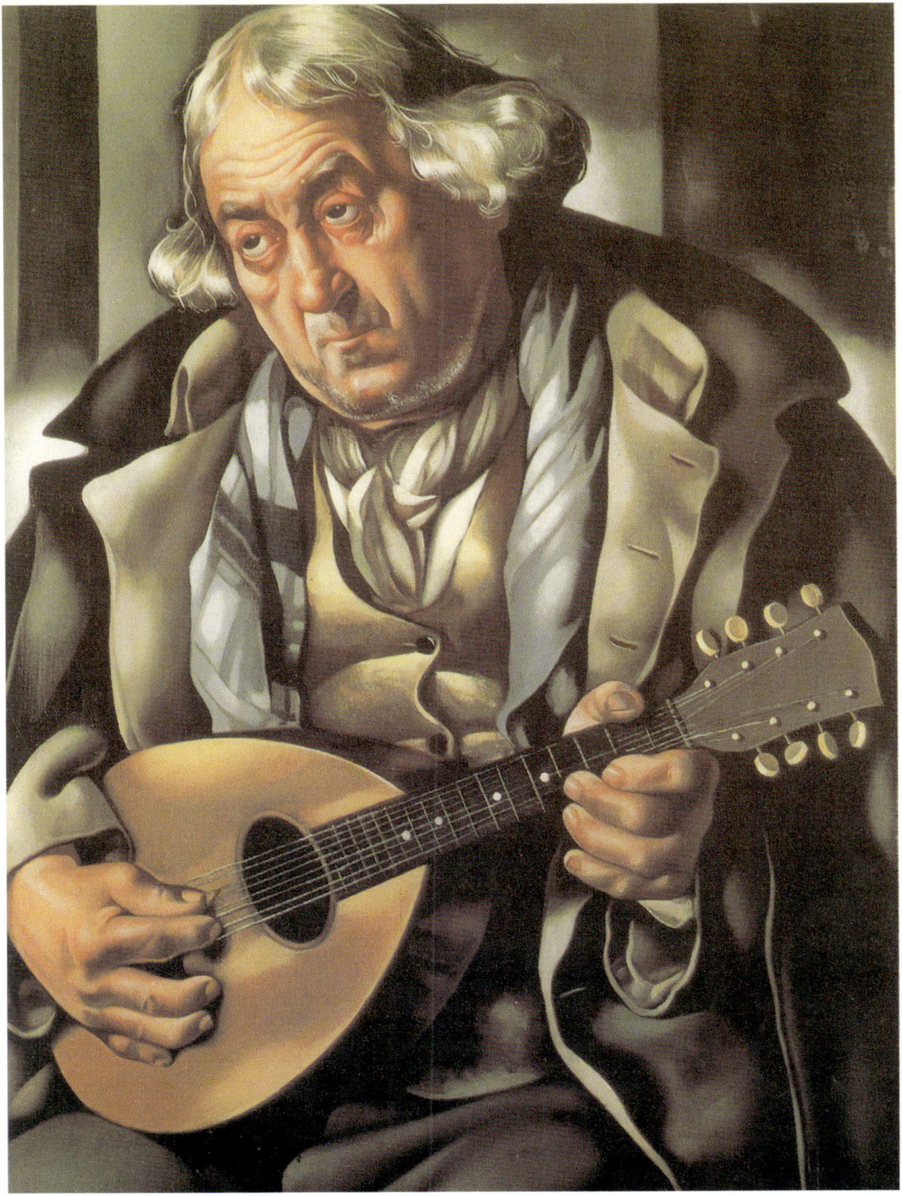

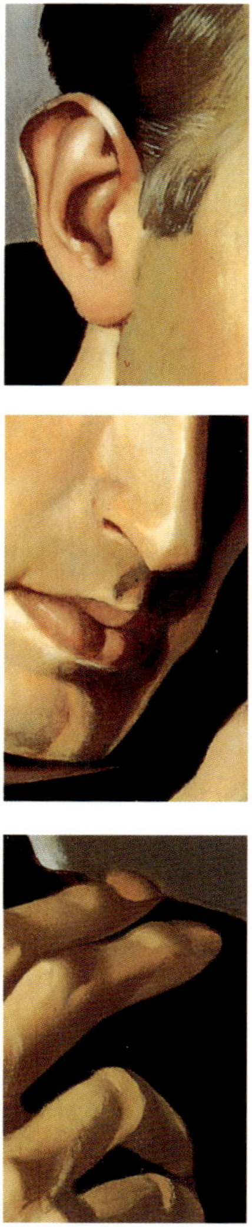

As Kizette de Lempicka-Foxhall was the chief source of information for the Charles Phillips biography that is likely to remain the most authoritative account of Tamara de Lempicka's life and her colourful and complex personality, it is inevitable that we see this turbulent mother-daughter relationship through the eyes of the daughter. However there is plenty of corroborative evidence from friends and admirers of de Lempicka and indeed from Tamara's own words that she could be a domineering and manipulative monster and that her relationship with her daughter was in many ways abusive.

Saint Anthony

c. 1936
Oil on panel, 34.9 x 27 cm
Private Collection

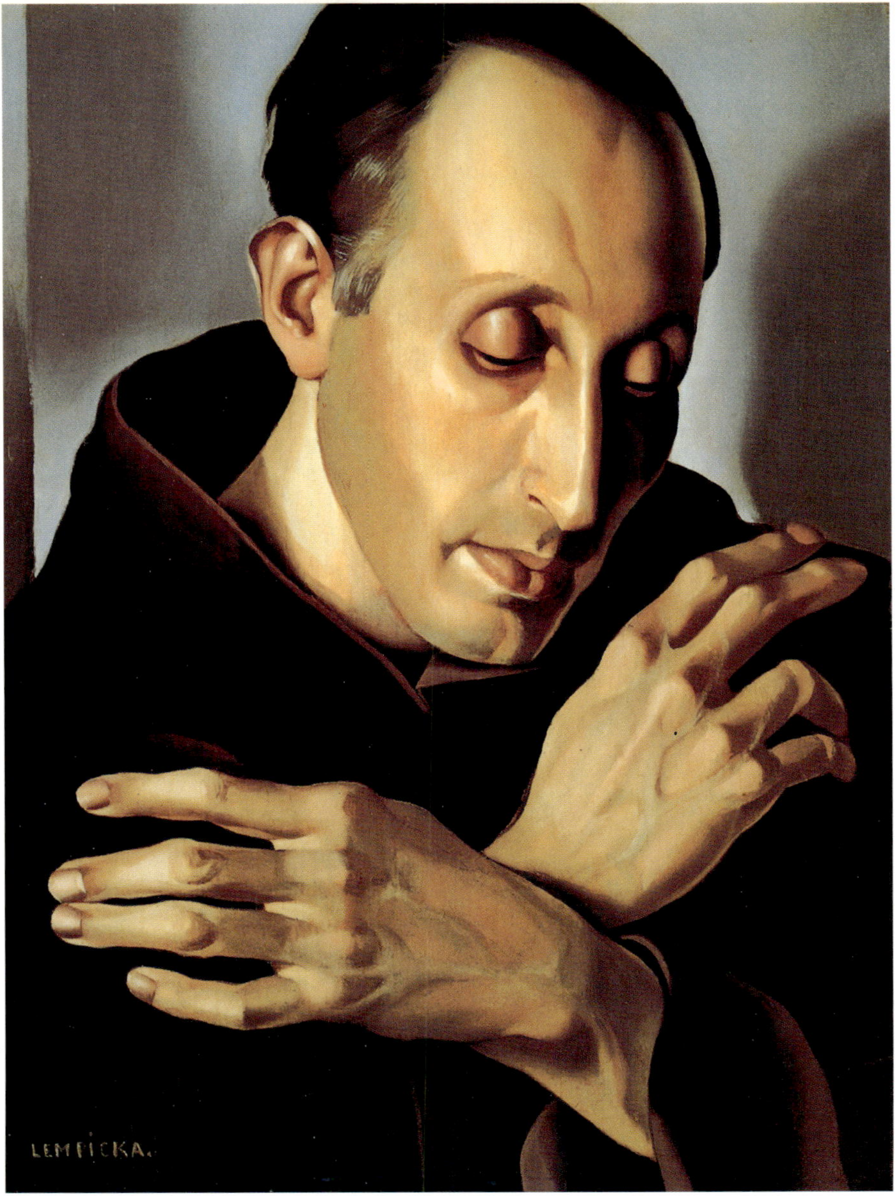
LEMPICKA.

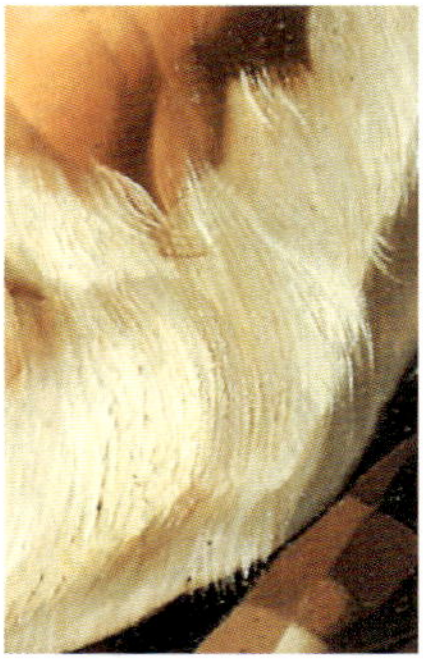
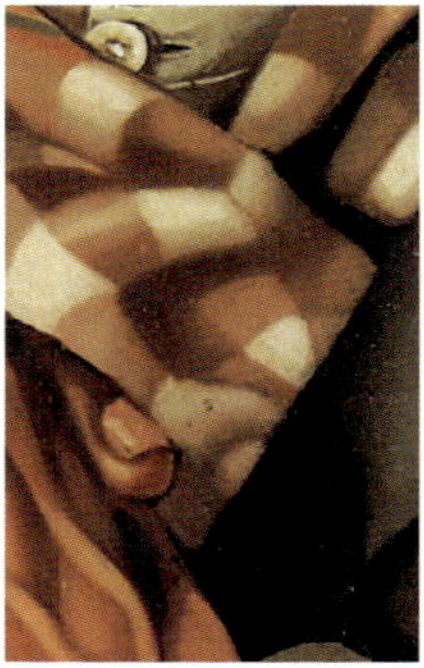
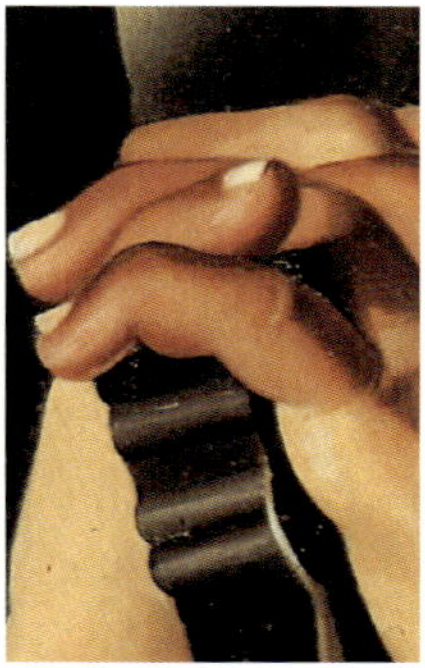

As a friend of both mother and daughter put it 'Anything Tamara did not like, she would change. Even her daughter. "I don't like your hair. Do your hair this way. Here change that dress. You must wear this. If you don't I won't take you out". She would not allow anyone to be themselves.'

Never very maternal, her chief interest in her daughter as a child, when she was not packed off to boarding schools, was as a model for such dubious portraits as *Kizette on the Balcony* of 1927 and *Kizette in Pink* where she appears as jail bait for paedophiles or the sickly *La Communicante* of 1929 with its fake piety. Even later on in life Tamara often seems to have treated her daughter as an embarrassing encumbrance. When Kizette came to visit her mother in New York she was introduced as her sister.

The Peasant Man

c. 1937
Oil on canvas, laif down, 40 x 28.5 cm
Private Collection

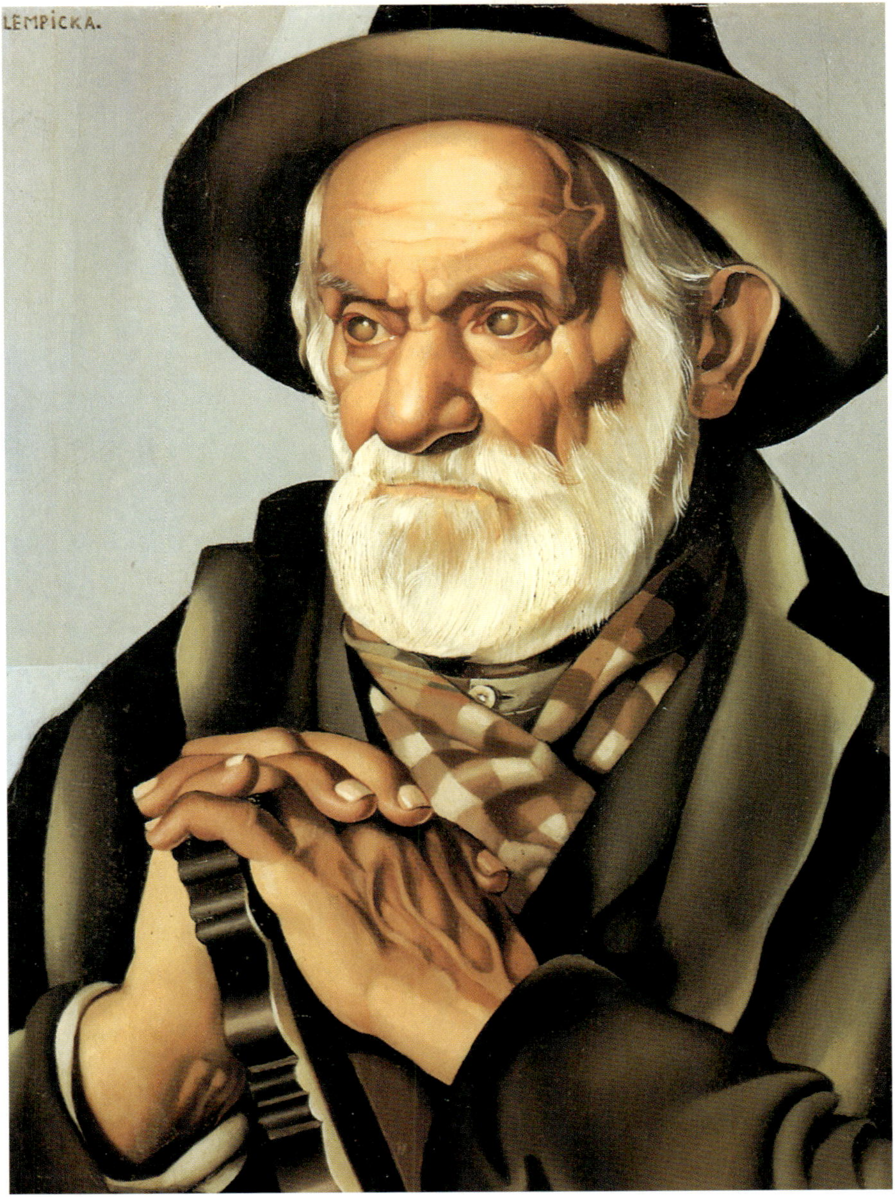
LEMPICKA.

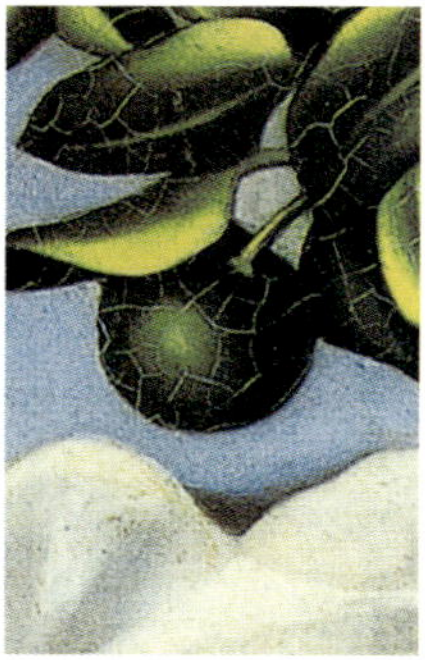

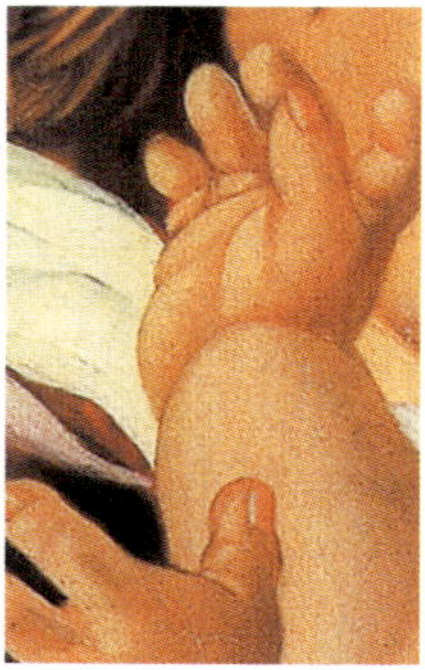

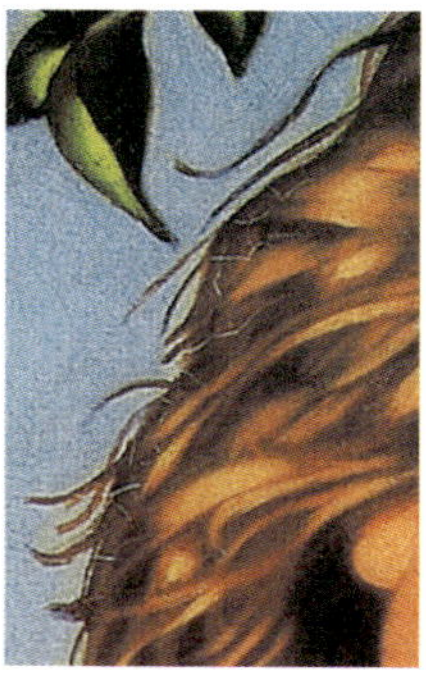

De Lempicka certainly sounds on occasion to have been the grandmother from hell as well. Amongst the countless anecdotes of her bad behaviour on a heroic scale one stands out as worthy of the great film script of her life. When Kizette's daughter Victoria (nicknamed *Putti* by Tamara) accepted a marriage proposal from a young Argentinian, Tamara was outraged not to have been the first to have been approached for permission. Her revenge was exacted on the day of the wedding reception "Kizette had invited dozens of guests to her house in River Oaks after the ceremony.

Quattrocento

1937
Oil on canvas, 55 x 46 cm
Private Collection

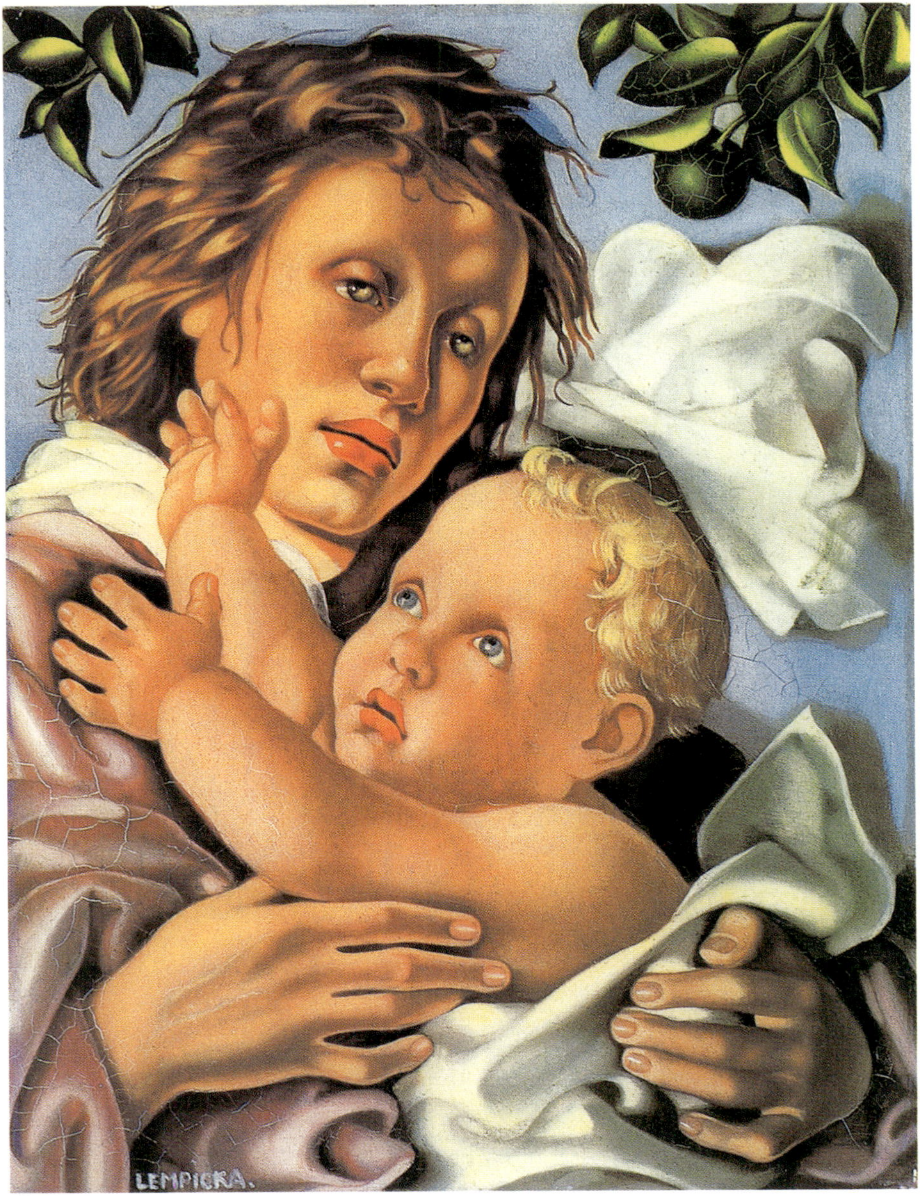
LEMPICKA.

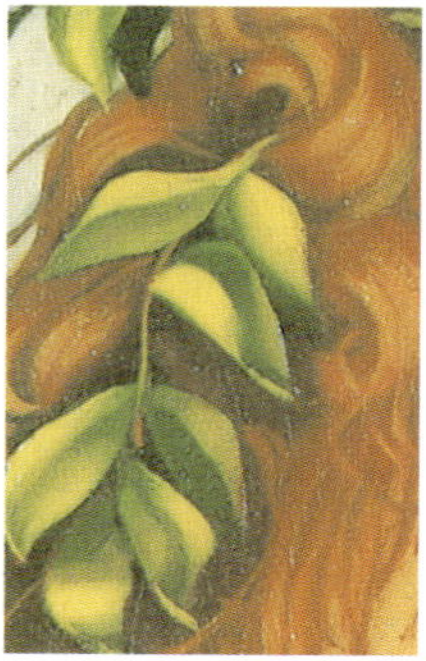

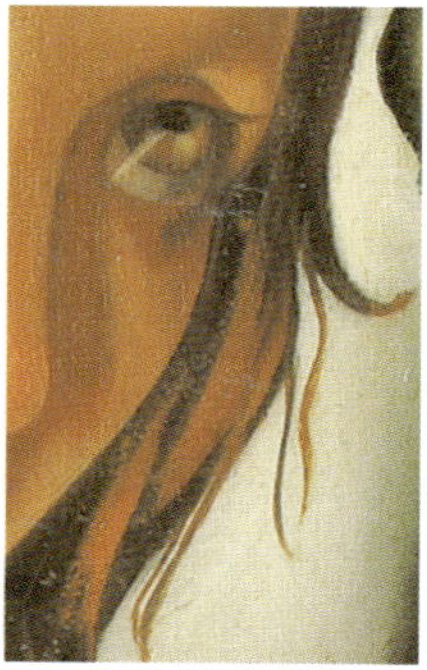

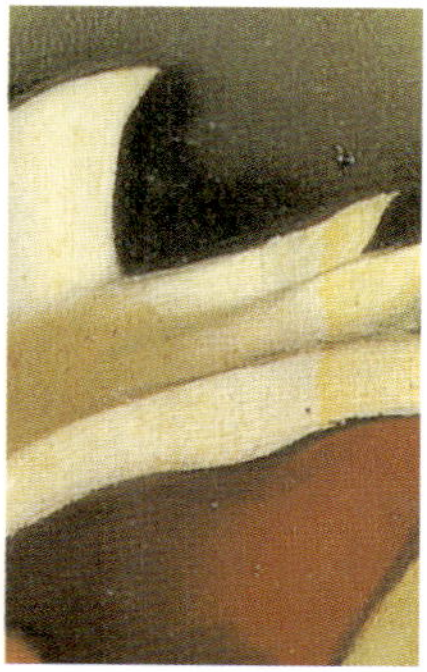

At ten o'clock that morning the doorbell rang and Kizette answered — to find the wife of the curator of Rice University's museum standing there with her two daughters and a number of grocery shopping carts. Tamara had donated to the museum all her antique serving pieces and silver, which Kizette already had properly in place, on the condition that the university pick them up that morning and at no other time. Kizette had to call the caterer and tell him to bring all the necessary dishes and silver".

Graziella

c. 1937
Oil on panel, 35 x 24 cm
Musée des Beaux-Arts du Havre

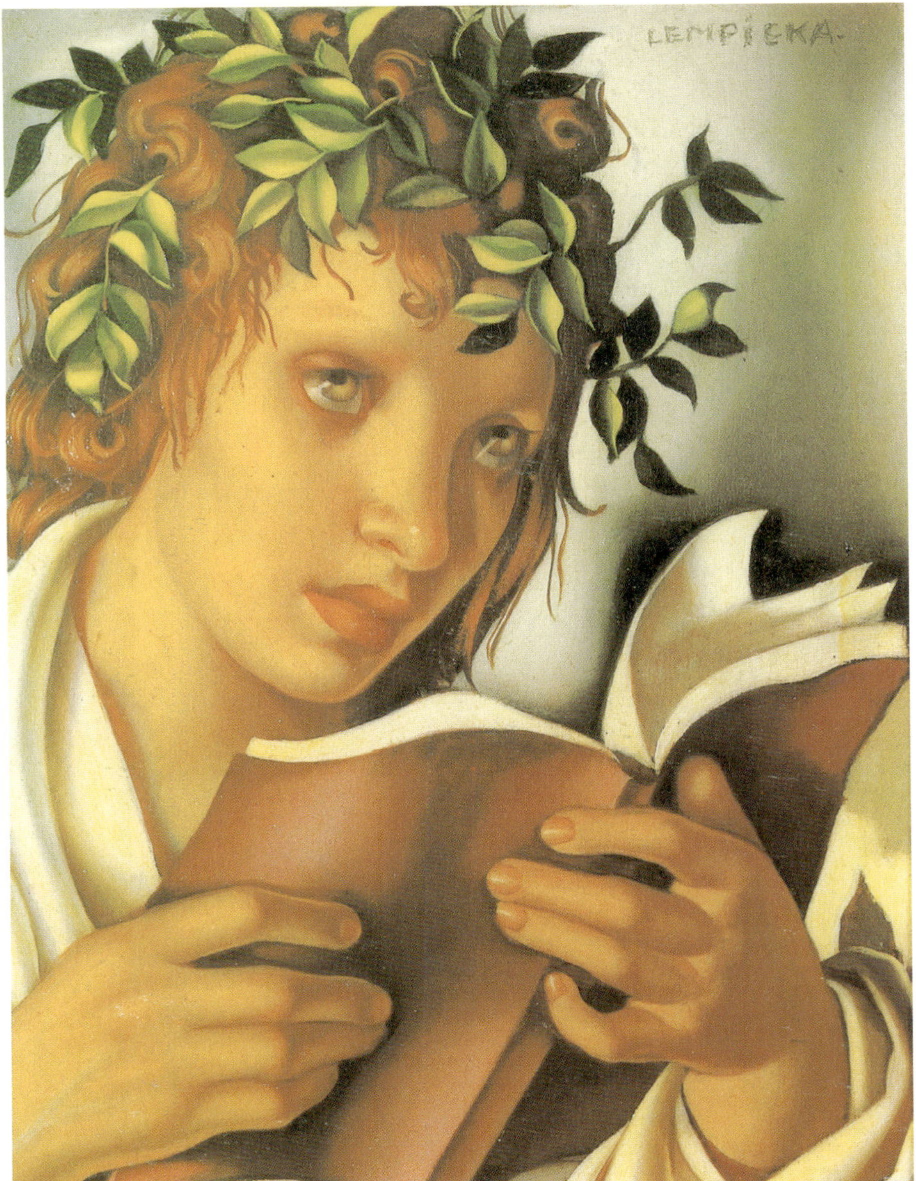
LEMPICKA.

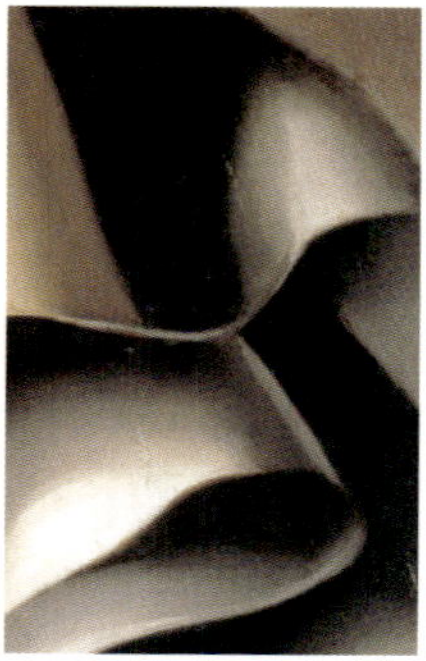

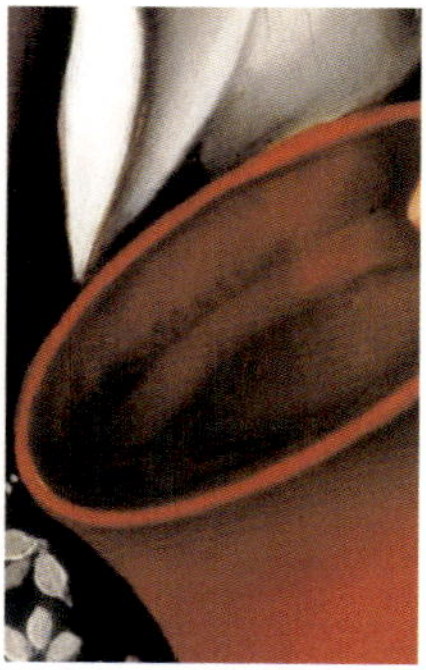

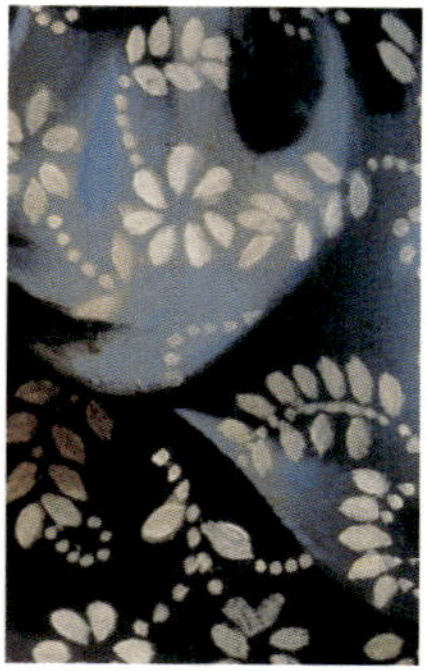

Happily de Lempicka's career did not end in bitterness and neglect but in a kind of triumphant coda as she lived long enough to see her earlier art rediscovered. With the triumph of the modernist aesthetic as cities were rebuilt after the Second World War, Art Deco came to be seen as a stylistic aberration by most "right thinking" people of taste. Ironically the wholesale destruction of Art Deco buildings in the 1960s and 1970s went hand in hand with the rise in nostalgia and appreciation of the style. As people increasingly stayed at home in the 1950s and 60s to watch television there was no further use for the great Art Deco picture palaces that were the most visible and popular expression of the Art Deco style in most cities.

Peasant Girl with Pitcher

c. 1937
Oil on panel, 35 x 27 cm
Private Collection

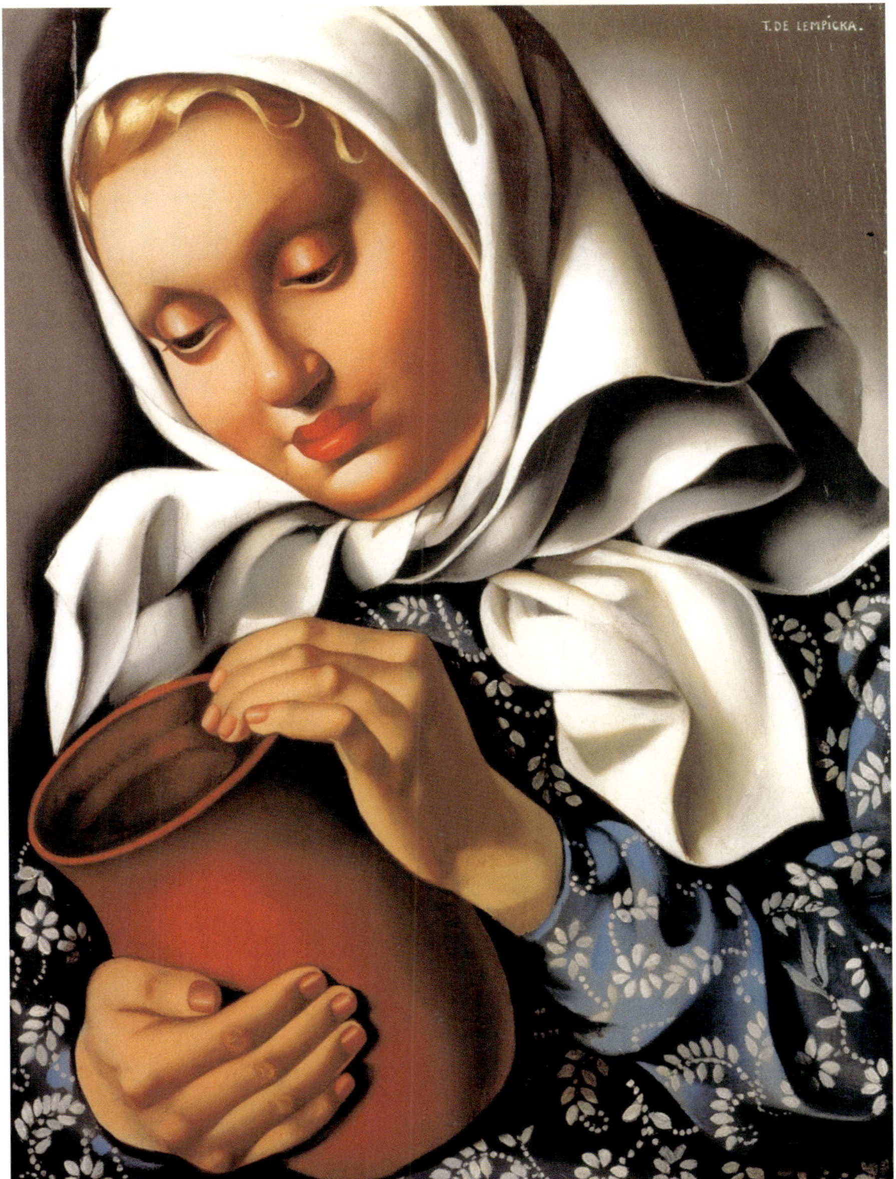
T. DE LEMPICKA.

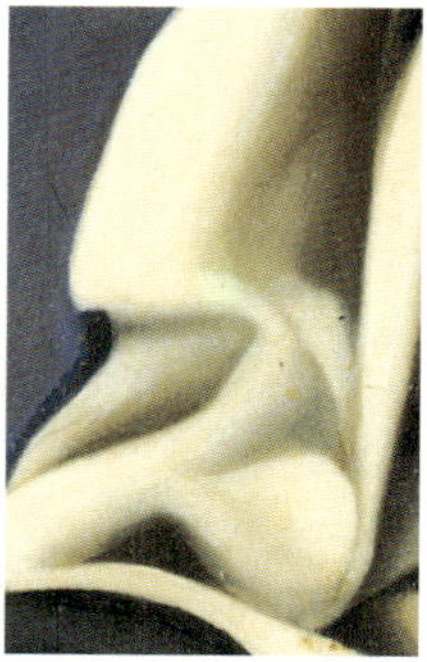

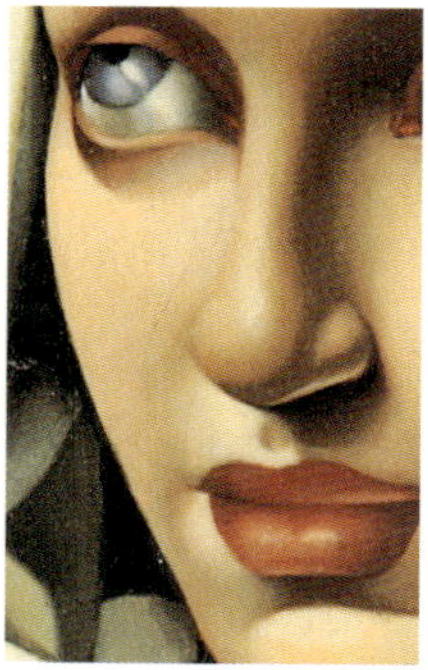

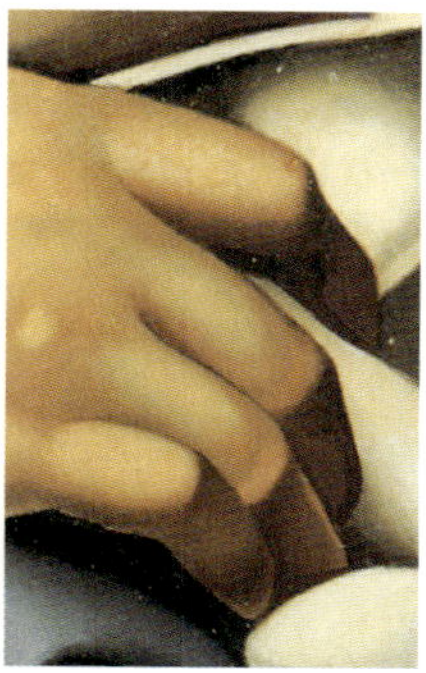

But as the Odeons, Paramounts and Roxys fell to demolition men or had their splendid interiors ripped out to make way for the construction of multiple screens, the televising of old Hollywood films on Sunday afternoons helped to create a new public for the style. When Edgar Brandt's magnificent wrought iron lifts for Selfridges were removed on safety grounds in 1971 they went straight into museums as did the most magnificent Art Deco glass and metal foyer from the Strand Palace Hotel (though it took the Victoria and Albert Museum more than thirty years to restore and display it). By 1980 there was a public outcry when the Jazz-Moderne Firestone Building by Wallis Gilbert on the Great West Road out of London was scandalously torn down.

Madonna

c. 1937
Oil on panel, 33 x 33 cm (diameter)
Musée départemental de l'Oise, Beauvais

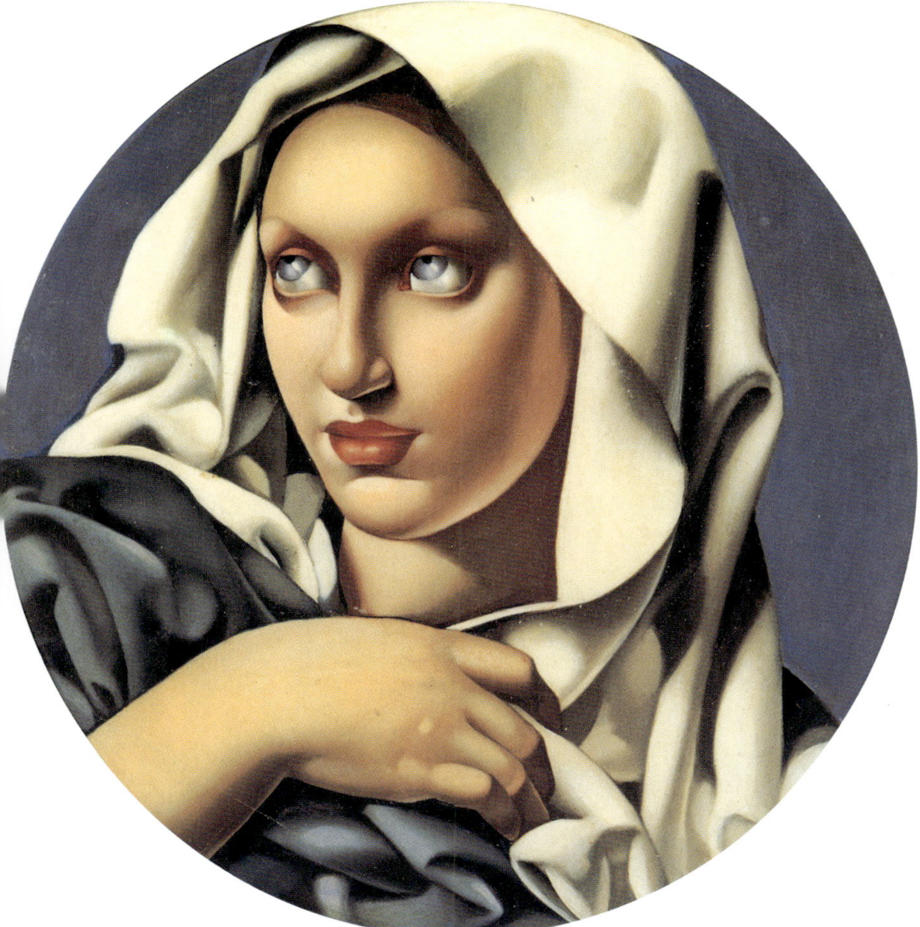

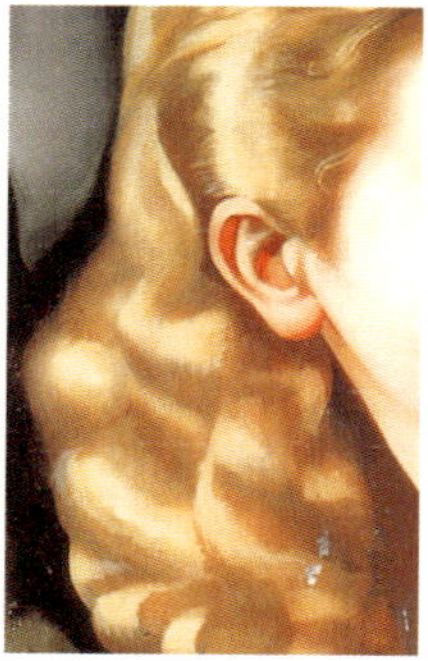

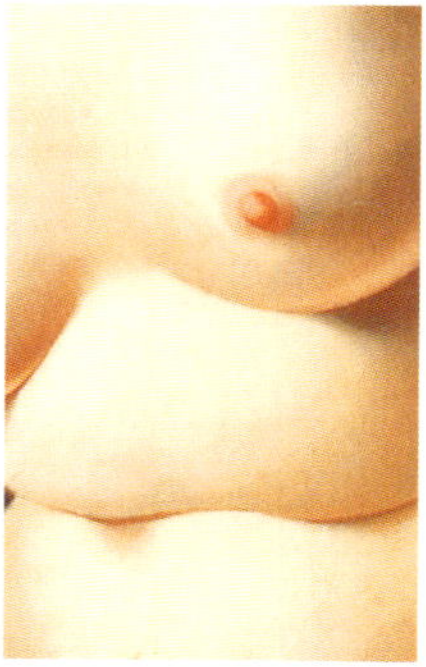

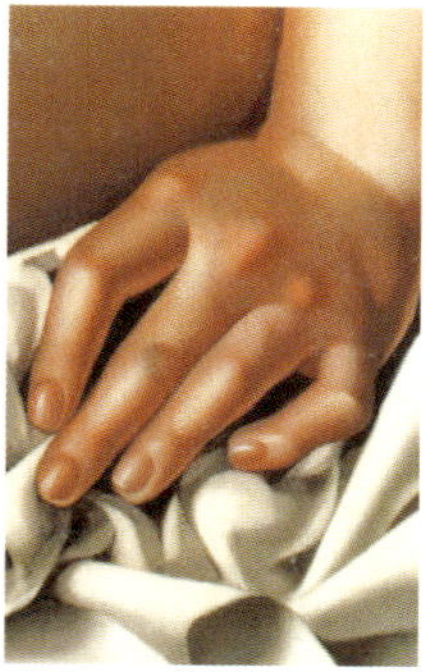

As early as 1966 the Museum of Decorative Arts in Paris staged a hugely successful pioneering exhibition entitled *Les Années '25*. Once interest had been aroused in the design displayed at the Paris 1925 Exposition des Arts Decoratives it was merely a matter of time before de Lempicka herself would be re-discovered, as academics and dealers began to pore through the periodicals and literature of the period and realised how much coverage she had received. In some cases French museum curators discovered that they already had works by de Lempicka in their store rooms.

Suzanne Bathing

c. 1938
Oil on canvas, 90 x 60 cm
Private Collection

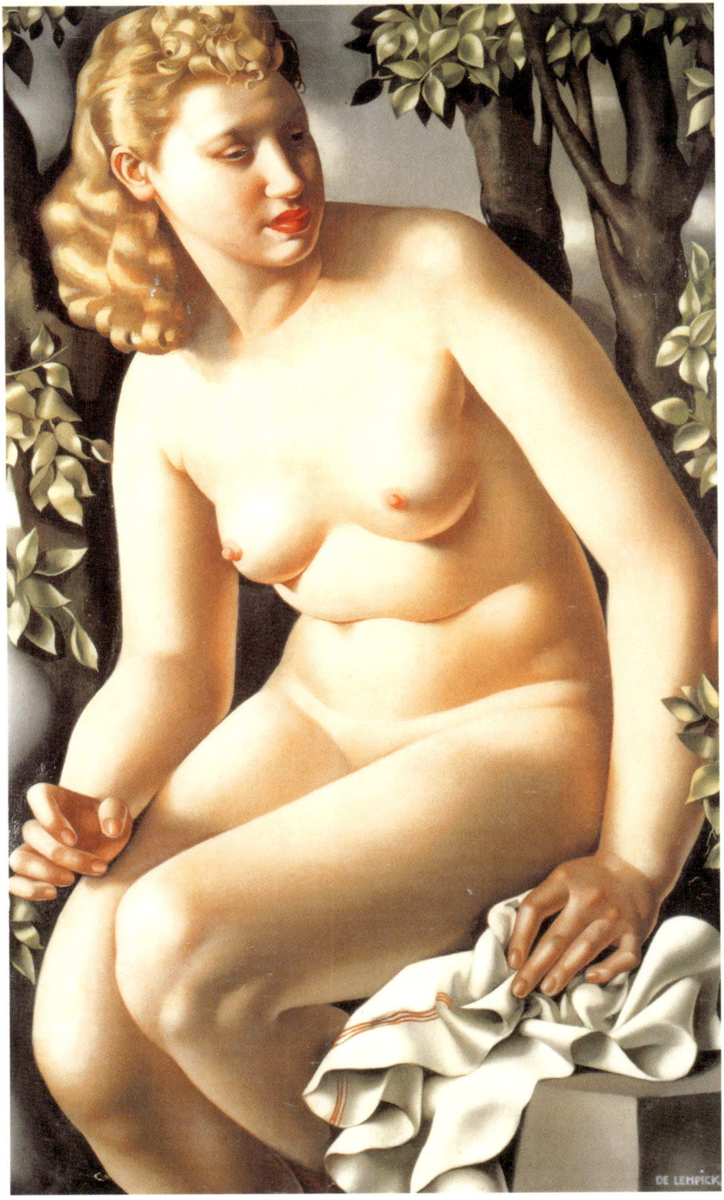
DE LEMPICK

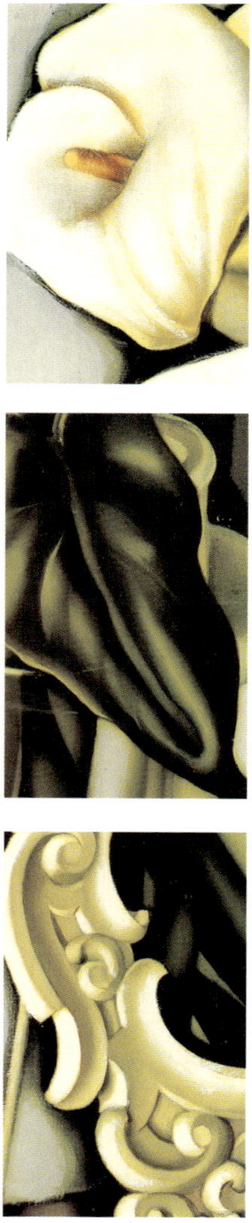

In 1969 four young Parisian dealers Alain Blondel, his wife Francoise, her sister Michele Roccaglia and her boyfriend Yves Plantin, planning to launch a new gallery in the currently revitalised quartier of *Les Halles*, began to speculate on "Whatever happened to Tamara de Lempicka". A glance through the Paris telephone directory showed her name listed under her rue Mechain address. By a happy coincidence she was in Paris and working in her studio, when, out of the blue, Alain Blondel rang her doorbell and asked to see her work of four decades earlier.

Still Life with Arums and Mirror

c. 1938
Oil on canvas, 65 x 50 cm
Musée National d'Art Moderne, Paris

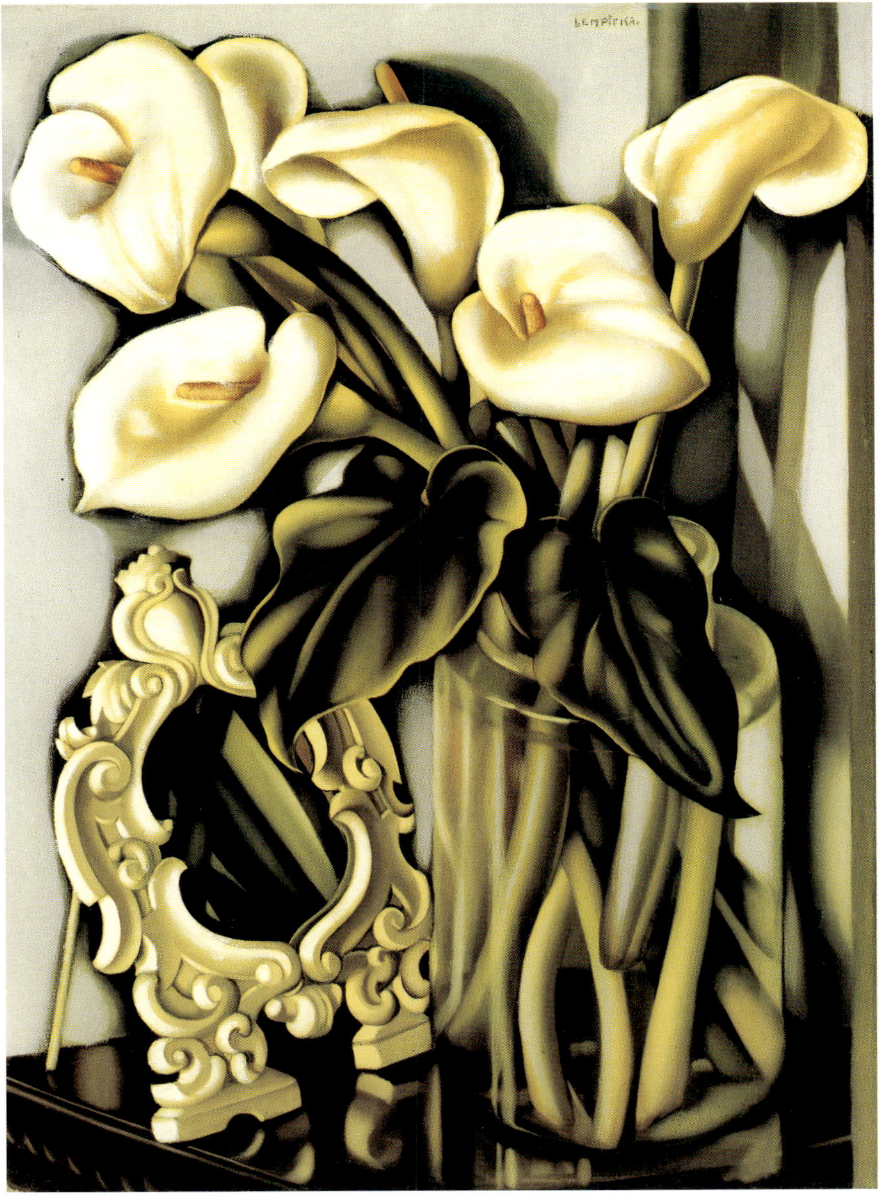
LEMPICKA.

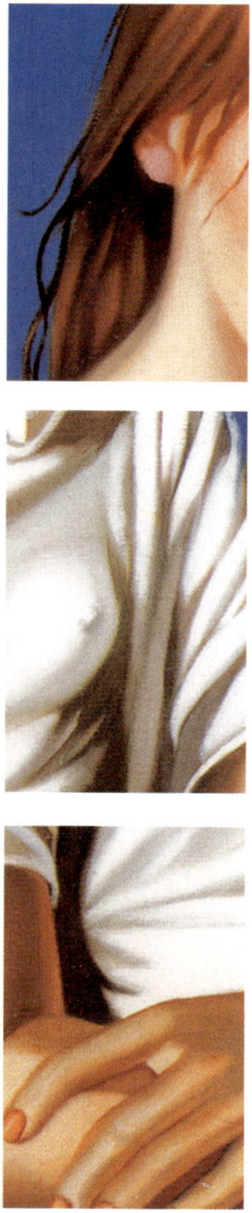

For someone who had probably resigned herself to oblivion it must have been a somewhat disconcerting experience. And it was with some misgivings and suspicion that she allowed him to explore her servant's quarters on the seventh floor Mallet-Steven's apartment block where she stored her old work. Tamara allowed Blondel to take some work away with him but it would be another three years before she was persuaded to allow Blondel and Plantin to launch their new Galerie du Luxembourg and relaunch her reputation with a retrospective exhibition.

Young Lady with Crossed Arms

1939
Oil on canvas, 50.8 x 40.6 cm
The Metropolitan Museum of Art, New-York

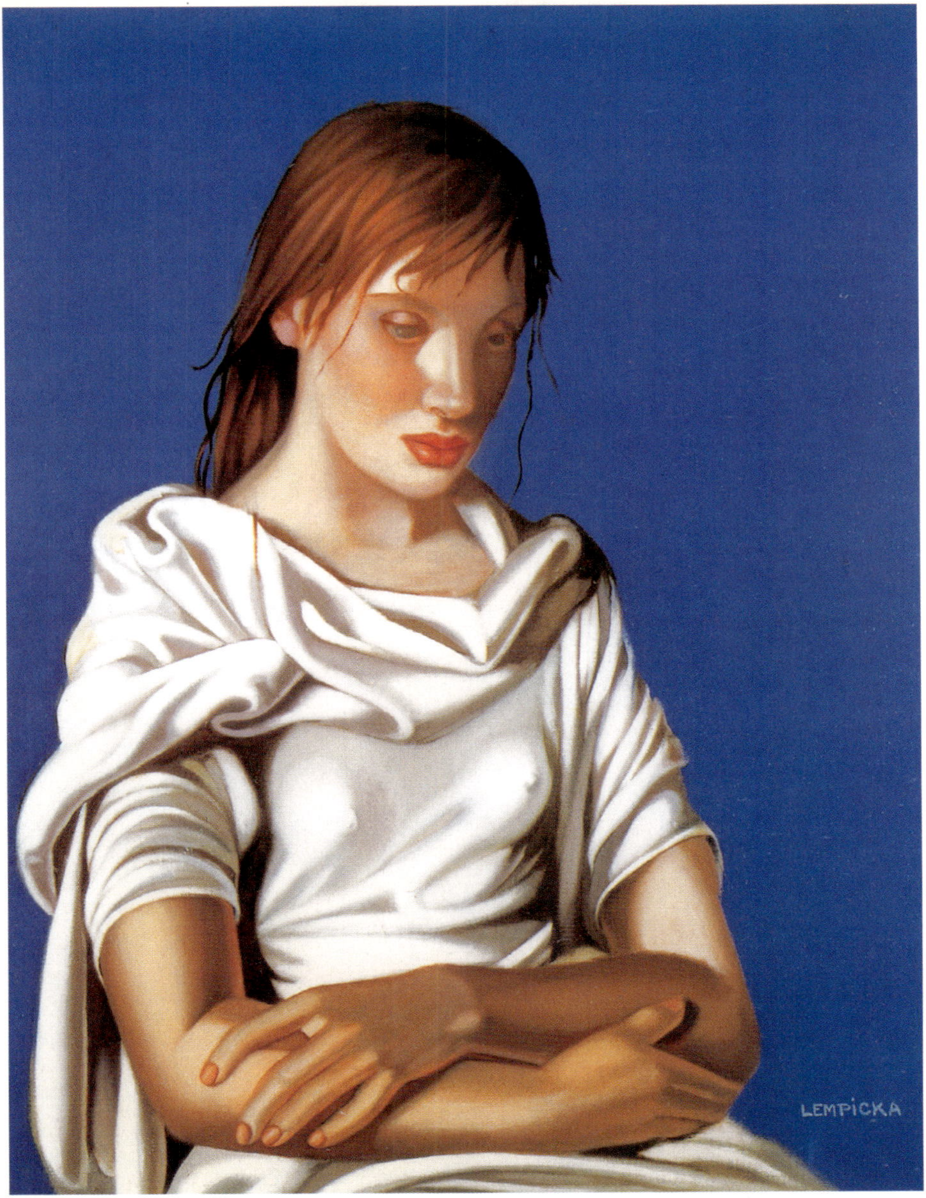
LEMPICKA

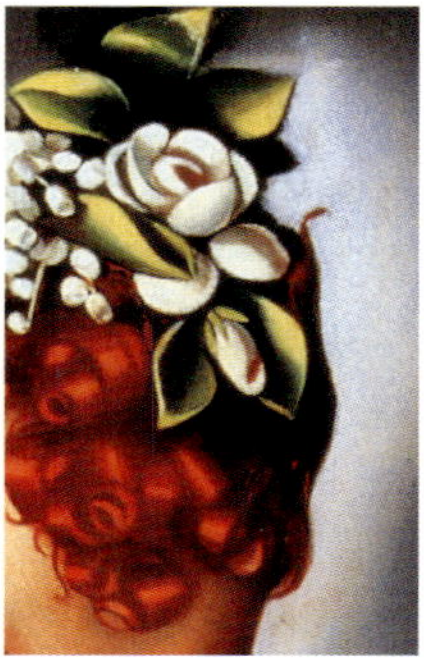

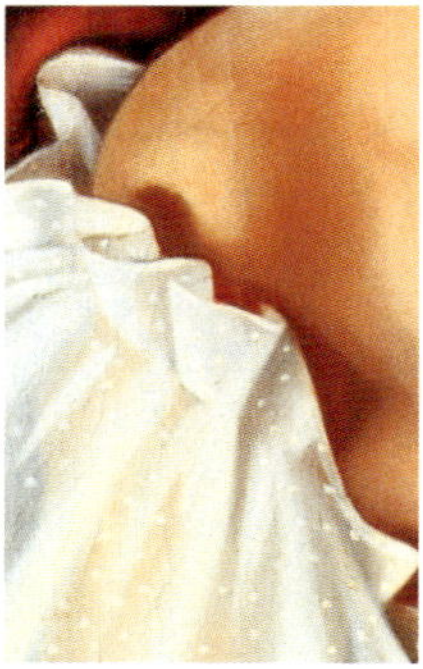

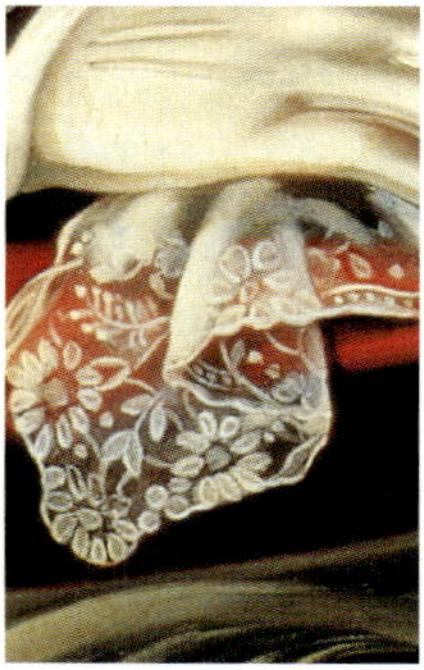

Virtually all the pictures that have since become so famous and widely reproduced were in this show and included the portrait of the Duchesse de la Salle, all the Boucard family portraits, the portrait of Ida Perrot, *La Belle Rafaela, Adam and Eve, The Woman with the Green Glove, Nana de Herrera,* the 1928 portrait of Tadeusz Lempicki, *Saint-Moritz* and the self portrait at the wheel of a green Bugatti. De Lempicka's prices were already rising sharply, but anyone who bought at this show would have made a very clever investment indeed as prices have continued to spiral ever since.

At the Opera

1941
Oil on canvas, 76.2 x 50.8 cm
Private Collection

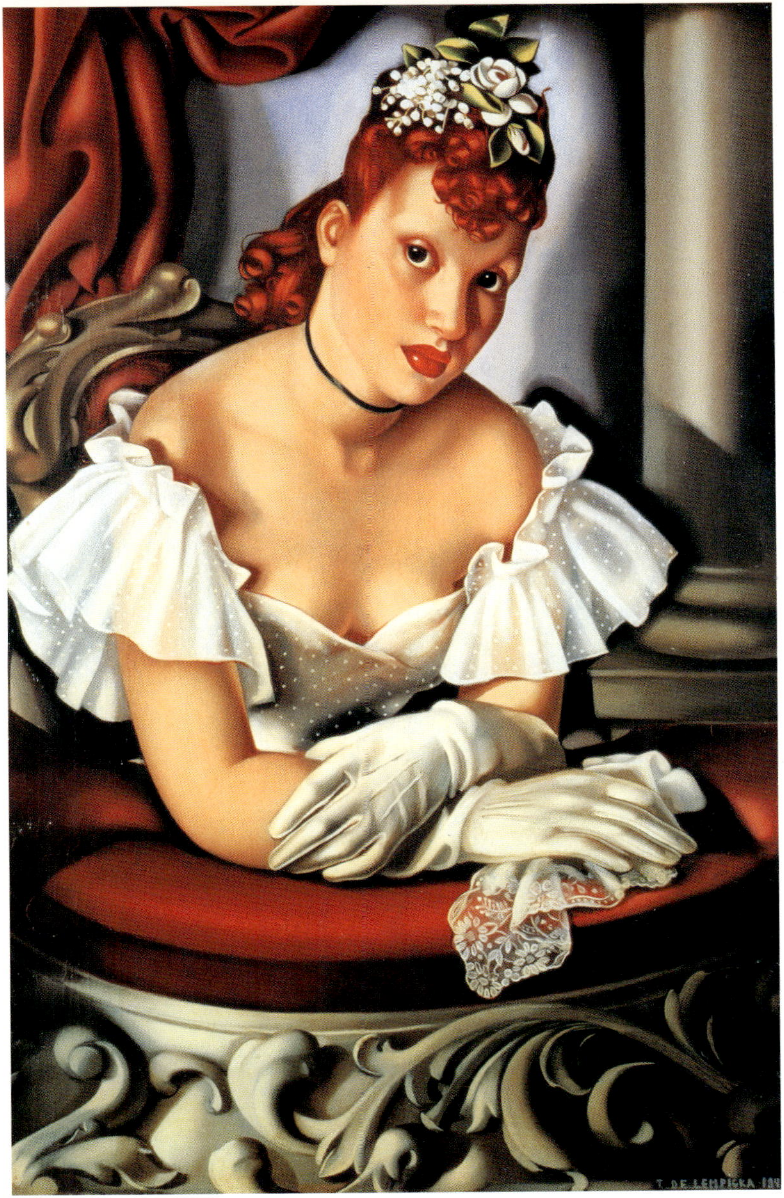
T. DE LEMPICKA

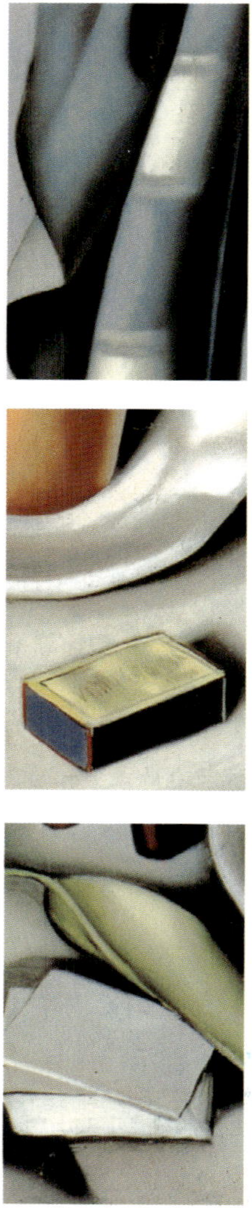

The outstanding success of this show and the ensuing press coverage brought de Lempicka's work to the attention of Franco Maria Ricci, publisher of the art magazine FMR which through its flair and sheer lavishness made it one of the most outstanding publications of the period. Ricci proposed to de Lempicka what every forgotten artist dreams of — a sumptuously produced and richly illustrated tome on her work. There was to be, however a sting in the tail.

Succulent and Flask

c. 1941
Oil on canvas, 55.9 x 45.7 cm
Private Collection

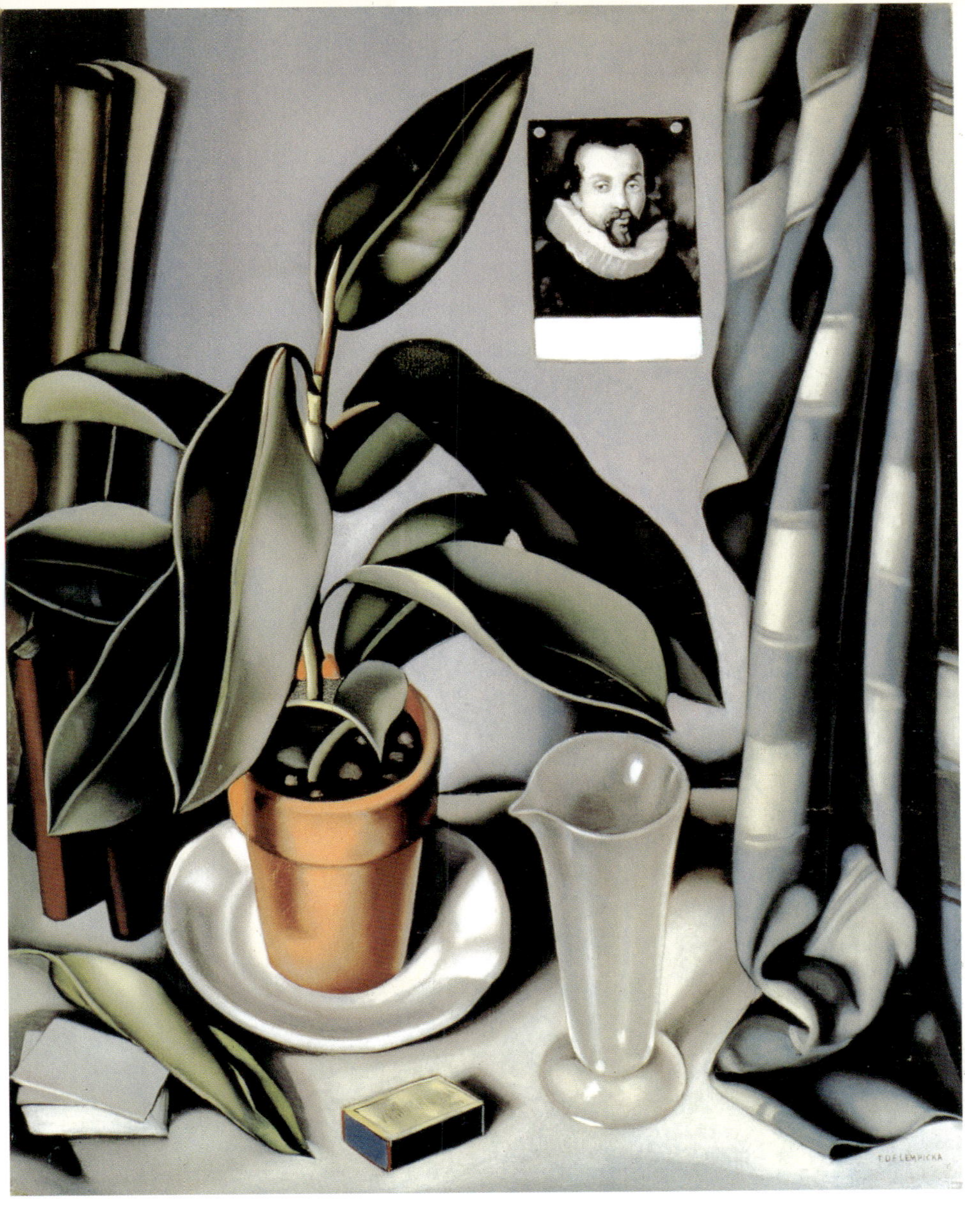
T. DE LEMPICKA

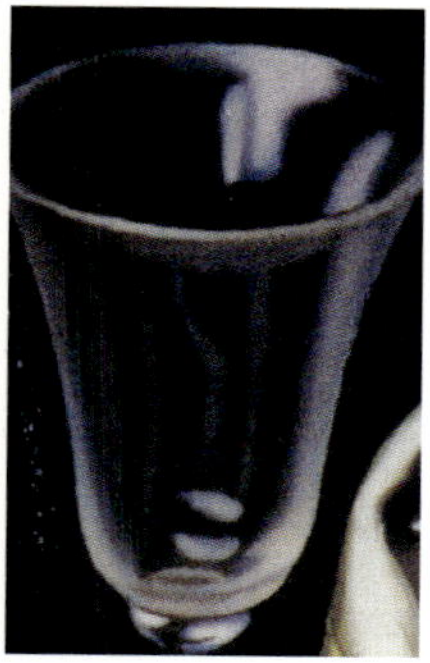

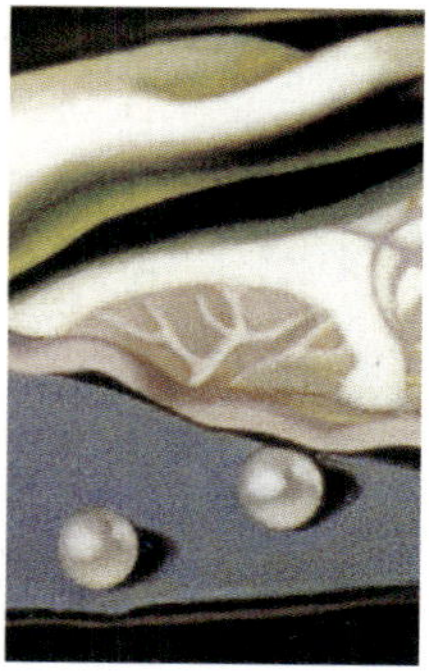

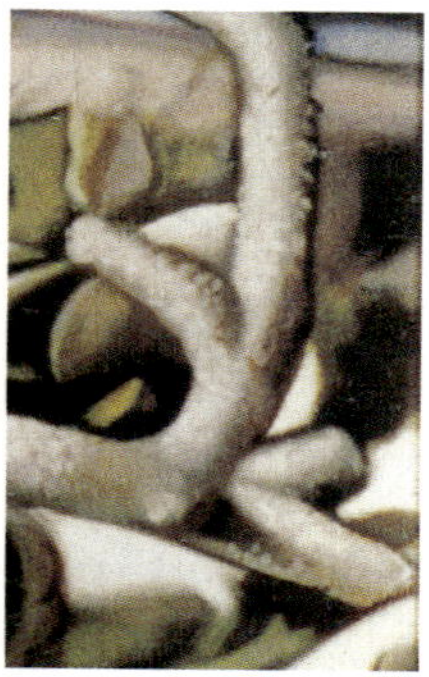

What de Lempicka did not know when she gave her consent to this enterprise, was that it would also include a scurrilous and extremely detailed account of Gabriele d'Annunzio's abortive attempts to seduce de Lempicka in the 1920s, based on the diaries of the poet's mistress and housekeeper Aelis Mazoyer. It was hardly surprising that de Lempicka felt deeply betrayed, but by the time the book came out in 1977, her reputation had already been consecrated by the acceptance of a donation of her work by Europe's most prestigious and glamorous museum of modern art at the Centre Pompidou.

The Seashell

1941
Oil on canvas, 40.6 x 50.8 cm
Private Collection

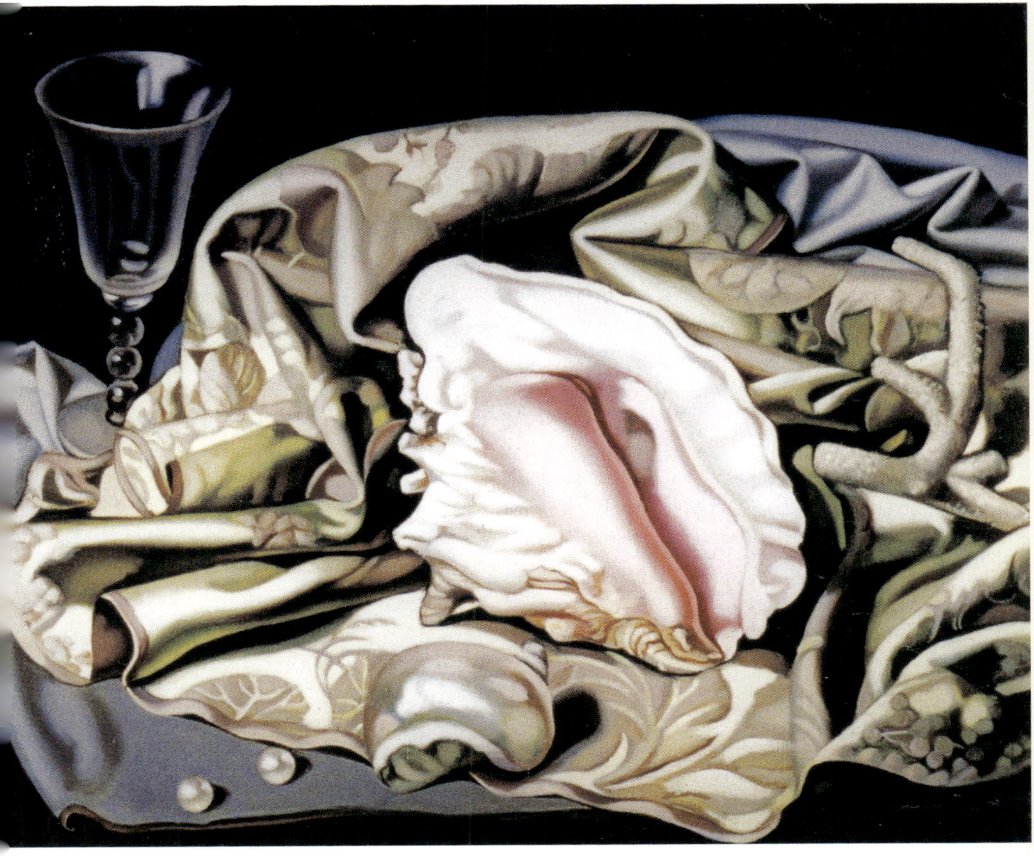

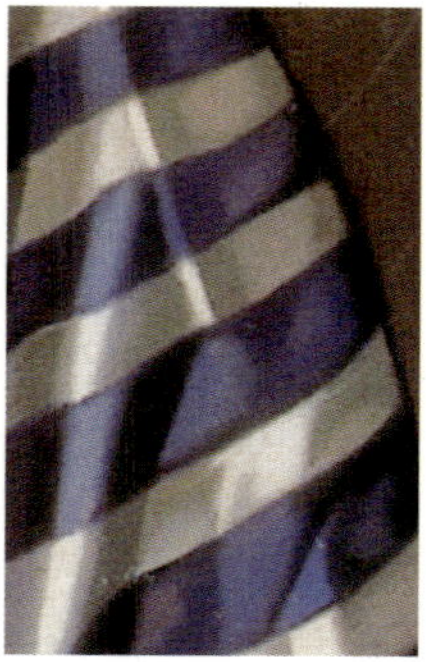

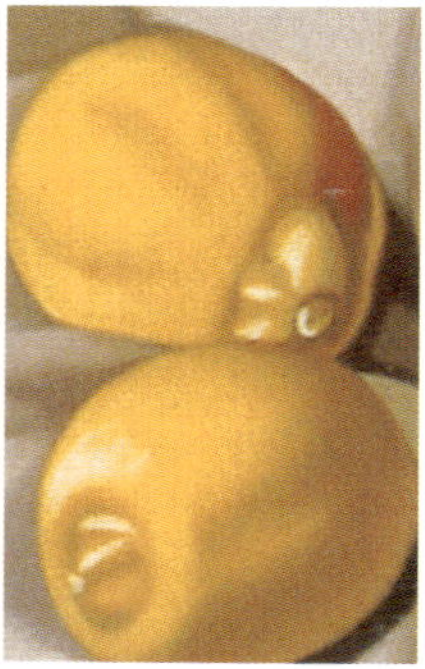

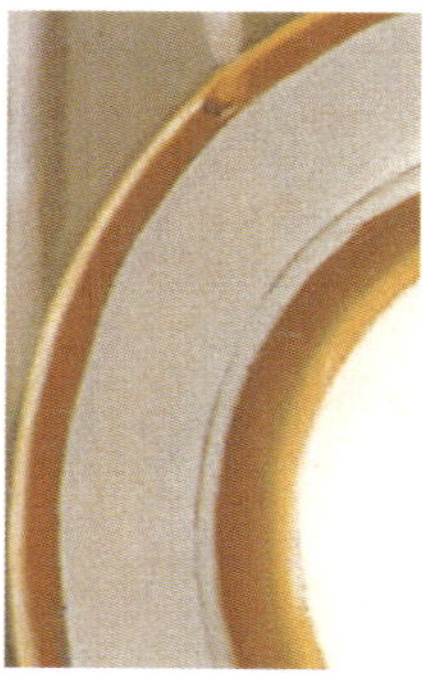

De Lempicka was to enjoy her belated fame for a further eight years, if "enjoy" is the right word for someone so little attuned to appreciating the simpler joys of life. Her irascibility in her dealings with her family and with the rest of the world was often self-destructive. In 1973 in the wake of the brilliant success of her show at the Galerie du Luxembourg, the respected Knoedler Gallery in New York offered to show her more recent work. De Lempicka sabotaged the whole enterprise with her excessive and imperious demands. In this case it may have been perhaps because she knew in her heart of hearts that her recent work was bound to be compared unfavourably with her best work from the 1920 and 1930s.

Still Life, Lemons and Plate

c. 1942
Oil on canvas, 55.9 x 45.7 cm
Dr and Mrs. Richard Hirschberg's Collection

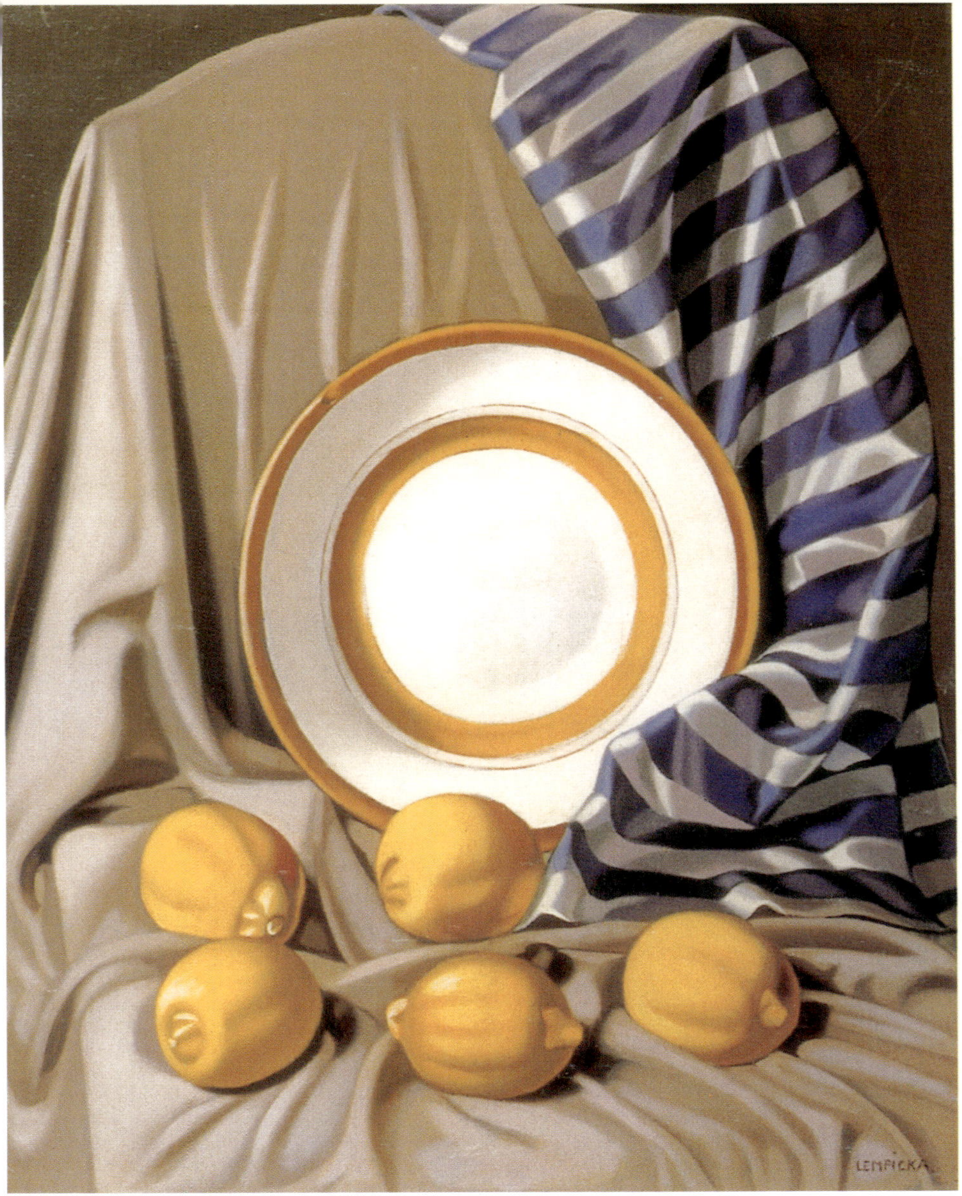
LEMPICKA

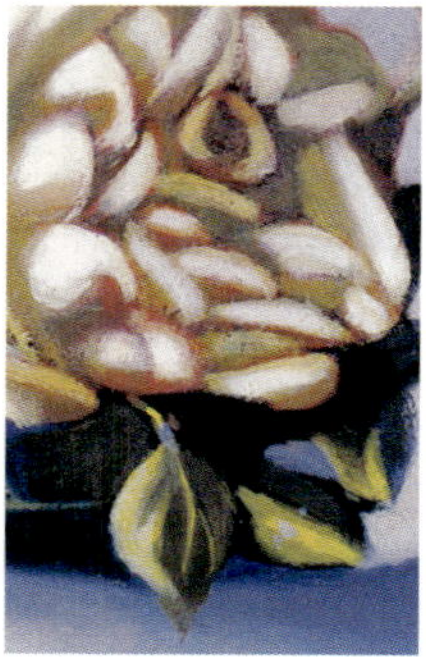

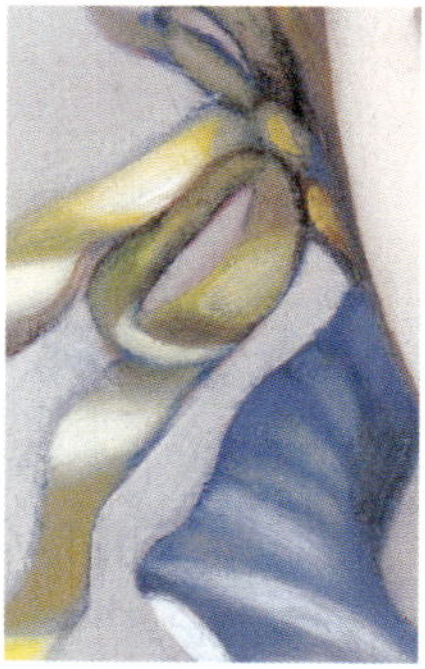

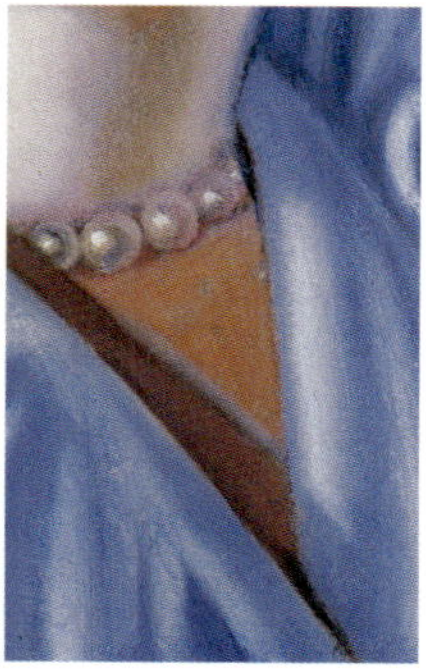

As her relationship with her daughter and her granddaughters became increasingly strained, de Lempicka spent more time away from Houston , at the Mexican resort of Cuernavaca where she eventually bought herself a house. In Cuernavaca, de Lempicka forged an intense but platonic relationship with the Mexican sculptor Victor Contreras, 40 years her junior. Despite his devotion to this proud and fascinating old lady, Contreras could not help being a witness to her increasingly cruel and unreasonable treatment of her daughter Kizette — especially as Kizette went through the ordeal of nursing her husband through the final stages of cancer. Tamara refused to accept that Kizette should put her husband first and used constant changes in her will in an attempt to blackmail Kizette to come to Mexico to nurse her rather than staying in Houston with her husband.

The Rose Hat

c. 1944
Oil on canvas, laid down, 30.5 x 20.3 cm
Private Collection

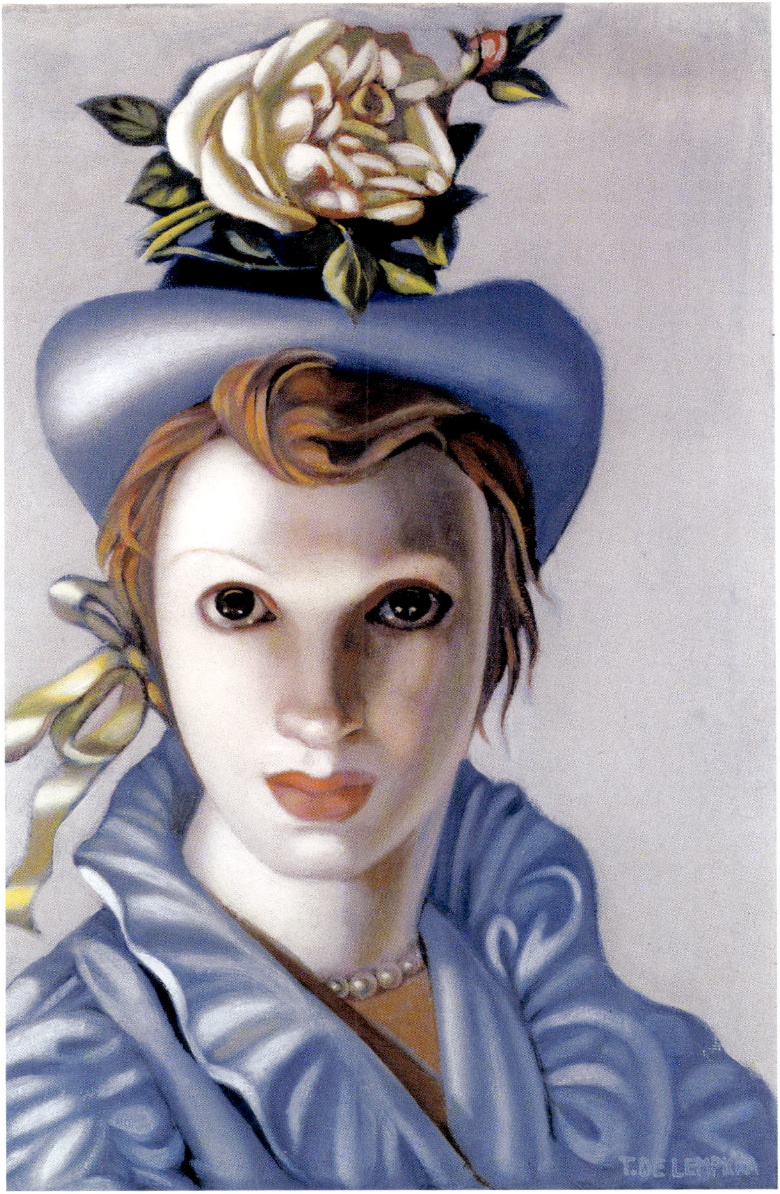
T. DE LEMPICKA

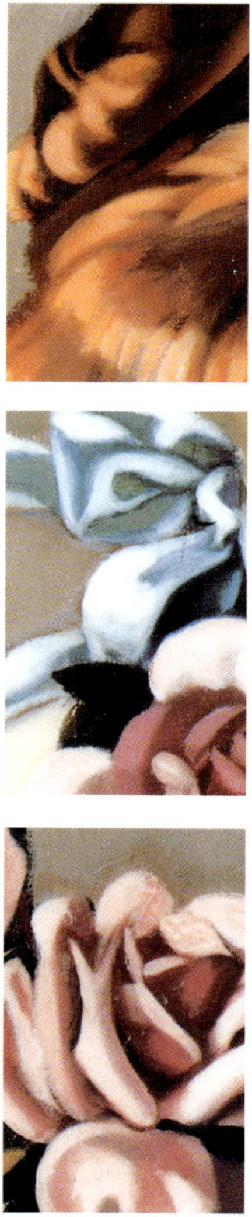

As Harold Foxhall pre-deceased Tamara, she did not put into practice her threat to cut Kizette out of her will altogether if she was not with her at the moment of her death. Nevertheless, she gave her Mexican house to Victor Contreras in a gesture intended to spite her daughter as much as to demonstrate her affection and gratitude to her Mexican companion.

On March 18 1980 after months of infirmity and nursed by her daughter as she had demanded, Tamara de Lempicka died. With a characteristic desire for control, she had made all the funeral and cremation arrangements herself. Before she died she confided in Victor Contreras that in one last great theatrical gesture she wanted her ashes to be scattered over the crater of the volcano Popocatepetl.

Redheaded Girl and Garland of Roses

c. 1944
Oil on canvas, 30.5 x 22.9 cm
Private Collection

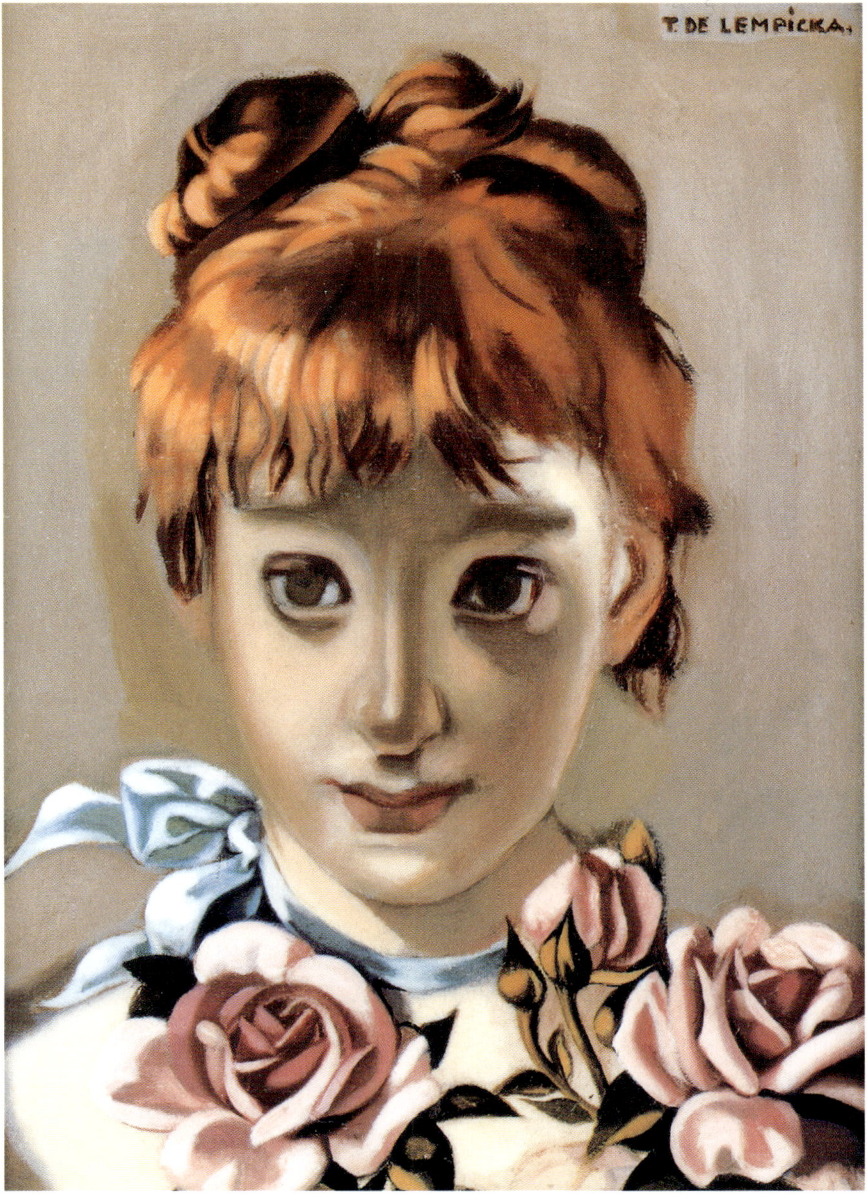
T. DE LEMPICKA.

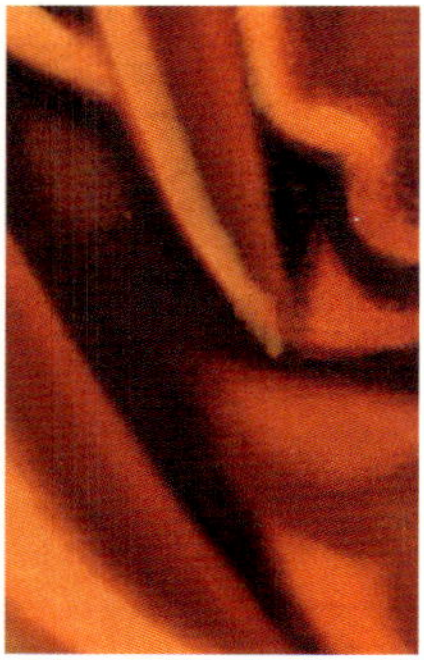

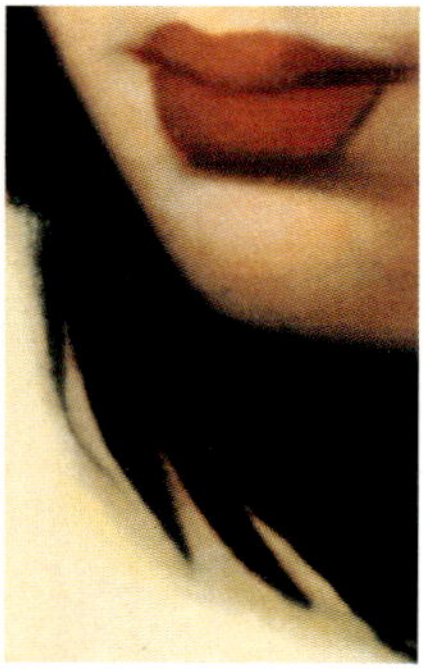

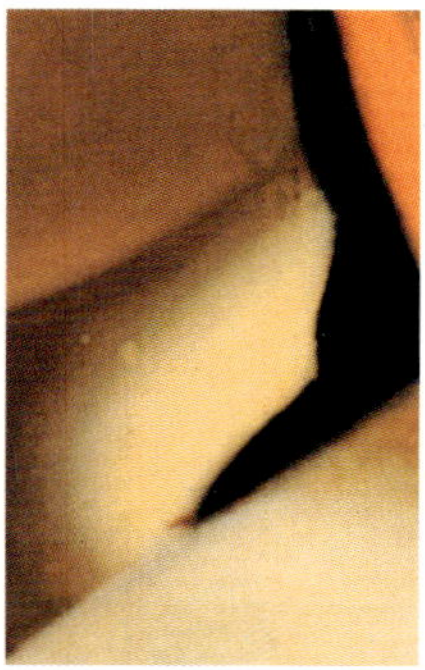

How good was Tamara de Lempicka as an artist? Do we believe the snobbish, disapproving critics who dismiss her art as meretricious and ephemeral or the celebrity collectors and the wider public who find her work beautiful and fascinating? Part of the problem is the tendency to demand from her what she does not intend to give. She does not offer the profundity of Rembrandt, the truthfulness of Velazquez or the directness and spontaneity of Frans Hals. She belongs to quite a different tradition of courtly portraiture that goes back via Ingres and Van Dyck's English and Genoese portraits to the icily beautiful Medici court portraits of Bronzino in the sixteenth century. These artists are more interested in beauty than truth and they offer portraits of a milieu as much as they do of an individual.

The Orange Turban II

c. 1945
Oil on canvas, 27 x 22 cm
Musée des Beaux-Arts du Havre

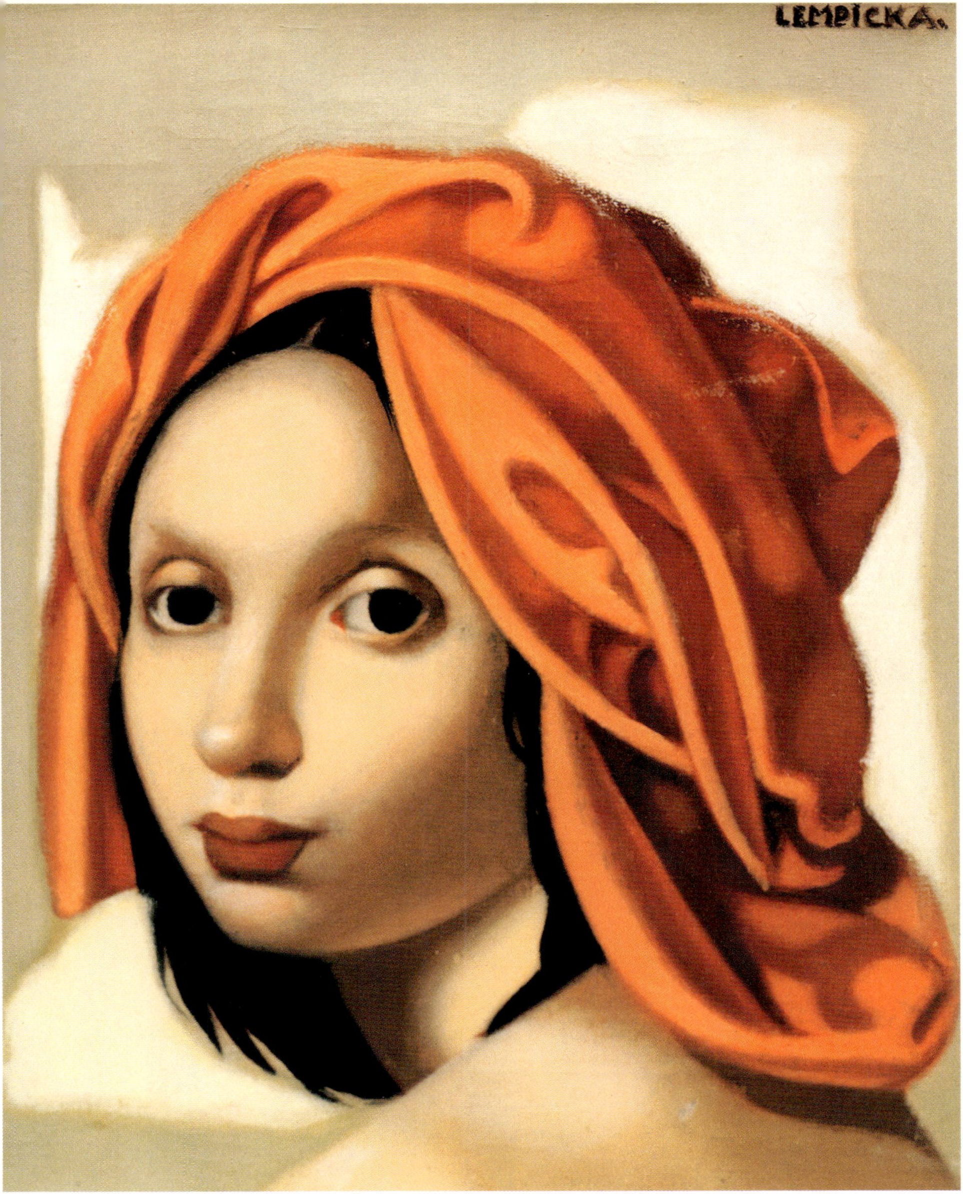
LEMPICKA.

Another problem for some, is de Lempicka's eclecticism. It is true that there is nothing especially original or ground breaking about her art and that she borrowed freely from others. One is reminded of Picasso's famous dictum that "Only bad artists borrow. Good artists steal". Judged according to this rule, de Lempicka is a very good artist indeed. What she takes she makes her own. Her borrowings are synthesised into a style that is utterly individual and immediately recognisable if all too easily imitated.

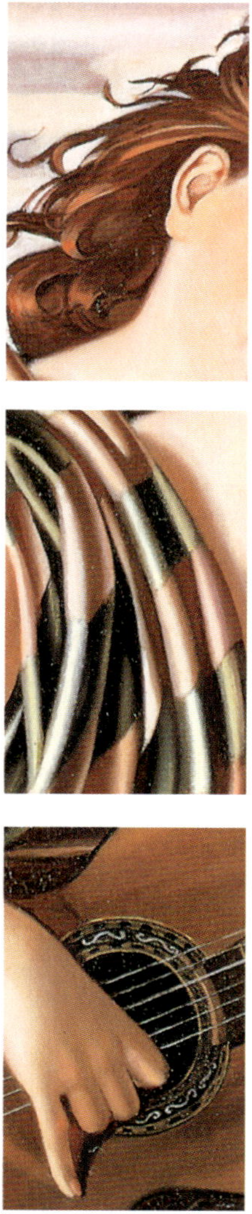

Amethyst

1946
Oil on canvas, 76.2 x 63.5 cm
Private Collection

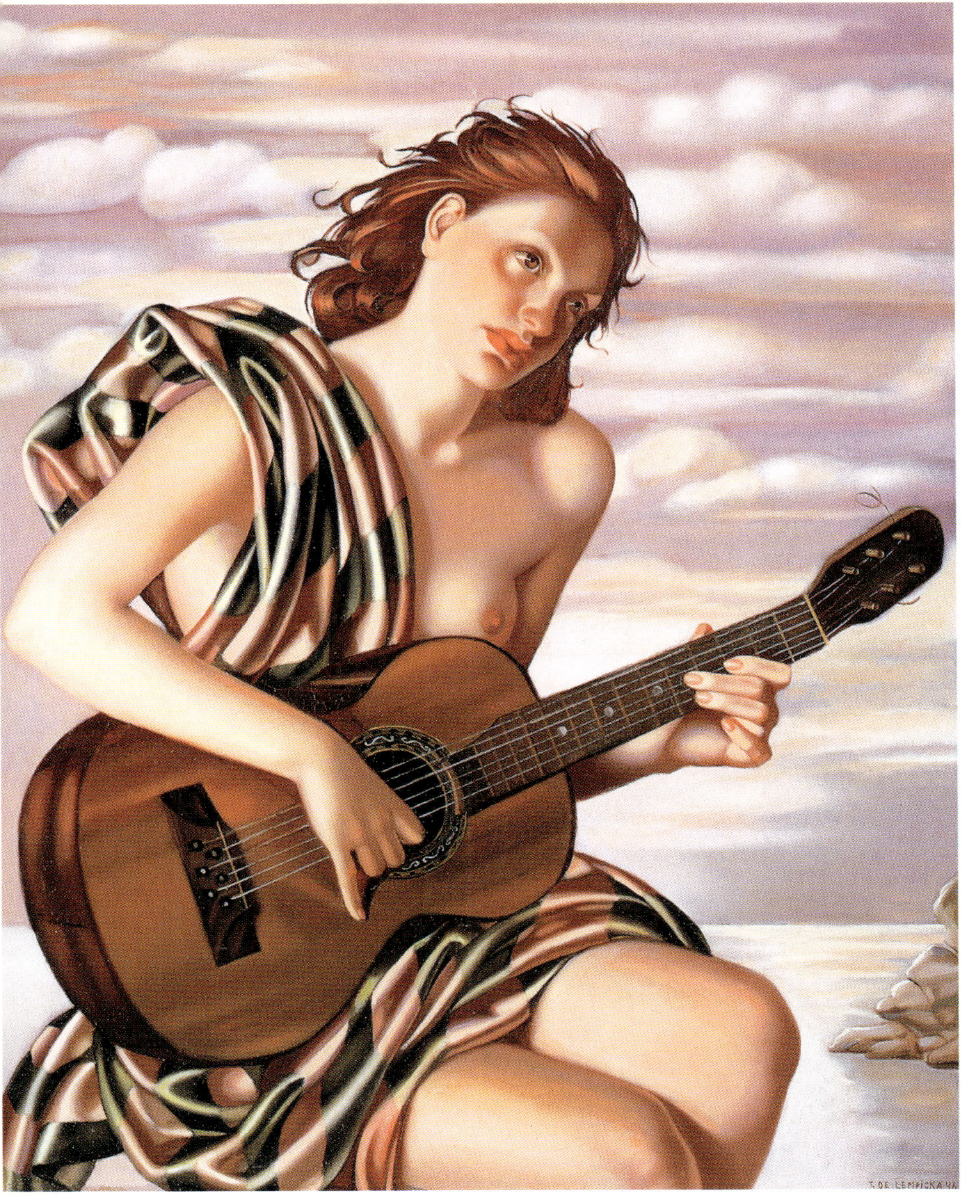
T. DE LEMPICKA

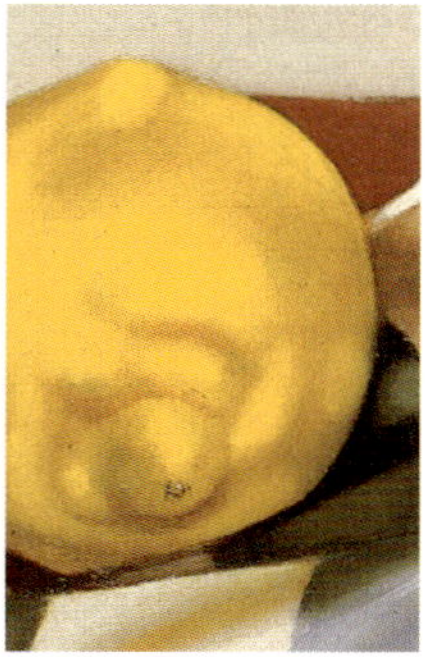
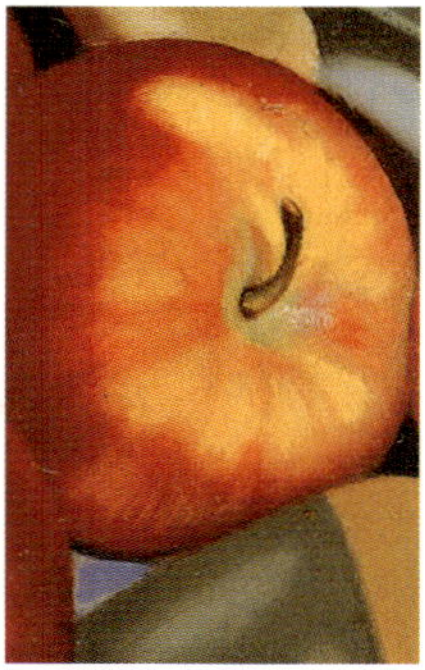
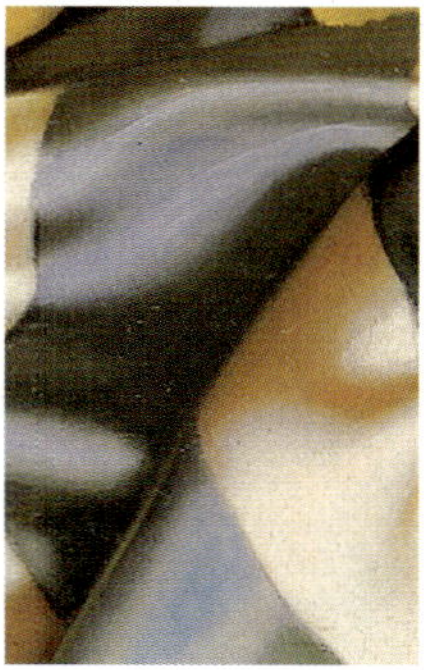

And here is another problem. In her Art Deco period de Lempicka painted to a formula that looks temptingly easy to reproduce. As anyone who has visited the Paris flea markets in recent years will know, de Lempicka has become one of the most widely faked and imitated artists of the twentieth century. There is nothing like imitation and over familiarity to spoil an artist's reputation and de Lempicka has suffered from both.

Still Life with Apples and Lemons

c. 1946
Oil on canvas, 30.5 x 40.6 cm
Private Collection

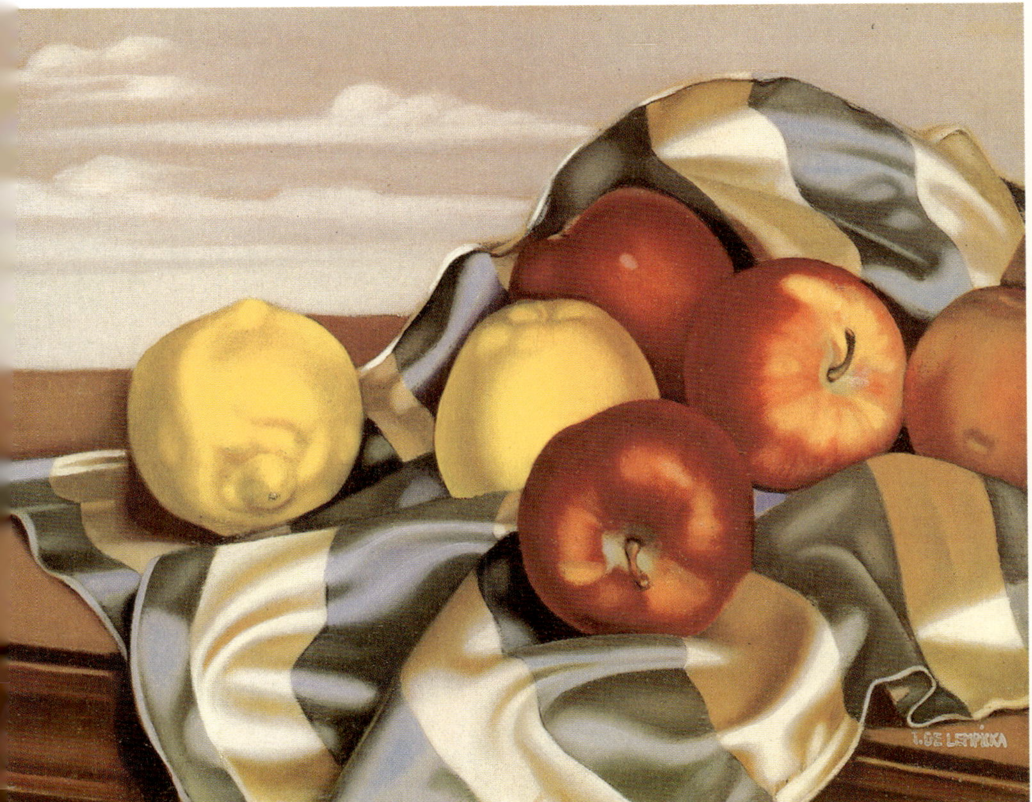
T. DE LEMPICKA

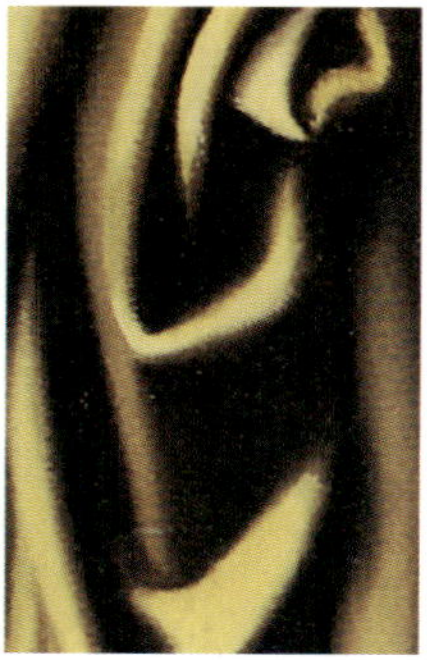
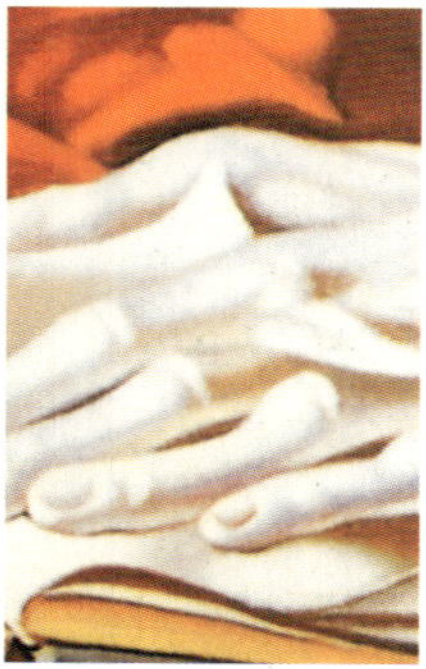
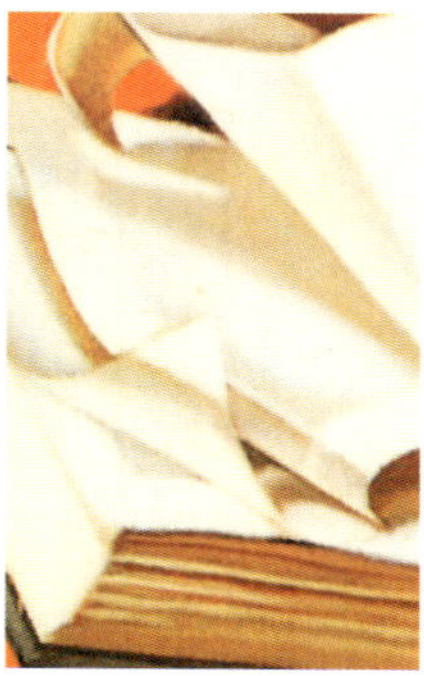

In the end de Lempicka's greatest achievement was that she had something to say about a certain class, at a certain time, in a certain place that no one else was able to say quite as memorably. Just as Van Dyck characterised the England of Charles I and Otto Dix created our image of the people who inhabited Weimar Berlin, Tamara de Lempicka gave us the images that from now on will always be used to conjure up Paris in *Les Années Folles.* The disapproving critic will just have to get used to the fact that Tamara is here to stay.

The Key

c. 1946
Oil on canvas, 48.3 x 35.6 cm
Private Collection

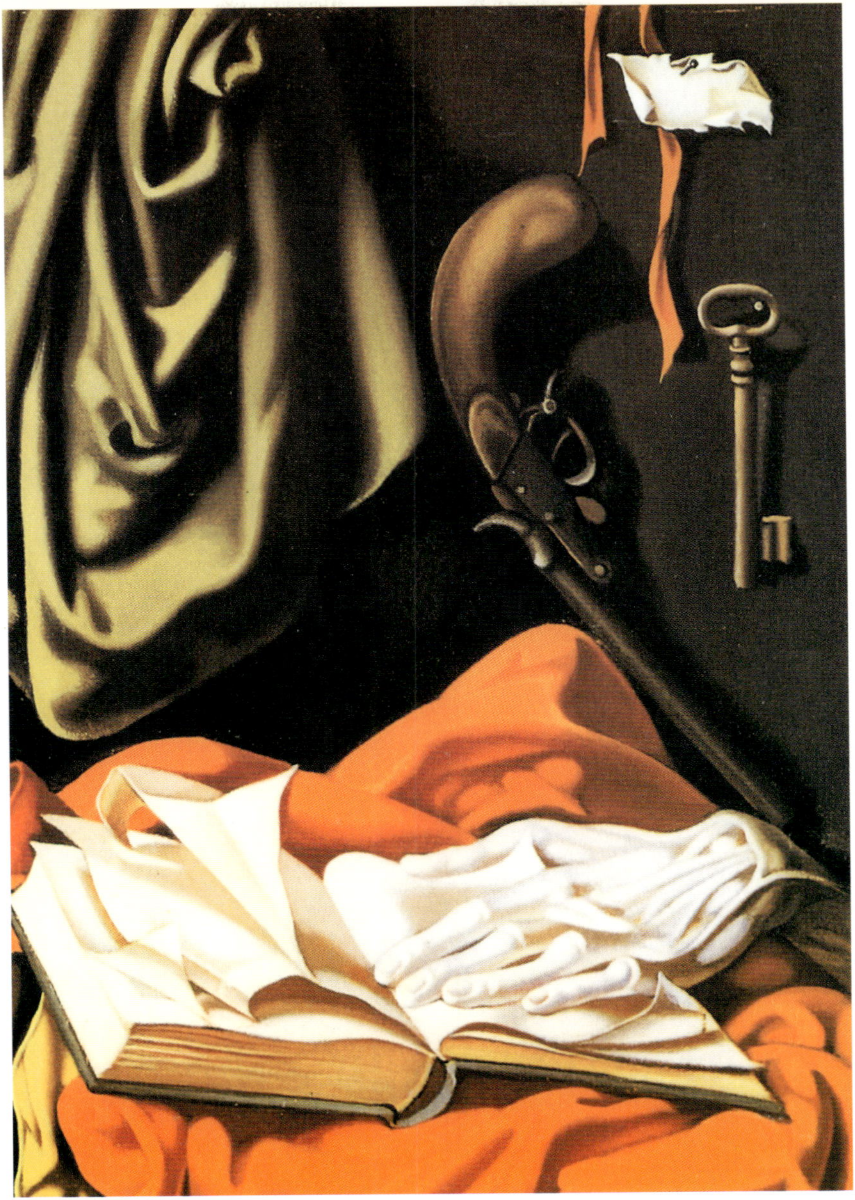

Index